OVERLOAD, CREEP, EXCESS

AN INTERNET FROM INDIA

Theory on Demand #45
Overload, Creep, Excess - An Internet from India

Authors: Nishant Shah, Ashish Rajadhyaksha and Nafis Hasan

Copy editor: Sunaina Dalaya
Cover Design: Katja van Stiphout
Design and EPUB development: Tommaso Campagna and Jasmin Leech

Published by the Institute of Network Cultures, Amsterdam, 2022

ISBN print: 9789492302922
ISBN EPUB: 9789492302922

Contact
Institute of Network Cultures
Amsterdam University of Applied Sciences (HVA)
Email: info@networkcultures.org
Web: www.networkcultures.org

Order a copy or download this publication for free at: www.networkcultures.org/publications
Subscribe to the INC newsletter: www.networkcultures.org/newsletter

institute of
network cultures

ADARSH BAALAK, AADHAAR BAALAK

GETS UP EARLY IN THE MORNING

SALUTES PARENTS

BATHES REGULARLY - BECAUSE SWACCHH BHARAT

USES AADHAAR FOR HIS SCHOLARSHIP

USES AADHAAR TO GET HIS MIDDAY MEAL

USES AADHAAR FOR HEALTH-CARE, LPG, PDS GRAIN...

LOGS TEMPLE VISITS WITH AADHAAR SERVER

PREACHES THE GOSPEL OF AADHAAR

USES AADHAAR TO AUTHENTICATE HIS TINDER MATCHES

REPORTS THOSE WITHOUT AADHAAR - FOR THEIR OWN GOOD

NEVER LEAVES THE HOUSE WITHOUT HIS "VOLUNTARY" AADHAAR CARD

HAS NO PRIVACY

ALWAYS ON THE RADAR

Research & Action | Find us on Facebook

CONTENTS

FOREWORD

CHINMAYI ARUN

When reading anything, we absorb the text through our particular gaze, infused with our background and history. Here, I offer a lawyer's reading of a textured, interdisciplinary book that will benefit from multiple readings. For lawyers like myself who tend to engage mainly with the creation and application of rules, this book's narratives are a revelation. They illuminate the past with political theory, design theory, philosophy, history, and sociology. The authors take a period of time that is very familiar, and show us everything we missed as we lived through it.

This book is an intertextual conversation across disciplines, generations, and geographies. Since the authors are long-time collaborators, it is also a conversation across time. This adds depth and warmth to their engagement with each other. You will see, in the three essays, the authors speak to each other's writing, and also to prior work, as they join voices to tell this story. Ruth Padel wrote of migrations, in her poem 'Time to Fly', that 'you go because the world rotates, because the world is changing and you've lost the key'. This book, by three individuals on three different continents, is also proof that wherever you may go, you can come together and remake the key.

This is a book for everyone who cares about citizenship, technology, and democracy, even though we have each formed our concerns and questions in different contexts. In the first part of this foreword ('Eye-opening'), I discuss the authors' repositioning of seemingly familiar history. The second part ('Crisis in India') will resonate particularly with those who are familiar with recent developments of law, politics, and technology in India, and have a visceral interest in the meaning of citizenship and democracy in India. This book shows us, step by step, how technology and law have changed what it means to be a citizen in India.

In the last part of my foreword ('Yes, all democracies'), the crisis discussed in this book is a crisis of democracy and citizenship that is building worldwide. The authors' pathbreaking scholarship offers important questions and theories for anyone with an interest in democracy. India is one of the most interesting democracies in the world and is a great choice of canvas for the authors' ideas. To understand these ideas is to understand India a little. But to understand India is to also understand how societies move toward and away from seeing themselves as democracies.

Eye-opening

The combined effect of the three authors' narratives of how technology has changed society is much more than the sum of its parts. This narrative is informed by their personal and scholarly understanding of the events that constructed and embedded the relationships between technology, state, and society in India. The authors are able to theorize these questions with a granularity of detail that is both satisfying and enriching. Ashish Rajadhyaksha, for example, reflects on the questions that the three authors were asking at the time that the universal identity system was proposed, and details the developments that changed both the nature of the system and the authors' view of it.

As an Aadhaar-skeptic who has written about the deficiencies of the statutory safeguards proposed for the system, I thought I had already read about, heard of, or conceived its worst outcomes. For example, I have always maintained that using statutory safeguards (as opposed to constitutional obligations) to contain Aadhaar's excesses can easily be undone by the first legislature that is willing to remove the safeguards. However, each of the authors surprised me by showing me dimensions of this project that I did not know about, understand, or envision.

Rajadhyaksha sketches out how the National Population Register and other developments that directly threaten meaningful citizenship were able to use or repurpose Aadhaar. While Nishant Shah has been coy about his past work, Rajadhyaksha has devoted several pages to reminding us of Shah's past work on Aadhaar's conflation of identity and identification. This work was so insightful that it was cited in Justice Chandrachud's 2018 dissenting judgment in the second Aadhaar case. But it is Nafis Hasan who shines light on previously unplumbed questions in the context of Aadhaar. He does this by showing us how the Indian government chose particular technologies and private actors to create its databases, and helps us understand how these choices affect citizens. Using a brilliant blend of empirical research and theory, he shows us how datasets are perceived as objective but can be compromised in several ways. The particular paths chosen by the Indian government leave citizens with the burden and labor of ensuring that their information is recorded correctly. This part of the book is not only visionary in its own right, it also shows us why Shah is right, now and in the past, about what these databases do to the individual citizen.

I wonder how the Supreme Court judges who wrote the privacy and Aadhaar judgments would read this book. Aadhaar, like many serious questions before the Supreme Court, triggered a conversation between the judiciary and the executive. In the case about the fundamental right to privacy, in particular, the judges made assumptions about the restraint the executive was likely to exercise in its invasion of privacy within the broad space offered to it. One wonders if they would rule differently if we could throw this book back in time to show benches past the future their combined rulings constructed.

Crisis in India

Indian readers will have lived through the period and events discussed in this book, and others may have witnessed similar developments in their countries. What we think we witnessed is transformed and reconstructed by the authors' narrative, framing, and retelling. If you were wondering how and why we got here – how citizenship is now based on a fragile and almost fickle digital ID, why protesting can get you arrested, and what the Aarogya Setu was doing on anybody's phone – this is the book to read. It offers compelling insights to show us how India got here, and ways to rethink where technology and society have taken our democracy.

In March 2015, many celebrated the Indian Supreme Court's decision in *Shreya Singhal* v *Union of India*, which was widely regarded as the first significant Indian judgment on online communication. During the litigation, big technology companies were rallying support and coordinating advocacy that would favor unrestricted online speech. Public attention was focused on online speech. In the meantime, data collection by these companies and by the state was expanding. The unique identification system was being put in place, and state surveillance was becoming more sophisticated and less accountable. Companies were competing to invent new ways to collect and use data. At the time, very little attention was being paid to privacy and to the ways in which these companies violated it. The companies would go on to argue for some years that granular privacy laws restricted innovation and were bad for the population. They would also go on to privately restrict speech in ways that would not have met the constitutional threshold if the state had ordered the restriction.

The connection between Shreya Singhal and the events discussed in the book is that this highly regarded judgment also displayed the judicial shortsightedness that would be displayed in the court's later rulings on privacy and universal identity. The judiciary failed to appreciate the extent to which the executive could censor information, if it was able to negotiate directly with companies and leverage their gatekeeping role without involving the citizens whose speech and information is made inaccessible. The advocacy in the case also assumed that companies' incentives would always lie in resisting censorship, and this optimism did not survive the test of time. The story of Aadhaar was similarly a story of not seeing what was in plain sight as well as what lay concealed, both of which powerfully affected the form that the system would take and the future it would create.

Parts of the book unearth new and important information. Other parts reveal what was hidden in plain sight or obscured by how we were taught to see. What, for example, has Aadhaar done to the meaning of citizenship and choice? Does this change depend on the demographic to which one belongs? Can this change be attributed only to Aadhaar or was the universal identity system a part of a series of changes made to what it means to be a citizen of India? For Indians, to read this book is to understand the many ways in which the last decade has changed how citizenship works. Rajadhyaksha characterizes these changes as 'creep'. While national attention focused on the questions framed and amplified by policy wonks and news media influencers, creep was taking place. Shah is looking at it from our point of view. We the user, or 'yousers' as he prefers to think of us, suffer from information overload. Hasan characterizes the problems as emerging in part from excess.

As Rajadhyaksha points out, it was difficult for many to understand the full implications of the Unique Identification number or UID in its initial stages. The trio who authored this book, along with my old friend, brilliant lawyer-researcher Sruti Chaganti, were among the first to study the project. Despite their meticulous work, they were — as we all were - looking at only one corner of the picture. It is not only Rajadhyaksha but also Hasan who surfaces everything that was unknown then. Hasan's chapter is revelatory because it shows us that the changes began long before any of us imagined they did. Shah shows us that it was not just the obscurement of changes in law and policy, but the overriding of our cognitive capacity to take in the world and to think, masked by the language of access and empowerment, that has made it difficult to participate in the democracy as we should. Together, the three authors offer an account of how technology has been used to gradually restrict and stunt the capacities that flow from citizenship in India.

Yes, All Democracies

Although this is a book that will certainly be of interest to Indians, the theory, the questions and the reimagining should be of interest to anyone with an interest in technology, citizenship, and democracy. It offers a rich interdisciplinary narrative of these questions that is unusual. The compound vision of this book might be turned on other countries, especially democracies that are skewing the way India has.

As a postcolonial democracy that is not ruled by colonial settlers, India is acutely sensitive to questions of power, equality, and control. When the information revolution began, India was one of the world's most interesting democracies. It was less than fifty years old then, and is less than a hundred now. It is also a country that was, and is, constantly learning and remaking itself, with a momentum toward change that has been steered in varying directions. India has moved rapidly toward increasing equality and then, perhaps even more rapidly, toward eradicating equality. It has invested heavily in the public sector and then privatized aggressively as it took its neoliberal turn.

The authors have a deep and nuanced understanding of the country. As you will see, this ease of navigating the past and its meaning allows them to reimagine narratives about technology and citizenship, and also allows them to show us how to ask the right questions and how to understand how technology and a democracy affect each other. Additionally, as international scholars, they are able to situate this narrative within a broader global and theoretical context. If Lisa Gitelman's book *Raw Data is an Oxymoron* discussed why there is no such thing as raw data, and danah boyd showed us the real nature of enmeshment of technology and human society, then these three authors show us the ways in which technology and private interest are entwined within democracy, and between citizens and states.

The phases of technology in democracy that this book takes us through – the euphoria, and use of the language of rights to allow technology to permeate society unrestricted – will be familiar to most people in most democracies. Similarly, the use of the language of freedom to usher in insidious changes of unfreedom has also been a global phenomenon. The cycle outlined by the authors is one that infects many democracies at different stages of having technological determinism creep into core administrative systems while the population remains hooked on entertaining videos. Like Shoshana Zuboff's widely read *The Age of Surveillance Capitalism* which describes the visible and invisible changes that technology was precipitating in one country, this too is a book that speaks to the world using India as its canvas.

As the authors took me through the last decade's events, I asked myself what it is about India that seems make it particularly fertile ground for all the most difficult questions of technology and society to grow. Perhaps it is the way forceful neoliberalism came into contact with strong constitutionalism in ways that affect a very large percentage of the people of the world.

Perhaps it is also the place that India occupies in both the creation and the consumption of technology, with populations and participation that are highly visible and entirely invisible in turn. This book not only helps us understand what has come to pass, but also helps us ask more questions.

SERIES INTRODUCTION

Overload, Creep, Excess: An Internet from India is part of a series of titles supported by the Centre for the Study of Culture & Society (CSCS), Bangalore, under the broad theme of **Culture and Democracy at the Millennial Turn**.

Turns of millennia are usually occasions to review forms of knowledge production for what they have achieved. In India, however, such an endeavor takes unusual turns. Politically bracketed by globalization at one end and the onset of religious majoritarianism at the other, as the current century has worn on it has turned into something far more significant than merely a political crisis as we come to terms with the insufficiency of several founding concepts of modernity such as nation, freedom, identity, governance, and indeed of power.

Paradoxically, as the current volume shows, this struggle is rendered especially stark when placed alongside a contrasting, and widespread, optimism that *also* defined the era. The sudden availability of new open access research tools once found only in wealthy Western universities now promised a delirious new freedom as the archives opened and transdisciplinary and transnational access led to the crumbling of timeworn disciplinary silos. Variously characterized as the time of the 'internet', it was also a time of transborder conversations that only a scant decade earlier might have been inconceivable, and of the pluralization of *spaces* for doing theory and *means* by which theory could be done. While the series defines these spaces and means diversely, a possible common thread that runs through them will be a focus on new practices of trans-institutional knowledge production, typically brought together by the triad of *pedagogy, research*, and *public engagement*, often contextualized by the onset of mass public digitization.

It was in the spirit of the times that CSCS, together with a range of new institutions, initiatives, and projects across India, saw its role as moving beyond the limits of the orthodox institution: inventing the term 'inter-institutionality', contending that the range of research resources and networks that good interdisciplinary work needed could never be supported within any single institution, however large or well-funded.

It is clear that this period did not last. One sign of its demise may well be the loss of faith in the internet's neutrality, signaled by meltdowns, funding crises, corruption, fears of neoliberal excess, terrorist threats, surveillance mechanisms, and new global ecologies that would soon engulf us in the new century.

As we turn back to the millennial moment, however, such diversity of both location and method allows us to re-view the dilemmas faced by academic practice in this fraught era of modern political history. The diversity of means, in the expanded space of the human sciences, may need to be viewed alongside the expectation that new practices of pedagogy and public engagement be given full recognition as research domains. Both came together – this series proposes – in the larger academic response mounted to the political challenges of the time. Across the literature we find outlined an era that was politically fraught, facing crises that were at once of the moment and requiring a larger historical frame, capable of some radical interdisciplinary/institutional barrier-breaking, and sustained if only momentarily by the temporary convergence of academic-activist drive and independent support.

***

This Volume

The origins of this book lie in a CSCS project assembled by the authors in 2010. The previous year, the 'Unique Identity for Every Indian Resident' project, better known as Aadhaar (support), had been announced with much fanfare by the Government of India. Known then as the Identity Project, it sought over three years to research the grassroots social impact of mass digitization through detailed field research across seven Indian states. The multiple outcomes and findings of that particular project, on paper, PDF, and video, are in the public domain. This volume is, among other things, a retrospective turn to that epochal moment, and the decades that both preceded and followed it, using insights that are very much of the present.

INTRODUCTION

Data Without Content, or the Medium With no Message

In February 2015, India's Supreme Court delivered a landmark judgment on the right to speech.[1] The issue was itself, certainly by today's standards, relatively insignificant – a Facebook post by a young woman in the small town of Palghar, in Maharashtra, that another young woman had 'liked' – that blew up when police arrested the two women under something named Section 66A of India's Information Technology Act, 2000, which redefined India's hallowed right to free speech into the digital era.[2]

The Court easily agreed with the primary argument of the petitioners on the specific question of free speech. This was the easier part, for, as legal scholar Pranesh Prakash wrote, it would have taken 'a highly clever lawyer and a highly credulous judge to make 'liking' of a Facebook status update an act capable of being charged with electronically "sending . . . any information that is grossly offensive or has menacing character"'.[3] Most lawyers also were agreed that, as Prakash elsewhere unambiguously asserted, ''liking' is protected speech under Article 19(1)(a)'.[4]

Justice Rohinton Nariman, who wrote the judgment, however went further. He took the debate beyond the relatively settled domain of the content of protected free speech and into a far more ambiguous and contested space, namely the legal nature and the properties of data itself. In seeking to regulate speech, the specific amendment to the Information Technology Act that was now being challenged had sought to define speech as *all* forms of digital storage and movement. 'Section 66A', Nariman said, 'casts the net very wide', for it effectively seeks to control 'all information that is disseminated over the internet'. Its diktat was being sought to be extended, he pointed out, over any 'computer, computer system, computer resource

---

1   Supreme Court of India, *Shreya Singhal* v *Union of India*, WP (Criminal) No. 167 of 2012 (24 March 2015), https://indiankanoon.org/doc/110813550/.
2   The original 66A said that 'any person who sends, by means of a computer resource or a communication device, (a) any information that is grossly offensive or has menacing character; or (b) any information which he knows to be false, but for the purpose of causing annoyance, inconvenience, danger, obstruction, insult, injury, criminal intimidation, enmity, hatred or ill will, persistently by making use of such computer resource or a communication device, (c) any electronic mail or electronic mail message for the purpose of causing annoyance or inconvenience or to deceive or to mislead the addressee or recipient about the origin of such messages, shall be punishable with imprisonment for a term which may extend to three years and with fine.
3   Pranesh Prakash, 'Social Media Regulation vs. Suppression of Freedom of Speech', *Kafila Online*, 19 November 2012, https://kafila.online/2012/11/19/social-media-regulation-vs-suppression-of-freedom-of-speech-pranesh-prakash/.
4   Pranesh Prakash, 'Adding Insult to Injury', *Outlook India*, 19 November 2012, https://www.outlookindia.com/website/story/adding-insult-to-injury/283033.

or communication device including attachments in text, image, audio, video and any other electronic record'.[5]

Could all of this data be even understood as speech? Speech in India has a specific legal history. The right to speech is a key right, defined by the Constitution of India as one of the cornerstones of the freedom that India's citizens had been promised with Independence. Such speech has had particular meaning. It has defined speakers as conscious subjects who know what they are saying, what meaning their speech can have, who take responsibility for what they are saying. If what they are saying is seen as dangerous, such danger 'should not be remote, conjectural or far-fetched' but should have 'proximate and direct nexus' with what is said.[6] Did all data disseminated over the internet produce such a speaker? If not, how was it speech?

But even that wasn't the real problem. The real problem was that, in defining objectionable speech, the Act 'refers only to the medium through which such information is disseminated'. It was, reversing the famous McLuhan dictum, as though the *message was now the medium*. 'Information of all kinds is roped in', Nariman went on. 'Such information may have scientific, literary or artistic value, it may refer to current events, it may be obscene or seditious', none of this apparently made any difference to the regulator. As a result, 'no distinction is made between mere discussion or advocacy of a particular point of view which may be annoying or inconvenient or grossly offensive to some' and the far more inflammatory 'incitement by which such words lead to an imminent causal connection with public disorder, security of State etc'.[7]

***

It may well be possible to read into Nariman's view of data's content neutrality, and the potentially inflammatory nature of *all* data in the paranoid view of the state censor, an inevitable if unintended afterlife to Tim Berners-Lee's original famous May 1990 conception of the ubiquity of information on the internet — when a 'web' of 'hypertext documents' would become intelligible across browsers everywhere. Now it was precisely the *illusion of its intelligibility* — the capacity of the digital delivery mechanisms to simulate speech in the way they assumed that universal accessibility automatically equated with damage — that allowed police and judicial authorities to read whatever they chose into it. It also made the sheer possession of any device traceable however remotely to seemingly suspect data into a non-bailable criminal act.

A scant three years later, in another Supreme Court case in 2018, Justice Nariman's premonition was graphically on view when the eminent historian Romila Thapar led a small group of senior academics to challenge the legality of the arrest of five human rights activists

---

5   *Shreya Singhal* v *UOI*.
6   Supreme Court of India, *S. Rangarajan Etc* v *P. Jagjivan Ram*, 1989 SCR (2) 204, 1989 SCC (2) 574, 30 March 1989, https://indiankanoon.org/doc/341773/.
7   *Shreya Singhal* v *UOI*.

and lawyers.[8] In their rejoinder, the police made a series of fantastical, ever-expanding claims of a nationwide conspiracy on the part of the accused to overthrow the Indian state. They based this entirely on 'material retrieved from the computers, laptops, pen drives and memory cards of [...] accused persons'. Such material, they asserted, revealed the arrested 'as active members of the Communist Party of India (Maoist), a banned organisation, and reflected a design of being involved in the commission of offences having the potential to destabilise the country'. They had been, the police added, arrested 'not because of their political activities' but for 'selecting and encouraging cadres in [...] banned organizations to go underground [...] mobilizing and distributing money, facilitating selection and purchase of arms, deciding the rates of such arms and suggesting the routes and ways of smuggling such arms into India for [...] training and laying booby traps and directional mines'.

None of this had been proved in any court. Instead, as Justice Chandrachud pointed out, the police claimed at a press conference to possess 'more than sufficient evidence against the five individuals' without indicating what this evidence was. Three days later, the judge continued, 'letters (many of which should form part of the case diary) were selectively flashed and read out' and 'leaked to the media', even though the concerned officer admitted – once again only on television – that 'the letters which had been read out by him were still undergoing forensic analysis together with the electronic devices'.[9] Since then, as regards the specific detainees of the Bhima-Koregaon undertrials, a US-based forensics company named Arsenal Consulting has shown, in its own analysis of some of the disks owned by them, that significant malware existed indicating the possibility of 'planted' evidence. Although Arsenal's report has been widely circulated, it too has not appeared in Court evidence since the National Investigative Agency has challenged the *locus standi* of this organization, and so it too hangs – like the data the police claim to have – in a liminal ghostly existence hovering over the actual legal process.

Possession

This book is centered around a proposition. 'Somewhere', says Nishant Shah in his essay, 'in the last few years, without us even realizing it, and in an almost non-dramatic fashion, we have foundationally changed our idea of who we are as information subjects'. The human being has become 'rehumanized', 'parsed, processed, and presented only through interfaces that render it recognizable'.

The essays in this book address a relatively recent development: the ever-expanding tsunami of data that surrounds, engulfs, and contaminates us all, passes through our devices and implicates us in multiple actions. We look at how the experience of both receiving and producing data has transformed several basic concepts of democratic politics such as

8   Supreme Court of India, *Romila Thapar* v *Union of India*, Writ Petition (Criminal) No. 268 of 2018, 28 September, 2018, https://indiankanoon.org/doc/52834611/. This concerned the arrest and incarceration without bail of several well-known activists, lawyers, and academics in 2018, known as the 'Bhima-Koregaon' case. On the occasion of the bicentenary celebrations of a colonial war celebrated by the Dalit community in Maharashtra, a political rally was held. It led to retaliatory violence, that in turn led to a major crackdown across the country. Most of the arrested are still in jail.
9   *Romila Thapar* v *UOI*.

citizenship, authorship, the right to life, to livelihood and to speech, and indeed our experience of the public domain itself. Such data defines us as much to the state as to online entities trying to access us, sell us things, troll us, qualify or disqualify us, even as we on our side relentlessly seek to understand and avail of an ever-expanding range of new and often unfamiliar rights, goods, services, and privileges available 'online'.

This transformation has taken place within a relatively short span of time. Although Nafis Hasan's essay explores an essential 70s-80s prequel, the book mostly covers a narrower period – between, as Nishant Shah has it, the Information Technology Act of 2000 and Facebook's Free Basics project of 2016 or, as Ashish Rajadhyaksha suggests, between 2009 (when in a single month India announced its massive biometric Aadhaar project and passed the draconian Section 66A) and 2020, which saw the Supreme Court judgment on the longest and severest internet shutdown the world has yet seen in Kashmir.[10]

In this time, we saw data – together with the manner of its gathering, its location, its securing, and the ability to interpret it – foundationally transform the basic armature of the modern state. In some measure the technological transformation was built, Hasan argues, on the arrival of RDBMS (or Relational Database Management System) to India. Introduced as a corporate technology, and responsible for much of the famous information technology boom of the 90s, it was the mounting of governmental functioning onto RDBMS that reinvented governance itself into something of a corporate-style service provider with the National e-Governance Plan (NeGP) of 2006, and also thereby into what Indian political scientist Partha Chatterjee has described as the 'tactically extended state'.[11] It transformed the modern state away from what Hasan calls the constraints of 'an overbearing fidelity to the organizational design of bureaucracy, to its hierarchies and rules, as well as to the computational design of information systems' and into a new era in which digital governance 'clogs the information highway, storms into the lanes, cracks, and crevices of daily life'.

A more complex register concerned the parallel morphing of several universal and 'unbound' conceptions of identity into unrecognizable avatars following the rise of targeted delivery of benefit alongside equally targeted surveillance technologies. We began encountering a new kind of subjectivity that surely rewrote the old Hegelian negotiation between subjec*tion*, or the condition of being a sovereign subject defined by the King and the State, and subjec*tivity*, or the individual egotistic interiorization of both the freedoms and responsibilities of the citizen-subject. Shah calls it a crossroads between being subjects *of* information (where we spend much of our life producing, consciously or otherwise, information about who we are, what we do, and how we relate to the world around us), subjects *to* information (as algorithmic data mining constantly produces information structures that determine various markers of who we think we are), and *subjective to* information (as we keep filtering

---

10   Internet shutdown for 552 days, starting August 4, 2019, when Article 370 of the Constitution was abrogated by Parliament.
11   Partha Chatterjee, *I am the People: Reflections on Popular Sovereignty Today*, Ranikhet: Permanent Black, 2019, p 73.

everything that does not directly pertain to us, produce a bias in favor of information that is customized for our specific needs, and eventually find ourselves in filter bubbles, 'echo chambers of network neighborhoods that protect us from people who are unlike us').

At all these stages we encounter informational excess as a condition of existence, as we turn into subjects 'whose *ontology* lies in information overload'. Such an 'ontology', says Shah, is pivoted around what may be the most basic, founding transformation taking place in our 'rehumanization': a move away from *representation*, upon which the entire polity of the 20th century was based, and into *simulation*. It is not, as we saw (in the Nariman judgment when free speech was being sought to be re-simulated into media of data storage and dissemination) a *break* from the past as much as it is the *re-signification* of the classical public sphere, morphing its key concepts such as democracy or rights into a new era that significantly redefines basic meaning-making languages that have historically founded our representation-driven 20th century. The shift from representation to simulation, paralleled by further transformations from author*ity* to author*ization*, also forces another transformation from older conditions of possibility to new structures defined by probability.

This ontology is manifested in permanent systemic crisis, but it is a crisis that, for perhaps the first time in history, has become *naturalized*. It has even turned into an everyday state of being. As human beings reconcile to their new condition (one that Hasan, on his side, names 'responsibilization'), they become ever-more dependent on 'information-overload managing technologies', even as these technologies in turn 'train' human users to meet technology halfway. At the heart of information overload, says Shah, is the argument that we are now in a cybernetic feedback loop with ourselves, where we produce and consume our own data, and engage with it through multiple terrains so that we no longer can see outside of the data streams into which we are permanently immersed.

Such humans are a new construct – 'yousers', Shah calls them – with new claims, new promises (including, as he points out, the promise of immortality that requires the older human to step out of the model of being either human or relevant and to enter this new world where Google would be their savior) and, most of all, transformed citizenship norms. We are possessed by a 'condition of informality' that defines 'our authorship, which in turn defines who speaks, on behalf of whom, in what voice, and with what authority'. It defines 'agency, choice, freedom, and truth'.

It also appears connected with what Hasan calls a *techne* of neoliberalism that, while demanding a lesser or leaner government, often actually *expands* regulation and domination through multiple seemingly autonomous entities not part of the formal state apparatus but guided instead by a corporate enterprise logic. Hasan sees it as a confluence of two interconnected trajectories. One is precisely technological – the 'electronification of governance' redefined an old command-driven, centralized planned economy into a new center-periphery imagination. The second is more ideological, a neoliberal transformation of the democratic state that allowed – often in the name of the very people whose rights were being taken away – the conversion of state benefit into elite privilege.

Being Possessed By

The authors of this volume first came together in 2010. This was a year after Aadhaar or the 'Unique Identity for Every Indian Resident' project had been announced with much fanfare by the Government of India, under which members of a large team were to research the grassroots social impact of mass digitization. 'The Identity Project' (as we named it) ran for three years, during which time we carried out detailed field research in seven Indian states, generated a mound of documentation, conducted four major workshops, and published three books.[12] The multiple outcomes and findings of that particular project, on paper, PDF, and video, have been p8ublished and are easily accessible.[13]

At that time, in 2010, we had sought – against, it must be said, considerable pressure from numerous friends, coworkers, and colleagues who offered grim forebodings about this new development and saw totalitarian designs behind it – to withhold judgment, and to try and understand what the digital ecosystem of governance might actually look like. It has been, as Ashish Rajadhyaksha's essay shows, an unfolding story, especially in the startlingly *déjà vu* manner in which the new Arogya Setu app evoked, in 2020, much of the voluntary/mandatory shadow dance that we had seen in the old Aadhaar playbook. As the last decade panned out, especially in the series of Supreme Court judgments between 2016 and 2018, it appeared that a new story could be told of the earlier period when, coinciding with the arrival of social media, a new apparatus of state regulation was also being assembled.

Such a retrospective retelling, Rajadhyaksha suggests, would now place the National Population Register (NPR) as a far more central player in the story of the first two decades of the present century than we recognized when it was passed into law in 2010, to create a register of India's 'usual residents', redefining both the Citizenship Act, 1955 and the Citizenship (Registration of Citizens and Issue of National Identity Cards) Rules, 2003. In 2010, it had appeared that Aadhaar, which had repeatedly claimed *not* to be mandatory and *not* about citizens but rather about residents, and had presented itself in far more social media-friendly terms than the NPR, had been in some conflict with the coercive approach of the NPR, which had made registration mandatory for all those who had either lived or intended to live in in India for six months or more. A retrospective timeline – especially outlined in detail by the 2018 Supreme Court judgment on Aadhaar – however suggests that the two were very much envisaged together and were indeed always meant to be two halves of a single picture.

Although this picture came together in public imagination only in 2019 with the passing of the Citizenship Amendment Act, 2019 and in the protests that followed, what it did

---

12   See Ashish Rajadhyaksha, *The Last Cultural Mile: An Inquiry into Technology and Governance in India*, Bangalore: The Centre for Internet & Society/Researchers@Work, 2011; Rajadhyaksha (ed.), *In the Wake of Aadhaar: The Digital Ecosystem of Governance in India*, Bangalore: Centre for the Study of Culture and Society, 2013; Atig Ghosh (ed.), *Branding the Migrant: Arguments of Rights, Welfare and Security*, Kolkata: Frontpage Publications Ltd., 2013.
13   The entire video archive is available on the open access platform pad.ma. See https://pad.ma/grid/title/list==zi:The_Identity_Project.

mean was that, even as information-starved Indians everywhere were both consuming and producing digital content, we were also being possessed by a larger ecosystem that governed us. Such a state, and its attendant crisis, has been often most directly evidenced in anxiety around access: both the *granting* of access and concerns about the *control and regulation* of practices that emerge.

In 2018, the Supreme Court judgment defined the condition of being possessed by data in yet another way: by calling it 'civil death'.[14] It described what was happening as a 'compulsory bartering away' of 'rights freely exercised, liberties freely enjoyed, entitlements granted by the Constitution and laws'. All these rights, liberties, and laws were being 'made conditional', and citizens were being compelled, in return, to give up their biometrics 'voluntarily', allow their biometrics and demographic information to be stored by the state and private operators, and then used for a process termed 'authentication'.

Such an operation has, said the Court, the '*propensity to cause the civil death of an individual by simply switching of Aadhaar of that person*'. If the Indian Constitution 'balances rights of individuals against State interest', Aadhaar 'completely upsets this balance and skews the relationship between the citizen and the State enabling the State to totally dominate the individual'.

Civil death, in this sense, may well be the extreme condition of such possession – where data is viewed as something of a life-support apparatus. More commonly, however, it redefines citizenship into a condition of suspended animation of what Hasan calls 'slow violence'. In his detailed example of the digitization of landownership records, he describes it as the routine 'violence of data repair' when actual people find themselves trapped in a legally precarious condition of 'temporal vacuity, a state of limbo, a temporary break from ongoing relationships' which, while not an extraordinary event of 'spectacular violence', is nevertheless an equally deadly 'circuitous low-grade suffering'.

Accidental Possession and Verifiability

In July 2020, Delhi University's much-respected professor of English, Hany Babu, was arrested by the National Investigation Agency, yet another target in the state crackdown on intellectuals, academics, and activists on the Left. As part of their inquiry, the Agency seized Babu's computer, and their 'forensic inquiry' claimed, in what had become a by-now familiar police playbook, that some sort of a 'disk partition' had existed in that machine between February and April 2019, and that this partition had contained 62 files with ''incriminating details' about his involvement in the Maoist movement'.[15] Hany Babu said he had made no such partition, possessed no such files.

---

14   'Gist of the Challenge to the Aadhaar Scheme as Well as the Act', Sec 59, Supreme Court of India, *Justice K.S. Puttaswamy (retd)* v *Union of India*, Writ Petition (C) 494/2012 (2018), https://main.sci.gov. in/supremecourt/2012/35071/35071_2012_Judgement_26-Sep-2018.pdf.
15   Sukanya Shantha, 'Elgar Parishad: NIA Arrests Hany Babu, 'Pressured Him to Implicate Colleagues, Others,' Says Wife', *The Wire*, 28 July 2020, https://thewire.in/government/nia-bhima-koregaon-hany-babu-arrest-gn-saibaba.

Eight months later, five senior academics – including several of Hany Babu's colleagues – went yet again to the Supreme Court with what appeared to be a far more basic anxiety than even the protection of their liberty: namely the potential loss of their research through unauthorized seizure of their computers and hard disks. Such seizure, they said, endangered decades of research work for their computers contained 'their life's work', 'extensive field work spanning decades or the results of scientific experiments or calculations', 'patentable material [...] or work that runs the risk of being plagiarised'. All such research work was 'irreplaceable'. In the hands of the police, it could 'run the risk of damage, loss, destruction' or – the academic's ultimate nightmare – 'even distortion'.[16]

The question of what data is may in these fraught times open up, together with an ontology, a parallel epistemic trajectory. Documents, as Lisa Gitelman says in the beginning of her book *Paper Knowledge*, are at base 'epistemic objects', 'recognizable sites and subjects of interpretation across the disciplines and beyond' and are thus 'evidential structures' – essentially there to document, to *know* and to *show* (along with their corollary, 'no show', or no proof).[17] While their digital variants may inherit some of these properties, these successor objects reveal a deeply disquieting elusiveness, where you (or rather, your device) could have chance encounters with other data or other human beings tampering with it, that can only be navigated in real time.

Raw data, says a well-known book, is an 'oxymoron' for data is everywhere, always already 'cooked'.[18] 'Access-centered discourse overrides the complex terrain of the human-technology relationship – usage, adoption, penetration, internalization, proliferation, nudging – and becomes the single point of obsession in telling the promise of the internet', writes Shah. There is a double bind of anxiety, defining both the concerns around privacy (and the draft Personal Data Protection Bill of 2019) or the multiple Terms of Service and of Intermediary Liability that define both informational control and access regulation. It is a role that the state in its orthodox avatar is often unable to perform, forcing new layers of '*state-like organizations* that would take up state-like functions in order to help deal with the threat of access'.

Shah's introduction of pornography into this picture, and his addition to the famous Rule 34 of the internet that claims that 'If something exists, there is [internet] porn of it', with a further Rule 35 that 'If there is porn on the net, people will access it', also brings a new political edge to transgressive access which he understands as a question of agency within the logics of regulation. In January 2018, when a news report appeared that a journalist had been able, via a WhatsApp group and an INR 500 bribe, to access the main databases of Aadhaar, the journalist, instead of being recognized as a whistleblower, was promptly

---

16   Krishnadas Rajagopal, 'Plea in Supreme Court to Save Academic Freedom', *The Hindu*, 30 March 2021, https://www.thehindu.com/news/national/plea-in-supreme-court-to-save-academic-freedom/article34200750.ece.
17   Lisa Gitelman, *Paper Knowledge: Towards a Media History of Documents*, Durham: Duke University Press, 2014, pp 1–2.
18   Lisa Gitelman (ed.) *'Raw Data' is an Oxymoron*, Cambridge: MIT Press, 2013.

charged with a criminal offence.[19] Among those who came to her rescue at the time was Edward Snowden. He contended that Aadhaar was 'creating a systemisation of the public' that was unrelated to its original agenda.

The incident, alongside the tantalizing ease of the hack, also brought to the fore the phenomenon of what we might call accidental possession. This is *data contaminated*, not in its content, not even by how you came across it, but most commonly in the way *it accessed you*. The idea that there exists only one single definable truth and any truth becomes a truth only when it is *verifiable*, as this entire teleology of truth-production got technologized (usually by interminable systems of authentication), it also produced strange fruit that produced the very opposite of their stated intentions when you found yourself caught within the irresistibility of its flow.

There has been, for example, the growing phenomenon of *impunity*, or what political theorist Anant Teltumbde calls the 'macabre spectacle' of extreme violence conducted in the full glare of the media.[20] When perpetrators of violence perform their actions in front of cameras, leaving no one in doubt as to what happened, but nevertheless force a legal challenge to the verification apparatus precisely from the excess of data they have produced, they point to one of the basic consequences of what Rajadhyaksha calls 'creep'. If the entire history of state digitization, from the Information Technology Act of 2000 through to Aadhaar 2009 to the Citizenship Amendment Act of 2019, unveils a relentless process of making 'creep' ubiquitous through the incessant production of information overload, it necessarily also opens a disquieting underside. Both the hacker's pornographic transgressions and its opposite, fears of police tampering, evoke the same crisis as do the perpetrators of violence on camera – the possibility that data in its very nature is always already contaminated, and that both the 'truth' it stands for as well as the apparatus of its verifiability remain compromised. What we see is, in a way, a new problem for democratic governance, and it points to one of the more bizarre consequences of the transition of the subject from a beneficiary of data practices into a source for data harvesting.

The Body, the State

Much of this book deals with the apparatus of the digital state. As the crisis of the informational subject reveals itself and reveals thereby the unprecedented challenges to the Directive Principles of the Constitution of India that define the responsibilities of the state, it necessarily opens up a larger question on the ideologies of the state apparatus itself – as distinct from the ruling ideologies of whichever government happens to be in power. There was once the idealism of a hierarchical, centralized, ordered state that regulated, along with its data itself, a parallel meaning-making apparatus on what the data meant, how it should be interpreted,

---

19   'Journalists Exposing Aadhaar Deserve Award, Not Investigation: Edward Snowden', The News Minute, 9 January 2018,
       https://www.thenewsminute.com/article/journalists-exposing-aadhaar-deserve-award-not-investigation-edward-snowden-74409.
20   Anant Teltumbde, *The Persistence of Caste: The Khairlanji Murders and India's Hidden Apartheid*, London: Zed Books, 2010, pp. 54, 137.

who should be given access to it, and how it could translate into policy. From the 80s, this idealism was replaced with a second idealism of the neoliberal state, this time premised on the seamless capacity of data to travel unhindered, to become both universally accessible and universally intelligible. Such a belief, which underpinned the protocols of networking and delivery of targeted benefit, was in some measure adapted from the early idealism of the internet, one that (we have suggested above) Justice Nariman's judgment of 2015 may well have brought to a close. We need, as we turn to a yet more recent chapter in both idealisms, to not only question their salience, but also to track – as Nafis Hasan does at the end of his essay – a yet further development, where once again the state is seeking to close down its borders to once more localize access: this time within the boundaries of the nation.

Already, in 2019, and long before the pandemic saw national borders being made tighter and more impregnable than perhaps ever in history, both the morphing of the colonial Section 144 of the Indian Penal Code (the right to public assembly) into the longest and most severe internet shutdown the world has seen in Kashmir (over 500 days) – a blanket shut off from data that threatened a 'civil death' type crisis of unprecedented proportions – as well as the extreme Emergency-like deployment, with the first COVID-19 outbreak, of the National Disaster Management Act, 2005 in March 2020 revealed further state reinventions through reinscribing real-life conditions into virtuality and back into real life, and also the central presence of the embodied informational subject in these makeovers. Overriding the question of how data challenges the sovereignty of the nation-state, what we may be witnessing is something opposite, namely the reinscription of data to make something of a massive digital cartography project in the re-encoding of the state. Its various *avatars*,[21] from hierarchical to networked to boundary-driven – and the corresponding *avatars* of its citizen, from resident (Aadhaar's favored term) to 'usual resident' (as used in the NPR) to beneficiary to 'natural person' and 'data principal' (as used in the Personal Data Protection Bill) – may well be best comprehended as simulations of the models of democracy rather than merely their digital renditions.

One result of this simulation process is the growing *weaponization* of concepts like 'sovereign national interest' and 'security and integrity of India' to define a new legal apparatus alongside the multiple new identity and biotechnological checks that regulate national borders. India's legal system has, says legal theorist Gautam Bhatia, in recent years taken a major turn.[22] Indian law has historically been constituted by two parallel regimes, the criminal justice system (or CJS) characterized by elements of due process, personal rights, and rigorous judicial review of state power, and a parallel 'preventive detention system' (PDS) in which none of these features obtain.

The two halves have been historically incompatible, but in recent years this incompatibility has been solved by the simple if deadly expedient of the return of the old colonial sedition law and its sequel laws, Terrorist and Disruptive Activities (Prevention) Act, 1987 (TADA),

---

21   Avatar, in this context, is a variant phase or version of a continuing basic entity.
22   Gautam Bhatia, *The Transformative Constitution: A Radical Biography in Nine Acts*, New Delhi: Harper Collins, 2019, p 257.

Prevention of Terrorism Act, 2002, and now the Unlawful Activities Prevention Act, 1967. All of these have been premised on custodial detention, on absolute executive (as against judicial) supremacy. Almost all are derived from unpredictable encounters with contaminated data.

Such weaponization of the apparatus of verifiability could be intentional and targeted, as with digital benefit and surveillance, or could emerge as a consequence of the sheer randomness of accidental possession – where you did not discover data as much as it discovered you, or when your inadvertent stumbling into a data ecosystem automatically criminalized you. Identity here becomes a life-and-death matter of dealing with essentially accidental encounters. If its extreme condition is the threat to life itself – when a person's digital identity gets obliterated, hacked, or simply shut off – mostly it is a slow-burning process of coming to terms with both the aspirational as well as targeted consequences of overload, to learn overnight when to be visible and when it is best not to be.

The focus on the embodied data-subject is thus no longer merely the bearer of data but an instantiation of the data practices into which the body finds itself immersed, voluntarily or otherwise. The weaponization of data as evidence to punish, control, and contain the body is therefore a corollary of digital misinformation and civil death. Both conditions are eventually tied to the idea of ownership defined not in terms of possession but of *distribution*. If data evidences are no longer about discrete bodies and institutions where ownership can be demonstrated, disrupted, or contained, then we could be looking at new challenges posed by the conditions of data circulation to meaning itself.

In the end, if Justice Nariman's pronouncements on data may have ended one kind of internet dream, his parallel point about making 'no distinction' between 'mere discussion or advocacy' and 'incitement by which such words lead to an imminent causal connection with public disorder' may well open up another possibility.[23] The signification of data through circulation exists within, but also breaches, the boundaries of the state. In either case, it defines several of our immediate political challenges, the subjective condition of being immersed in informationality, or the consequences of being disconnected from it.

---

23   *Shreya Singhal* v *UOI.*

THE INSIDIOUSNESS OF INFORMATION OVERLOAD

NISHANT SHAH

Introductory Note

In 2018, there was still a breathless excitement about information access, expansion, and bounty, leading to futurescaping scenarios of interactive smart cities, self-driving autonomous vehicles, and 5G inspired virtual environments that we shall all live and interact in. The promise of the internet (and all things included in that catch-all term) was still expressed in the boundless, limitless, and accelerated information which forms the basis of Big Data dreams as well. However, somewhere around that time, there also emerged a different conversation — about excessive data streams, relentless notifications, algorithmic manipulation, and the capacity to discern the veracity, validity, or value of the information that was circulating so fast that any meaningful interaction with it became difficult. The proliferation of 'fake news', in particular, made it clear that the extraordinary and uncontrolled spread of digital information had suddenly erupted as a critical and unforeseen problem.

In addition, with more and more people finding a voice online — we were globally celebrating some powerful hashtags like #metoo and their local consequences — there was also increased backlash, online violence, and abuse directed at them through institutional and informal organization. The excess of information, or information overload, was no longer just an information design and data management question; it had become a weaponized mode of address, leading to silencing, intimidation, and harm. While we were processing these questions, the COVID-19 pandemic shrunk our lives into rectangles on screens and the weariness of increased digital engagement — encapsulated in the cultural zeitgeist as 'Zoom fatigue' — led to people's disengagement from decision-making. People were relying more on automated algorithmic structures to curate the information that they engaged with. We were slowly recognizing the unbearable lightness of digitization and the insufferable weight of information, realizing that the thrill of plenty was now manifesting as the tyranny of overload.

Information overload became the unspoken state of digital being and it took us by surprise. The assurances of search engines, database management, algorithmic curation, peer-2-peer dissemination, wisdom of crowds, intuitive information shaping, and emancipation from the task of remembering everything by putting it into storage seemed to have done their rhetorical work so well that when we started recognizing information overload, it felt like it was new, sudden, and unexpected, and we didn't quite know how it happened. This essay is an attempt to first recognize and identify this state of information overload as a cultural and political, not just technological, question. It examines the cost of being in this perpetual state of crisis of informational overload and how it shapes our conversations about action and activism. More urgently, it refuses the framework of unexpectedness and surprise and shows how information overload is not the bug but rather the feature of computational network design, and one that has been a long time in the making.

This essay looks at significant milestones, judgments, policies, acts, regulations, controversies, and cultural phenomena that have shaped and signaled the rise and making of information overload. It takes pastiche historicization to break the pattern of responses that accompany the newness of digital media crises: the finding of new digital tools to counteract the existing digital tools and pathologizing the user as the corrupt variable responsible for these crises. When it comes to digital media, the crisis of the now invariably looks for solutions in the future, as if the immediacy of the crisis also precludes all historicity. In this essay, by focusing on the infrastructural production of overload and the informational shaping of the user, I examine how we got to this state of information overload and the crisis of the informational subject.

The first section tries to understand how the state of overload was designed and naturalized through regulatory and policy frameworks on the one hand, and the favoring of specific forms of informational behavior on the other. The second section establishes that the user, who is often seen as the agential unit of digital cybernetic feedback loops, is compromised in agency and autonomy through the championing and the perpetuation of informational overload. Both sections together present a specific account of how we got to this point where information overload is so ubiquitous and insidious that we do not even recognize it as a critical condition and do not understand the materiality and historicity of how it came about. Through an archive of milestones in India – some popular, some lesser studied – this essay offers a way of reading some of the most pernicious problems of our times as a result of the engineering, cultural shaping, and political proliferation of the state of overload.

I.

Informationally Yours: Overloaded

In July 2020, when India, and the rest of the world, was reeling from the COVID-19 pandemic, a YouTube video went viral in the country.[1] Made by a self-described *YouTuber and influencer* Shubham Mishra, the video shows Mishra sitting in his car, uttering profanities in unchaste Hindi. He threatened a stand-up comedian Agrima Joshua with physical violence and even rape. Mishra, a staunch nationalist and a moderately popular influencer, who regularly created offensive and threatening videos in the name of *calling truth* for his roughly 2.5 million followers, was aggravated by a stand-up routine or set that Joshua had performed

[1]   The video, a piece of misogynist vitriol, was later deleted by the original uploader. While many clone copies exist, I find it important not to center his voice and give him more hyperlink attention. However, the following write-up in *The Free Press Journal* offers a comprehensive summary of the case at hand. See 'Remember Agrima Joshua's Vile Abuser Shubham Mishra? He's Out on Bail Now', *The Free Press Journal*, 18 August 2020, https://www.freepressjournal.in/entertainment/remember-agrima-joshuas-vile-abuser-shubham-mishra-hes-out-on-bail-now.

a year earlier in 2019. In that set, Joshua mocked the Indian government's plans to build a massive statue of the beloved nationalist icon Chhatrapati Shivaji Maharaj off Mumbai's shoreline and the way people on the crowdsourcing platform Quora were exaggerating and embellishing the features of the proposed statue – laser eyes to kill terrorists, solar cells to power the entire state of Maharashtra, and GPS trackers to identify enemies, for example.

In his three-minute video, like a professional social media berserker, Mishra managed to at once profess his love and loyalty for Shivaji, appoint himself as the vanguard of all communities aggrieved by this attack on their religious/nationalist leader, and call for the cancelling of such *progressive* stand-up comedies. Announcing his respect for women, he went on to lambast Joshua, call her the 'N' word (coincidentally doing it while Black Lives Matter was taking global anchor in its second uprising), and casually threaten her with rape and death while inviting his followers to join him in teaching Joshua a lesson.

The video, which has since been deleted and re-uploaded multiple times, went viral amidst polarized responses from those supporting Mishra and those appalled at the blatant display of toxic masculinity and aggression woefully naturalized in the entertainment-hate complex of digital social media. The renewed interest in this video a year later led to a series of quick attacks on Joshua in a manner that has become all-too-familiar by now. The ruling right-wing party in Maharashtra unleashed an army of trolls who started threatening and intimidating Joshua for insulting their beloved warrior king Shivaji. Pratap Sarnaik, a member of the Maharashtra legislative assembly representing the nationalist party Shiv Sena, wrote to the home minister of Maharashtra Anil Deshmukh to prosecute the comedian for making contemptuous comments against Shivaji.[2] Deshmukh himself tweeted to his affronted populace that he had 'instructed CP (Commissioner of Police) Mumbai and IG (Inspector General) Cyber to take legal action expeditiously', and urged everybody to 'maintain calm' and let the law take its course.[3] Caught in the storm, Joshua tweeted an apology video and took down the offending recording, even as angry mobs echoed Mishra that Joshua should be taught a lesson. They ignored her apology, ransacked the café where the comedy sketch had been hosted, and committed multiple acts of vandalism and destruction.[4]

This narrative of digital bullying, intimidation, harassment, threat, violence, and incitement to sexual assault that Joshua experienced – in an intense viral cycle – follows an all-too-familiar trope of women's experiences on digital social media in India. It exemplifies the

---

2   *The Quint* published a detailed report on the story. See, 'Comic Joshua Gets Rape Threat for Joke on Chhatrapati Shivaji', *The Quint*, 13 July 2020, https://www.thequint.com/news/india/comic-agrima-joshua-gets-rape-threat-for-joke-on-chhatrapati-shivaji.

3   'Agrima Joshua Case: Maha HM Anil Deshmukh Asks Mumbai Police to Take Legal Action against Comedian over Chhatrapati Shivaji Maharaj Remark', *The Free Press Journal*, 11 July 2020, }https://www.freepressjournal.in/mumbai/agrima-joshua-case-maha-hm-anil-deshmukh-asks-mumbai-police-to-take-legal-action-against-comedian-over-chhatrapati-shivaji-maharaj-remark.

4   'Agrima Joshua Row: Comedian Posts Video Apologizing to Members of Political Parties', *The Free Press Journal*, 11 July 2020, https://www.freepressjournal.in/india/agrima-joshua-row-comedian-posts-video-apologizing-to-members-of-political-parties.

2018 Thomson Reuters Foundation report that pegged India as one of the most dangerous countries for women[5] and the 2020 Global Press Freedom Index which ranked it 142 out of 180 countries for erasure of the right to free speech.[6]

The Joshua–Mishra story might well have ended here, except for an unexpected narrative twist. Outraged by Mishra's particular brand of misogyny, a growing movement began protesting the impunity with which Mishra, together with a slew of hate-spewing influencers, was apparently able to continue unaffected. Following a public outcry, the National Commission for Women (NCW) took cognizance of the case,[7] and Mishra was arrested by Vadodara Police on charges of obscenity, outraging the modesty of a woman, provocation to break public peace, public mischief, and criminal intimidation. Police also seized his phone and booked him under the Information Technology Act, 2000, for publishing and transmitting lascivious material.

The Joshua–Mishra story is unremarkable in how such incidents have become normalized on the Indian social web. However, some responses were significant. Many of those responsible for joining the social media outrage that had led to Mishra's arrest were surprised, alarmed, and angry, but also genuinely shocked to see their favorite video-sharing platform hosting such content. Several were apparently discovering such content for the first time on the web. There were heated discussions on the YouTube video, on Quora and on Reddit, about how this might be *scripted content*, a *publicity stunt*; how this amount of hatred is *not natural*. People were busy examining Mishra's previous videos (his followers and video views increased tenfold in the process) trying to present this instance as anomalous, hinting at a larger conspiracy theory of who might have *put Mishra up to the job* or what might have *triggered him* to use such language. It seemed impossible to view casual misogyny as the naturalized state of digital entertainment in influencer cultures. There appeared an overwhelming felt need to find deeper, somehow more profound, explanations alongside hidden conspiracies that might have made this video at all possible.

Mishra's supporters, too, were analyzing his loathsome diatribe, seeking to prove that, while admittedly violent and hateful, it did not either explicitly or conclusively threaten Joshua with rape. Progressive liberals were, they claimed, twisting Mishra's profanity-laden words and misinterpreting them because he was standing up for national honor. In his own apology video, which he was forced to make after being threatened with legal action, Mishra reiterated that he had not attacked Joshua, but rather defended the honor

5   Belinda Goldsmith and Meka Beresford, 'India Most Dangerous Country for Women with Sexual Violence Rife - Global Poll', *Reuters*, 26 June 2018, https://www.reuters.com/article/women-dangerous-poll-idINKBN1JM076.

6   '2020 World Press Freedom Index: "Entering a Decisive Decade for Journalism, Exacerbated by Coronavirus"', Reporters Without Borders, https://rsf.org/en/2020-world-press-freedom-index-entering-decisive-decade-journalism-exacerbated-coronavirus.

7   Tanvi Akhauri, 'Shubham Mishra Has Been Arrested, but the Problem of Offence-Taking Still Persists', *shethepeople*, 13 July 2020, https://www.shethepeople.tv/home-top-video/shubham-mishra-arrested-agrima-joshua/.

of his people. He was indeed the *victim* here, of conspiracy, of being baited by the secular press and media to suit their own agendas of nation-hating.

For Mishra's supporters and critics, this in-your-face video and its production and reception were deemed suspicious. Debates arose on both sides on what, to use Kellyanne Conway's phrase, the 'alternative facts'[8] were, how the video could not be taken at face value, and how it didn't necessarily mean what it said.

I point here to the ease with which both outraged factions slipped into the examination of conspiracy, unable to see the obvious. Together with the large amount of information generated around this entire phenomenon, a critical new mode of subjectivity was created: that of being *informationally overloaded*. I propose that the natural propensity to take almost *any* digital content and expect something *more*, something *hidden*, something *extra* than what meets the eye or is available on the surface indicates a particular condition where blame, responsibility, and culpability become ever negotiated and constantly oscillating values without fixity. The production of Joshua, as a perpetrator who had to apologize for her acts, and the presentation of Mishra, as a victim being wronged by angry Twitterati, are not exceptional, but rather a regular occurrence in an ever-expanding zone of crises produced by social media.

Information overload produces, then, a state of permanent crisis – one that allows for inversions and suspensions, and allows for fixed values to come *unstuck*, enabled by a set of paradoxes that frame our debates around contemporary digital social media. In an attempt to unravel these paradoxes, this essay provides a symptomatic reading of three major *digital crises* that have emerged in India (along with the rest of the world) over the last two decades that saw an astonishing democratization of digital technologies even as it saw the digitization of democracy. Building through these crises, the sections in this essay help us understand the implications of a naturalized information overload, and how such a condition allows us to unpack the almost paralyzed debates on misinformation, verification, fake news, and post-truth – contexts that destabilize nearly all our conversations on political governance, from climate to social justice.

The Information (Overload) Crisis

I begin this section with a fundamental proposition: In the last few years, without us even realizing it, and in an almost nondramatic fashion, we have foundationally changed our idea of who we are as information subjects. We increasingly define information as a *condition* of our existence, a condition of naming ourselves and each other. Our informational condition is now also what defines our authorship, which in turn defines who speaks, on behalf of whom, in what voice, and with what authority. Our questions of agency, choice, freedom, and truth are all tied to conditions of informationality.

---

8   Aaron Blake, 'Kellyanne Conway Says Donald Trump's Team Has 'Alternative Facts.' Which Pretty Much Says It All', *The Washington Post*, 22 January 2017, https://www.washingtonpost.com/news/the-fix/wp/2017/01/22/kellyanne-conway-says-donald-trumps-team-has-alternate-facts-which-pretty-much-says-it-all/.

It appears also to be widely accepted that such a condition of informationality exists at three different levels, in the three kinds of relationships we have with information. First, as subjects *of* information, where we don't need personal and social media or smart and quantifying devices to tell us that, primarily, when we talk about anything at all, we talk about ourselves. A large part of our everyday life is spent in producing information about who we are, what we do, and how we relate to the world around us. It is not a surprise that, with the rise of easy-to-access digital devices, we built *social media* which built something that was not *new* as much as it was a documentation of our authoring of our selfhood immersed within this informational condition.

At a second level, informationality also makes us subject *to* information, as it shapes our informational realities and the contexts we live in. Our identities, subjectivities, opinions, choices, tastes, preferences, and desires are continuously designed and influenced by a variety of other information hubs. This is at the heart of communication and marketing, and this is also the hold, in analogue media, of advertising and propaganda. It is, then, not surprising that with the rise of algorithmic data mining practices we are being written more and more into information structures that *determine various markers of who we think we are*. An emerging global concern of invisible data being stored and circulated and manipulated and reintroduced into our lives is essentially a recognition that we are more written against than writing.

Third, and perhaps most significantly, informationality also makes us *subjective to* information. Not only do we produce habits of filtering information that do not directly pertain to us, we also have a *positive bias* toward information that is relatable, accessible, and customized to our specific needs. These needs box us into filter bubbles in digital networks, and explain why so many of our conversations are in echo chambers of network neighborhoods that protect us from people who are unlike us. We are aware that information can be excessive, intense, and paralyzing, and hence we have learned to selectively filter out the streams that can sustain our modes of being. This relationship is historical as well as ingrained in our daily practices of life, labor, language, and love. And because this relationship is so central to our very biological, social, political, and emotional survival, we have guarded it fiercely across history.

One of the ways in which we have protected ourselves within such a relentless informationality is by thinking about what constitutes a reasonable amount of information for a human person to process, analyze, and execute. Hence, the much used, abused, and sometimes dismissed notion of information overload. The moment you read this phrase, I know you have a reaction to it – you are either rolling your eyes, shaking your head in empathy, or bookmarking it for later because right now you have a dozen other tabs open that are competing for your attention.

While information overload has been talked about extensively in the last decade or so, connected with precarious labor in attention economies, with scattered and fragmented lives shaped by #FOMO (Fear of Missing Out), and data circulation in digital networks, it is good to remember that it is not as contemporary a concern as it appears. Ann Blair, a historian of information, points out that in the Judeo-Christian traditions of the West, the concern around *too many books* surfaced as early as in the 1st century, where in Ecclesiastes we are cautioned: 'But beyond these, my son, be warned: there is no end to the making of many books, and much study wearies the body.'[9] This warning was echoed in moral philosophy where Seneca, in his *Treatises*, mourned the dangers of abundant information:

> Even for studies, where expenditure is most honorable, it is justifiable only so long as it is kept within bounds. What is the use of having countless books and libraries, whose titles their owners can scarcely read through in a whole lifetime? The learner is, not instructed, but burdened by the mass of them, and it is much better to surrender yourself to a few authors than to wander through many.[10]

Similarly, even at the height of the accumulation craze in the mythical libraries of Alexandria in Egypt, the concern about *How much is too much?* was very much alive. As Kathleen Fitzpatrick shows in her history of information design, *Planned Obsolescence*, it was the idea that too much unfiltered exposure to information might paralyze the reader that gave rise to librarians as custodians and keepers of the keys rather than as access points and facilitators of knowledge.[11] Mark Rose talks about scribal cultures in the 5th and 6th centuries A.D. in England, where the Church educated young men to take the sacred duty of copying the Holy Writ for circulation across the land.[12] However, not just anybody could become a scribe. Apart from privileges of birth and gender, the to-be-scribe also needed to show moral fortitude and the capacity to deal with the excessive information he would be exposed to in the course of his literary education. Even when scribes were finally granted an epiphany and tasked with the holy book, they were kept in cloistered isolation so as not to transmit any possible madness that may emerge from excessive sensory and information overload.

At the turn of the 16th century, with moveable type democratizing information access, the concern around information overload took on a more gendered tone. As Virgina Woolf, in her 1929 novel *A Room of One's Own*, reminds us, in her commemoration of Aphra Behn, 'the blue stocking with an itch for scribbling', the trope of too much information leading to more depravity was also used as a justification for keeping women from reading or writing literature.[13] Kate Millet, in her seminal 1970 thesis *Sexual Politics*, reminds us that there was a systemic relationship between madness and reading, where the woman was considered too fragile to deal with the cerebral processing that came as a part of too much exposure to information.[14]

In the late 19th century, the arrival of mass communication, especially the telephone, opened the door to anyone being able to call to give you information – spammers, cold callers, wrong numbers, heretics with dubious content, strangers with predatory intent

---

9   Eccles. 12:12 Christian Standard Bible.
10 Ann M. Blair, *Too Much to Know: Managing Scholarly Information before the Modern Age*, New Haven and London: Yale University Press, 2010; all citations in this paragraph are from pp. 14–16.
11 Kathleen Fitzpatrick, *Planned Obsolescence: Publishing, Technology, and the Future of the Academy*, New York and London: New York University Press, 2011.
12 Mark Rose, *Authors and Owners: The Invention of Copyright*, Cambridge, Massachusetts: Harvard University Press, 1993.
13 Virginia Woolf, *A Room of One's Own*, London: Hogarth Press, 1929.
14 Kate Millett, *Sexual Politics*, Garden City, New York: Doubleday & Co., 1970.

—putting us all in the continued danger of lapsing into a state of excessive information that would leave us uncertain about our own identities. The anxiety at this point was not about our *ability* to discern credible information from lies, but about an *instability in our sense of self* and its well-being.

So strong was this idea of sudden bursts of information overload as harming the self, that it even translated into facetious-sounding but earnestly written editorials vilifying and demonizing the technology apparatus itself. Carolyn Marvyn, a historian of information technologies, in her book *When Old Technologies Were New*, fishes out an editorial from *The Electrical Review* that relates the story of an affluent Chicago woman who was looking for a housekeeper she could entrust her children to while she traveled for a family emergency. A housekeeper who was tending to another house recovering from scarlet fever was recommended. As Marvyn recounts, '...she was urged to expedite arrangements by telephone'. At first, she was 'aghast at the proposition, and was sure there would be great danger of infection' by wire, her fears a metaphor for all the elements of the world beyond domestic control. After weighing the arguments of a knowledgeable friend, she concluded:

> Well, I suppose I must risk it. I'll have a servant call up the house and tell them be sure that the housekeeper changes her clothes and the sick children aren't in the room where the telephone is; then I may feel justified under the circumstances in talking with her.

In 1894, *Electrical World* had reported that the 'editor of a prominent Philadelphia daily newspaper had cautioned his readers not to converse by phone with ill persons for fear of contracting contagious diseases.'[15]

This idea of information overload – either caused by unexpected information, excessive information, shocking information, dangerous information, or misinformation, all resulting from what Alvin Toffler described in 1970 in his famous *Future Shock* as 'an information explosion' – has been naturalized and brooded over.[16] For those of us old enough to have lived through the turn of the millennium, we still have memories of the Y2K scare where the entire world order was going to collapse, as time-counting mechanisms of modern-day computers, unable to grasp the millennial turn, would throw us into an information chaos. The crisis-that-never-happened was perhaps best enshrined in the iconic Nike advertisement that showed a jogger 'just doing it' in a world slowly deteriorating into Y2K anarchy.[17] The biggest worry about Y2K was not just that infrastructure would crash – satellites collapsing, planes crashing, banks coming to a halt – but a sudden savagery that we would all regress into because the machines that regulated our information consumption would give up on their task of information regulation.

---

15   Carolyn Marvin, *When Old Technologies Were New: Thinking About Electric Communication in the Late Nineteenth Century*, Oxford: Oxford University Press, 1988, p. 81.
16   Alvin Tofler, *Future Shock*, New York: Random House, 1970.
17   Nike Y2K - Jogger, https://www.youtube.com/watch?v=q_7YmvH3pYw.

I give you this huge, ahistorical, symptomatic overview to go back to my proposition – that somewhere, in the first two decades of the 21st century, our relationship with information shifted, and that this shift is perhaps best characterized by information overload. This is not, as my sketchy history shows, a new phenomenon – every technology that sought to expand knowledge documentation and information production has triggered worries about who we will become. In short, we have always worried about what happens when we lapse into information overload.

What is, however, *new* for the digital turn that we live in is that we may have, perhaps for the first time in history, *stopped worrying about information overload*. Or, to make it clearer, we no longer think about information overload as the exceptional moment when we get bombarded with too much information. Such a condition is not evidenced through isolated incidents, nor does it require special coping mechanisms and skills to deal with it and escape it. Our overflowing inboxes, our continuous stream of notifications, the smart devices we see, and the smarter devices that are invisible but watch us, have all created a new informational subject – a subject whose *ontology* lies in information overload. This has become our naturalized state of being, not a futuristic phenomenon or a momentary condition to be separated and dealt with in isolation.

If the older information subject was a subject worried about information overload and how to escape it, the new information subject understands itself *through* the condition of incessant information. This is why we participate in the continuous mining of data by devices that give us beautiful visualizations masquerading as profound self-knowledge and truth. It is perhaps why we subject ourselves to the ever-expanding field of algorithmic surveillance that gives us convenience for privacy. This may also be why we see ourselves as willfully participating in polarized positions that are neither illustrative nor reflective of our subjective selves, but performative of the networked mechanics that shape the digital.

I seek to establish this naturalization of information overload as a *condition* of crisis, which not only engineers and perpetuates the contemporary crises around automation, fake news, algorithmic polarization, and filter bubbles, but is a *crisis in itself*, which needs to be unpacked beyond the questions of usage, penetration, regulation, and control that are often addressed when dealing with information overload.

The Information Overload (Continual) Crisis

The information overload crisis, as in the case of the Joshua–Mishra controversy, can be studied – and has indeed been mainly analyzed – at the level of content: in editorials, analyses and conversations about the nature of hate speech and the polarizing formats of digital engagement. However, such analyses do not always help us understand the phenomenon where *both* Mishra and Joshua are presented as victims, and how *all* the narratives seem to be received as potentially fake and are thus at once informationally overwhelming as well as deficient in credibility. This particular condition of information overload as both *saturated* and *depleted* by informationality has to be understood as *itself* a crisis as opposed to the *reason* for a crisis. It establishes information overload not as a future horizon or a historical event but a *specific condition of the digital* perpetuating and generating itself as a continuous condition.

In technology studies, and particularly in critical code and software studies, such a crisis has received a lot of attention. The French media philosopher Bruno Latour proposed the idea of 'reversible black-boxing', where he takes the example of a broken overhead projector to propose that, upon breakdown, a technological object transforms from being an enclosed object to a network of different agents – actants – making up the performance or idea of the object.[18] This framework has found much traction because it recognizes the breakdown as a state of crisis where the user's attention is directed from the system as an enclosed object to an awareness that the system is constituted by different parts.

It is possible to take the Joshua–Mishra case as an instance where the expected smoothness of social media gets interrupted by the intrusion of the legal apparatus that seeks to regulate the content and its distribution. It is important to notice that the Terms of Service of digital services and the Information Technology (Intermediary Guidelines and Digital Media Ethics Code) Rules, 2021 were ineffective in actually curbing the spread and the visibility of this hate speech. Despite multiple people reporting the videos and the call for action, neither Instagram nor YouTube took responsibility for censoring and removing such content. Even as people were commenting on the broken nature of this social media engagement, amplified by discussions in traditional media, it was clear that multiple agents were needed to make sense of this digital crisis. The swift intervention of the law, the arrest of Mishra, the stepping in of different celebrities and politicians, the response from the political party that sought to investigate Joshua as also culpable, all suddenly make themselves visible in the infrastructure of otherwise opaquely transparent interfaces of our digital devices where these crises play out.

American sociologist Susan Leigh Star builds on Latour's work in her 'call to study boring things'.[19] She seeks to understand crisis as located in neglected and invisible systems – not systems that work and might break, but systems that have long stopped working, but are still around, forming a massive infrastructure of what German media theorist Wolfgang Ernst calls 'undead media'.[20] While Star was particularly interested in thinking of 'computers as information highways' and 'as symbolic sewers' to open up the back ends of global information flows, which otherwise remain 'buried in inaccessible electronic code', Ernst, by contrast, was identifying the crisis in the time criticality of digital computational media which converts the computer into 'a complex time machine' and manifests it as 'equiprimordial' (temporally undistinguishable).[21] Media do not have a historical past, says

---

18   Bruno Latour, 'A Collective of Humans and Nonhumans: Following Daedalus's Labyrinth', in Bruno
      Latour, *Pandora's Hope: Essays on the Reality of Science Studies*, Cambridge, Massachusetts: Harvard
      University Press, 1999, pp. 183–184.
19   Susan Leigh Star, 'The Ethnography of Infrastructure', *American Behavioral Scientist* 43.5 (1999):
      377–391.
20   Wolfgang Ernst, *Digital Memory and the Archive*, Minneapolis: University of Minnesota Press, 2013, p.
      57.
21   Wolfgang Ernst, *Sonic Time Machines: Explicit Sound, Sirenic Voices, and Implicit Sonicity*,

Ernst: while in operation, they exist outside of historic time in a state of micro-temporality, a synthesis of the past and the present in the now.

New Media theorists Hertz Garnett and Jussi Parikka draw on Ernst's idea of crisis as constituted in the very operation of media, and propose that *all media is always in a state of degeneration* and hence always on the precipice of obsolescence – a state of continual crisis. Hertz and Parikka present 'planned obsolescence' as a crisis horizon that can both be bent and differed as art and design practices 'resurrect, reanimate, and reappropriate' discarded dead media, turning them into new assemblies of 'zombie media'.[22] This resonates with Lauren Berlant, who, in their exposition on *Cruel Optimism*, reminds us that the naturalization of crises of 'life-building' has so overwhelmed our experience of living that 'adjustment seems like an accomplishment'.[23] Critical Code studies theorist Wendy Chun begins her book by claiming that 'new media exist at the bleeding edge of obsolescence', thus necessitating a continued state of 'updating to remain the same'.[24] Chun argues that the 'twinning of crisis and code/habit' (perhaps a perfect description of social media engagement) 'has not diminished crises, but rather proliferated them through an unending series of decisions and unforeseen consequences that undermine the agency they promise'.[25] In her characteristically pithy way, Chun announces that in 'new media, crisis has found its medium: and in crisis, new media has found its value, its punctuating device'.[26]

Information overload as a condition of crisis is itself critical because it does not seek to dissolve itself or offer any resolutions for the short-lived but intense moments of engagement it generates. Rather, it normalizes a state of continual crisis, manifested in different events that rise and fade without the crisis ever going away. It is from this sense of a crisis that we shall now try and make sense of how digital discourse and practice have been shaped in India.

This essay lays out the story of the internet in India as a story of the naturalizing of information overload. It tries to make sense of current debates around disinformation, fake news, post-truth, and governance as structured and informed by such naturalization. In order to do this, it establishes three paradoxes that mark the naturalization and anchors these paradoxes in *social media crises* that have pockmarked the history of the internet(s) in India. I hope to retell the story of infrastructure, governance, regulation, and policy through the often-overlooked questions of affective, libidinal, and lived experiences of the people. This will hopefully also return our focus back to the human actors who are often a part of the technological crises, but are made invisible by the focus on the technological terrain and the idea of the user as the predominant way of describing and resolving these crises.

Amsterdam: University of Amsterdam Press, 2016, pp. 64, 80, xxii.

22   Garnet Hertz and Jussi Parikka, 'Zombie Media: Circuit Bending Media Archaeology into an Art Method', *Leonardo* 45.5 (2012): 424–430.

23   Lauren Berlant, *Cruel Optimism*, Durham: Duke University Press, 2011, p. 3.

24   Wendy Hui Kyong Chun, *Updating to Remain the Same: Habitual New Media*, Cambridge, Massachusetts and London: The MIT Press, 2016.

25   Chun, *Updating to Remain the Same*, p. 70.

26   Chun, *Updating to Remain the Same*, p.74.

Your Access/Accessing You

On August 25, 2015, the state government of Gujarat imposed an unprecedented internet shutdown on the entire state.[27] For the state, which had built itself up as the poster child of digital development, through reurbanization, opening up public sector projects for private investments and offering tax breaks to information technology companies to build their development-making centers in the state,[28] this was an unexpected and unprecedented move. The promise of economic and inclusive growth, enshrined in the ruling party's slogan *Sabka saath, sabka vikas* (Everyone's support, everyone's development), and the image of Gujarat as a new IT state that was investing in the digital future, made this an unexpected site for a shutdown. While other parts in the country have a continued history of internet shutdowns, these were generally in states that saw conflict, where the suspension of digital access and civil liberties appeared necessary for security and sovereignty.[29]

The movement that ushered Gujarat into this state of digital emergency has a 22-year-old politician, Hardik Patel, as its poster child. The convener of the Patidar Anamat Andolan Samiti (PAAS), a political body that advocates for minority rights for the Patidar community[30] by including them in the category of Other Backward Class (OBC),[31] Patel has been actively involved in organizing massive rallies since the summer of 2015.[32] The on-the-ground rallies have also been accompanied by a popular social media campaign which included YouTube videos, messages, memes, and even two Android apps that mobilized the community through weak people-to-people networks.

It took a small but dedicated core team of young political leaders to put together the *Maha Kranti* Rally (The Epic Revolution Rally) that engulfed the whole state.[33] While

---

27   Aarefa Johari, 'Gujarat Internet Ban: On Day Six, Citizens Have Had Enough of Being Patronized by the State', *Scroll.in*, 1 September 2015, https://scroll.in/article/752538/gujarat-internet-ban-on-day-six-citizens-have-had-enough-of-being-patronised-by-the-state.

28   Pooja Thomas, 'Museum as Metaphor: The Politics of an Imagined Ahmedabad', in Arvind Rajagopal and Anupama Rao (eds) *Media and Utopia: History, Imagination and Technology*, New York: Routledge, 2017, pp. 133–148.

29   Examining this phenomenon of lockdowns and internet shutdowns to show how 'disinformation' continues to travel in these shutdowns to shape state propaganda and messaging, I have also written about this case in another journal paper: Nishant Shah, '(Dis)information Blackouts: Politics and Practices of Internet Shutdowns', *International Journal of Communication* 15 (2021): 2693–2709.

30   To know more about the political context of the Patidar community, see Gopal Kateshiya, 'Gujarat Protests: Who are the Patidars, and why are they Angry', *The Indian Express*, 27 August 2015, https://indianexpress.com/article/explained/simply-put-who-are-gujarats-patidars-and-why-are-they-angry/.

31   Ashish Chauhan, 'Jat Fire Tempts Patidars to Action', *The Times of India*, 22 February 2016, https://timesofindia.indiatimes.com/city/ahmedabad/jat-fire-tempts-patidars-to-action/articleshow/51086440.cms.

32   'Patidar Reservation: Social Media Spreading Sardar Patel Movement Like Wild Fire', *DNA*, 22 August 2015, http://www.dnaindia.com/india/report-patidar-reservation-social-media-spreading-sardar-patel-movement-like-wild-fire-2117056.

33   'Stir Over OBC Status: Govt Proposes Talks; Hardik Plays Hardball', *The Indian Express*, 23 August 2015, http://indianexpress.com/article/india/india-others/stir-over-obc-status-govt-proposes-talks-

each major city in Gujarat was organizing the coordinated demonstration, the biggest protest gathering was planned in Ahmedabad. Beginning at the massive Gujarat Mineral Development Corporation (GMDC) ground, the rally attracted more than half a million members of the community, who, after some political speeches, held the city under siege, marching to the district collector's office. Patel, who was one of the speakers rallying up the crowds, announced that at the end of the rally he would go on an indeterminate hunger strike until the chief minister of the state herself came to receive the memorandum. Both he and his immediate allies were arrested for not having the adequate permissions to stay on the ground after the rally. Although they were later released, tensions had already escalated and the city saw the deployment of police and paramilitary forces to disperse the agitating crowds that were already demonstrating acts of mob violence. Ten people (police and protestors) would eventually be killed across the state. The state government of Gujarat imposed physical curfews in a few cities along with a complete shutdown of the internet.[34]

The story of PAAS, and the electoral and political results it led to, merits another analysis. Here it is important to place its role in the blocking of internet access, and thus to tell a somewhat different story of the promise of access that has shaped the history of the internet in the country.

Access has been one of the primary drivers of digitalization and investment in internet infrastructure that was supposed to leapfrog the country into a digital revolution. In fact, the very first definition in the Information Technology Act, 2000 is for the term access.

Access with its grammatical variations and cognate expressions means gaining entry into, instructing, or communicating, with the logical, arithmetical, or memory function resources of a computer, computer system, or computer network.[35]

Even in this definition, both the conditions and means of access are clearly nuanced. Access was not just about usage *but any meaningful interaction with the entire digital ecosystem*. Access was discussed in the context of unauthorized access; storage, retention, and retrieval; licensing and public access; availability and perpetuity; security and legitimation; denial and maleficent blockage of access; privacy and replication of information; and markers of public space.[36] In that very first laying out of the regulations

---

hardik-patel-plays-hard-ball/.

34   'Gujarat Shuts Down Internet during Exams', *The Hindu*, 29 February 2016, http://www.thehindu. com/todays-paper/tp-miscellaneous/tp-others/gujarat-shuts-down-internet-during-exam/ article8294672.ece.

35   'The Information Technology Act, 2000', *The Gazette of India*, June 2000, https://www.indiacode. nic.in/bitstream/123456789/13116/1/it_act_2000_updated.pdf.

36   See 'The Information Technology Act, 2000', p. 4 (unauthorised access), p. 6 (storage, retention, and retrieval), p. 9 (licensing and public access), p. 11 (availability and perpetuity), p. 15 (security and legitimation), p. 15 (denial and maleficent blockage of access), p. 20 (privacy and replication of information), p. 22 (markers of public space). The page numbers here correspond to the actual gazette and can be found at: shorturl.at/kuyS4.

of legal and acceptable forms of transactions in the digital networks, access was clearly one of the most cited and critical clauses.

I have explained earlier that both the emphasis on access as well as the conditions of its possibility are mirrored by Access to Technology (A2T) developments across information societies in the face of digitalization. Access has been fetishized as the aspired-to end of all technological infrastructure, and also as the point of danger that allows for criminal practices to proliferate. Access to technology remains central in IT4D portfolios which look at universal access as the endgame. Government practices recognize lack of access to digital infrastructure as an axis of discrimination and seek to invest in creating access opportunities.[37]

Access, here, typically carries a double bind of anxiety. On the one hand, it generates anxiety about the need to *grant* access. On the other, and immediately afterward, it triggers concerns about the *control and regulation* of practices that emerge. Access-centered discourse overrides the complex terrain of the human-technology relationship – usage, adoption, penetration, internalization, proliferation, nudging – and becomes the single point of obsession in telling the promise of the internet. More than 15 years after India's first Information Technology Act, 2000, we see this double bind emerging, where we celebrate the participation of young people in 'Digital India' economies, while also shaping their behavior by banning undesirable content. Likewise, in the world of user-generated content, there is a celebration of the participatory cultural processes, of peer-to-peer sharing and distribution, and of remixed and reused genres that show the possibility of creative explosion in the age of ubiquitous access. At the same time, there is a growing concern that these new regimes of cut-and-paste creativity are leading to an explosion of information that is being mined by predatory algorithms and data mining practices that make the subjects extremely vulnerable. Access is often thought of as a one-point entry into the digital world.

Yet, in the Information Technology Act, 2000, access was more a *condition* than it was an interaction, and this becomes clearer in the amendments made to the Act in the Information Technology (Amendment) Act, 2008. On the one hand, access became closely tied to the *infrastructure of access*, specifically looking at the emergence of 'cyber cafes', and examining the idea of 'cyber security'.[38] On the other, there arose a particular focus on the extended practices of information and data protection, 'access, use, disclosure, disruption, modification or destruction',[39] recognizing the threats that come when ubiquitous access becomes the norm. The amendments mainly concentrated on the potential for transgression that emerged with web sociality. They thus envisaged the instituting of controllers with extraordinary access to computers if 'he has reasonable

---

37   Nishant Shah, 'In Access: Digital Video and the User', in Joshua Neves and Bhaskar Sarkar (eds) *Asian Video Cultures: In the Penumbra of the Global*, Durham: Duke University Press, 2017, pp. 114–130.
38   'The Information Technology (Amendment) Act, 2008', *The Gazette of India*, February 2009, p. 3, https://eprocure.gov.in/cppp/rulesandprocs/ kbadqkdlcswfjdelrquehwuxcfmijmuixngudufgbuubgubfugbububjxcgfvsbdihbgfGhdfgFHytyhRtMTk4NzY=.
39   'The Information Technology Act, 2000'.

cause to suspect' that the computing network was used to break the laws set out through this regulation.[40]

The Information Technology (Amendment) Act, 2008 recognized the role of service providers and those who would be made responsible for providing access, and thus also for mitigating any threat that emerged out of the access. What such recognition did was to enable the government to 'issue directions for interception or monitoring of information through any computer resource',[41] that would eventually introduce the intermediaries as critical to shaping the conditions of access.

On the one hand, the amendments to the Information Technology Act, 2000 clearly acknowledged the internet as a cultural force. On the other hand, the amendments were primarily aimed at containing and regulating the internet, focusing on usability and agency, because of its ability to disrupt 'public order' and because it could 'have [a] debilitating impact on national security, economy, public health, or safety',[42] all of which needed to be more monitored and contained for better governance. The *promise* of access was not merely one public agency and the right to informational technologies. It was also about training the public into becoming responsible and responsive, and for training regulatory units to meet the expectations of these emerging technologies. The design and regulation of technology was thus simultaneously the design and regulation of the *intended user*, creating the need for devices that shall train the user to become the technosocial subjects to now be shaped around the promise of access.

Meeting Technologies Halfway

Digitalization was aspirational, arriving before it was experienced and heralded before it materialized. The accent of digitalization was virtuality, but access to the digital went beyond infrastructure. Infrastructure was a way by which the digital user was shaped to meet technologies halfway. This was not in itself an unexpected or unprecedented development. In the mid-1960s, in the United States, when the first idea of mass digitalization was being floated, Douglas Engelbart was examining, as a part of his 'Augmenting Human Intellect' project of 1962, how to develop 'new techniques, procedures and systems' to enhance the 'effectiveness of the individual's basic information-handling capabilities in meeting the various needs of society for problem solving in its most general sense'.[43] Engelbart's ambitious and influential research came up with many conclusions and recommendations for humans and computers to work together, some of which pioneered and shaped the Graphical User Interface as we know it – from the first prototypes of a Macintosh by Alan

40 'The Information Technology Act, 2000', p. 12.
41 'The Information Technology (Amendment) Act, 2008', p. 27.
42 'The Information Technology (Amendment) Act, 2008', pp. 27, 29.
43 Douglas C. Engelbart, 'Augmenting Human Intellect: A Conceptual Framework', Summary Report, SRI Project No. 3578, Stanford Research Institute, October 1962, https://www.dougengelbart.org/content/view/138.

Kay to the production and introduction of the mouse and the GIMP design.[44] However, implicit in almost all of the findings was the idea of information overload and information processing.

In staging the problem, Engelbart proposed that 'the entire effect of an individual on the world stems essentially from what he can transmit to the world through his limited motor channels.' However, most problems we directly grapple with do not rely on our motor skills but on innate sensory inspection and cognitive capabilities. Engelbart thus broke human capabilities down into four classes: Artifacts, Language, Methodology, and Training, all of which could be stored as information on computer-controlled systems, which could handle massive amounts of information and display it when needed, thus enabling a transfer of knowledge and the adaptive invoking of expertise whenever required for dealing with new problems. Engelbart's basic presumption was that the human subject was not entirely capable of explicitly recognizing its knowledge and, when confronted with it, not always able to discretely and efficiently process that information or to make the most effective decisions. The human, in Engelbart's proposal, needed *augmentation* – because we are continually paralyzed by the informational overload of our own knowledge and perception. We needed an external augmentation device that would offer prosthetic help to move from ineffective to effective, and then to brilliantly effective, when faced with complex problems. A *device*, then, which would, as it were, allow us to access our own information through intelligent filters, so that we can cope with massive information without being overwhelmed by it.

The production of the device was not a straightforward digitization process of deep mining the human subject for information, however, though that would become one of the logical fallouts of the process. Engelbart's own efforts were directed at training machines that can learn from human actions and interventions and, subsequently, training humans to be able to work with these machines. Augmentation was not just an *expansion* but also a *reworking* of human capabilities to work with these machines of expansion. So much so that he wrote a tutorial on 'Games that teach the fundamentals of computer operation', where he devised a way by which 'a group of common laymen' might be taught how to 'coax sophisticated information-handling behavior from an organization of simple physical elements [...] to simulate various kinds of simple elements by organizing them into a network' whose behavior is obviously more sophisticated than that of any single element.[45] Whimsical, overly elaborate, and long-drawn as this game might be, it does signal a pivotal moment in technology design, where it became clear that for the *human* to be effective,

---

44   Adam Fisher documents the process by which Douglas Engelbart pulled off the presentation that was retroactively dubbed 'The Mother of All Demos', and paved the way for Alan Kay's historical presentation. See Adam Fisher, *Valley of Genius: The Uncensored History of Silicon Valley (As Told by the Hackers, Founders, and Freaks Who Made it Boom)*, New York and Boston: Twelve (The Hatchett Group), 2018.
45   Douglas C. Engelbart, 'Games That Teach the Fundamentals of Computer Operation', *IRE Transactions on Electronic Computers*, March 1961, https://ia800203.us.archive.org/13/items/GamesThatTeachFun damentalComputerOperationsEngelbart/1961-Games-That-Teach-Fundamental-Computer-Operations-Engelbart.pdf.

new information-overload managing technologies would be necessary. Subsequently, for these *technologies* to be effective, the human user would have to be trained to meet technology halfway.

In India, some of the earliest manifestations of this human-technology access and co-design was in the problem of access that was both at the level of infrastructure penetration and systemic unevenness. Through the 1990s, as the first wave of telephone connectivity was receding, the infrastructure of telephony was quickly transformed to become the basic infrastructure for all digital access. People close to the ground, and especially those who were aware of the back-end costs of digitalization, had already recognized that reducing access to infrastructure would not be enough. While it remained necessary to develop the digital ecosystem, a promise of mass connectivity would need more: the design of a user who could indeed be installed and meet the technology development demands.

Hence, Simputer, the first 'local' computing machine, proposed in 1998 as a 'low-cost, usable and *useful* and usable to the common man' solution. The Simputer group, located at the Indian Institute of Science in Bangalore, under the leadership of Vijay Chandru, found that the 'high cost of initial acquisition' made computation unimaginable for the average person. They also recognized that the 'equally high cost of maintenance and upgrade', and the 'complete lack of user-friendly interface' combined with English as an alien language to a vast majority in the country, made computation prohibitive.[46]

The Simputer — A 'Simple Computer' or, as its co-inventor Swami Manohar writes, 'if you prefer ridiculously complex recursive acronyms, 'simputer stands for Simple, In-expensive Multi-lingual PeopLE's :-) comPUTER'.[47] (I am as intrigued by this proposition of access for and by the people as I am by the fact that back then, before the world of emojis had exploded on us, Manohar was already using smileys in his documenting of the project.) The Simputer was a prototype to be designed and commercially sold for under Rs 5,000 to address three key application areas: 'Transactions, Communication, and Information'. It was supposed to facilitate economic transactions, establish interpersonal communication, and give access to the 'right information at the right time' so as to 'dramatically improve the quality of life at all levels',[48] including in political and electoral participation and governance.

The 'make or break' point of the Simputer was its interface. Or, as the pithy statement said, 'The simputer IS the user-interface'. For a country struggling with massive illiteracy, functional literacy, and semi-literacy problems across multiple languages, a text-based interface was exclusionary and thus futile. The Simputer group was already zeroing down on voice inputs and speech outputs in local languages, 'augmented by a minimal single-line display' as the best, indeed the only feasible, option. Combined with a user interface

---

46   Swami Manohar, 'The Simputer: Access Device for the Masses', p. 1, http://www.simputer.org/simputer/
       history/paper.pdf.
47   Manohar, 'The Simputer', p. 1.
48   Manohar, 'The Simputer', p. 2.

of the TV remote, this produced the Simputer as a phone with a keyboard – a concept that sounds quaint from the contemporary vantage point, but was revolutionary for that time.[49]

The Simputer, in recognizing the need for a visually dense interface, telephonic connectivity, and simple navigation structures, was already preempting the mobile revolution that leapfrogged India into the information age. However, the really visionary qualities of the Simputer, even though it never quite made it in the mass market, was its way of predicting three critical points in access infrastructure that bring us back to the phenomena of access and disconnectivity we discussed earlier.

The scientists behind the Simputer indicated that the infrastructure of the future would be dynamic. Devices with their own IP address, new protocols to manage these dynamic IP addresses, and hyperconnectivity through Local Area Networks, all this would be part of the architecture managing the projected massification of the internet. In the standardization, they saw a clear hierarchy: the *application* was the responsibility of the intermediary, but the *infrastructure* would be a state enterprise. The state, in their vision, would hold ownership over the entire ecosystem from spectrum to device in order to facilitate a comprehensive suite of transactions. Standardization would necessitate not only the setting up of technical protocols, but also a clear guideline on what can and cannot be said. The state, then, would have to evolve into the digital system to become the primary service provider rather than just a regulator. The state must access the digital before the user does.

However, before the state could access the digital, digital technologies would have to first reach the physical user. With its emphasis on costs and the chief ambition of being 'inexpensive', the Simputer advanced the concept of 'smart card' access. The project underestimated the seduction of private ownership and was thinking of communal access devices where entire communities would use one Simputer to manage their needs. This also led to the possibility of a cloud-based, modular infrastructure where, based on the personalized login of a user, the same device could become temporarily personal, thus allowing for multiple ownership and usage paradigms: a structure that (we saw) had been implemented by cybercafes in the late 1990s. With smart card access, the Simputer was already proposing that individual voter identities, electronic cash repositories, and other essential services be tied together to form a specific profile which in turn served as an access point to the expanding universe of computational information services. *The individual would have to thus be first accessed by the digital technologies before s/he could be authorized into the system.*

Lastly, the Simputer focused on questions of security. The Simputer group recognized that putting this information, data, and 'money' on the digital network came with additional risks of theft, loss of control, and hacked leaks that put the individual in vulnerable conditions. Security concerns were central, but were also a known risk that had to be taken. The personal risk of security breaches is, the Simputer suggested, negligible when compared

---

49   Manohar, 'The Simputer', p. 3.

to the far more real threat posed by the digital transaction ecosystem to the regulatory state. The digital transaction ecosystem identified anonymous transactions, unverified identities, direct access communication between people, and undocumented movement of information as posing serious challenges to the state, even as the state reconfigured itself in digital space. The model of the Simputer thus showed that both the digital infrastructure and the governance ecosystem access each other and share the information around the user before the user could be given access to the promise of the digital revolution.

It is telling that the Simputer had already embodied the basic paradox of information overload and access. In order for the user to access the information superhighway, the user needed to be *made accessible*, thus meeting demands of both state and technology for legibility as well as intelligibility. The user needed to be designed toward specific protocols and behaviors in order for a digital transformation to emerge. This also preempted the fact that universal access was not only about building access infrastructure, but that it was also about leapfrogging users into a techno-governmental regulation model that would shape them to meet technologies halfway.

The Simputer was part engineering, part science fiction, part fantasy. It imagined a future that we have now naturalized, even though it never managed to be a significant player in that future. It preempted the principles of the mobile revolution as well as the rapid transitions of the Indian state toward 'Digital India' policies. However, more than anything else, the Simputer presented the first model of a *user who would be designed and regulated*, both because of the user being information-hungry as well as informationally overloaded, alongside a new model of a fresh state-technology nexus to sift credible data from the mass of unnecessary information that surrounded it.

What You Get is What You Want

The digital turn, we have argued, was aspirational. We may take this a step further and argue that the aspiration was for transgression. The dramatic changes in media practices that the digital ushered in have found many terms – convergent media, post-media, disruptive media, collaborative media, connected media. Regardless of the name, what marks digital media practices is their power of transgression, the capacity to not just blur boundaries but produce an aggressive disregard for any boundaries at all. The promise of access as unleashing *unbounded* access in turn produced unbound practices that became central to how we saw the potentials of access.

It is impossible to make an exhaustive list of all the transgressions that digital media practices enabled. Perhaps the most evocative embodiment could be the playful and provocatively fictive 'Rule 34' meme that asserts that 'If something exists, there is [internet] porn of it'. In memetic truth, Rule 34 shows how nothing is off limits when it comes to the internet, and how *accessing the web is to already be in a state of transgression*. It is easiest to understand the state of both transgression and access by looking at the burgeoning phenomenon of net porn. This is particularly true in India, which has the dubious honor of being among the top ten consumers of online pornography ever since MMS-enabled phones became popular.

India's regulatory authorities have used every technological means at their disposal to try to stop the libidinal flow of pornographic content – from censorship to blocked ISPs, from individual penalization to intermediary liability. The fact that nothing has worked leads me to build a Rule 35: 'If there is porn on the net, people will access it'. Transgression here means not just accessing the forbidden or blurring the boundaries. The potential of transgressive access is in its capacity to engineer desire, expression, and freedom. I propose that transgressive access needs to be understood as more than an adolescent glee of breaking rules. Transgressive access needs to be understood as a question of agency within the logics of regulation.

It is perhaps possible to tell the story of access as transgression bookended between two of the largest public debates around transgression, morality, and pornography in India. The first instance of transgressive access that is also the most popular (but forgotten in viral time) is the story of the famous DPS MMS (Delhi Public School Multimedia Messaging Service) case. A short, grainy, low-resolution clip that portrayed two students, allegedly studying at the Delhi Public School in New Delhi, went viral in 2004. The pornographic clip, shot by the male student using his then cutting-edge camera-enabled phone, shows the face of the female student performing fellatio as he verbally encouraged her. The male student leaked the video after he was dumped, and the clip first made its appearance on the closed networks of the school. In the friend-of-a-friend logic of digital networks, the clip soon went viral on the internet. Arguably one of the first instances of user-generated pornography in India, it became the origin point of the spy cam – the hidden cam, the POV, and other invasive and amateur pornographic conventions – that has now been mainstreamed and naturalized across various porn tubes.

When the MMS first emerged on the digital landscape of smutty social media in India, however, it took the country by storm. As Namita Malhotra points out in her landmark monograph examining the intersections of law, pleasure, video, and porn in India, everybody was looking for it.[50] On the pervert-2-pervert network, the need to see 'real people' with 'bodies like ours' having 'Indian sex' caught on video resulted in spikes on search engines and local sharing networks. The clip also found its way into grey markets where it was sold as 'real sex' as opposed to 'imported porn'.

Even as the clip went viral, an enterprising student, Ravi Raj, at the Indian Institute of Technology Kharagpur decided to capitalize on the demand and put the clip up for auction on the site Bazee.com where it appeared as an e-book under the scintillating title *Item 27877408 – DPS Gurl having fun!!! Full video + Bazee points*, priced at Rs 125. The state regulatory apparatus, which had no way of recognizing and controlling the 'nether spaces of p2p networks' or 'covert exchanges on mobile phones' found its first engagement with this e-commerce transaction and immediately banned the offensive clip.[51]

A public interest litigation was filed against the clip and a bizarre case ensued. Once all the bodies involved in the making and circulation of the clip were identified, nobody could be

---

50   Namita Malhotra, *Porn: Law, Video & Technology*, Bangalore: The Centre for Internet & Society, 2011.
51   Shah, 'In Access: Digital Video and the User'.

found guilty. Ravi Raj was taken into custody for possession and intention to sell pornographic material but was acquitted in juvenile court and expelled from his university. The male student who was the clip's producer/actor/distributor was also acquitted: his crime, according to the presiding judge, was of being part of a society that is rapidly being influenced by Western Culture. The female student, the most visible body of the video, was recognized as a victim, and mechanisms were set in place to protect her identity and her future. When none of these three obviously responsible people could be charged with the crime, the state sought a 'symbolic resolution' by extraditing the CEO of Bazee.com, Avnish Bajaj, from the United States and recognizing him as 'the foreign-educated man who had been touched by the spread of such sleaze'.[52] Bajaj was an easy target: it was over his visible body that the case was resolved, at least for the public. He won the case, pitting 'Terms of Service' against the Information and Technology Act, 2000, and thus claimed innocence as an intermediary.[53] We shall discuss intermediary liability shortly, but it becomes interesting that in this one case, where several transgressive bodies were identified, and several more desiring bodies were accessing the transgressive material, that the blame eventually was put on the technology itself.

The court judgment argued that the true culprit in this case were 'the gadgets…which make possible certain kinds of technological conditions' that caused '…obscene material to be published'. The technology – which offered access to a 'listing which informed the potential buyer that such a video clip that is pornographic can be procured for a price' – was what needs to be controlled and regulated.[54] The ensuing regulations addressed the control of access to technology. Those found in possession of the clip could be fined and prosecuted. The police in Mumbai were given the authority to carry out digital frisking of people's phones to check for the objectionable content.

The concern was not about obscenity or pornography, but about the fact that the digital was now producing ways to sidestep the state's authorial positions, and producing mutable, transmittable, and transferrable products which could be accessed without regulation or control. *The crime was thus not individual but collective.* The culprits were not the four people in the case, but an entire technosocial country participating in the proliferation and consumption of the video clip. Access, an avowed goal of the state's ICT4D visions, suddenly produced the *user as a potential criminal* whose crime was to access the digital, making such an act in itself into an act of transgression. The *potential* of transgression thus made access into a point of regulation and control: making access into possibly the most contested space of digital engagement, thereby also turning access into infrastructure.

Transgressive access was not just about infrastructure *of* access. It was also about memory making and archiving. Wendy Chun, in her work on Software Studies, points out that 'the

---

52   Shah, 'In Access: Digital Video and the User'.
53   *Avnish Bajaj* v *State (NCT of Delhi)*, 105 DRJ 721 (2008). The presiding judge was Justice S. Muralidhar. For details, see https://indiankanoon.org/doc/309722/.
54   Shah, 'In Access: Digital Video and the User'.

role of the digital is to make memory into storage'.[55] Chun points out that, as physical computation, memory refers to actual storage. The web's infinite capacity to remember is tied to its material capabilities of storage or information and data. Obsolescence, corruption, and erasure of storage can easily invalidate memories and remove entire archives without any respite.

Transgressive access thus meant that the user, who only had spectatorial memories so far, was also suddenly equipped with archival storage mechanisms. To access something on the web was to also have the potential for storing it. The personal archive for public distribution directly challenged the state's authority of being the custodian of histories and guardian of memories.

This was evidenced in another famous case around pornography in India, this time enshrined in the illustrated figure of 'Savita Bhabhi'. Created under the pseudonym of 'Deshmukh', India's first adult comic strip series on the now banned website SavitaBhabhi. com depicted the fantasy-filled sexual adventures of a 'housewife' whose husband was traveling a lot for work, which gave her space to engage in pornographic encounters. The 51 stories published in this series destabilized the home as the bearer of family values and foregrounded a woman's agency and sexual desire. They also made the site the 82nd most visited Indian website in 2009.[56]

In 2009, the Department of Telecommunications (DoT) issued an order asking all internet service providers in the country to block access to the website. The Controller of Certifying Authorities, N. Vijayaditya, explained in an interview that even though there was no legal order for the ban, they were proceeding with it as a sign of respect to the voices of protest from conservative quarters in the country. [57] While Puneet Agarwal, a second-generation Indian entrepreneur in the United Kingdom, eventually acknowledged responsibility for the website and even spearheaded the 'Save Our Savita Bhabhi' campaign, he did not challenge the ban, giving into 'family pressures'.[58] And, thus, Savita Bhabhi disappeared from the Indian web.

In this case, however, when the official distribution channels got pulled down, the users who had been accessing the series revealed that they were not just accessing but also archiving all the content. User-generated torrents of archives marked by obsession, animated by passion, and sustained through personal libido began appearing on social

55   Wendy Hui Kyong Chun, 'The Enduring Ephemeral, or the Future is a Memory', *Critical Inquiry* 35.1 (2008): 148–171.
56   Ariana Rodriguez, 'India Bans Adult Cartoon Site SavitaBhabhi.com', *XBIZ Newswire*, 28 June 2009, http://newswire.xbiz.com/view.php?id=109797.
57   Sruthijith K.K., 'Govt Bans Popular Toon Porn Site', *Hindustan Times*, 20 June 2009, https://www.hindustantimes.com/entertainment/govt-bans-popular-toon-porn-site/story-M7UO7XgStS9Cfrvfziok6J.html.
58   Vinita Chaturvedi, 'I Keep a Low Profile to Promote Savita Bhabhi Better: Puneet Agarwal', *The Times of India*, 11 April 2013, https://timesofindia.indiatimes.com/entertainment/hindi/bollywood/news/i-keep-a-low-profile-to-promote-savita-bhabhi-better-puneet-agrawal/articleshow/19493624.cms.

media. Savita Bhabhi was given a viral lease of life as pervert users suddenly became defenders of free speech and protectors of the public memory that was being erased by the regulatory authorities. While the official platforms – the legal owners, the intermediary suppliers, and regulated channels – could be regulated and controlled to make Savita Bhabhi disappear, the personal archives emerging from access could not be subjected to the protocols of the gatekeepers. The checkpoints and chokepoints of regulation could control the conditions of circulation, but not the potentials of access. Transgressive access in this case was not just a retaliation against the state: it challenged the state's ability to write memories and histories. Access became more than infrastructure – it became a point of archiving – and thus also challenged older forms of regulation and control of information, much as it did in the case of the DPS MMS.

This idea of information access as not just *enabling* transgression, but being *itself* an act of transgression immediately dovetails into the second paradox of information overload: the information you get and the information you want. On the one hand, access to information is seen as a right, a necessary condition for participation and inclusion in the information (overload) networks. Indeed, because information overload is also at the basis of the economic and regulatory models of digital governance and development, it is important to have all users 'accessible' on the premise of 'having access'. However, the peer-2-peer and distributed modes of information dissemination and circulation mean that this access, an act of transgression, is continually seen as a state of crisis, where it is simultaneously both a right and a threat.

Informationally Overloaded Threats

The regulation of information – its access, ownership, proliferation, and infrastructure – clearly imagines the rise of people participating in information production spaces as a threat. In the hands of young users, the access to and ownership of information became a way of bypassing social conservatism, leading to the proliferation of sexual desires and identities. When equipped with information infrastructure of proliferation, engaged citizens turned into active protestors, as in the case of the PAAS agitators. As computing became ubiquitous, every household with an internet connection became a potential hub for piracy, with pirate crackdowns becoming a major concern. Minority and marginal voices found an amplified presence, sparked off by the tragic case of Rohith Vemula and the discussions around caste-based discrimination.[59] Survivors and victims of violence found platforms to voice their struggles, creating lists that called out systemic perpetrators, as in the case of the #LOSHA (List of Sexual Harassers in Academia) and the #metoo conversations. When used by populist vigilantes, these platforms have mobilized lynch mobs that have hurt and killed people through social participation. The democratization of the internet might have started as a romantic invitation to participate in the political economies of the digital transformation, but the consequences and results of this engagement have been extremely threatening to ways of life and living.

---

59   For details, see https://en.wikipedia.org/wiki/Rohith_Vemula.

The history of internet regulation has largely been a series of often futile attempts using older models of censorship, blackouts, and control. Many foolhardy attempts at blocking domain names, installing censoring mechanisms, banning content, removing platforms, and hiring 'content clean-up crews' litter the landscape of controlling and curtailing access. As Ashish Rajadhyaksha points out in his landmark monograph *The Last Cultural Mile*, there was an inherent conflict in these mechanisms of control: the state was trying to introduce regulatory mechanisms that were relics of a centralized information model, on to a system that was necessarily peer-2-peer and distributed, and hence had different mechanics.[60]

As network engineer and theorist Duncan Watts points out in his 'Small World Phenomenon', the digital network is essentially a collection of small worlds – each world self-contained and self-referential, but with an infinite capacity for expansion and replication.[61] The regulation of physical computation networks like the internet needs a different mode of control, one which sets up instances of governance for every 'small world' and yet has the capacity to scale that to each world that is simultaneously generic and unique. Martin Warnke, a system theorist and digital cultures critic, along with Carmen Wedemeyer, explains this as a 'scale-free' event.[62] Warnke argues that because the physical computing networks do not work through the law of medians, but of correlations – looking not at averages but at unique relationships – it is impossible to govern the space through regulations and laws which are limited in their scale, scope, and speed. Our older forms of regulation were devised around the law of silos, of contained, scaled, carefully demarcated spaces, whereas the internet is necessarily a space of bleeding overlaps, circulating traffics, and flows of information which cannot be regulated or contained.

In the face of this networked logic, the state is often unable to be the vanguard, arbitrator, or gatekeeper of informational control and access regulation. As one of the peers – nodes in a flattened network – the state can serve as a hub through which different nodes operate, but it cannot be a central node from which this control emerges. Hence, it became necessary to think of a new layer of *state-like organizations* that would take up state-like functions in order to help deal with the threat of access.

The need for such a layer was already visible in the DPS MMS case, where the regulation was seen to be the responsibility of a platform like Bazee.com. However, the Terms of Service of service providers like Facebook, Google, or WhatsApp does not hold them accountable for the nature of the content. The service provider – also known as intermediary – consisting of telecommunication companies, platform providers, application owners, device manufacturers – was generally imagined as neutral, whereas the informational relationship and its content was a direct relationship between the state and the citizen-user. In the face

60   Ashish Rajadhyaksha, *The Last Cultural Mile: An Inquiry into Technology and Governance in India*, Bangalore: The Centre for Internet & Society/Researchers@Work, 2011.
61   Duncan J. Watts, 'Networks, Dynamics, and the Small-World Phenomenon', *American Journal of Sociology* 105.2 (1999): 493–527.
62   Martin Warnke and Carmen Wedemeyer, 'Documenting Artistic Networks: Anna Oppermann's Ensembles are Complex Networks!', *Leonardo* 44.3 (2011): 258–259.

of new networked logics, through the 1990s it became quickly clear that the logic and logistics of the central governmental regulation were not going to work. Especially with the rise of hate speech, gendered violence, terrorist recruitment, fake news, and personal attacks, it has become apparent that the intermediary can no longer be treated as a neutral delivery mechanism.

The Information Technology Act, 2000 (Section 79) provided intermediaries with qualified immunity, where, as long as they follow the prescribed due diligence and do not conspire, abet, or aid an unlawful act, their lack of 'actual knowledge' of the content and the failure to remove or disable access would not be punished. However, this condition of what constitutes 'actual knowledge' has been quite vague. Thus, in the intellectual property case of *MySpace Inc vs Super Cassettes Industries Ltd.*, the Delhi High Court read the Information Technology Act to declare that in the case of copyright infringement, a court order is not required and an intermediary must act to remove the content upon receiving knowledge of the infringement.[63] Similarly, in at least two cases of sexual abuse and lynching through mob violence, the government has indicated that the responsibility of finding solutions is on the service providers who, if they remain mute spectators, would otherwise be 'liable to be treated as abettors' and 'face legal action'.[64]

In April 2011, the Government of India published Intermediary Guidelines that prescribe, among other things, guidelines for takedowns by intermediaries, thus controlling both the conditions of access and the afterlife of access.[65] These guidelines also mark the beginning of post-access politics: control and contestation around access, not just as the point of engagement but in the continued interaction with, and ownership over, the content produced. Under these guidelines, *access became conflated with agency*, where the intermediary was required to 'publish rules and regulations, privacy policy, and user agreement for access or usage of the intermediary's computer resource'.[66] The control was not just about the moment of access, but about what happened once access had been established: control, in short, also of *usage*. Similarly, the intermediary was to be held responsible not only for monitoring the access to its 'computer resources', but also the control over 'removal of access to any information, data, or communication link by an intermediary after such information, data, or communication link comes to the actual knowledge of a person authorized by the intermediary'.[67] The guidelines help us understand that access is a two-way link; they monitor not only persons accessing but also persons being accessed. They identify persons who might be violated because of

---

63 *MySpace Inc.* v *Super Cassettes Industries Ltd.*, 236 DLT 478 (DB) (23 December 2016). The case was presided over by Justices S. Ravindra Bhat, Deepa Sharma. For details, see https://indiankanoon.org/doc/12972852/.

64 Cyril Sam and Paranjoy Guha Thakurta, 'Part 1: Is Facebook in India Truly Independent of Political Influence? Not Really – It has Backed Modi and BJP', NewsClick, 22 November 2018, https://www.newsclick.in/part-1-facebook-india-truly-independent-political-influence.

65 'Notification', New Delhi, 11 April 2011, *The Gazette of India Extraordinary* Part II-Sec.3(i), https://dispur.nic.in/itact/it-intermediaries-guidelines-rules-2011.pdf.

66 'Notification', 3 (1).

67 'Notification', 3 (3 b).

other persons accessing *their* data and information and recognize the need for grievance redress mechanisms as part of access regulations.[68]

Such an extension of access control into the afterlife of engagement has had some alarming consequences. The Centre for Internet & Society in Bangalore, along with the Google Foundation, carried out investigative research with a small group of intermediaries to determine 'whether the criteria, procedure and safeguards for administration of the takedowns as prescribed by the Rules lead to a chilling effect on online free expression.' Legally and informationally wrong takedown notices were sent to the intermediaries.[69] A large majority of them, without any scrutiny, immediately removed the content, showing the possible 'chilling effects' on free speech that result from such intermediaries' power.[70] The question of the *threat* of access found its solution in controlling the very *conditions* of access by putting the responsibility on intermediaries and allowing their terms of service and takedown powers to override what might be fundamental individual freedoms. This, coupled with algorithmic detections and no-obligation removal practices, produced a different notion of regulation: where any action or expression was removed even *before* it was officially charged with a criminal or objectionable intent, and which considered *all* information – indeed considered the very act of access – as potentially criminal.

Rightful Information Overload

This right to information has been both a utopian promise and a fundamental prerequisite for information overload to become our naturalized setting. This right began as a question of access and infrastructure shaped as a problem of hardware penetration. However, over the last 30 years, it has become a question of agency, identity, and expression, so much so that universal access is no longer positioned simply as *good to have* but as a fundamental right. Lack of access to the net is discrimination, and a preventive mechanism for the realization of one's true self. So strong has been this idea of access as *right* that it culminated in one of the largest cases of public consultation and protest around internet policy in India.

It all began with Internet.org, a Facebook-led not-for-profit initiative that seeks to build infrastructure and conditions of universal access. Its mission states that 'the more we connect, the better it gets' and sets out to overcome 'issues of accessibility, affordability and awareness' in the hope that 'one day everyone will be connected'. One of the largest initiatives under the umbrella of Internet.org is a program called Free Basics by Facebook, that 'provides people with access to useful services on their mobile phones in markets where internet access may be less affordable'. The underlying condition of Free Basics is to help improve the lives of people who are hitherto underconnected or unconnected.

---

68   'Notification', 3 (11).
69   Rishabh Dara, 'Intermediary Liability in India: Chilling Effects on Free Expression on the Internet 2011', *The Centre for Internet* & Society, 10 April 2012, https://cis-india.org/internet-governance/intermediary-liability-in-india.
70   Dara, 'Intermediary Liability in India'.

Free Basics partners with mobile operators to build universal access infrastructure that gives people 'access to basic websites for free'.

Mark Zuckerberg, the CEO of Facebook, has already been identified as moving the company from being a 'directory of information' to a 'social network' to a 'core social infrastructure' of connectivity.[71] In his 2013 white paper, 'Is Connectivity a Human Right?', Zuckerberg announced a new milestone for making internet access available to 5 billion new users. Recognizing the infrastructure-deficit of emerging network societies, his proposal was to expand access with a marginal role for governments as regulators of the spectrum, and then give the responsibility to secure the right of access to intermediaries: technology and telecom industries. Free Basics thus actively sought partnerships with telecommunication and ICT intermediaries in order to build what they saw as universal access.

Given that the Indian government had already recognized access as a critical pillar for development and growth, it did not come as a surprise that Internet.org was welcomed to partner with the government in its quest to create access across the country. The program was first launched in 2015 as 'Free Facebook', with viral television and digital media campaigns showing young millennials in India holding up notecards saying, 'I want free Internet'.[72] Facebook proposed pairing up with Reliance Telecommunications in order to offer free access to a selected set of websites for all consumers of Reliance mobile phones.[73] Effectively, Free Basics was the gateway to users being connected for the first time as it provided them with initial free access that also tied them to the Reliance-Facebook nexus as the basic infrastructure for their internet. In a country like India, where 350 million existing users access the internet through mobile phone, and almost 70 percent of its 1.2 billion population wait for future connectivity, this was a massive market share. Universal access clearly became the philanthropic strategy toward securing a loyal customer base of new users who were being 'platformed' into this new ecosystem. The right to access was in the service of expanding the consumer of private telecom ecosystems.

This blatant use of developmental rhetoric to create a future monopoly was severely critiqued by technology advocates, technology entrepreneurs, information activists, and internet researchers. Apart from this transparent ploy of market expansion, however, #SaveTheInternet groups[74] also challenged Facebook's claims to universal access as threatening two core principles of free and democratic access in the country.[75] They claimed that in its 'walled-

---

71 Anna Lauren Hoffmann, Nicholas Proferes and Michael Zimmer, '"Making the World More Open and Connected": Mark Zuckerberg and the Discursive Construction of Facebook and its Users', *New Media and Society* 20.1(2016): 199–218.
72 Lauren Smiley, 'How India Pierced Facebook's Free Internet', *Wired*, 1 February 2016, https://www.wired.com/2016/02/how-india-pierced-facebooks-free-internet-program/.
73 'TRAI Tells Reliance to Put Facebook's Free Basics Platform on Hold', *The Free Library*, 23 December 2015, https://www.thefreelibrary.com/ TRAI+tells+Reliance+to+put+Facebook%27s+Free+Basics+platform+on+hold-a0438721289.
74 https://savetheinternet.in/.
75 Nimisha Jaiswal, 'Why Indians Are Turning Down Facebook's Free Internet', *GlobalPost*, 13 January 2016, https://theworld.org/stories/2016-01-13/why-indians-are-turning-down-facebooks-free-internet.

garden' design, Facebook was creating a restrictive environment and overriding the principles of zero rating and net neutrality in the country. They started a massive campaign, pulling in one of the largest comedy groups, All India Backchod (AIB), into their fold and a public mobilization toward saving the internet and the principles of net neutrality.[76] They showed how Free Basics could create a discriminatory preference of Facebook's selected websites while downgrading access to the others. They demonstrated how this building of a *super* super information highway would throttle innovation and smaller services, which might be disruptive to Facebook's future services. Through blogs, hashtags, twitter campaigns, comedy videos, and print media, the #SaveTheInternet group mobilized more than a million emails and comments to TRAI[77] in response to their consultation paper on service differentiation in less than a month, asking for a free and democratic internet that does not get compromised in the quest for universal access.

The Cellular Operators Association of India launched their countercampaign #SabkaInternet (Everybody's Internet)[78] arguing that Free Basics was a way to leapfrog the population into mobile connectivity. Facebook responded to the #SaveTheInternet email campaign with its own public relations promotions of Internet.org as a 'step towards digital equality'. Massive banners, emotionally charged advertisements promoting its mission to 'connect the unconnected', became a part of its strategy.[79] They created poster children – a farmer who looks up weather information and commodity prices and learns new framing techniques; a woman finding access to independence and a break from patriarchy as she gains access to education through digital services – in order to position themselves as the new saviors helping unconnected India transform into Digital India. Mark Zuckerberg took center stage, talking with Prime Minister Narendra Modi, visiting different parts of the country to promote technology empowerment dialogues, and reassuring everyone that while user growth was good for Facebook, it was only part of a larger mission for a more diverse ecosystem.

Despite its large advertising machinery, Facebook's Free Basics lost ground. The Telecom Regulatory Authority of India (TRAI) ruled against its 'differential pricing' and 'zero-rating plans' which allowed mobile phone companies to offer only a few services for free.[80] The judgment endorsed the position taken by the #SaveTheInternet group that in a yet-to-be-connected country like India, 'allowing service providers to define the nature of access

76   'Indian Comedians Explain Net Neutrality in Free Basics Battle', *Web We Want*, 13 January 2016, https://webwewant.org/news/indian-comedians-explain-net-neutrality/.
77   Rahul Bhatia, 'The Inside Story of Facebook's Biggest Setback', *The Guardian*, 12 May 2016, https://www.theguardian.com/technology/2016/may/12/facebook-free-basics-india-zuckerberg.
78   Mohul Ghosh, 'Is #SabKaInternet a Deliberate Attempt by COAI to Confuse People?', *Trak.in*, 2 December 2016, https://trak.in/tags/business/2015/04/22/sabkainternet-deliberate-attempt-coai-to-confuse/.
79   Nash David, 'Digital 'Equality' Not So Equal: Is an Aggressive Facebook Turning Free Basics into a Movement?', *Firstpost*, 24 December 2015, https://www.firstpost.com/india/is-an-aggressive-facebook-turning-free-basics-into-a-movement-2557360.html.
80   Telecom Regulatory Authority of India, 'Prohibition of Discriminatory Tariffs for Data Services Regulations, 2016', *Gazette of India*, 8 February 2016, https://trai.gov.in/sites/default/files/Regulation_Data_Service.pdf.

would be equivalent to letting TSPs shape the users' internet experience.[81] India became the first country that fought against the lobbying powers of Facebook and retained the conditions for free and democratic access, guarding these conditions as critical to the fundamental rights of the citizen. Even with the government's flagship programs in 'Make in India' and 'Digital India', which seek to create a 'digitally empowered society and a knowledge economy',[82] and despite its close association with tech giants like Facebook, Microsoft and Google, it had to succumb to the idea of access as such a fundamental right that it could not be transferred to intermediaries. It also resulted in the #SaveTheInternet group launching themselves into the Internet Freedom Foundation, with an explicit mission to 'defend freedom of speech, privacy, and our digital commons' in the face of the new technosocial nationalism.[83]

The story of Free Basics, its reversal and the continued promotion of universal access, becomes a logical bookend to the story of the internet itself as it got concretized in the Information Technology Act, 2000. It offers an illustration of disconnectivity in far more insidious ways than internet blackouts, regulation of content, or the moderation of expression. It shows how companies benefitting the most from maintaining information overload and all its paradoxes continue to exclude users who participate as data subjects from the new data owners produced in these conditions. The subject remains informationally circumscribed but also severed from the regulation of the digital spaces and, ironically, information overload remains the way by which this exclusion is engineered.

Stitching Things Together

At the core of the argument around information overload is an attempt to historicize this as a crisis-in-the-making. While the history of computation and the internet has often been written as a history of information access, I have attempted to rewrite it as an history of informationally overloaded access, showing how access is both a multidirectional process as well as a transformative paradigm. It has been well noted that production digitalization is not merely an infrastructural project but a technosocial revolution that rewires circuits and bodies, people and societies. Through the lens of information overload, it becomes possible to see how the infrastructures of digital spread move beyond the hardware of computational networks and incite an entire ecosystem of regulatory, political, and technological actors to create conditions of informationality that anticipate and write a subject to occupy it.

Or, in other words, the story of digital expansion is the story of creating people into becoming users. The success of digital connectivity lies in transforming the subjects into users. They are defined by their presence in these digital systems which access them through informationally overloaded circuits. In this narrative, digital networks such as the internet find their cybernetic nodes in digital users, and the development is thus co-constitutive and

81   'Prohibition of Discriminatory Tariffs', p. 10.
82   'PM's Remarks at the Launch of Digital India Week', 1 July 2015, https://www.narendramodi.in/pm-s-remarks-at-the-launch-of-digital-india-week-175128.
83   Internet Freedom Foundation, 'About IFF', https://internetfreedom.in/about/.

interactive, where technologies course through bodies, converting them into digital nodes, which, when assembled, form the layered and stacked network of information transactions.

The problem may well be that the idea of users as agential, and thus in control of the systems of digital networking in which they are installed, may well be misleading. Overwritten in informationality and superseded by the processing power of rapid computing, the user – often the end point of these technologies – is also *excluded* from decision-making practices and processes of digital developments. Such a realization is especially significant given the rhetoric of unlimited choice, individual customization, filter bubble existence, and network neighborhood architecture often presented in the guise of human-centric design of the digital ecosystem. In the following section, I narrate a symptomatic development of digital technologies in India to show how the human user, an infrastructural presence in the growth of these technologies, also remained excluded from their ownership and decision-making.

The first section has been an exposition on the making of digital access systems, and the way they *create* and *validate* specific human users as legitimate operators of these spaces. In the next section, I focus on the making of this user – how different computational logics, network principles, and technosocial standards naturalize the making of this user – and particularly consider the questions of power, agency, and choice as they unfold in these informationally overloaded systems.

II.

The Portrait of You as a User

In the summer of 2020, Netflix released a globally trending documentary called *The Social Dilemma* which centered the voices of some of the people who worked in the early years of the Silicon Valley expansion to create the monopoly of the GAFA (Google, Amazon, Facebook, Apple) companies over our attention and data economies. Largely male, white, and rich, these woke voices presented themselves in a *mea culpa* – they screwed up, they set out to save the world and ended up ruining it; they believed in the emancipatory powers of digital technologies but don't quite understand how these technologies produced the conditions of dread that we now see in our digital futures. Apart from the fact that the documentary failed to address or even acknowledge the voices of critiques, activists, and researchers who have been actively foreshadowing the future, it also failed to acknowledge that these technological problems are not merely technological problems – they are profoundly human and fiercely intertwined in the shaping of our collective and singular identities.

As the film went on, the very people now confessing to their oops moments began positioning themselves as the new warriors who were going to learn from mistakes (that they consciously made during the times of emerging tech) and were now going to build better and more humane technologies to set the world right into order. Each well-curated and crafted message ended with hope that we will only need new technological frameworks, new tools of regulation and control of these technologies, and all would be well. Without any sense of irony, when they talked about their own personal interventions in the field of data surveillance, predictive algorithms, and acute information profiling, they kept resorting to ways of stepping out of information overload. They did not mention information overload *per se*, but in their discussions on design hacks, UIX manipulations, data seductions, algorithmic correlations and profiling, their message was very simple: these technologies have now produced such an overwhelming amount of data and information that, at a very human level, it will be impossible to actually understand, process, and fathom our informational societies leave alone rebuild them. The message was clear: those who can afford it, will find data bubbles where they can escape the onslaught of information overload. The rest of us will just have to bear with it and put our trust in other technologies that will counter the attacks of the current technologies.

Alternatively, if we were to extrapolate from their implicit messages, the only way to fight these current technologies of information overload is to develop yet more technologies of counter-information overload. In many ways, this debate is reminiscent of the first propositions by Alan Turing during the Second World War to break the code of encrypted Nazi information by developing decryption machines. Alan Turing's so called 'Turing Test' is often misrepresented as some kind of purity standard that digital computation has to pass in order to qualify as intelligent. However, a closer reading of Turing's essay, 'Imitation Game', presents a more interesting formulation. Turing wasn't interested so much in whether a computer network takes the semblance of intelligence or not. He was more invested in the idea that a computer network can perform a manipulation and ordering of abstract symbols (like numbers or language) and thus compute all possible predictions in any value (like a sum or a sentence) and eventually approximate it in such a way that the process of composing that value would become intelligible to a human reader.

Turing's imitation game was not about a computer imitating a human and fooling us into accepting it as sapient intelligence. He was rather proposing that computer networks are more adept at *manipulating structures and symbols that we may think of as human language* and can thus produce complex results that can no longer be understood or decoded by human faculties. The imitation machine, then, would be the answer to the encryption produced by one machine. At the level of both scale and complexity as well as of speed, the measure of one machinic process would be another machinic process, or rather, the best imitation of a machine would be another machine so that when machines start speaking to each other, the human in the information circuit would either become unbearably overloaded or outright excluded from this information transfer.

Turing was effectively warning us that if we continued to reduce language to nothing more than granular arrangement of data, strip it off all the different contexts, bodies, and affects that give it meaning, we would soon find language becoming a paralyzing rather than a generative force because then the logical machines would take over. The original proposition of the Turing Test – that in a purely text-based environment mediated by a digital screen we might no longer be able to discern whether the person we are talking to is male or female – is signaling that when it comes to information overload, *context collapse is the natural mode of informational existence*, that the individual capacity for discernment, interpretation, and engagement with information is simultaneously both redundant and futile. So much so that the very basic identification of the sex of the person, manifest in so many different ways in embodied interactions, might collapse, thus introducing in us a fundamental existential crisis where we would no longer be able to rely on our capacity to tell a truth, to recognize or engage with truth. The Turing Test was not about being fooled by machines, but about realizing that we were rapidly emerging into a system where our human abilities and histories of truth-telling might be replaced by systems and networks of verification, where the human subject is both ontologically unstable and epistemologically rewritten.

I invoke Turing to come back to our conversation around information overload because, as we have seen earlier, nearly all conversations around information overload have been staged and rehearsed as technological conditions. They typically invite two pre-wired responses: one, that if we only created enough regulations and controls, the technologies would become better; or, two, that we needed to educate and rehabilitate users into coping and negotiating with information overload. In both these responses, the user remained either a problem to be solved or a unit that has to be aligned to the state of continued crisis that we experience in our unceasing and unrelenting state of being informational. The user thus gets defined only as a transactional entity of the computation network. In order to put the questions of agency, affect, embodiment, and intentions into the conversation around information overload and usership, I propose the term 'Youser' – a portmanteau of 'you' and 'user' – in order to anchor the questions of information overload and the movements that naturalize it as personal questions that affect the very making of our bodies, selves, identities, and desires.

The idea of a youser suggests that we need to let go of both the romantic fantasies of 'stepping out' of these networks of information overload as well as futuristic impulses of finding a 'cure', as if this is just a phase or a temporary state of being. Instead, I hope to map out specific transitions that digital computation-driven information overload enables, and suggest an in-betweenness there that might find resistance, critique, and collectivity, to question informationally overloaded futures otherwise presented to us as both definite and inevitable.

Making of a Youser

The idea of the youser was perhaps most visible in two almost science-fiction-like predictions that were made in 2014 by two of the biggest digital technology actors, showing us the imagined future of data-driven realities. Google announced the backing of a life-extension company called Calico that aimed to cure not disease but death itself, thus promising immortality. Such immortality would be achieved through extensive data mining of the human code. A company that combines biotechnology, artificial intelligence, deep-learning algorithms, and pharmaceutical experiments was now sure that deep data mining that allowed for unprecedented and unfathomable intimacy of code with human biology would also allow for the production of super drugs to reverse aging and thus defy death itself.

It was surprising and revealing to large swathes of people who identify Google largely as a digital information organization company that the quest of organizing the world's information is not merely a question of sorting and processing information: it also entailed converting the world into information. As Google built larger and more comprehensive databases where user data got organized, stored, and processed, it also started creating a profile of the user that both mimicked and overrode the knowledge that users had about themselves. In the ambition to cure death, Google's vast data empire established itself as a digital force that could rescue the human from its fragile, mortal conditions. In offering this hope of being saved, Google could immediately trigger a future that it defined, because it became clear that the older human had to now step out of the model of being either human or relevant and enter this new world where Google would be the savior.

That same year, billionaires Peter Thiel and Elon Musk announced their quest for immortality through singularity by investing in a Thiel Fellowship that encouraged young innovators to 'hack' the human body, encode it exhaustively into data, and thus find ways of transferring the data into android smart machines that continued to live on our behalf long after our bodies were claimed by death.

In both visions, concerned in the end with human mortality, the human-technology intersections are clear. In Calico's vision, human biology is a code that needs to be broken and intercepted so that it can be infiltrated by genetic information that makes us live beyond our natural capacities. In Thiel's proposition, the body is merely a shell that houses the human: it can be discarded once the 'essential makeup' of the human gets transferred to more durable hosts. In this singularity vision, the human body is clearly being positioned as both undesirable and accidental and in need of a reengineering that can cure its mortal uncertainties.

While both seem to mimic science fiction fantasies — and indeed both of them heavily reference immortality quests drawn from popular and historical sci-fi — what they also do is signal a changing model of the human within new data realities. This model of the human-in-technological-transition, liberating and frightening as it is, betrays three intertwined tropes in the discourse around technology and the human, especially with the rise of the digital: the *human as discrete* from the technological conditions; the *human eroded* through the technological engagement; and the *human and the technological as contingent and paradoxical in their codependence*.

The 'discrete human' has been scathingly critiqued by Asha Achuthan, who argues as a feminist epistemologist of science and technology that such a discrete human has been at the heart of the radical transformation caused by Information and Communication Technologies for Development (ICT4D) in developing networked countries like India.[84] Achuthan posits, through a political history of nation-building, that despite the change in political ideologies of statecraft and governance, even as technologies of governmentality leapfrogged into different forms, the human as a 'user' always remained discretely removed and separated from the technological. Achuthan argues that the production of the digital

---

84   Asha Achuthan, *Re:Wiring Bodies*, Bangalore: Researchers@Work and The Centre for Internet & Society, 2012.

and human as ontologically discrete, and in need of reconciliation, perpetuates the idea that technology is prosthetic and dependent upon human desire and agency for its meaning.

It is a trope that Bruno Latour argues against when he recommends that we 'inquire into the existence of things and into all the relations in which things enter as well as the behaviours and values they exhibit, in order to exist'.[85] Latour resists imagining technology as neutral, but also warns us against seeing human existence as the teleological means of technological forms. He shows that while reified practices of technology are marked by intention and desire, the singular focus on transactions and actions as the end point of existence willfully remains innocent of the politics that accompany the practices that make the human and the thing coexist as a parity.

The second trope of the human being eroded through technological engagement is underlined by the contemporary vision of a postapocalyptic future where the human has been dislocated from its centrality in our contemporary Anthropocene.[86] It is a vision where the human-technology interaction is seen as a process of extraction, where the idea of 'use' is not as simple as a human using technology. As Rosi Braidotti emphasizes in her formulation of the 'post-human', the dislocation of the human from its centrality is not just a conceptual tool, it is also a recognition that the idea of the human at the center of the universe, creating use value for all of its resources, is no longer valid; the human is perhaps more *used* than *using* in the future.[87]

Malavika Jayaram points out in her analysis of e-governance structures in emerging networked societies that there is a conceptualization of the human as a data pod, harvested for data that seeks to *replace* rather than *represent* the human subject.[88] This is what I have elsewhere described as *subject of/to technology*,[89] where the very idea of the human subject has been under renegotiation. On the one hand, the human is sought to be reconfigured in the digital matrix, and on the other hand, the human is parsed, processed, and presented only through interfaces that render it recognizable. The call for rehumanizing technology, or mapping the human subject, presumes that the human and the technological are unknown to each other, creating, in the process, opaque structures of dependence and manipulation.

The third trope sees the human and the technological emerge as paradoxical, each as the context for the other. As Arjun Appadurai argues in the unravelling of the conflicting

---

85   Bruno Latour, *An Inquiry into Modes of Existence: An Anthropology into the Moderns*, Cambridge, Massachusetts: Harvard University Press, 2013, p. 93.

86   Eric Hörl in exchange with Paul Fiegelfeld and Cornelia Kastelan, 'The Anthropocenic Illusion: Sustainability and the Fascination of Control', in Christoph Behnke, Cornelia Kastelan, Valerie Knoll, and Ulf Wuggenig (eds) *Art in the Periphery of the Center*, Berlin: Sternberg Press, 2015, pp. 352–368.

87   Rosi Braidotti, *The Posthuman*, New York; Wiley, 2013.

88   Malavika Jayaram, 'India's Big Brother Project: The World's Largest Biometrics Identity Program', *Boston Review*, 19 May 2014, https://bostonreview.net/world/malavika-jayaram-india-unique-identification-biometrics.

89   Nishant Shah, 'Subject to Technology: Internet Pornography, Cyber-terrorism and the Indian State', *Inter-Asia Cultural Studies* 8.3 (2007): 349–366.

'scapes' that mark modernity, the fixity of geography and genesis are no longer granted to the modern migratory subject who encounters technological transactions in essentially transitory states.[90] The modern subject, for Appadurai, remains bound in technology and media, which then produces all-encompassing and inescapable situations that define the ethnic, ideological, and financial determinants of everyday life.[91] Appadurai's argument for thinking of the contemporary moment as a moment of fusion – where the inextricable nature of our technologized subjectivity brings forth what Woodhouse and Patton call the 'technosocial regime'[92] – is important to look at new intersections of politics, policy, and practice. This technosocial subject resonates with Donna Haraway's ironies that define the cyborg. As she says in *Simians, Cyborgs, and Women*: 'Irony is about contradictions that do not resolve into larger wholes, even dialectically, about the tension of holding incompatible things together because both or all are necessary and true. Irony is about humour and serious play. It is also a rhetorical strategy and a political method.'[93] This technosocial subject, then, does not have the burden of either reconciling or choosing between staged paradoxes, but finds its existence in a continuous negotiation between the two.

This technosocial subject is what I call a youser. The youser, defined by the information overload and circumscribed in the technologies that support it, is no longer outside the computational networks and no longer seeks to escape its matrix. However, unlike the dramatic declarations of Google and Elon Musk, the youser is not constructed overnight. The production of the youser does not carry the same speed and scale of many of our popular social media practices where entire lifetimes get lived and transformed in short-lived trends. Instead, the production of the youser is an insidious process. It takes a long time, and when the shifts happen, they happen almost imperceptibly, as transitions get naturalized and new modes of being and becoming are established as the status quo.

It is important to call out these transitions in order to unpack the processes by which the youser is engineered, produced, verified, and created, and see the possibilities of escape and resistance to this insidiousness of information overload that we have now come to experience as the default of our digital lives.

---

90   Arjun Appadurai, *Modernity at Large: Cultural Dimensions of Globalization*, Minneapolis: University of Minnesota Press, 1996.

91   Arjun Appadurai's notion of scapes looks at the boundlessness of subjectivity in the age of late modernity. Appadurai posits that the two fixities of geography and genesis are no longer granted to the modern migratory subject who encounters modernity and its value systems in a state of transitory transactions. This produces the subject as caught in various binds of ethnicity, ideology, and technology that produce it at the center of distinct and divisive contrary forces. See Appadurai, *Modernity at Large*.

92   Woodhouse and Patton describe technosociality as 'a system where people and technologies combine to work as heterogeneous but functional wholes'. See Edward Woodhouse and Jason W. Patton, 'Design by Society: Science and Technology Studies and the Social Shaping of Design', *Design Issues* 20.3 (2004): 1–12.

93   Donna J. Haraway, *Simians, Cyborgs and Women: The Reinvention of Nature*, New York and London: Routledge, 1991, p. 180. I particularly want to reference Donna Haraway's invocation of irony as a reading and a political strategy that allows for these contradictions to emerge as distinct and not necessarily in need of resolution.

From Representation to Simulation

In her much cited and often critiqued 'The Cyborg Manifesto', Donna Haraway cryptically introduces the shift from representation to simulation as marking the transition from 'comfortable old hierarchical domination to the scary new networks... (of) informatics of domination'.[94] Haraway does not expand upon this shift, though she was already writing with others who were examining simulation as a new order of 'reality making' in a world of symbols that ruled the abstractions provided by the new social relations tied to science and technology at the turn of the century. The works of Baudrillard[95] and Deleuze[96] are often invoked in thinking through the question of simulation, and the practices of hacking simulations[97] are offered as a way of breaking the simulations open. I am not taking either of those routes, nor am I seeking to develop toolkits on how to work with them. I am more interested in the shift itself – from representation to simulation – as a computational network phenomenon that controls and shapes the politics of informationality. While Haraway does not herself unpack this shift, it is interesting to go down this particular rabbit hole and understand what simulation might mean within a computational network.

Namita Malhotra reminds us, in her analysis of born-digital pornographic objects, that these are essentially simulations.[98] At the back end of a digital video are numbers. These numbers become pornographic images, like bodies without organs, only when they are rendered through a simulation software, such as a web browser or a video player. In fact, one of the continuous struggles in preparing standards for a unified language of the web has been that different simulation software compilations render this material differently, thus reminding us that there is nothing authentically real about digital objects: they are inherently 'fake' and capable of being 'faked'.

Duncan Watts complements 'fake' digital media in his description of the mathematical networks that power computation.[99] Watts admits that the mathematical model of a social network is 'in place of the real thing', and it does not have fidelity to the external world. Computational networks might have a correlation with the world that they seek to describe and model, but they are not in a state of mimesis. They are not 'realities' that can be understood by measuring them up against a physical phenomenon or event. The network is an abstraction of modified information and of the connections made between them. This nonrepresentational characteristic of the network enables a decontextualization of the information that it circulates. Thus, even a stable information set in a network is subject to change as new connections are made, even though there might be no change in the 'real

---

94   Haraway, *Simians, Cyborgs and Women*, p. 167.
95   Jean Baudrillard, *Simulacra and Simulation*, trans. Sheila Glaser, Ann Arbor: University of Michigan Press, 1983.
96   Gilles Deleuze, *Difference and Repetition*, trans. Paul Patton, Columbia: Columbia University Press, 1994, p. 69.
97   Jaron Lanier, *You Are Not a Gadget: A Manifesto*, New York: Alfred A. Knopf, 2010.
98   Malhotra, *Porn*.
99   Duncan Watts, *Small Worlds: The Dynamics of Networks between Order and Randomness*. Princeton Studies in Complexity #36. Princeton: Princeton University Press, 1999.

state' of the individual or phenomenon that is the source of the information being abstracted. This break from fidelity enables new conditions within which we measure the veracity of information.

This means that the computational network is necessarily *in a state of simulation* and can no longer live up to the expectations of the 'real' and the 'truthful': concepts premised on a representational paradigm that presumes a material external reality to the represented object, an external gaze that can be used as a verificatory tool when there is doubt about the meaning of the representation. To put it bluntly, within any computation network of simulations everything is 'fake news'.

Such an eschewing of ontologies of the real is a characteristic of what Albert-László Barabási calls 'scale-free networks'.[100] As Barabási explains, such a network doesn't only have a lack of fidelity with the external world, it doesn't even have any central median value or scale by which other elements of the network might have an ascertained value. A scale-free network is thus an indeterminate system, where each element has a relational value only in the transactional connection that is established between the two.

The shift from representation to simulation, then, is not just aesthetic but ontological. It invalidates the meaning-making foundations of our representation-driven expressions and languages. It propels us straight into the world of 'deep fakes' and 'alternative facts', not as aberrations to a human truth, but as new 'cyborg unities' that are corrupt, instable, and without fixity. This shift is also not a futuristic one: it is coded into the very nature of computational networks that drive our digital communication practices. Thus, the 'you' in 'youser' of information is created *as* a simulation, a fake, an approximation without an original. The youser has to be understood as something created through manipulated information, decontextualized data, faked circulation, and doctored rendering, needing neither certainty nor external verification. This youser now needs to be understood as a 'cyborg body' that circulates to create informational instability. As Haraway had prophesized, 'we can no longer go back materially or ideologically'.[101]

This shift from authority to authorization – (where we essentially depend on one set of digital protocols to validate the others) – is a telling symptom of information blackouts. It establishes a digital regime where the representational touchstones of verification are no longer going to be enough to determine the veracity of a digital object. And it is worth noting that, despite the high-profile media trial around this doctoring of evidence and the disproving of the sentiments, the viral reach and accelerated spread of the video was so vast that it started a nationwide rhetoric of branding JNU students as 'anti-national' and facilitated draconian control and clamping down of free speech and organization on the campus by the right-wing political party in power.

A similar pattern emerges in WhatsApp lynch mobs, where it is not just the instability of truth in a born-digital simulated object, but the speed of its circulation that leads to a fabricated

---

100 Albert-László Barabási, 'Scale-Free Networks: A Decade and Beyond', *Science* 325.5939 (2009): 412–413.
101 Barabási, 'Scale-Free Networks', p. 62.

reality. So it was in the case of the well-documented[102] instance in the district of Bidar, when Mohammad Azam, a software engineer working with Google, had gone off on a long pleasure ride in his car with a relative and friends. One of the members of the group, who was visiting from Qatar, had a box of chocolates with him. At a stop where they were stretching their legs, when he saw a group of schoolchildren passing by and looking at them, he offered to share some chocolates.

What the group did not know was that the entire region was bristling with WhatsApp videos with no provenance warning people of child abductors. Even though there had been no cases in the villages of kidnapping, communities were firmly convinced that multiple children had gone missing. When somebody reported the men stopping in the village and offering chocolates to children, a mob quickly assembled. They started abusing the group. The group fled in their car. However, the information of their arrival had passed much faster than their travel, and in the next village of Murki, they were faced with an angry mob that forced the car to stop. The mob dragged the occupants out of the car and beat them up with sticks and stones. By the time the police arrived, Azam was dead, while the others had sustained critical injuries and were taken to the hospital.[103]

Even though the group that was lynched bore all the markings of affluence and middle-class respectability, the mob insisted on misreading them as kidnappers. In their police reports, the survivors from the group talked about how all their explanations, their identification, and efforts to have a conversation were overridden and they were framed only as confirmed kidnappers who had come to abduct children. In other testimonies, people also note how mob participants saw videos that they had access to and used them as verifying evidence, claiming that the people in their videos resembled the group that they were attacking. And even when the group could escape the first mob, the speed with which information was passed to the connections in the next village eventually turned fatal for the traveling company.

This predominance of authority of digital objects – without recognizing them as simulated and potentially modified – and using them as a way of establishing representational truths, overriding the authority of the individuals but trusting the authorization of the digital information – is the way by which the youser become operational. It is no longer a question of verifying information but of producing information that pretends to be representing a reality and only ends up simulating the small world that works through connections, circulations, recontextualization, and computational realities.

---

102 IANS, 'Google Techie's Lynching in Karnataka: How an Act of Kindness Turned Deadly', *Business Standard*, 16 July 2018, https://www.business-standard.com/article/current-affairs/google-techie-s-lynching-in-karnataka-how-an-act-of-kindness-turned-deadly-118071500351_1.html.
103 Reuters, 'Bidar Lynching: He Looked Like terrorist, Says Villager, Days After WhatsApp Rumour Leads to Death of 1 in Rural Karnataka', *Firstpost*, 30 July 2018, https://www.firstpost.com/india/bidar-lynching-he-looked-like-terrorist-says-villager-days-after-whatsapp-rumour-leads-to-death-of-1-in-rural-karnataka-4848181.html.

From Possibility to Probability

The reason why networked authorization works over human authority and discretion is not only to do with the life cycle of rumors and speed of information. It has also to do with the epistemic choices of networked computation. At the heart of counting are two knowledge-making systems. One deriving its laws from logic, and the other from mathematics. In contemporary computation, drawing from Watts' 'small world' hypothesis, it is clear that we have established logic as the default mode of meaning-making. With self-containing systems at its core, the logical world of computation creates a system of referential meaning-making that depends on deduction and reduces the probability of event occurrence. Logical probability insists that if a thing happens once, then the chances of it happening again are large; and if it happens enough times, it is the naturalized order of things so that other alternatives of things happening are reduced.

In her work expanding the second order of logic, Maria Manzano argues that within the first and second order of logic, 'we will never find a strongly complete deductive calculus... (because) compactness, which could be proven from strong completeness, fails'.[104] She draws from the history of logic to remind us that 'a complete calculus can never be obtained', and yet computational networks continue to demand and affirm stability and validity of a probability driven approach. Clemens Apprich characterizes this as the 'hermeneutical paradox' where, '[i]n order to filter a message out noise, to literally discriminate data to extract information, the discriminatory patterns within the communication process have to work behind the scene'.[105] The logical fallacy that *first* computes all the possibilities and reduces them to a probability coefficient, and *then* uses that probability coefficient as a way of predicting and shaping behavior and events, is deeply located in the four principles of social media as characterized by Jose van Dijck and Thomas Poell: *programmability, popularity, connectivity*, and *datafication*. As they argue, in our data-driven computational networks, computation now 'refers to the ability of networked platforms to render into data many aspects of the world that have never been quantified before'.[106] These quantifications, unprecedented in their volume and velocity, being constantly consolidated and circulated, provide the platform basis for a whole new structure of *governance* which tries simultaneously to predict and shape the behavior of the users and redefine our understanding of both engagement and participation.

With this logic of pattern recognition and probability indices, the youser becomes a symbolic construction that only makes sense within the confined and closed universe of a computational network system. The youser has no fidelity, no engagement, and no faithfulness to the person(s) that they might refer to. The idea of the youser is not so much to *describe* the user as it is to *hide* that fact that our digital networks are more expansive

---

104 Maria Manzano, *Extensions of First-Order Logic.* Cambridge Tracts in Theoretical Computer Science, Series # 19. Cambridge: Cambridge University Press, 1996, p. 5.

105 Clemens Apprich, Wendy Hui Kyong Chun, Florian Cramer, and Hito Steyerl, *Pattern Discrimination,* Minneapolis: University of Minnesota Press, 2019, p. 102.

106 José van Dijck and Thomas Poell, 'Understanding Social Media Logic', *Media and Communication* 1.1 (2013): 9.

and more opaque than we understand when we bring them down to mere transactions made by the user.

The creation of the youser is not wedded to these principles of logic. Yousers are grounded in the mathematical realms of possibility mapping. The first order of mathematics insists that, at any given space-time confluence, there is an almost infinite possibility of things that can happen. Even in making something as simple as a natural number, there is recognition that the value can be infinitesimally granulated so that it only approximates the number but never quite achieves it. Or, to make it more legible, the value of 1 is an infinite possibility of the number '0.999999…' stretched to such infinite levels that it might as well be 1. Mathematical possibility makes transparent the pragmatism of choice, but in doing so it also denies the precluding of all the other things that might happen outside of computed events.

This mathematical uncertainty is closer to human perception and cognition than it is to the logical certitude of computation networks. This uncertainty replaces *scale* with *intensity* and *speed* with *depth*, offering a different register of information within the digital realms – imagining a network of quantum computers invested in calculating different possibilities of human negotiation rather than predicting the scripted routes of controlled behavior. It privileges the making and structuring of authority, and the negotiations with it, rather than the deployment and penalization of authorization that is central to shutdowns.

Perhaps this tension between logic and mathematics is the most visible in conspiracy theories that accompany particular crises. Take the terrifying Facebook streaming of two consecutive mass shootings that occurred at mosques in Christchurch, New Zealand, during Friday prayer on March 15, 2019. The attacker, a white supremacist, was charged and convicted of 51 murders, 40 attempted murders, and terrorist activity.[107] In an attempt to reconcile the population with this heinous act, both the video and the manifesto that it was linked to were banned in New Zealand,[108] effectively putting a temporary lockdown both on the video's circulation and its capacity to make connections.

However, the erasure of the perpetrator as a Facebook user via modes of internet censorship did not stop a global response and viral consumption of the phenomenon.[109] Additionally, it led to an enormous conspiracy theory group emerging in far-right global mainstream media as well as on the fertile grounds of Reddit where detailed forensic analysis of the video insisted that the entire shooting and its subsequent regulation were

107 Kristen Gelineau and Jon Gambrell, 'New Zealand Mosque Shooter is a White Nationalist who Hates Immigrants, Documents and Video Reveal', *Chicago Tribune*, 16 March 2019, https://www. chicagotribune.com/nation-world/ct-mosque-killer-white-supremacy-20190315-story.html.
108 Charlotte Graham-McLay, 'Spreading the Mosque Shooting Video is a Crime in New Zealand', *The New York Times*, 21 March 2019, https://www.nytimes.com/2019/03/21/world/asia/new-zealand-attacks-social-media.html.
109 BBC, 'New Zealand Man Jailed for 21 Months for Sharing Christchurch Shooting Video', *BBC News*, 18 June 2019, https://www.bbc.com/news/world-asia-48671837.

staged in order to forward a 'liberal left agenda' that would take guns away from people.[110] This wasn't just a small faction, but these conspiracy theories found huge traction in different media forms and in viral posters and memes that offered 'rational' evidence to their irrational analyses.

This particular form of resurgence of a user who has been removed by regulation as a youser that is still circulating and replicating is in the realm of the mathematical possibility that abounds the digital web, so that even when faced with factual or logical resistance, the informationality of the youser only grows in intensity and popularity. From anti-vaccine movements to flat-earth conventions and global climate change deniers, these dabblers in possibility mapping continue to exploit the strength of correlative causality embedded in digital networks to create these alternative 'small worlds'. They find each other through weak ties of topical interest and the algorithmic correlation of weak ties to form a sustained community consolidated on unregulated platforms, where they emerge as a collective force rather than merely fringe elements of irrational thought. Thus the 'content possibility' that enables irrational argumentation, conspiracy theories, and absurd fantasies, none of which get either detected or filtered by the computational networks of weak ties because such networks are only tied to 'network probability' that maintains a mythical neutrality toward the information, the theories, and the fantasies being circulated.

The networks pretending agnosticism to content, its traffic and the management of its connections allow for such discourses to emerge uncontrolled into a domain of speculation. Networks facilitate these practices even as they try to establish regulation over social media platforms. And even when legal and governance measures, depending on the fallacy of logical erasure, remove users from these platforms, the networks of circulation and possibility continue to proliferate and replicate such yousers on the social web's horizons of possibility.

From Memory to Storage

Computational networks encourage overproduction of information. This happens in part by making users encounter their own information and its relationships, and partly by circulating all information at the same scale and speed, making it almost impossible to take parsing or verifying practices as human practices. In fact, the new mode of countering or blocking information is to flood the topics, hashtags, or viral events with counter-information and misinformation so that human users are so overwhelmed by the information that they disengage from it. This disengagement, however, does not mean a lack of information. It merely means that the responsibility of presenting this information is now given to machine learning and customization practices that we call artificial intelligence. It establishes a new model of information circulation, where the human user is created by an algorithmic data harvest and the targeted information provided to the user is also curated and filtered by

110 Ben Strang, 'Thousands Don't Believe Official Christchurch Terror Attacks Story', *RNZ*, 4 April 2019, https://www.rnz.co.nz/news/national/386367/thousands-don-t-believe-official-christchurch-terror-attacks-story.

another algorithmic network. The human in this computational network – sandwiched between two sets of self-verifying and mutually complementary algorithms – has diminished the agencies that protect free speech and expression.

This is the death of memory – the capacity to remember, the ability to forget, and the need for willfully remembering wrong. This is the relegation of the youser into a database, an information stream that is beyond the capacity of the human, trusted only to the verification and authorization principles of algorithmic machines that mimic human agency and make machine decisions. The role of the digital self is to be bereft of memory, but in the midst of abundance of storage. The responsibility and capacity for memory has firmly been relegated to other things that perform that task.

Both in our bodily practices and data preservation, we persist in being creatures of storage. A look at our hard drives will tell us that we have stored more data than we remember or will ever read. A glance at our digital histories and archives shocks us because just the storage of our self has taken up so much data property that increasingly we are unable to read anything more than the data that we have produced – we have become queries that retrieve the data that algorithms sort for us. Our relationship with our data, as informationally overloaded subjects, is necessarily one of *dis*information. Given the volume, velocity, and vectors of our data, it is now a given that everything we can know about our data is wrong, and that we will be corrected only by the algorithms of storage that will do our remembering for us. We complain about information overload now, not because we cannot remember enough, but because we are aware that digital storage is always going to exceed our capacities of memory, and hence we see ourselves moving into storage. What you can tell about yourself is now wrong. And if your memory is challenged with storage, you know that you are going to lose the battle.

Insidousness Overload

In contemporary discourse around the future of digital technologies and the lives lived in those futures, many anxieties get foregrounded. Questions of automation, machine ethics, information extraction, data surveillance, algorithmic censorship, infrastructural silencing, and violence by misinformation have not only become theoretical speculations but lived realities in our increasingly networked societies. The formulation and intervention in these areas are rich with different multilayered approaches and poly-vocal narratives that give attention to the social, technological, embodied, affective, and material consequences of these unfoldings.

Most of these formulations and interventions are circumscribed by a few characteristics. They recognize the problems post facto. The focus on case studies, production of actual events, and reliance on a case-driven narrative invariably means that the problem with all its violence and consequences, often borne by those who are the most vulnerable, is allowed to flourish. The scale with which these problems proliferate in digital circuits also means that countermeasures are slow, lag behind, and not effective in reaching the root cause of these problems.

The identification of the frictions and dangers focuses on dramatic unfolding. While many of these problems are quite spectacular (as also referenced in this essay), it is obvious that these spectacles are neither representative nor comprehensive in understanding the underpinning principles and motivations that create them. They are both, invisible and offered as natural progression, thus making it difficult to identify them when they are being operationalized. In reality, despite knowing these concerns, we become willing actors contributing to the development of these shifts because of the incentives and gratifications that are offered.

There is a tacit understanding that while these technological developments are problematic, they are aimed at the social good and need to be protected and championed. From the market logic of *too big to fail* to the technosocial framing of *technology for social good* or its predecessor concept of *information technologies for development*, most definitions of both good development and bigness are unable to recognize their structurally exclusionary and discriminatory character. The conventional counter to technological problems is inevitably more technology of a similar kind with a slightly different orientation.

What remains problematic to these circuits is the location of the human within them. Visual and popular narratives insist on ease of access and convenience as the end point of users' interactions with these technologies, and continue under the seduction of the visual interface to create new operational conditions that nudge, train, and produce users into becoming a different kind of subject.

The lens of information overload that I have presented here offers two ways of breaking through these much-repeated modes of inquiry and intervention. In information overload, I identify the axiom that information overload is a computational network necessity, not a human one. In showing the different ways by which information overload is being naturalized, I show how it creates a subject that is rendered vulnerable, fragile, helpless, and in need of rescuing by the very technologies that create this subject position to begin with.

In the shift from user to youser, I show how the technological user is not just being led into new forms of practice and transactions, but rather into an entirely new mode of being and becoming. By making the principles that engineer these transitions explicit, I show that the youser is already in the making, and that access to and of digital technologies has to be complicated to produce a more nuanced idea of who is being accessed, for what purpose, and how this access is creating a new template of a technological user.

Through all this, I want to emphasize that the digital condition (as opposed to digital technologies) is insidious, and it doesn't merely amplify or augment reality, but replaces it, gently, without fanfare, and then demands and forces us to accept it, spending our energy and focus in filling up the positions and profiles that are created in this new reality. This essay is an attempt to provide a framework where we can think through our digital conditions to create spaces for intervention rather than just making meaning, and to make transparent the ways by which we are seduced into becoming yousers of an insidious informationality.

The history of the digital conditions has been written as the history of digital access. However, digital access is an insidious process that diverts our focus and energy on explicating, understanding, and making meaning of it. In this role, we are always going to be informationally overloaded, temporally lagging, and structurally reactive, falling into predicted futures with scripts where our roles have already been written.

THE AMBIVALENCE OF 'CREEP': A BIOPOLITICAL HISTORY OF CITIZENSHIP IN DIGITAL TIMES

ASHISH RAJADHYAKSHA

Introductory Note

This essay was written in April and June 2020, during India's first COVID-19 lockdown, and bears the marks of that astonishing moment. The lockdown, as is well known, was announced on March 24, 2000 under the Disaster Management Act, 2005 by the sudden appearance of India's prime minister on national television giving four-hour notice before effectively shutting the country. All access to the physical public domain was declared illegal and all travel suspended, leaving millions of Indians not only in a space of considerable legal jeopardy, as they could not prove their identity, their address or their need to travel, but also in a physically precarious space that threatened their very survival.

It did seem, that April and May, that several things had come to a head. It also seemed that an unusual clarity had somehow descended upon us all – not only a clarity about what was being attempted by the government, but also where it was coming from. Eight months earlier, in August 2019, similar restrictions on public movement had been enhanced by the longest and most severe internet shutdown the world has seen, in the state of Kashmir. And a scant four months earlier, nationwide protests had taken place against the 2019 amendment to the Citizenship Act, 1955, whose incendiary Section 2 (1)(b) was widely construed as directly targeting Muslim migrants. The protests clubbed together four disparate initiatives by the state: the Citizenship (Amendment) Act, 2019 (CAA) together with a revised Unlawful Activities (Prevention) Act, 1967 (UAPA) that could now designate individuals as terrorists, the National Register of Citizenship (NRC), and the technology that was believed to have been the one that enabled it all, India's much-discussed Aadhaar or biometric authentication system.

That April, as the jailed students (under UAPA) of the Jamia Millia Islamia University came together with the parallel images of millions upon millions of India's displaced migrants walking across the length of the subcontinent, or taking whatever means of transport they could to escape the stranglehold of quarantine, something appeared to click together. Even as images of the laborers incessantly evoked the Partition of India, the last time such a scale of subcontinental upheaval had taken place, it became clear that questions of identity – and the regulatory mechanisms defining it – needed, historically, conceptually, and politically, to take on a similar span. You could not account for the Disaster Management Act or the several technologies of 'contact tracing' it brought in (most notably the Arogya Setu health app) without at the same time looking at the history of legislation that went back to the Information Technology Act, 2000 (IT Act), and to several other acts, bills and rules redefining citizenship that went hand-in-hand with new digital technologies 'targeting' India's populace as recipients of state benefit.

This essay retells what is to some a familiar story – or at least a recent and well-known moment in history – from that particular, if temporary, vantage point. There is wide acceptance that India, like several other nation-states in different parts of the world, is seeing a totalitarian turn in its governance. This is not new. India has previously seen, in 1975, the formal suspension of civil rights, and has also seen in several regions within the nation – from Kashmir to Chhattisgarh and across the Northeast – military action under special powers that looks a lot like the Emergency, with significant curbs on public movement, the imposition of censorship, and the incarceration of political dissidents.

What may well be new, however, was the political weaponization of the massive digital infrastructure assembled since the 90s. This infrastructure, which initially saw the famous information technology revolution in the early 2000s, followed by the targeted delivery of state benefit to consumers, beneficiaries, and citizens (label depending on the nature of the benefit), also undergirded a massive neoliberal state apparatus whose consequences may only now be apparent.

For all its immediacy, the story may well go back a long way. The fragmentation of 'the people' – the 'we' who wrote the Constitution of India – into multiple rights and duties also dispersed 'the people' into numerous new categories. These include, among others, the 'natural person' and 'digital principal' of the draft Personal Data Protection Bill, 2019, the 'terrorist' of the UAPA, and the 'hacker' of the IT Act. Negotiating one's digital existence includes new questions basic to the idea of identity, ranging from bodily incarceration and what one major Supreme Court judgment called 'civil death' to an increasingly invisible 'virtuality'.

This story is told here in bold strokes, over five parts that foreground the conception of 'creep' or the phenomenon of how tools, devices, structures, or modes develop a purpose far removed from their initial conception. The first part, addressing the embodied sovereign subject, opens vexed questions of citizenship going back to India's Independence and beyond. The second more specifically addresses Aadhaar, the promise and the revision, suggesting a tactical maneuver – of two Aadhaars, one small and nimble, the other a larger data guzzler acting at the behest of the state – and an element of 'creep' literally built into the system. The third addresses Justice D.Y. Chandrachud's much-celebrated dissenting judgment on the 2018 Aadhaar case in the Supreme Court, locating his view within a tradition of social science addressing the question of identity in the Indian subcontinent. The fourth looks at the basic transformation in the conceptions of 'people' and 'citizen' as India moves into a new, many argue, more draconian regime of digital management of civil society. The fifth part primarily addresses the Kashmir internet shutdown and looks at the link between freedom of speech and the right to free movement in the public domain – a right directly threatened by the 2020 lockdown.

I.

'The Time is not Right': The Sovereign Body

On April 10, 2020, three weeks into the first COVID-19 lockdown, Safoora Zargar, an MPhil student at Delhi's Jamia Millia Islamia University, was arrested by Delhi Police. She was a member of a student body that had been active in the agitations that had convulsed the nation since early December 2019, ever since Parliament passed the CAA.[1] Now she was accused of organizing a protest at East Delhi's Jaffrabad metro station in support of a planned nationwide strike.

The agitations over December and January had been generally peaceful, often led by women, their most visible manifestation the very public occupation of Shaheen Bagh in deep eastern Delhi.[2] Although right-wing pro-Hindutva hotheads had repeatedly threatened retaliation, nobody was quite prepared for what now followed Jaffrabad or what Zargar's protest would be accused of having started.

A day after the Jaffrabad metro sit-in, a man named Kapil Mishra, member of the right-wing Bharatiya Janata Party (BJP), proclaimed that the protesters in Delhi had three days to wind up their movement, a period of grace determined by American President Donald Trump's visit to India at the time. That grace period never materialized: violence broke out that very night and over the next five days, even as Trump was being feted by the president of India, 53 people were killed and thousands lost their homes, many forever.

It is widely accepted that Delhi police did nothing to stop these riots. On February 26, 2020, the Delhi High Court heard an emergency plea to urgently step in and ensure both accountability and immediate police action. A two-judge bench chastised the police for their failure in bringing to book the pro-BJP leadership whose inflammatory speeches as well as active role in the riots had been widely recorded. That night, the bench was replaced and one of the justices, S. Muralidhar, transferred. The following day, another bench accepted with alacrity the solicitor general's claim that the abnormality of the situation, with passions inflamed everywhere, made it not 'conducive' for any action against the riot instigators. The authorities were given six weeks to comfortably rethink their strategy.

---

1   The Citizenship (Amendment) Act, 2019 or CAA was passed on December 11, 2019, amending the Citizenship Act, 1955 with a focus on religious 'minorities' from India's neighboring states, explicitly excluding Muslims. Although there have been several earlier amendments to the original Act (in 1992, 2003, 2005, and 2015), this was the first time that religion was specifically mentioned as a criterion for citizenship. The earlier December 2003 amendment had introduced the concept of illegal immigrants, thereby also reversing a basic principle of citizenship, namely the right to the soil as against inheritance and descent. The 2003 amendment also introduced the controversial National Register of Citizens (NRC), implemented in practice only in Assam.

2   Shaheen Bagh is best known among a series of protests that broke out after the 2019 amendment to the Citizenship Act, 1955. It was a peaceful sit-in organized primarily by women in northeast Delhi between December 15, 2019 and March 24, 2020 when, after the COVID-19 lockdown was announced on March 23, police had dispersed the gathering.

Even as tensions remained high and thousands of people who had lost their homes continued to seek temporary shelter and basic help, the COVID-19 pandemic came upon us. In late March, a nationwide lockdown was declared, initially for three weeks but extended four times thereafter, leaving millions of migrant laborers stranded in conditions of extreme hunger and penury. This lockdown was authorized by an unusual emergency measure: a time-bound Order issued on March 24, 2020 invoking the Disaster Management Act, 2005. The Ministry of Home Affairs decided that it was 'satisfied that the country is threatened' and that 'effective measures' were needed.[3] Every extension thereafter became an excuse to add ever-greater authority to the home ministry. 'It can be tempting in these circumstances to argue that the executive's powers are limitless', warned legal theorist Gautam Bhatia, 'that, if the government so chooses, fundamental rights can be suspended at will. The pandemic [...] is an existential threat and the paramount need to save lives takes precedence over all other interests.' However, 'any temporary measures they impose have a disturbing habit of entrenching themselves into the landscape [...] well after the crisis has passed.'[4]

Zargar, meanwhile, was taken to Tihar Jail and charged with non-bailable offences under the draconian UAPA. This Act itself has seen significant modifications since it was first introduced in 1967 mainly as an anti-terrorist measure. In 1967, it had mainly targeted organizations, or 'unlawful associations', usually either Maoist or Muslim, trying to 'bring about [...] the secession of a part of the territory of India from the Union, or [...] disrupt the sovereignty and territorial integrity of India'.[5] A major shift, of some relevance to the argument that now follows, was the 2004 amendment that began recognizing 'persons' as also potential terrorists, making it possible to give such organizations an identifiable name and a face, thereby also making the UAPA the instrument of choice for suppressing political dissent.

This was the Act under which Zargar was arrested, followed by arrests the next day of human rights activists Gautam Navlakha and Anand Teltumbde for their involvement in the

---

3   On March 20, 2020, even before the National Disaster Management Authority (NDMA) emergency Order was declared, the Ministry of Electronics & Information Technology (MEITY) had issued its own 'advisory': to 'curb false news/misinformation on corona virus' it would invoke the Information Technology (Intermediary Guidelines) Rules 2011 to initiate 'awareness [...] of authentic information' along with 'immediate action to disable/remove such content' hosted on social media platforms. See Advisory to Curb False News / Misinformation on Corona Virus issued to 'All Social Media Platforms' by MEITY, dated March 20, 2020.
4   Suhrith Parthasarthy, Gautam Bhatia, and Apar Gupta, 'Privacy Concerns During a Pandemic', *The Hindu*, 29 April 2020, https://www.thehindu.com/opinion/op-ed/privacy-concerns-during-a-pandemic/article31456602.ece.
5   See Sections 2(i) and 2(ii), https://www.indiacode.nic.in/bitstream/123456789/1470/1/a1967-37.pdf. The Unlawful Activities (Prevention) Act was originally passed in 1967 and repeatedly amended, mainly defining terrorism, who terrorists are, and what the 'security and integrity of India' is. It was replaced by the Prevention of Terrorism Act (POTA) in 2002, but in 2004 it incorporated most of POTA's language. The July 2019 amendment was to enable the state to impose draconian preventive detention measures to enable people to be jailed without trial, and also to designate individuals, as against groups, as 'terrorist'.

aftermath of the Bhima-Koregaon crackdown in 2018.[6] In a public letter he wrote shortly before surrendering, Navlakha pointed to how the amendments to the UAPA had advocated 'stringent punishment' without any checks and balances, such as 'stricter procedures regarding evidence, especially electronic'. As '[legal] procedures, which otherwise provide tighter rules regarding evidence' become 'elastic', jail 'becomes the norm, and bail an exception [...] [the] process itself becomes punishment'.[7]

When Zargar and her fellow students were taken to Tihar, their phones were taken away, their passwords extracted under duress, and when they expressed apprehension that fake evidence may be planted, the magistrate at the Patiala House Court refused to monitor the cases for once again, as the Delhi High Court too had said, the 'time was not right'. This time the reason was the 'circumstances ensuing in the nation due to pandemic' that made it 'not feasible to call for weekly reports and to monitor them'.[8] Zargar, who was several months pregnant when she was arrested, had been at the time of writing placed in solitary confinement, in her own interest according to the police, who officially renamed it as quarantine.[9]

Ten days after her arrest, Delhi Police, clearly on the defensive, asserted on Twitter that they had done their job 'sincerely and impartially' and would not be 'deterred by the false propaganda and rumors floated by some vested elements'. The arrests, they said, had been made 'based on analysis of scientific and forensic evidence, including video footages, technical & other footprints'.[10]

****

This essay does not deal with the specific legal situation that Safoora Zargar and her colleagues face. Nor does it deal with the condition of migrant labor during the pandemic, trapped as they were in a major crisis of identity, somewhere between work and home. I shall attempt instead to address what seems to be a techno-normative maneuver that brings together several of the key issues in which both the arrested students and the stranded laborers find themselves

---

6   Bhima-Koregaon refers to an event in colonial India when, on January 1, 1818, a Mahar regiment of the East India Company defeated the Peshwa Bajirao II. The event is commemorated annually by Maharashtra's Dalit community since Dr. B.R. Ambedkar led a commemoration ceremony in 1927. In late December 2017, a political event was organized in Pune's Shaniwar Wada mainly by Dalit Bahujan groups. On January 1, 2018, the 200th anniversary of the original event, Dalits were attacked by some local right-wing groups protesting the celebration and they retaliated with roadblocks and a call for a statewide *bandh* (general strike). Over several months thereafter, many prominent lawyers, activists, and academics have been targeted by the police under the UAPA and jailed without trial.

7   Gautam Navlakha, ''My Hope Rests on a Speedy and Fair Trial': Gautam Navlakha Before His Surrender', *The Wire*, 14 April 2020, https://thewire.in/rights/gautam-navlakha-bhima-koregaon-nia-surrender.

8   Sruthisagar Yamunan and Shoaib Daniyal, 'As Delhi Police Crack Down on Student Leaders, Courts Cite Lockdown to Justify Lack of Scrutiny', *Scroll*, 29 April 2020, https://scroll.in/article/960591/as-delhi-police-crack-down-on-student-leaders-court-cites-lockdown-to-justify-lack-of-scrutiny.

9   Safoora Zargar was eventually granted bail on June 24, 2020, after spending four months in jail.

10   @DelhiPolice, 'Important Information', Twitter post, 20 April 2020, 10:38 AM, https://twitter.com/DelhiPolice/status/1252101893628796933.

implicated. The National Population Register or NPR, the 'video footages, technical & other footprints' that the police claim to have as the basis for Zargar's arrest, the modified UAPA, and the astonishing Emergency powers that the pandemic vested in the hands of the state at the time of writing all come together to allow the authorities to say that both Zargar and the migrant laborers were quarantined, jailed or stranded *in their own best interests*. The authorities were to decide as much 'with sincerity' as from the arsenal of scientific and forensic evidence they claim to possess what that interest should be.

I suggest that we are seeing something of a state-created technological unilateralism that fundamentally reinterprets the concepts of both sovereignty and citizenship. At the time of writing, India's state apparatus, as though a *parens patriae* gone rogue, had started deploying digital technology to create a combination of legal, administrative, and technological conditions for arrogating for itself the absolute, imperial right to *own the people*.

Such an absolute right, although most graphically represented by carceral control of subjects, springs primarily from the data that the state now possesses on those subjects. As data (together with the sole right to interpret it) becomes state property, so does its unique authority to define the social good get weaponized. A populist abstraction of the 'people' has increasingly been turned against actual people, who no longer have any say in what is being done in their name and apparently for their own good. Citizens as conscious and autonomous subjects, capable of comprehending the responsibilities that go with key constitutional rights, are replaced by populations to be 'managed' and symbolized by individuated bodies, identifiable and incarcerable.

India has had a historical ambivalence around citizenship. The modern citizen-subject, a thinking person who could qualify for a unique individuated subjectivity, has historically been separated from another kind of undifferentiated subject, literally a *body to be enumerated*, to be fed, housed, incarcerated, quarantined. As a result, citizenship has a component part that is viewed as an entitlement, requiring qualifiers, impossible to make available for all. Niraja Gopal Jayal, in a complex argument which will appear many times in this essay, identifies a differentiated citizenship, of status (or 'thin' citizenship) as against practice ('thick' citizenship).[11] Within reform language, the first is meant to lead to the second in the assumption that, in the fullness of time, status would eventually translate into practice. Both race and class defined many of its subjective qualifications when India became independent, even though the Constitution of India explicitly defined *residence* (or *jus soli*) as the overriding qualification for citizenship. Over decades, however, residence has been replaced by *jus sanguinis* (blood-based descent), specifically so in the 2004 amendments to the Citizenship Act, 1955.[12]

---

11   Niraja Gopal Jayal, *Citizenship and its Discontents: An Indian History*, Cambridge, MA: Harvard
      University Press, 2013, pp. 84–85.
12   The crucial amendments were the introduction of the 'illegal migrant' in section 2(i)(b) and the new
      requirement in Section 3(i)(c) that 'both [...] parents are citizens of India' or 'one [...] parent is a citizen
      and the other is not an illegal migrant'. See https://www.indiacode.nic.in/bitstream/123456789/4210/1/
      Citizenship_Act_1955.pdf.

At the same time, there has remained the enduring recognition of people who are either not, not-yet, or not-quite citizens, who nevertheless have to receive basic welfare, even if not necessarily any other entitlements. Colonial India – in which an articulate nationalist elite campaigned for the citizenship rights of subaltern Indians in the British Dominions even as they 'accepted without question their own privileged class position within India' – saw a definitional shift take place, early on, in the concept away from civil and political rights to social and economic rights, says Jayal.[13] It also led to an especially troubled career for what Jayal calls social citizenship.[14] A universal and 'difference-blind' citizenship was replaced by a group-differentiated constitutional identification of various special 'backward' categories, primarily of caste but also gender and other social categories. While such a recognition of backwardness went far toward acknowledging diverse forms of historical discrimination, the flip side has been that delivery of *economic* benefit did not necessarily extend to *social* rights.[15] Indeed, special care was taken to ensure that this did not happen. It was necessary that the right to food and shelter, to education and to vote, should not automatically translate into the associational privileges of citizenship. 'To become a citizen required being marked, but paradoxically the very act of getting marked meant the entrenchment of one's exclusion from substantive citizenship', says Jayal.[16] Politics would thus produce some of its most elaborate contours in India as a fight for social justice.

****

Digital platforms arrived in the 2000s with the intention of delivering state welfare with a utopian promise. They were to accurately identify intended recipients and make sure those recipients got their benefits in a direct and unmediated mode. 'Leakages', it was claimed, both of misdirected benefit and corrupt middlemen, would be eliminated.

The experience has been rather different, even as digital governance enhanced the Indian state's enumerative capability to historically inconceivable levels. As populations turned into targeted beneficiaries identified by whatever category of 'backwardness' or lack of that qualified them for benefit, many entered the digital gateway on terms that would freeze their status on the poverty line, their qualification for property, and their creditworthiness. Somewhere along the way, a divide between entitlement and welfare also got frozen. The

---

13   Jayal, *Citizenship and its Discontents*, p. 14.
14   Jayal writes, 'Social and economic rights everywhere—including in India—remain poor cousins of civil
      and political rights. This hierarchy of rights—civil and political on top, social and economic below—
      appears invincible, though it continues to be frequently attacked. However, the very fact that the
      grammar of rights is being constantly reinvented through struggle is in itself a testimony to the power of
      an idea of citizenship in which the core mainstream rights—civil and political—are simultaneously the
      weapons of achieving the rights on the margins and of the marginal populations, as well as the object or
      that which is sought to be undermined'. See Jayal, *Citizenship and its Discontents*, p. 162.
15   Aadhaar (Targeted Delivery of Financial and Other Subsidies, Benefits and Services) Act, 2016
      (henceforth Aadhaar Act), Section 2f, defines benefit 'as any advantage, gift, reward, relief, or payment.
      in cash or kind, provided to an individual or a group of individuals and includes such other benefits
      as may be notified by the Central Government'. For details, see https://uidai.gov.in/images/targeted_
      delivery_of_financial_and_other_subsidies_benefits_and_services_13072016.pdf
16   Jayal, *Citizenship and its Discontents*, p. 19.

potential redrawing of the blurry and porous character of the 'last mile problem' often enhanced social divides as it recast them into a new form of socio-technological rigidity. New questions of source codes and encryption arose even as a new battle over coercion and aspiration came to define, since 2000, the primary location for social rights in India.

Divides between aspirational rather than received identity would sharpen after 2004 when the arrival of social media – whose associational rights as defined by Apple and Facebook appeared to be beyond the control of and perhaps were even antagonistic to the enumerative apparatus of the state – represented far friendlier digital possibilities for much of the same demographic that digital governance was also fashioning as its target. A technological battle for control now ensued in India, between coercive measures to regulate what came to be known in the Personal Data Protection Bill, 2018 as 'data fiduciaries'[17] and conciliatory ones such as Aadhaar's various attempts to dress itself as cool and media friendly.[18] Various social media platforms struggled to make their peace with the IT Act's many amendments, Facebook going the furthest in proposing nothing less than the abolition of net neutrality, the holy grail of internet freedom, in return for partnership with the Indian state.[19]

There was a larger history at play here when a week into the first pandemic lockdown the central government announced the launch of a smart phone app named Aarogya Setu or 'Health Bridge' as a single-point solution for contact tracing, believed to be an essential part of fighting the pandemic. Would *health* now be added to multiple existing criteria for social exclusion? At the time of writing, the app revealed four parts to its operating system. The first recorded some basic demographics: name, age, gender, and travel history. The second, a kind of automated health check, gave a diagnosis for any symptoms you wished to list out: temperature, oxygen saturation levels, and so on. The third gave periodic updates on the pandemic. The fourth, in all probability intended to be the key section for future use, was a digital 'e-pass' that worked like a kind of health data aggregator to certify that you are 'green' and thus healthy enough to access public utilities. The e-pass, clearly templated on China's Alipay Health Code,[20] was designed to continuously record your geographic location, while your Bluetooth (which is required to be permanently open) range recorded all other Aarogya Setu apps that might come within 6 feet of you, thus enabling contact tracing if anybody in your chain of access ever tests positive, while recording your whereabouts in relation to designated containment zones. Everybody who installs this app gets a static digital ID; so far it appears that some 90 million have done so.

---

17   See Committee of Experts under the Chairmanship of Justice B.N. Srikrishna, *A Free and Fair Digital Economy: Protecting Privacy, Empowering Indians*, Ministry of Electronics and Information Technology, Government of India, 2018, Chapter 1, Section C.
18   An early pitch by Aadhaar was to use the UID number as a Facebook identity.
19   Nishant Shah's essay in this volume discusses Free Basics in some detail.
20   China's Health Code was introduced in February 2020 as an e-passport reporting real-time health conditions in which applicants, after providing information such as travel history, residence, and medical records, receive a QR code that identifies their risk level as red, yellow, or green. Alipay and WeChat are among other agencies of the provincial government that receive personal data and issue health codes.

As it has rolled out, Aarogya Setu's safeguards have been stressed by Rahul Matthan, a lawyer representing the Government of India on matters of technology and privacy law and tasked with putting together the legal framework for the app. The data would, he asserted, remain inside your phone; it would be extracted only if you came into actual contact with anyone who tested positive for Covid-19, unless, that is, it was needed for research or other such use.[21] Your digital ID, tagged onto your name and your data, would be anonymized unless you came under any threat of exposure. This data would be deleted from your phone every 30 days and, if at all it was pulled into any cloud, would be deleted from there within 45 or 60 days. The bottom line was that the app only existed for the limited purpose of fighting the pandemic. Most importantly, said Matthan, its implementation was voluntary. If you didn't want it, you didn't have to have it; even if you did have it, you could switch off the Bluetooth and the GPS anytime or simply uninstall the app.[22]

Many of these claims have unraveled, some quite spectacularly. On April 12, 2020, a middle-aged woman sitting down to dinner with her husband and daughter in an apartment in the Mumbai suburb of Kalina suddenly encountered the proverbial knock on the door: a team of officials of the Brihanmumbai Municipal Corporation (BMC), two policemen, and an ambulance outside, responding to a 'complaint from the PMO office' that she had tested positive for COVID-19.[23] The woman protested and her neighbors confirmed that she hadn't gone anywhere, that she had rigorously observed the lockdown, that no stranger could have possibly come within 6 feet of her. Her protestations came to nought and she was taken away to be hospitalized and tested. She had apparently installed the Aarogya Setu app earlier that day, leaving many to puzzle out just where the bug lay, and not least why she had been treated like a criminal. Two days later, when a pizza delivery boy in Delhi working for the food delivery service Zomato tested positive, Zomato and several other local delivery services began using 'Aarogya Setu compliance certificates' issued by a commercial entity named 'Suraksha Store', in partnership with the Department of Consumer Affairs, for a fee and in return for a host of further data.[24] While initially termed voluntary, no effort was being made any longer to even pretend that the app installation was voluntary.[25] The Ministry of Personnel, Public Grievances and Pensions issued an office memorandum that 'all officers, staff (including outsourced staff)

---

21 'Notification of the Aarogya Setu Data Access and Knowledge Sharing Protocol, 2020 in Light of the COVID-19 Pandemic', Ministry of Electronics and Information Technology, Government of India, 11 May 2020, Section 8 ('Principles for sharing of response data for research purposes'), https://www.meity.gov.in/writereaddata/files/Aarogya_Setu_data_access_knowledge_Protocol.pdf.

22 Rahul Matthan, 'The Privacy Features That Are Built into Arogya Setu', *The Mint*, 8 April 2020, https://epaper.livemint.com/Home/ShareArticle?OrgId=b5a81ef7.

23 Hemal Ashar, 'Woman With No Travel History, No Symptoms, Whisked Away by BMC', *Mid-day*, 18 April 2020, https://www.mid-day.com/articles/coronavirus-outbreak-woman-with-no-travel-history-no-symptoms-whisked-away-by-bmc/22737204.

24 Suraksha Store, https://www.surakshastore.com/.

25 An Aarogya Setu Tracker, set up by the Internet Democracy Project, has listed some 45 agencies who made this app mandatory or required people who have it to behave in a certain way (for example, curfew violators being forced to download the app or Resident Welfare Associations refusing entry without the app and a 'health certificate'). See Tanisha Ranjit, 'When and Where is Aarogya Setu Mandatory? We're Keeping Track', Internet Democracy Project, 8 May 2020, https://internetdemocracy.in/2020/05/aarogya-setu-tracker/.

working in Central Government should download 'Aarogyasetu' app on their mobile phones, immediately'. All these employees, 'before starting for office' should 'review their status on Aarogyasetu and commute only when the app shows 'safe' and 'low risk' status'.[26] On April 29, 2020, an Order extending the lockdown under the Disaster Management Act required private corporations to ensure their employees had the app as a condition for reopening. In 2020, reports were coming in that the app might be required to be compulsorily preinstalled on all new smartphones, and may well be uninstallable.[27]

By late May 2020, all of the above was still happening under the Disaster Management Act, 2005. There was no clarity on when and if the technology would be pulled down, what kind of dedicated legislation would be put in place to run this in the longer term, especially once the Act was withdrawn, how such legislation would handle any conflicts with the Personal Data Protection Bill or who would oversee its use. Meanwhile the 'e-pass', the fourth and possibly deadliest part of Arogya Setu's OS, was recommended as a travel requirement on all journeys by land or air and on the Delhi Metro whenever these services reopened.[28]

Much of this is because the likely true uses of the Aarogya Setu app, like of all digital governance, are an evolving story, and if precedent is anything to go by, the story will be one of creep. Already, on April 10, 2020, a wing of the Information & Broadcasting Ministry put out a tender for a 'Covid-19 Patient Tracking Tool' along with a handheld thermal imager and an optical fever-sensing system. The tracking tool, probably something like a wristband, was meant to 'pair with Arogya Setu' to identify what it now quite unambiguously names a 'suspect', to 'identify a suspects behaviour, see what he or she does on specific days of the week, where does he or she order food from, where does the suspect go for regular walks, where does he/she work during the day, where does he/she sleep at night'; identify 'close contacts, frequent contacts as well as occasional contacts'; 'trace where this person has been'; 'collect information like where the suspect has spent most of his/her time and who all he or she has met'; and 'identify common friends'. Basically, the tracking tool was meant to be an 'intelligence investigation platform & tactical tool to detect, prevent and investigate threats to national security using CDR, IPDR, Tower, Mobile Phone Forensics Data.'[29]

This is unambiguously surveillance language. The tool's purposes as a kind of health surveillance mechanism are independent of its founding intentions. Aarogya Setu's contact-

---

26   Office memorandum issued by Ministry of Personnel, Public Grievances and Pensions, 29 April 2020, https://www.scconline.com/blog/post/2020/04/29/central-government-employees-asked-to-download-aarogyasetu-app-on-their-mobile-phones-immediately/.

27   {Prasid Banerjee and Shreya Nandy, 'Govt's Arogya Setu App to be Installed on Smartphones by Default Soon', The Mint, 29 April 2020, https://www.livemint.com/technology/apps/govt-s-aarogya-setu-app-to-be-installed-on-smartphones-by-default-soon-11588170539557.html.

28   'After Delhi Metro Opens, You May be Denied Ride Without Mask', Arogya Setu Pass', The Mint, 23 April 2020, https://www.livemint.com/news/india/after-delhi-metro-opens-you-may-be-denied-ride-without-mask-aarogya-setu-pass-11587649373682.html.

29   # Ivan Mehta, 'India Wants to Build an Ultra-intrusive 'Wristband' to Track Coronavirus Patients' Every Move', TNW News, 22 April 2020, https://thenextweb.com/in/2020/04/22/india-wants-to-build-an-ultra-intrusive-wristband-to-track-coronavirus-patients-every-move/.

tracing capability, at this moment its primary reason to exist, has been questioned by many, for example, by Professor Subhashis Banerjee of the Indian Institute of Technology Delhi in a remarkable presentation for the Internet Freedom Foundation.[30] The scientific-technical questions about whether the tool works or not need not detain this argument since all it takes is to shift focus and figure out a different, and perhaps infinitely more effective potential purpose for this mechanism.

A day after the app was announced, on April 3, 2020, a memo from the Cabinet Secretariat, Rashtrapati Bhavan, noted that 'technology experts, academicians and private companies' had offered a wide range of 'technology products and applications' with which to fight this pandemic. The memo announced the decision 'to create an enabling mechanism through a public-private partnership model to develop and implement a 'Citizen App technology platform, on-boarding all citizens in combating Covid-19'.[31]

You only need to call it what this Cabinet Secretariat memo calls it, namely a *Citizen* App, and other possibilities emerge. They also take us back to where the story originally began for Safoora Zargar: back to the National Population Register and the original reason for the Shaheen Bagh protests.

The Body Corporeal: Revisiting an Old Project

The argument I present below is a revisionist account of the past two decades. It seeks to produce a hindsight account of a transformation in the embodied national subject, enabled by the *technological appropriation* of what I'm calling an 'ambivalence' that is inherent to the concept of citizenship in India.

The ambivalence has been, in brief, this. As thin and thick citizenship straddles two increasingly separate spheres – in shorthand, those of *entitlement* and *right* – it has also allowed a further ambivalence, as actual human beings, concretized into various manifestations, become discrete subsets of the abstracted 'people'. Such ambivalence opens a two-level operation of citizenship, an increasingly segregationist approach when the constitutional privileges of citizenship get selectively and diversely distributed to actual people. While normative segregation is historically part of what Sudipta Kaviraj (quoted later in this essay) famously called the 'enumerated' community, what may not have been adequately discussed is the ways by which it has been further enabled by digital technology in terms of controls over data gathering, aggregation, and analytics, but also in terms of *whose* data was being gathered and the rights of both access and control it promises to that person in the process of converting her into a data subject.

30   Subhashis Banerjee, 'Covid Surveillance and Privacy in India', Internet Freedom Foundation, 1 May 2020, https://forum.internetfreedom.in/t/webinar-covid-surveillance-and-privacy-in-india-may-01-2020-5-50-pm/440.
31   Memo issued by Rashtrapati Bhavan for the 'Constitution of Committee for Developing and Implementing a Citizen App Technology Platform for Combating Covid-19', dated 3 April 2020.

Just a little over a decade ago, my coauthors in this volume, Nishant Shah and Nafis Hasan, the lawyer Sruti Chaganti and I led a large team on a major project to research the grassroots social impact of the Aadhaar project, or the 'Unique Identity for Every Indian Resident', that had been announced with much fanfare by the Government of India in February 2009. This paper is not about those findings, but it nevertheless emerges from that experience to make a larger argument set in April 2020, the time of writing this essay, even as we see Aarogya Setu reprise the old Aadhaar playbook in startling detail. My revisionist account then, the one I provide here, was not available to us in the period 2009–2011, even though a hindsight reading of several of the findings of the Identity Project do provide initial signs of how things might pan out in the decade that followed.

In February 2009, when the Unique Identification Number (UID) (as we still called it then, the term 'Aadhaar' was yet to enter common usage) was announced, there were admittedly reasons to worry. But there was also palpable excitement. The IT revolution still retained the last gasps of its 90s fervor and much of its history was still being written. Although many friends and colleagues perhaps more in tune with the times than us brought up grisly specters of Big Brother, we decided we weren't going to jump the gun, we wouldn't predetermine what would happen, for there were two, perhaps three, essential reasons for why we believed this might yet be a political and technology game changer. For one, it promised a technological flattening of hierarchies that had been historically inbuilt into citizen-based identity, and we felt this entire enterprise was very likely going to have unpredictable consequences that we wanted to study in real time. Secondly, it appeared, at least initially, that this flattening would not happen from above, but rather in a way that did not delegitimize the market – it would adopt market-consonant approaches to bridge what we believed was the one ambivalence that needed the deepest possible study: the proverbial 'last mile'.

Thirdly, and most importantly, and shorn of all excess claim, we understood the UID's claims to be twofold. One, to issue a unique, randomized, dumb number. Such a number would have no intelligence attached to it and it would be issued to all Indian residents (as against citizens, an important distinction).[32] And, two, to assemble an easy verification mechanism in which that demographic identifier would connect to biometrics – to prove that I am who I say I am, even if I have no other document to prove this. My identity would be my scientific, culturally unmarked, body. My identity thus would lie solely in my bodily existence. It would not be dependent on another's endorsement.

Such a biopolitical definition of the citizen would be autonomous from the cultural credentials of citizenship – such as status, family, education, or employment – to which numerous Indian residents had no access. The demographic data would be name, date and place of birth, gender, parents' names and UID numbers (optional for adult residents) and address (permanent and present). This data would, as the 2016 Aadhar Bill later

---

32   As per the Aadhaar Act, Section 2(v), an Aadhaar number can be issued to a resident who has been residing in India for at least 182 days in the 12 months immediately preceding the date of application for enrolment.

reasserted, explicitly exclude 'race, religion, caste, tribe, ethnicity, language, records of entitlement, income or medical history of an individual'.[33]

In 2008, Nandan Nilekani published *Imagining India: Ideas for the New Century*, one of the more useful books in the 'ten easy ways to reboot India overnight' genre obligatory for tech tycoons. Many also saw it as a book-length job application for the post of head of the UID authority. The following February, the Unique Identification Authority of India (UIDAI) was set up and it published a working paper, *Creating a Unique Identity for Every Resident in India*. Read together, Nilekani's book and the working paper have the synergy of a virtual manifesto of tech solutionism — of what was wrong with the country, what needed doing, where the hope lay, and what the UID would now do to realize that hope.

Among its founding principles, the UID was above all *not* going to provide a citizenship record; it would be available to *anyone who resided in this nation*. It was not — repeat *not*, repeat *ad infinitum* not — an identity card. It would only be a 'mechanism that uniquely identifies a person, and ensures instant identity verification'. Its purpose, once such a unique identification took place, was to 'transform the delivery of social welfare programs by making them more inclusive of communities' and also 'enable the government to shift from indirect to direct benefits, and help verify whether the intended beneficiaries actually receive funds/subsidies'.[34] It would thus eliminate 'gatekeepers' and link 'investors, farmers and citizens directly to both information and resources, and [provide] rapidly democratizing access', since 'unprecedented access to information and resources' was the only thing that would transform 'both political and economic power structures'.[35]

As Partha Chatterjee has argued in multiple contexts, independent India had found ways to expand key developmental systems of welfare beyond its normative citizens by creating parallel forms of classification and enumeration that divided society into elementary units of *population*.[36] Unlike the citizen, he said, a population is descriptive and empirical, not normative. In 2009, it appeared at least possible that such a concept of nonnormative identity could pitch the bodily self as tagged identifier into a flatter, more equitable digital ecosystem of both governance and social acceptance. That identification had purposes other than merely those of surveillance. That, as a result, the rose-tinted digital future just might if not fight then at least bypass the hierarchies of social exclusion that analogue citizenship had seemingly written in stone.

It all seemed to come down to a particular interpretation of what, to use prevalent terminology, was widely known as the last mile problem. Such a problem was typically referenced by the so-called Rajiv Gandhi 15-paise formula, namely that only 15 paise of every rupee meant for a poor beneficiary actually reached that person. 'Across our

---

33 Section 2(k) of the Aadhaar Act.
34 UIDAI, *UIDAI Strategy Overview: Creating a Unique Identity Number for Every Resident in India*, Planning Commission/UIDAI, Government of India, April 2010.
35 Nandan Nilekani, *Imagining India: Ideas for the New Century*, New Delhi: Penguin, 2008, p. 122.
36 Partha Chatterjee, 'Beyond the Nation? Or Within?', *Social Text* 56 (1998): 57–69.

creaky subsidy distribution systems', writes Nilekani, 'leakages average 50 per cent and more. The inefficiency of these state schemes has gotten even worse over the last two decades'.[37] Benefit does not reach beneficiaries because of leakages either due to theft or corruption. This is tolerated in India mainly because, said Nilekani, the benefit was seen as *subsidy* (i.e. an entitlement) and not *benefit*.

The last mile problem was not new to the Indian political system, but what was perhaps new was its translation into a communication paradigm. In its classical form, the 'last mile' is a communications term defining the final stage of providing connectivity from a communications provider to a recipient.[38] The last mile *problem* referred to situations in which intended beneficiaries do not receive the communicated signal due to either a break or distortion in the system at the receiver's end. The term has been widened to include problems that affect schemes of public policy, from disaster relief to housing and food subsidies, where benefits go astray and do not percolate to those for whom they are intended. The UID would now, declared its book-working-paper manifesto, eliminate this problem once and for all. It now promised both accurate identification of and targeted delivery to intended recipients.

New questions arose in our project and new data needed to be studied. What of flaws, not in the methodology but in the very theory of 'targeting'? When creating new group-differentiated (as against universal) definitions of public distribution to recognize special 'backward' categories deserving of special benefit, would the shortcuts to which Chatterjee points – the workarounds of normative protocols – not create potentially more problems than they solved? Could the mere redefinition of politics and democracy into a communications model be a sufficient solution for the shadowy, secondarized, and often covert domain of negotiated state operation that now arose? Was it not inevitable that techno-managerial solutions would paper over what might become foundational cracks between the theory and practice of democracy?

What happens, Amartya Sen famously asks, when large forms of public good are not divisible into targeted individual use?[39] Does not delivery of something like 'shirts and apples' always trump the delivery of, say, a 'malaria-free environment'? What happens then when, as the marketplace enters this targeting mechanism, individuated developmental goals start getting available only for a fee? What happens when uncomfortable tracking mechanisms begin being built into the delivery that reveal not the beneficiary's need, but her ability to pay for them?

37   Nilekani, *Imagining India*, p. 373.
38   The Last Mile Problem is used in supply chain management as the hardest, most expensive, and time-consuming part of the supply chain process, amounting up to 53 percent of the total cost of shipping. It has however taken on an entirely new set of local inflections, involving battles between the state and the market on who can bridge this last mile better, or what it means. See Ashish Rajadhyaksha, *The Last Cultural Mile: An Inquiry into Technology and Governance in India*, Bangalore: Centre for Internet & Society/Researchers@Work, 2011.
39   Amartya Sen, 'Markets, State and Social Opportunity', in Amartya Sen, *Development as Freedom*, New York: Alfred A. Knopf, 2000, pp. 126–128.

The problem was further enhanced by another view. A slight shift in the kaleidoscope showed the last mile being routinely bridged by diverse local actors and low-end economies: rather like a boatman who plied you across a river when the bridge had collapsed, or a tout who walked you through an incomprehensible bureaucratic maze.

As a communication model the flaw could be somewhat precisely identified. The model worked only when the receiver was seen to also be a *sender* of a kind, and this sender could only become one if she was given some agency. 'The art of 'targeting'', says Sen, 'is far less simple than some advocates of means-testing tend to assume [...] since the potential beneficiaries are also *agents of action*' (emphasis mine).[40] Such agency of action was possible only if assignation of identity went along with the capacity to *talk back* – to act on juridical citizenship rights, such as being able to vote or litigate – and it worked even better when peer-to-peer structures enabled recipient-senders on the periphery to communicate without having to go through any apparatus of centralized gatekeeping.

How, in delivering state benefit using communications language, does one view the recipient as also a sender? A sender of what? Who is qualified to receive what the senders were sending? How might senders exercise some control over the data being generated in their name, and ostensibly with their knowledge? How to enable two-way and peer-to-peer structures? Back in the late 60s, the scientist Vikram Sarabhai had proposed terrestrial television as a single-point solution to what he said were the two key problems of last mile delivery in India: *linguistic diversity* and *geographical distance.*[41] Considered the classic example of India's fascination with technological leapfrogging, or the use of the latest available technology to jump intermediate steps within the developmental curve to 'catch up' with the developed world,[42] the Sarabhai model would inaugurate a developmental fascination with communications media in its innate capacity to link *connectivity* to the key tenets of democratic citizenship. This paradigm, first deployed with radio, has provided the major rationale for successive technological developments: the wave of portable transistors in the 60s, the terrestrial transponders of the first televisual revolution in the early 80s, the capacity of satellite since the SITE and INSAT series, and the arrival of wired networks (LANs, cable, fiber optics) followed by wireless technology (WLAN, WiMAX, W-CDMA) from the 90s, all of which seemed to have battled this two-way and peer-to-peer problem and found many provisional solutions one way or another.

Nilekani's use of the term 'electronification' appeared to consciously evoke this history – he himself has welcomed a popular science historiography casting him in the tradition of Visveswaraiah and Sarabhai[43] – and his upbeat assumption that 'entrepreneurial energy' would 'work its way through infrastructure barriers and connect markets, thus building

40   Sen, 'Markets', p. 135.
41   NAMEDIA, *A Vision for Indian Television*, New Delhi: Media Foundation of the Non-aligned, 1986.
42   A.S. Bhalla, 'Can High Technology Help Third World 'Take-Off'?', *Economic & Political Weekly* 22.27 (1987): 1082–1086.
43   For example, by Arun Mohan Sukumar in his much-discussed book *Midnight's Machines: A Political History of Technology in India*, New Delhi: Penguin Viking, 2019.

innovative, interlinked networks from scratch',[44] appeared at least worth hearing out for its possibility of defining bodily identity in a way that did not entirely rip it from its survival conditions.

It is perhaps worth remembering that the arrival of a new ecosystem – combining mobile networks, satellite communications, offline enrolment and verification – did offer promise. There were the inevitable glitches, but it appeared, at least initially, that the UID, for the first time, was bringing to the table a mix of agencies to improve direct benefit service delivery and direct cash transfers to poor beneficiaries.[45] How effectively it would do this was yet to be seen, but the proposition was at least before us.

Despite this long history of development communication, two-way and peer-to-peer structures have been incommensurable with the hierarchical self-image of the Indian state. One consequence, as a bureaucrat pointed out during our Identity Project interviews, was that 'everywhere the state usually steps in when markets fail; in India, markets step in when the state fails'. Access to various kinds of community-market mechanisms that were often hidden, rendered covert and even illegal (the criminalization of bribery, for example) appeared through our field studies a far more trusted lifeline to survival for much of the population than often discredited state benefit, not least because, even at the time, all such state benefit came inevitably with the threat of surveillance, even in, and perhaps especially during, times of crisis. Again, to quote Amartya Sen, the role that markets play 'depend[s] [...] not only on what they can do but also on what they are allowed to do'. While the interests of some people are served by the smooth functioning of markets, there are 'groups whose established interests may be hurt by such functioning'. Confronting such influences has to occur 'not merely through resisting – and perhaps even 'exposing' – the seekers of profit from captive markets, but also [...] taking on their intellectual arguments as proper subjects of scrutiny'.[46]

Little Aadhaar, Big Aadhaar – 'The Poisoned Well' and the Origins of Creep

The idealism with regard to Aadhaar as a revolutionary technology didn't last long. Perhaps, barring our project, the optimism over Aadhaar was never really recorded, and so it is worth noting, momentarily, the excitement of the brief period when the UID (not yet Aadhaar) presented itself as at least potentially a radical break from unidirectional hyper-centralization. Nilekani's contention, in *Imagining India*, that information technology, 'untouched as it were by the legacies of the *sarkar raj*, could be a powerful leverage for better public services [...]

44   Nilekani, *Imagining India*, p. 274.
45   The agencies included government ministries with development schemes for the poor, such as the Ministry of Rural Development's Mahatma Gandhi National Rural Employment Guarantee Scheme (MGNREGS), the Ministry of Labour and Employment's Rashtriya Swasthya Bima Yojana (RSBY), the Department of Food and Public Distribution's Targeted Public Distribution System (TPDS); Life Insurance Corporation of India and Ministry of Petroleum and Natural Gas; banks and other financial institutions offering outreach through banking correspondents; and service-oriented agencies such as mobile phone companies.
46   Sen, 'Markets', p. 120.

could play a bigger and more powerful role in the economy than anyone had guessed or attempted before'[47] was part of the giddy romance of the internet. It was also the moment from where the story would begin to unravel.

Early warnings were less to do with the enrolment procedure itself and more about the UID being a populist mechanism upon which central and state governments were mounting their own diverse schemes with diverse ideological purposes. Many revealed a gargantuan KYR-plus desire for gathering ever-expanding and infinitely more intrusive data about all those it enrolled, well beyond what Aadhaar itself asked.[48] We were, it appeared at times, seeing an optical double image: of two Aadhaars, a lithe lean-and-mean Aadhaar, up front and visible, and a massively data-guzzling Big Aadhaar lurking in the shadows. This ghost-image effect would be key to the creep that now followed.

The UID itself was no more than one, albeit crucial, cog in a very large wheel that was the National E-Governance Plan (NeGP) announced in 2006 by the then-Department of Electronics and Information Technology to promote e-governance through a series of mission mode projects to deliver various services online.[49] As the only cog that sought to define the wheel itself, the UID now became something of an in-house ideologue for Digital India as a whole (and so gradually became indistinguishable from it), taking it upon itself to explain how all manner of programs would work, from health care to microfinance, to mediate their populist differences, all the while 'pitching' the usefulness of its key central feature – direct cash transfers under the overall umbrella concept of financial inclusion. *Interoperability*, and Aadhaar's unique ability to offer it, was going to be the key to the success of the NeGP. Inevitably this proved complex, not least because of turf wars, but more significantly because of seeming ideological differences between different populisms to which Aadhaar's own delivery mechanism claimed, increasingly ineffectually, to be neutral.

Was it, to take only one contradiction, mandatory or was it not? Aadhaar itself repeatedly asserted (as Aarogya Setu is currently doing) that it was not, but that meant little when government schemes that *were* mandatory mounted an 'interoperable' arrangement upon it: it rapidly became, as Jean Drèze would say, 'like selling bottled water in a village after poisoning

---

47   Nilekani, *Imagining India*, p. 365.
48   All Aadhaar registrars were permitted to ask for additional information for their own purposes – also known as KYR+. To take one instance, that of Andhra Pradesh (AP), KYR+ included information regarding caste membership, NREGS job card no., SHG no., pension card no., bank account details, LPG connections, etc. Typically, KYR+ forms contained some mandatory fields and some non-mandatory fields. However, from what The Identity Project witnessed at the enrollment centers, residents did not seem to distinguish between the two, nor were they appropriately advised at the Enrollment Centre. So, while UIDAI-mandated Enrollment Forms asked residents to volunteer their bank details, in the AP KYR+, residents were asked to furnish their bank account details without any discernible distinction between it being a mandatory or a voluntary field.
49   The NeGP, launched in May 2006, was a 'mission mode' plan to bring into a single system all government services available to the citizens of India via electronic media. It initially comprised 27 'Mission Mode Projects' (MMPs). It was a long-term ancestor to the present Digital India and UMANG (Unified Mobile Application for New-age Governance) initiatives.

the well, and claiming that people are buying water voluntarily'.[50] Drèze was one of the early critics of the program, fearing the damage it would cause to the National Rural Employment Guarantee Act (NREGA), especially its insistence on being the sole payments gateway for cash transfers. Drèze and Reetika Khera spoke of a 'potent recipe for chaos' if workers of the Mahatma Gandhi Rural Employment Guarantee Scheme (MGNREGS) were deprived of their bank passbooks, inserted into a system where there was no internet connectivity, and required single bank operating procedures.[51] Drèze also noted with some apprehension a proposal in 2010 by the Planning Commission that the National Food Security Act should impose the 'mandatory use of UID numbers which are expected to become operational by the end of 2010'. 'No UID', says Drèze, 'no food'.[52] So much then for the UID's much-touted voluntary nature.

While some differences between Aadhaar and the government schemes on which it was mounted were foundational, like the vexed 'mandatory' question, other differences (mostly procedural issues) appeared like a dispute internal to the joint family that was the NeGP, to be resolved within. The real battle emerged when a hairy outsider moved into the neighborhood scarcely a year after the UIDAI was set up, clearly with hostile intent: the National Population Register or NPR.

Between 2010 and 2012, Aadhaar would fight a bitter, occasionally personal, and clearly ideological battle with the NPR that saw its very existence threatened more than once. Eventually it was – or so it appeared at the time – the price Aadhaar paid for its survival that proved pivotal to the turn digital governance took, a *longue durée* origin of the issues framing the 2019 protests against CAA.

Unlike Aadhaar, which to date presents its voluntary status like some act of faith, the NPR flaunted its compulsory nature. Unlike the Census of India, which worked on the premise of anonymized data, the NPR's register would be public, causing a problem when the single-point Registrar General of the NPR was also the Census Commissioner. Aadhaar was pivoted on the *individual* as the basic social unit. The NPR's basic social unit was instead the *family*, represented by its head who became legally liable for every member of his family. NPR brought in 15 data sets, including marital status, educational qualifications, and occupation. While family, marriage, occupation, and education sent out their own alarm bells, the most worrisome was the category of '*usual* resident' (not resident). You had to have physically lived in the space you gave as your address for a minimum of six months. You had to be *socially known* there, and had to pass a 'social audit'. Such an audit would happen in the following way: Your biographical data along with your photograph and your Aadhaar number would be publicly 'displayed in the local area for inviting claims and objections', to be 'scrutinized by local officials' and 'placed in Gram Sabhas and Ward Committees'. This process of social

50   Jean Drèze, 'Unique Facility, or Recipe for Trouble?', *The Hindu*, 25 November 2010, https://www.
      thehindu.com/opinion/op-ed/Unique-facility-or-recipe-for-trouble/article15714630.ece.
51   Bharat Bhatti, Jean Drèze, and Reetika Khera, 'Experiments with Aadhar', *The Hindu*, 27 June 2012,
      https://www.thehindu.com/opinion/lead/Experiments-with-Aadhaar/article12916184.ece.
52   Drèze, 'Unique Facility'.

audit, said the NPR, was necessary to 'bring in transparency and equity'. [53] Aadhaar's Proof of Address (POA), in accepting a wide range of documents and in its introducer mechanism, was in sharp contrast far more relaxed.

The war spilled out in the open when the NPR announced that it too would be gathering biometric data. What initially began as a relatively minor spat over quality of data and the usefulness of iris scans became a turf issue, sought to be resolved (in January 2012) by dividing up the country into two halves, giving the NPR control over one half and Aadhaar the other.[54] When that didn't work, a compromise was reached in which NPR data would be sent to Aadhaar for deduplication, but if the two data sets didn't match, NPR's data would prevail. Other capitulations rapidly followed: the NPR, it was decided in 2010, would include, alongside demographic data and biometric data, the Aadhaar number. The final nail perhaps was this: India's Identity Card, whenever it is issued to all of India's 'usual residents' over 18 years, would have the Aadhaar number on it. In a full turn of the wheel, Aadhaar finally *de facto* became the one thing that it has always specifically said it is not.

Despite this capitulation there were, as technologist R. Swaminathan wrote, 'genuine divergences in the objectives of NPR and UIDAI. Their worldviews are from different eras. While one is rooted in a mindset of exclusion and security, the other is inclusive and participative.'[55] The NPR made no secret of what its chief proponent, former Home Minister P. Chidambaram, was trying to set up: '21 sets of databases [...] to achieve quick seamless and secure access to desired information for intelligence and enforcement agencies', including a DNA data bank, the NATGRID, and a series of others such as the Crime and Criminals Tracking Network and Systems (CCTNS) and a National Counter Terrorism Centre, all of which were intended to work together to make a devastating and unimaginable impact on surveillance.[56]

---

53   All references to the NPR taken from the Census of India's FAQs: https://censusindia.gov.in/2011-common/faqs.html. This particular FAQ, outlining the social audit, is no longer on the Census website.
54   See 'Nandan Nilekani, Home Ministry End UIDAI Tiff, to Divide Data Collection', *The Economic Times*, 28 January 2012, https://economictimes.indiatimes.com/news/politics-and-nation/nandan-nilekani-home-ministry-end-uidai-tiff-to-divide-data-collection/articleshow/11655516.cms?utm_source=contentofinterest&utm_medium=text&utm_campaign=cppst
55   # R. Swaminathan, 'UIDAI-NPR Row: Identity Politics of a Different Kind', Observer Research Foundation, 7 April 2012, https://www.orfonline.org/research/uidai-npr-row-identity-politics-of-a-different-kind/.
56   The plan, according to newspaper reports, was that from May 2011, the National Intelligence Grid (NATGRID) would integrate 21 existing databases with central and state government agencies and other organizations in the public and private sector such as banks, insurance companies, stock exchanges, airlines, railways, telecom service providers, chemical vendors, etc. Eleven government agencies (including, among others, the Research and Analysis Wing or RAW, Intelligence Bureau, Directorate of Revenue Intelligence, and Income Tax Department) would be able to access sensitive personal information of any individual, such as bank accounts, insurance policies, property owned or rented, travel, income tax returns, driving records, automobiles owned or leased, credit card transactions, stock market trades, phone calls, emails and SMSes, websites visited, etc. A National Population Registry would be established by the 2011 Census, during which fingerprints and iris scans would be taken along with GPS records of each household. According to the home ministry, the central intelligence agencies and state police have plenty of information that is not shared or because there is no umbrella

II.

'Algorithms of Connectedness': Theorizing Creep

> Function creep: the gradual widening of the use of a technology or system beyond
> the purpose for which it was originally intended, esp when this leads to potential
> invasion of privacy – Collins Dictionary

The epic conflict between Aadhaar and NPR, and the eventual capitulation of the former, appeared to have been enabled by a relentless creep of some sort. It was as though the traditional ambivalences inherent to the definition of citizenship had led to a shadowy, sinister, sleight of hand movement in which one thing was being claimed and another attempted.

The conflict itself was largely technology-driven, but the problem itself – and its terminology – appeared to arrive in arcane language, of *citizenship* versus *population*, whose import would perhaps be more familiar to students of Foucault and Partha Chatterjee than either technologists or political activists. If Aadhaar was, in Chatterjee's sense, a populational database, the National *Population* Register, contrary to its name, was explicitly a register of *citizenship*. Indeed, the NPR was born under the 2004 amendment of the Citizenship Act, 1955, with several new clauses reversing basic constitutional norms that had returned the emphasis on ancestry, directly targeting 'illegal' migrants. Although the terminology was itself a minor matter, it nevertheless pressed an alarm button. Was this purely creep? Could this terminological confusion be illuminated by another rather more complex *theoretical* social-scientific explanation, with a rather longer time span, that might say something about the Indian state itself as it mutated in the early years of the new millennium?

These fine distinctions didn't seem so arcane in 2013 when Bezwada Wilson of the Safai Karmachari Andolan (a movement for the elimination of manual scavenging in India) and S.G. Vombatkere impleaded themselves in the ongoing Supreme Court Writ Petition challenging the Aadhaar program. Wilson, along with a few other co-petitioners such as transgender and sexual minorities, brought in specific concerns, namely identities thrust upon them that would *add to* citizen discrimination, not take away from it.

In a long conversation with *Frontline*, Wilson outlines his issues with Aadhaar. The central purpose of identity has to above all enable its *repudiation*. This was because 'identities of Dalits and Adivasis should never be permanent; they should be able to transcend them'. Dalits are 'segregated in such a way very clearly, demarcated in villages'. The problem manual scavengers face is how to 'come out of the identity and destroy it forever [...]

---

organization to collate all the information, which any or all the agencies can share to generate real-time intelligence. The NATGRID enables quick extraction of information, data mining, pattern recognition and flagging 'tripwires' of suspicious or unusual activities (Brijesh Pandey, 'Natgrid Will Kick in from May 2011. Is the Big Brother Threat for Real?', *Tehelka*, 13 November 2010). Also see, Usha Ramanathan, 'A State of Surveillance', International Environmental Law Research Centre, 2010, http://www.ielrc.org/content/w1002.pdf.

any marginalised community, any manual scavenging or vulnerable community wants to destroy its existing identity; that is our whole struggle'.

> My basic problem is that [Aadhar facilitates] keeping identity forever. This is against my principle. Because it is a caste-ridden society and we already have identities. You don't need any Aadhar; [people are] already branded so we don't need any fingerprints or iris recognition [...] So you are branding; even if I come out of this and get liberation also, but in your Aadhaar, my occupation, where I come from, everything will be there. Once you get the data, you can segregate in any way by means of technology. See, you never used identity to support us, never purposely did a proper survey to identify and rehabilitate us. Now you want to give us an identity?[57]

The ghostly illusions of two separate Aadhaars, one small, nimble and upfront, and one large and shadowy in the background, were now intense. On the face of it, Aadhaar's explicit mandate was to facilitate the entry, to identify the biological body shorn of cultural markers: it was *designed* so that it didn't have to ask the *safai karmachari* (a cleaner/someone engaged in manual scavenging) his occupation. On the other hand, the NPR *did* list occupation, as did identification surveys such as the Prohibition of Employment as Manual Scavengers and their Rehabilitation Act, 2013 that Wilson excoriates when he points out that *safai karmachari*s are 'immediately identified' and 'asked why are you here for a job when there is 100 per cent reservation for your community'.[58]

The issue wasn't creep alone. It was creep stalking a more fundamental slippage. We seemed to be looking at a designed ideological ambivalence in the interoperability system. In a curious twist of fate, Aadhaar not only capitulated to the NPR, it became the NPR's public face. Chameleon-like, even as it adopted the colors of whatever initiative it came in under, it would end up becoming that initiative. As further mismatches emerged, such slippages became routine: of Aadhar promising something only to have its interoperable partner take it away — just one of numerous instances being when Aadhaar's culturally sensitive 'third gender' category produced mismatches with PAN Cards (presently being cross-linked with Aadhaar) that had built no such category.[59] Little Aadhaar increasingly became like an invitation to the parlor of an elite Big Aadhaar citizenship club that professed nondiscrimination and entry to all, only to reveal covert hierarchies and fine print designed to reinforce segregation.

In 2017, the Supreme Court gave its much awaited omnibus judgment on Aadhaar and privacy law. Although the five-bench judgment cleared Aadhaar by a 4:1 majority, what

---

57   Akshay Deshmane, 'The Dalit Identity Dilemma', *Frontline*, 28 April 2017,
     https://frontline.thehindu.com/cover-story/the-dalit-identity-dilemma/article9629313.ece.
58   Deshmane, 'The Dalit Identity'.
59   Pankul Sharma, 'Only Male or Female Can Get PAN Card, Transgenders Told', *Times of India*, 15 March 2018,
     http://timesofindia.indiatimes.com/articleshow/63321785.cms?utm_source=contentofinterest&utm_medium=text&utm_campaign=cppst.

caught attention was Justice D.Y. Chandrachud's extraordinary dissenting opinion.[60] At a thousand pages, nearly twice as long as the main judgment itself, it was, says legal commentator Gautam Bhatia, a 'dissent for the ages'.[61] Among numerous sharp observations, Chandrachud caught and dissected the creep with clinical precision. It is true, he noted, that Aadhaar itself 'excludes storage of individual information related to race, religion, caste, tribe, ethnicity, language, income or medical history'.[62] However, when 'Aadhaar is seeded into every database, it becomes a bridge across discrete data silos, which allows anyone with access to this information to re-construct a profile of an individual's life' and so 'the mandatory linking of Aadhaar with various schemes allows the same result in effect'.[63] Section 7 of that Act has become an ever-expanding single window 'for the government to route more benefits, subsidies and services [...] and expand the scope of Aadhaar'. This section listed benefits that ranged from

> schemes for children [...] [to] meals under the Mid-day meal scheme, painting and essay competitions [...] [to] scholarships on merit, [from] schemes relating to rehabilitation of bonded labour and human trafficking [...] to access to tuberculosis care, pensions, schemes relating to labour and employment, skill development, personnel and training, agriculture and farmers' welfare, primary and higher education, social justice, benefits for persons with disabilities, women and child development, rural development, food distribution, healthcare, panchayati raj, chemicals & fertilizers, water resources, petroleum and natural gas, science and technology, sanitation, textiles, urban development, minority affairs, road transport, culture, tourism, urban housing, tribal affairs and stipends for internship for students.[64]

So that 'from delivery to deliverance, almost every aspect of the cycle of life would be governed by the logic of Aadhaar'. A legal and administrative creep was riding on the technology that, you wonder, could *surely* not have been entirely unintentional.

> When an individual from a particular caste engaged in manual scavenging is rescued and in order to take benefit of rehabilitation schemes, she/he has to link the Aadhaar number with the scheme, the effect is that a profile as that of a person engaged in manual scavenging is created in the scheme database. The stigma of being a manual scavenger gets permanently fixed to her/his identity. What the Aadhaar Act seeks to exclude specifically is done in effect by the mandatory linking of Aadhaar numbers with different databases, under cover of the delivery of benefits and services.[65]

---

60   Supreme Court of India, *Justice K.S. Puttaswamy (retd) and Another* v *Union of India and Others*, WP (C) 494/2012 (2018). For details see https://main.sci.gov.in/supremecourt/2012/35071/35071_2012_ Judgement_26-Sep-2018.pdf.

61   Gautam Bhatia, 'The Aadhaar Judgment: A Dissent for the Ages', *Indian Constitutional Law and Philosophy*, 27 September 2018, https://indconlawphil.wordpress.com/2018/09/27/the-aadhaar-judgment-a-dissent-for-the-ages/.

62   *Puttaswamy* v *UOI*, Dissenting judgment. Part H, Proportionality: 247.

63   *Puttaswamy* v *UOI*, Dissenting judgment. Part L, Conclusion: 14m.

64   *Puttaswamy* v *UOI*, 2018. Dissenting judgment. Part H, Proportionality: 246.

65   *Puttaswamy* v *UOI*, 2018. Dissenting judgment. Part H, Proportionality: 247. Emphasis is mine.

If Aadhaar and its linking process are the only visible part of an iceberg, the insight is sharp enough to clue us into how this double act fits into our larger project, of rewriting our digital past over two decades as precisely a history of the management of an ambivalence. It will, if we do it right, provide a new genealogy to where we found ourselves in 2020, to internet shutdowns, and to Aarogya Setu. And perhaps, with it, an even longer ancestry to the anti-CAA/NPR movements that the pandemic momentarily sought to suppress. We may even know at last what we are really up against.

'Tommy Singh' and the Indifferent Network

In 2015, in a remarkable essay that Justice D.Y. Chandrachud would in fact quote in his dissenting judgment, Nishant Shah produced a technologically informed understanding of the slippage. At the very center of the self-definition of the Aadhaar project, he pointed out a 'curious conflation [...] between the notions of iden*tity* and iden*tification*', both terms 'constantly used interchangeably'. 'The UIDAI authority, both in its name, and in its documents framing the technological infrastructure that would serve as the scaffolding for effective e-governance in India, centrally talked of identification.'[66]

Such a conflation of two opposing concepts of identity – one based on individual choice, the second explicitly without choice – would open a 'new understanding of the individual'.[67] The person whose data was being recorded was increasingly less you and me as we presumably understood ourselves – as people capable of individual subjective choice – and more a you-me looking in a distorting mirror and seeing an image of ourselves created out of 'predictive and self-correcting algorithms that develop correlations, curations and connections between disparate individuated transactions'. It was part of the design, said Shah, that you and I found ourselves in a digital ecosystem, caught in between two paradoxical imaginations of the individual. On the one side we were a 'data subject' and on the other a 'quantified self'. The data subject was offered a specific capability: of being imagined in such a way that she was 'no longer confined to the biological discreteness of [...] existence'. Such a person became available to the world 'through an extended relationality enabled by digital traffic flows of ideas, ideologies, and interactions' – became thereby a *blurred entity*, in turn blurring the lines between public and private. On the other hand, a 'quantified self' posited a very different sort of individual: as 'atomic', as no longer an actor but 'produced through a series of actions, understood as a networked entity that can be mined for data and information, ranging from genetic blue-prints to socio-cultural profiles'.

This conflation triggered multiple anxieties. These were in part 'about the fallibility of historical precedent', but mostly about 'the unimaginability of the post-human futures that the individual embodies'. They would sometimes manifest themselves as a 'fear for the loss of individual and human control and growing power of digital networks'. At other times they would 'call for accepting the emergent digital networks of life and love' in order to enable us to build

---

66   Nishant Shah, 'Identity and Identification: The Individual in the Time of Networked Governance', *Socio-Legal Review* 11.12 (2015): p. 28.
67   Shah, 'Identity and Identification', p. 24.

entirely new and perhaps 'more transparent and accountable systems of governance and regulation'.[68]

Shah's 'data subject', blurring the lines between public and private, was (to return to the terminologies used at the top of this section) our *citizen*. Such a subject was defined primarily through the capacity for *choice*: to choose how to best reflect her identity or, as Wilson's Dalit and Adivasi example requires, to repudiate it. Faced up to this kind of citizen-subject was another 'quantified self' that possessed none of these freedoms of either choice or repudiation. Here your identity was handed down by a machine, an identif*ication* produced by a complex algorithmic arrangement that collated all the data produced by you and about you and decided something about you — whether you were above or below the poverty line, if poor what your bodily needs were, if rich what your net worth was and what luxuries might be advertised to you. This was a *populational* procedure, where you were viewed as just a number to whom a certain benefit had to be delivered or a luxury sold, not a thinking and feeling human being.

Even as anxiety levels about privacy skyrocketed, the popularly held view came to be that a right to privacy could only be realized when my private self was walled off and made technologically entirely separate from the data-gathering mechanism. A more complex view was its opposite, to see how my two selves — the blurred choice-based self in which inhere my citizenship entitlements and the hypervisible, enumerative identification apparatus of the population that produced another self of me — could be *better synced*, so that the right of choice was not entirely lost when the process of enumeration kicked in. There was a third view that would directly confront us with the fear of state governance: where the second identity might entirely replace the first, freezing us all into faceless beneficiaries.

Shah proposes on his side the concept of an 'indifferent network'. He suggests that in its very indifference lay its potential, and outlines his argument with the metaphor of the dog on the Aadhaar card. This was a famous episode that had caused much hilarity on the internet, when a bona fide Aadhaar ID was made in Bhind, Madhya Pradesh, for a dog named Tommy Singh, son of Sheru Singh, born on November 26, 2009.[69] The incident, says Shah, led to several expected responses, most of them variations on the fond hope that 'these networked phenomena [might build] an implicit relationship with the exterior and with the human subject'. This hope was itself never unpacked or questioned. Inevitably, when questions are posed about the relationship between networks and reality, 'instead of looking at how networks fail to represent and map the exterior, the problem is posed as the exterior not measuring up to the parameters and models that the network produces'.[70]

---

68   Shah, 'Identity and Identification', p. 26.
69   Subash Jain, 'Man Arrested for Getting Aadhaar Card for Dog', *Hindustan Times*, 3 July 2015, https://www.hindustantimes.com/india/man-arrested-for-getting-aadhaar-card-for-dog/story-MVtobqWtsrLXm01OkCBSvK.html.
70   Shah, 'Identity and Identification', p. 36.

Shah saw Tommy Singh rather differently. The famous Aadhaar dog was not a failed stand-in for a person, but as a 'stand-in for the data scattered across databases which, because of their correlation now identify this dog as a resident of India, and probably even feed it into the National Population Register which was linked with Aadhaar in the last census'.[71] Such data has no exteriority; it exists inside a self-referential network that develops its content only in the way it travels.

From here Shah made two prescient and radical propositions. Firstly, a blanket statement that the *individual*, whether human or canine, 'has no space in the computational logic that informs our new structures of governance'.[72] The dog in Aadhaar's imagination is in the end 'as much an actor or an individual or the bearer of an identifier/identity as any other human being enrolled into the system'.[73] It can become such an actor only if we recognized that we were looking at an 'indifferent network'. Such a claim of indifference clashed directly with the PR claims made by the 2009 UID working paper which spoke of the caring nature of a data network 'committed to mapping the individual in all its difference through the constantly expanding databases of quantified measurement'. The facts, to Shah, were rather different: networks were the very opposite of caring, indifferent to 'the individual and its expressions'. Under the black-and-white ambivalence-free conditions of digital governance, the fiction of the 'reasonable man', which has been at the heart of legal regulation and justice, has been absolutely replaced by another set of tools for producing reason and rationality. These tools of reason are self-learning and iterative algorithms that make connections at speeds unfathomable to human faculties. As networks propelled by such tools grow, they 'reinforce this inherent paradox of the individual as unique – having a unique identifier – but also the individual as [...] an actor that can be mined for data, queried, and stored in mobile data sets'.[74]

Herein, says Shah in his second proposition, lies the hope. Identity, which had in its analogue construction included the right *not* to be identified, has been 'flipped so that identification through identifiers, and the data that accrues [...] becomes the only form of identity in the time of database governance'.[75] At the same time, when a networked governance database system 'does not treat the appearance of the dog as a glitch, but just another data set which helps make new correlations and predictions possible', then, linguistically speaking, '*the network is actually closer to the etymological understanding of identity* than how we recognise it in common utterance'.[76]

The possibilities of analogue blurriness morph into those of network indifference. If in analogue conditions the Dalit and the Adivasi claim the right to change or repudiate their historical identity, in the time of digital indifference a dog too can become an enumerable entity. A new techno-social framework has to be imagined if we are to account for 'the

---

71   Shah, 'Identity and Identification', pp. 33–34.
72   Shah, 'Identity and Identification', p. 27.
73   Shah, 'Identity and Identification', p. 38.
74   Shah, 'Identity and Identification', p. 38.
75   Shah, 'Identity and Identification', p. 31.
76   Shah, 'Identity and Identification', p. 38.

machine function of identification' that can offer new 'inroads into looking at what happens when our identities are mediated, mitigated, facilitated, and contained by the ways in which networked technologies of authentication and verification operate'.[77]

As we worry about how such mediated identities may once more be 'wedded to the human expression of identity', Tommy Singh suggests a new possibility. It is one of 'reconceptualising the individual as a networked subject, constituted by processes of mediation between older categories of being and new logics of digital computation'. Instead of being seen as contradictory and perennially at war, these two logics could instead be reintegrated 'towards a more robust framework for governance'.[78]

'Who is a person?': Identity Collapse, Psychological Numbing, and the Citizen-Killer

So where does identity lie? Partha Chatterjee asks this very question in the context of a major identity crisis that occurred at a crucial historical moment in late colonial India that shaped several principles of governmentality in times to come.[79] This was a famous dispute, much retold in popular fiction and cinema, of a dissolute *zamindar* (landowner) in rural Bengal who died of syphilis and was ritually cremated. Years later, when a *sannyasi* (a Hindu mendicant ascetic) appeared in Dhaka claiming to be the dead man, the British establishment was ranged, in its determination to prove the reincarnated figure an impostor, against an Indian side that included most (though not all) of his family that was equally committed to proving that he was indeed the erstwhile landlord returned to life. A fierce legal battle would begin in Calcutta[80] and go all the way to the Privy Council in London, taking us to the very gist of both the possibilities and limitations of identity as posing a very real crisis of state.

The British administrative answer clearly saw identity, as Aadhaar does, as bodily property. As such it was something unique, decipherable, and entirely unshakeable. Bodies were entitled to only one identity, and there could be no choice in the matter. The full powers of the colonial apparatus were therefore applied to reveal (unsuccessfully in the end) that the *sannyasi* had to be a fraud. Reading in the possibility of the second covert self the 'secret history of Indian nationalism', Chatterjee offers a political interpretation for where the colonial fault lines lay in this extraordinary dispute over who the *sannyasi* said he was. A founding principle, upon which the entire apparatus of sovereignty stood, was in its control over naming a person as a man and a citizen, and in ensuring that *all* human beings possessed a technically and socially verifiable identity. The apparatus of governance would pivot over a 'narrow (assumption) that insists on physical and psychological continuity based on normal causes and verified by scientific method'.[81]

---

77   Shah, 'Identity and Identification', p. 30.
78   Shah, 'Identity and Identification', p. 27.
79   Partha Chatterjee, *A Princely Impostor?: The Kumar of Bhawal and the Secret History of Indian Nationalism*, Princeton, N.J.: Princeton University Press, 2002.
80   In 2001, the government of West Bengal officially changed the name of the city to Kolkata.
81   Chatterjee, *A Princely Impostor?*, p. 126.

Arun Mohan Sukumar speaks of another trajectory of colonial anxiety, of what happens if this founding principle of governance fails, in projects that took place as recently as the 90s. In his history of technology in independent India, Sukumar says that the failure of India's vaccine and genome projects were in large part due to 'the subcontinent's long and dismal history of using biological attributes of Indians to serve in the British Raj'. From the mid-19th century, Sukumar shows how fingerprinting had been explicitly linked to criminal tracking, and the Indian Evidence Act of 1899 was the world's first legislation recognizing this technology. And so it was that when India first piloted automated fingerprint detection in 1992, it was the 'historical provenance of techniques and technologies that involved harvesting information from the human body [that] made them unpalatable to Indians young and old'. [82]

'Partition took place when human rights movements were more or less unknown, in a world just getting accustomed to genocide and ethnic cleansing', writes Ashis Nandy, in an extraordinary series of texts that reveal the crisis of selfhood that that episode in our history caused to the question of identity. Nandy has been interested in the social history of elusive 'multiple selves', a fundamental challenge to the question of who a person is, and in one such example he links this multiplicity to a situation of 'psychological numbing', when normal human beings took part in genocide as a condition of normalcy. In an intriguingly titled essay ('Coming Home: Religion, Mass Violence and the Exiled and Secret Selves of a Citizen-Killer'),[83] Nandy discusses a man named Madanlal Pahwa. He was a participant in the plot to assassinate Gandhi, for which he was convicted and did 17 years in jail. A largely forgotten man in his 80s, he lived in Bombay, disconnected from contemporary politics when Nandy and Rajni Bakshi met him. Over many conversations, Pahwa defended his extreme views but called himself a humanist, claimed to be a *kattar* Hindu (hardcore Hindu) when growing up but remembered the *qawwali*s (a style of Sufi devotional music) at the *mazar* (Muslim shrine) of Baba Farid Shakarganj during his childhood, admitted to numerous acts of violence and killing in many cities, but said he felt no hatred for either Muslims or for Gandhi. Pahwa saw no internal contradiction between these multiple selves, saying mostly that what he did was a consequence of the times.

Chatterjee connects the two eras, and two selves, thus. 'Just as the anti-absolutist desire for individual liberty produced the dictum in the reformed criminal law that one must be presumed innocent until proven guilty', so we find a 'corresponding desire for the welfare of populations'. This latter desire – very familiar to today's urban migrants seeking to find some way by which they may return home – is reflected in the further dictum that '*one must be presumed to be an impostor until proven otherwise*'. The two maxims, presumed innocent till proven guilty and presumed impostor by default, are 'not contradictory, but entirely consistent within the domain of modern governance'.[84]

---

82   Sukumar, *Midnight's Machines*, pp. 114–115.
83   # Ashis Nandy, 'Coming Home: Religion, Mass Violence and the Exiled and Secret Selves of a Citizen-Killer', in Ashis Nandy, *Regimes of Narcissism, Regimes of Despair*, New Delhi: Oxford University Press, 2013, p. 65.
84   Chatterjee, *A Princely Impostor?*, p. 366.

Justice Chandrachud apparently saw no such possibilities in modern governance in his expansive dissenting judgment. Although his conclusions were different, framed largely along classic constitutional lines, he nevertheless recognized the key category that was now in serious danger, in a way no legal or policy document of the time seemed to have done – namely the pared down networked subject surviving on a tenuous identity lifeline.

One of the central contentions of the petitioners in that 2017 Supreme Court Writ Petition was that 'at its core, Aadhaar alters the relationship between the citizen and the State', that it 'diminishes the status of the citizens' in the way it sets them up in some kind of trade-off, a *bartering process.*

> Rights freely exercised, liberties freely enjoyed, entitlements granted by the Constitution and laws are all made conditional, on a compulsory barter. The barter compels the citizens to give up their biometrics 'voluntarily', allows her biometrics and demographic information to be stored by the State and private operators and then used for a process termed 'authentication'.[85]

The petitioners did not see any of the negotiations that were enabled between different data sets swirling within Shah's indifferent networks. To them, the bartering away of choice-based citizenship had only one inevitable result: the subordination, and eventual stamping out, of basic citizenship rights by the enumerated self. And if for any reason such devastation did not occur, the state possessed one final nuclear option: the ability to – in the Court's chilling phrase – cause 'civil death' by simply switching off any person's Aadhaar connection. Deletion, blocking or rendering inaccessible an Aadhaar identity was potentially equivalent to extermination.

Chandrachud's dissent, effectively agreeing with the petitioners, quoted Shah's essay at some length, adopting experience of tension internal to identity – pulling people apart as it reintegrates them into technologically-enabled data subjects. While accepting the argument that the 'quantified self' is produced through data as it gets distributed across various systems and this 'curates [...] a comprehensive profile of an individual', he reads a rather darker, grimmer consequence into this than Shah himself may have intended. To Chandrachud, such quantification poses an unambiguous danger to citizenship rights, for he reads the 'flipping' of the right as undermining your ability to be identified *at all*, as it becomes, slowly and stealthily, *the only form of identity* you have available to you under database governance. This, he ruled, violated freedoms and liberties guaranteed by Part III of the Constitution premised on choice in the means of identification for proving identity. 'Requiring an individual to prove identity on the basis of one mode alone will [...] violate the right of self-determination and free choice'.[86]

For all the technological novelty of digitization, for Chandrachud the issue was still one of freedom classically framed. It bore similarity then to Safoora Zargar's solitary confinement

---

85 *Puttaswamy* v *UOI*. Dissenting judgment. No. 45. Emphasis is mine.
86 *Puttaswamy* v *UOI*. Dissenting judgment. Part G3: Identity and Identification, No. 185.

claimed as quarantine, where she is currently fighting for the right to be spoken of in the basic terms of liberty and self-determination. Central to both was the *control by the state of the bodily subject* emanating from the invasive 'curation' of that body into an identity tag. Perhaps the most dangerous aspect of Zargar's incarceration is the claim that this is being done for both her own good and that of society. It is the way technology defines sovereignty, integrating the 'social good' into the production of her identity as a terrorist and a candidate for UAPA treatment, that we need to analyze next.

In many ways, control over the bodily subject remains the defining center of the modern state's existence. It is, as Giorgio Agamben says, the founding principle of its sovereignty. There is some similarity between the decultured and pared down bodily identity (a blank-slate *tabula rasa* that, we felt in 2009, may have had some salience to the UID's basic system of creating unique identities) and Agamben's well-known conception of 'bare life'.[87] If the basic paradigm of state control over bare life originates in the concentration camp, the origins of sovereignty too lie in various 'States of Exception'.

Such States of Exception lie in zones needing surveillance, benefit, or other special attention. They may be spaces controlled by the Armed Forces Special Powers Act, 1958. They may be spaces of drought, or natural or man-made disaster. (Or they may be the 'containment zones' of the present pandemic when all humans are defined only as either COVID-positive or asymptomatic). The main point is that such States of Exception gradually morph and expand, so that gradually 'exclusion and inclusion, outside and inside, *bios* and *zoē*, right and fact' all come together to become a 'zone of irreducible indistinction', and the concentration camp becomes an increasingly normalized everyday condition.

Such an everyday normalization of extreme control appears relevant to Justice Chandrachud's anxieties over how the state deals with the sovereign body: and what might happen if the survival of such a body, controlled by the state, came to be leashed to its Aadhaar alter ego almost like a kind of RFID tag. It defines the further possibility that pulling the Aadhaar plug on any person might ensure a body-endangering 'civil death'.

In 2020, such a sovereign body dominating the Indian political horizon was that of India's migrant workers, who – ever since the invocation of the Disaster Management Act and the lockdown – literally started walking, in their millions, across the length of the country, going home, often asserting their determination never to return. The pandemic was used to block their departure in every way possible: through closed borders, suspension of transport, and multiple other means, of which one is especially relevant to our argument.

The full story of the largest physical migration the subcontinent may have ever seen, determinedly returning from city to country, reversing the foundational move that had defined the 20th century, will of course be told some day. Meanwhile, at least *some*

---

87   Giorgio Agamben, *Homo Sacer: Sovereign Power and Bare Life*, Stanford: Stanford University Press, 1998.

of the reasons for this blocking are blatantly obvious. These people provide the labor that keeps the urban economy going, from manufacturing to services; their departure threatens its collapse. The point here is that Aadhaar, as a portable identity, was surely *designed* for just such a cataclysmic event: especially when both the central and several state governments, realizing that they may have created a problem far larger than the pandemic, began making various kinds of delivery of benefit, of food and shelter, and in limited cases of transportation, available to bona fide returnees.

What happened next allows us to open an entirely new inquiry into the genealogy of key instruments of governance in independent India, including those over which Justice Chandrachud had agonized. The promised aid mostly never arrived. Numerous laborers, who had been living in spaces provided by labor contractors with no money and no food, found themselves disqualified from taking the trains being provided because they didn't have their village address on their Aadhaar card, and so couldn't prove that their destination was their home. Most of these people had gotten these cards only when they had come to the city, as a mandatory requirement to open a bank account and thus to receive their wages and other 'benefit'. Most would have been without proof of address (POA) and would have used 'introducers' – an innovative feature of Aadhaar in which undocumented people could get their identity if 'introduced' along a certain procedure, and which had in fact signed an MOU in July 2010 with a national coalition of several organizations specifically to design a strategy for migrant workers[88] – and most would have had to give their temporary workplace as their address. Aadhaar, by refusing to believe where they came from, was now *preventing* them from proving who they were.[89] It is hard to describe their condition – without aid, unable to go back home because they couldn't prove that it was home, unable to cross state boundaries – as anything but a form of civil death.

By now a pattern has surely emerged in the inevitable creep. Instead of tracking the delivery of benefit, the system had inverted itself into tracking the beneficiary. The onus lay on the migrant laborer to prove *her* identity against the overwhelming *default assumption that she was not who she said she was*. As several states too began closing their borders to returnees for fear of virus contamination, loss of identity began alarmingly to resemble political statelessness. The multiple tensions – layered with the historical memories of famine, disease and both natural and human catastrophe – into which the human body was now inserted revealed several of Justice Chandrachud's explicit fears about the state's near-totalitarian capacity to shut off the identity lifeline.

Inevitably, the images of men, women and children, old and young, in bullock carts, on trains, in trucks, on bicycle and overwhelmingly on foot, trudging down streets and railway tracks to cross the nation, evoked the migrations that followed the Partition. This was not just image

88 See Memorandum of Understanding between the UIDAI and the National Coalition of Organisations for Security of Migrant Workers (represented by Aajeevika Bureau), executed on 29 July 2010, to avert crises precisely such as this one. For details, see https://uidai.gov.in/images/mou/partners/Coalition_of_Migrant_Workers_NGOs.pdf.
89 # See Jawhar Sircar, 'A Long Look at Exactly Why and How India Failed its Migrant Workers', *The Wire*, 29 May 2020, https://thewire.in/labour/lockdown-migrant-workers-policy-analysis.

recall, although there was something relentless about the similarity between what we saw now and what we had seen in the mid-40s.

There was an additional reason. Then as now, amid the baffling determination of vast numbers of people to go 'home', in the astonishing incapability of both the central and state administrations to deliver benefit, whether as food, money, shelter or transport, lay a basic *collapse of identity*. I mean identity collapse in two ways: one, a globally familiar economic paradigm of invisibilizing the poor; and, two, a paradigm that may be closer to the subcontinent, in which who you are depends foundationally on your ability to name a *home*, such as (if not only) a nation. Who could these people be, if not citizens of *some*where?

As in Saadat Hasan Manto's legendary short story of the Partition, the location of the village of Toba Tek Singh is the only identity of the lunatic Bishan Singh, who – utterly confused by the political division taking place – finally finds himself 'after fifteen years on his feet' 'face down on the ground' with India on one side and Pakistan on the other, and his village of Toba Tek Singh 'in the middle, on a piece of land that had no name' – so too these migrants found themselves in an identity abyss and told to quarantine themselves in it.[90]

III.

Careers of Corporeality

The body corporeal – the body incarcerated – is a classic empty signifier. It thus possesses a potential for meaning that can appear both terrifying and uncontrolled, across religious and political ideologies. The institutions of its (political, sexual, subjective) containment define the repressions of the modern public sphere. Control over such a body is thus a crucial signifying site for state sovereignty. When an identity is lashed to that body, it is a key aspect of that control for its putative elusiveness can be a source of anxiety as much for the sovereignty of the state as for its subjects.

Such elusiveness of identity can occur both when a body loses its identity and when identity exists independently of any bodily anchor. Both phenomena trace back at least to colonial times and may well precede it by several centuries in other social-religious traditions. Here we look at more recent history to track, post-2000, the political, legal, and administrative morphing of bodily signification.

Sometime around 2012, legal scholar Kalyani Ramnath, still a student at the National Law School in Bangalore and participant-blogger on the CSCS Identity Project site, was developing an interesting take on India's historical ambivalence around citizenship. Like many legal scholars, she too took the problem back to founding documents, but instead of going to the

---

90   Saadat Hasan Manto's classic 1955 short story 'Toba Tek Singh', in which the newly formed
      governments of India and Pakistan exchange some Muslim, Sikh and Hindu lunatics, revolves around
      Bishan Singh, a Sikh inmate of an asylum in Lahore, sent under police escort to India, who eventually
      finds himself in the no man's land between two barbed wire fences.

Citizenship Act, 1955 she went instead to the Constitution's well-known Directive Principles of State Policy (DPSP).

These Principles have been, it is well known, controversial. Viewed as Ambedkar's explicit intervention bringing a moral and ideological edge to the document, they have also been critiqued as relegating social and economic rights to a section of the Constitution 'that was explicitly and intendedly noncognizable in a court of law', says Niraja Gopal Jayal.[91] The launch of neoliberalism, more or less since the onset of globalization, however, saw these Principles returned to curious prominence.

Since the 80s, an 'expansive interpretation of Article 21' saw the Supreme Court read a variety of unenumerated rights into the Constitution, says Jayal.[92] These included the right to shelter, to pollution-free environments, to privacy and medical aid, and to elimination of bonded labor. This trend only accelerated with globalization. 'Curiously', says Jayal, 'neoliberal ascendance has also been a period in which many social and economic rights have come to be legislated, and the air is thick with many more such rights signalled in activist slogans as well as judicial pronouncements'.[93] By the 2000s, the overuse of the language of rights – and early signs that they were serving a purpose that might be precisely the opposite of what was intended – had set up multiple alerts. In 2004, Jean Drèze, speaking of the Right to Food campaign launched in Rajasthan and mounted on Article 21,[94] was deeply concerned that this right not be reduced to a purely justiciable aspect. The complex reasons for this right needed, more than ever, a return to an Ambedkarian 'revolutionary conception of democracy' that existed in the umbrella protections of the Directive Principles.

---

91   Jayal, *Citizenship and its Discontents*, p. 151.
92   Jayal, *Citizenship and its Discontents*, p. 166.
93   Jayal, *Citizenship and its Discontents*, p. 174.
94   The prevalence of 'hunger amidst plenty' in India took a new turn in mid 2001, as the country's food stocks reached unprecedented levels while hunger intensified in drought-affected areas and elsewhere. This situation prompted the People's Union for Civil Liberties (Rajasthan) to approach the Supreme Court with a writ petition on the 'right to food'. Initially, the case was brought against the Government of India, the Food Corporation of India (FCI), and six state governments, in the specific context of inadequate drought relief. Subsequently, the case was extended to the larger issue of chronic hunger, with all states and union territories as respondents.
     The legal basis of the petition is simple. Article 21 of the Constitution is a guarantee of the right to life, and imposes upon the state the duty to protect it. This right is fundamental. The Supreme Court has held in previous cases that the right to life includes the right to live with dignity and all that goes along with it, including the right to food. The petition argues, in essence, that the response to the drought situation by central and state governments, in terms of both policy and implementation, constitutes a clear violation of this right. The bulk of the petition attempts to establish this using (government and field-based) data from Rajasthan.
     The petition points out two aspects of the state's negligence in providing food security. The first is the breakdown of the public distribution system (PDS). The failures of the PDS arise at various levels: its availability has been restricted to families living below the poverty line (BPL), yet the monthly quota per family cannot meet the nutritional standards set by the Indian Council of Medical Research (ICMR). Even this is implemented erratically: a survey in Rajasthan indicated that only one-third of the sample villages had regular distribution in the preceding three months, with no distribution at all in one-sixth of them. The identification of BPL households is also highly unreliable. All in all, the assistance provided to BPL households through the PDS amounted to less than INR 5 per person per month.

Kalyani Ramnath's inquiry, written in this time and context began (in a short and provocative essay she wrote in 2012) with the famous first three words of the Constitution. Although the entire document is as though written in the name of 'We the People', as it unfolds, there is a strange disappearance of 'the people' as active agents. As she tries to puzzle out this disappearance, she encounters another slippage that would be of some relevance in the early 2000s. From the larger and more abstract category of the 'people' emerges a second and very much more concrete subset, that of 'citizens'. Not all people can be citizens.

> The Constitution of India is not drafted in the name of citizens, although in practice, many of the Fundamental Rights (to speech, assembly or religion) may be claimed only by them. As with many other constitutions, it is drafted in the name of 'We the People', a phrase prominently placed in the Preamble, never again to appear in any of the other provisions.[95]

The 'people' reappear in force in the Directive Principles, for it is of course in their name that the social revolution is being envisaged. What ends up getting outlined, however, sounds to her like a rather 'random assortment of principles, presenting a confused, fragmented 'moral' vision for a social revolution' – such as 'improvements in agriculture, health, education and legal aid services', *panchayati raj* to attempt to put in place a uniform civil code, and to ban cow slaughter – in all of which the 'people' exist only as a moral force to whom the state has a duty.[96]

In contrast to such 'people' and their abstract moral authority, citizens emerge far more concretely as those who *did things for the State* in return for the rights they received. Even as the Directive Principles reveal an imagination of 'the people' to whom duties are owed, they also 'simultaneously reveal the state's expectations from them', says Ramnath, thus creating from the people a subset of citizens who are 'productive people', workers, 'imperative to building a modern nation-state'.

> The slippages in the constitutional text [...] offer insights into the nature of 'the people'. Education, public assistance and creation of just and humane conditions of work for everyone and a just social order are what the state owes to its people. Adequate means of livelihood and free legal aid are only promised to 'citizens'. The same was the case with the proposed uniform civil code. Finally, a living wage and participation in the management of industry are promised only to workers, reflecting an emphasis on providing equal opportunities for productive labour.[97]

In a way, the Directive Principles speak 'to a multitude' for they are addressed to all people – including 'citizens, workers, women and men in differing degrees'. This multitude is expected to be empowered and productive. But what if some of them are and some not?

---

95   Kalyani Ramnath, ''We the People': Seamless Webs and Social Revolution in India's Constituent Assembly Debates', *South Asia Research* 32.1 (2012): 58.
96   Ramnath, ''We the People'', p. 59.
97   Ramnath, ''We the People'', p. 61.

The social consequences of living in a nation-state are, then, firmly tied not only to official recognition of a political identity, but are also rooted in the ability of 'the people', in all the varied understandings of that phrase, to contribute to the building of the nation-state. The state may well choose to ignore non-productive lives while embarking on different aspects of its social revolution [...] choose to exclude many others in its grand march towards a transformed social situation, for example, by branding the undocumented as 'illegal' or treating the poor as dispensable.[98]

Building on Ramnath's argument, I want to outline a particular techno-normative maneuver that took place in the dichotomy she discovers between 'people' and 'citizens'. The 'people', already a conceptual abstraction, an anonymous mass, were now also *technologically* anonymized in specific ways. As recipients of state benefit, they did nothing but receive – they could, as Jayal says, only consume. What they *could* produce was *data*. And in a sharp departure from the practices of anonymization by the Census, this data had an unprecedented capability to be tagged to its bodily producers.

Meanwhile, 'citizens' who had the capability to self-define as *productive people* were further qualified to become (to use language from the Information Technology (Electronic Service Delivery) Rules, 2011) *persons*, more precisely *natural persons*.[99] A key qualifier of such personhood was their *right over data*: specifically the right to own what the IT Rules name Sensitive Personal Data (SPD) – listed there as passwords, financial information (such as bank account or credit card or debit card or other payment instrument details), physical, physiological and mental health conditions, sexual orientation, medical records and history, and biometric information.

From the early 2000s, privacy law dominated the debate on digitization. And dominating the privacy debate were the *entitlements* of what the B.N. Srikrishna Committee, set up in 2018 to outline a data protection law, named *Data Principals*.[100] These were legatees of our citizen-subjects capable of individual subjective choice, the small populational percentage of 'natural subjects' who actually qualified for privacy. Although the Committee did cast a wide net around data, with significant sections on identifiability, anonymization, community data and nonconsensual data gathering processes, it was firm in its core commitment that 'the primary value that any data protection framework serves must be that of privacy'. Srikrishna worries about what else should be included in SPD – he considers, for example, adding trade union membership – and is inevitably bothered by the special conditions under which consent is suspended in the name of 'larger public interest'. There is little evidence here of Justice Chandrachud's many concerns about the conditions under which the corporeal gets coercively identified by data over which the person has no control, or tagged by technologies, or the possibility of switching off tagging

98   Ramnath, "We the People", pp. 61, 66.
99   Ministry of Communications and Information Technology, Notification on changes to the Information Technology Act, 2000, issued on 11 April 2011, https://www.meity.gov.in/writereaddata/files/GSR3_10511%281%29.pdf.
100 Committee of Experts under the Chairmanship of Justice B.N. Srikrishna, *A Free and Fair Digital Economy*, Chapter 1-C.

to cause 'civil death'. Such a body goes simply missing in the Srikrishna Committee report. It appears only in two contexts: as the entity requiring anonymization, or as the entity submitting to involuntary consent.

As social rights for a new category of meritocratic 'productive citizen' came to be inverted into a segregation logic for *elite* privileges, these rights also inverted several of the beneficiaries of the group-differentiated 'backward' categories of the Constitution. Although antipoverty programs were confined to target populations and meant for the poor, Jayal points to a 'curious bifurcation' that occurs as elites find themselves in a position to cherry-pick which services they should appropriate and which they had no need for. Some services, such as water and electricity, although subsidized in the name of the poor, become 'effectively available only to the nonpoor and are sometimes almost exclusively appropriated by the well-off', whereas others, such as public education and health, for which the elites have no desire, are allowed to decline, since 'the classes that have political voice do not have any stake in their improvement, while the classes that are entirely dependent on these services lack the voice to effect such change'.[101]

In contrast to the 'Data Principals' defined by the draft Personal Data Protection Bill, 2019, another category of biopolitical 'person' came to be parallelly created in this time: for example, by the 2019 amendment of the UAPA which introduced an amendment allowing for a 'person affected by inclusion of his name in the Fourth Schedule as a terrorist'.[102] Although these were also named physical manifestations of abstract corporeality, they were bodies to be feared and contained. They had no control over the data that they produced, as the overt purpose of such data increasingly became surveillance. As the need to demonstrate sovereign control became a growing political concern, the legislation of the time typically visibilized these bodies, I hope to show below, into those of the *peasant*, the *illegal migrant*, the *terrorist*, and the *dissident*.

The 'propensity of formal citizenship to *legitimize and entrench inequality* is reinvented every day in social and political practice' writes Jayal.[103] And it happens 'not least through such a severance of welfare entitlements from the status of citizenship'. 'Not being universal, social and economic provisioning [...] did not attach to citizenship in the way in which civil and political rights were integrally linked to it', and so benefit came commonly to be described using the 'language of relief, charity, and alleviation'.

As I track the genealogy of identity in the many judgments, Rules, White Papers and Acts that took place — roughly between 2000, when the first Information Technology Act was passed, and 2019, when the CAA and UAPA were both amended — I shall try and show how targeting — or the 'determination of eligibility' — became what Jayal calls a 'defining marker of the normative aspiration contained in the idea of citizenship'. While

---

101 Jayal, *Citizenship and its Discontents*, p. 194.
102 Unlawful Activities (Prevention) Amendment Bill, 2019, Section 6-iii-c, https://egazette.nic.in/
      WriteReadData/2019/210355.pdf.
103 Jayal, *Citizenship and its Discontents*, p. 170.

the ever-growing number of rights being extended to an abstracted mass of beneficiaries 'cultivate the impression of improved access to substantive citizenship for disadvantaged groups', what they did was in fact something else. The 'severance of particular sets of rights from the civic status entrenched already existing hierarchies of citizenship, through a *paradoxical inversion* that places those who need or get social rights far below those who do not'.[104]

Degrees of Connectedness

The identity question that arose to prominence between 2004 and 2008, the key years of the first term of the UPA government,[105] was almost entirely framed within the emerging managerial logic of delivery of services and benefits. By 2007, one account shows that 151 Centrally Sponsored Schemes existed for delivery of benefit, entailing annual expenditures of about INR 72,000 crore, of which 30 key schemes alone accounted for INR 64,000 crore.[106] To give a flavor of both the opportunity and worry characterizing the time, I summarize a sample case made by three influential theorists, Devesh Kapur, Partha Mukhopadhyay and Arvind Subramanian, on what they wanted India to do.[107]

Kapur et al. begin – as did Nilekani in *Imagining India* – with leakage, and the Rajiv Gandhi '15 paise for every rupee' model. To solve this, they propose a complex segregation of beneficiaries. The core argument is disarmingly direct: if 27.5 percent of India's roughly 1.13 billion people are below the poverty line, and if they form approximately 70 million households, then what needs to be done is simply to transfer INR 2,140 each month in cash to these households, enabling them to 'buy the entire monthly PDS entitlement of 35 kilograms of rice or wheat in the open market, even at relatively high current market prices'.

It was breathtakingly simple, but there was one problem. It was how to *identify*. Given the scale and importance of what was being envisaged, it was 'vital to realise that *establishing an individual's identity is more important than establishing her eligibility*'.[108]

Partha Chatterjee wrote, coincidentally, another essay in the same journal in the week after Kapur et al.'s sweeping single-point solution for all of India's economic troubles. It focused on the key weak point in their argument, as he addressed the same transformation taking place in India, but read rather different things in it – things that, although not apparently connected with his book *A Princely Impostor?* discussed earlier, may still allow us to extend the argument he made there.[109] If in *A Princely Impostor?* Chatterjee was speaking of identity

---

104 Jayal, *Citizenship and its Discontents*, p. 194.
105 The United Progressive Alliance or UPA is a coalition of parties formed soon after the 2004 general election.
106 Devesh Kapur, Partha Mukhopadhyay and Arvind Subramanian, 'The Case for Direct Cash Transfers to the Poor', *Economic & Political Weekly* 43.15 (2008): 37–43.
107 Kapur et al., 'The Case for Direct Cash Transfers', p. 38.
108 Kapur et al., 'The Case for Direct Cash Transfers', p. 39. Emphasis is mine.
109 Partha Chatterjee, 'Democracy and Economic Transformation in India', *Economic & Political Weekly* 43.16 (2008): 53–62.

in colonial India, here he was speaking about the identity of another elusive category, namely India's *peasantry*.

Chatterjee too notes, with Kapur et al., the spread of technologies distributing 'education, health services, food, roadways, water, electricity, agricultural technology, emergency relief and dozens of other welfare services' that have 'penetrated deep into the interior of everyday peasant life'.[110] To him, however, it leads to a rather different crisis of identity than it does Kapur et al. The entire slew of government policies are devised to '*reverse* the effects of primitive accumulation'. There is a loss of an *economic* identity as 'more and more primary producers, i.e., peasants, artisans and petty manufacturers [...] lose their means of production', but these victims of primitive accumulation find themselves unlikely to be absorbed in the new growth sectors of the economy. As a new economy takes over, we find a 'degree of connectedness between peasant cultivation, trade and credit networks in agricultural commodities, transport networks, petty manufacturing and services in rural markets and small towns, etc, that makes it necessary for us to categorise all of them as part of a single, but stratified, complex'.

Their role in this new economy is rendered 'marginalised and [...] useless as far as the sectors dominated by corporate capital are concerned'. On the other hand, leaving them to 'the passive revolution under conditions of electoral democracy' would be to 'leave these marginalised populations without the means of labour to simply fend for themselves'.[111]

It also carried the major risk of 'turning them into the 'dangerous classes''. In another instance of the dependence on tagging, these peasants find themselves entirely dependent on state agencies for their benefit and end up focusing their skills on 'manipulating and pressurising these agencies to deliver these benefits'. Chatterjee would perhaps agree that the migrant laborers left stranded in the lockdown in March, April and May of 2020 were precisely this 'dangerous class' of his dispossessed peasantry, left stranded physically as well as in the way they fell through the cracks between the sudden withdrawal of state welfare and the inability of the new economy to define their existence.

Diverse forms of dangerousness and diverse victims have been in the air since late 2019 when (as we well know!) the Citizenship Act, 1955 was amended for the second time in two decades. The agitations that convulsed the nation led to sustained legal scrutiny of not only the amended CAA itself (and of its incendiary Section 2 (1)(b) that 'any person belonging to Hindu, Sikh, Buddhist, Jain, Parsi or Christian community from Afghanistan, Bangladesh or Pakistan, who entered into India on or before the 31st day of December, 2014 [...] shall not be treated as illegal migrant')[112] but also to the link between this CAA, its earlier 2004 amendment, and the NPR. We return, inexorably, to 2000, when the Information Technology Act was first passed, and to 2003, when the Rules on Registration of Citizens

---

110 Chatterjee, 'Democracy and Economic Transformation in India', p. 2.
111 Chatterjee, 'Democracy and Economic Transformation in India', pp. 57, 62.
112 Citizenship (Amendment) Act, 2019. For details, see https://egazette.nic.in/
     WriteReadData/2019/214646.pdf.

and Issue of National Identity Cards was approved. The 2003 Rules were the first time when a 'Local Register of Indian Citizens' was defined, when 'individuals whose Citizenship is doubtful' would be weeded out.[113]

It was also the first time that the question of *illegal migrants or foreigners* would begin to receive visibility as the defining feature of citizenship. The very theory of identity now meant, first and foremost, isolating these people, when in 2004 the Citizenship (Amendment) Act declared *descent*, rather than *birth*, as providing the right of citizenship. That same year, 2004, the UAPA was also amended, and would over the next two decades find several famous targets in some of the country's best known political dissidents: Binayak Sen, a doctor and vice president of the People's Union for Civil Liberties (PUCL); Maoist leader Kobad Ghandy; all the lawyers, academics, and social scientists arrested after the Bhima-Koregaon agitation; Assamese peasant activist Akhil Gogoi; Telugu poet and activist Varavara Rao and many others, before coming in 2020 to Safoora Zargar and other students from Jamia Millia and Jawaharlal Nehru University (JNU). The two Amendments were separate, but need to be read together for the new 'dangerous class' – fusing migrants, terrorists, displaced peasantry, and political dissidents – to emerge.

The Data Fiduciary Arrives

On March 3, 2006, the Department of Information Technology (at the time still inside the Ministry of Communication and Information Technology) was tasked with setting up a 'Unique Identification for BPL Families'. Over the next 18 months, several ministries would go into overdrive to create a mechanism for what a key strategic vision document published that August called a 'Unique Identification of *Residents*'. There are rumors that this document was written by Wipro, briefly hired by the Planning Commission as a consultant for the design phase and program management of the pilot, and which had already submitted a document titled 'Does India Need a Unique Identity Number?'[114]

Through 2006, these documents and discussions pivoted on residents – that is, on *everybody* – and not only citizens. A 2008 Expert Committee on Metadata and Data Standards defined the purpose of its Personal Identification Codification Standards to 'identify *each and every person uniquely* at the national level' to ensure 'interoperability of information related to individuals collected by various Govt./non Gov. organizations', to 'ensure data integrity and smooth horizontal and vertical data exchange related to the individuals across the domain applications'.[115] The data being sought would be elaborate: name, gender, marital status, language, religion, occupation, education, and a few other categories. There would be different recipient agencies for the date being generated. Language and religion data would be sent to the Registrar General of India for the NPR.

113 Citizenship (Registration of Citizens and Issue of National Identity Cards) Rules, 2003, https://censusindia.gov.in/2011-Act&Rules/notifications/citizenship_rules2003.pdf.
114 See Gopal Krishna, 'Where is WIPRO's 'Strategic Vision on the UIDAI Project' Document?', *Countercurrents*, 7 August 2011, https://www.countercurrents.org/krishna070811.htm.
115 Expert Committee on Metadata and Data Standards, 'Personal Identification Codification', Draft version 8, August 2008.

Occupation data would go to the Ministry of Statistics and Programming Implementation, Education data to the Department of Higher Education, and relationship (to head of family) data, interestingly, to the Indian Council of Social Science Research (ICSSR) and the Anthropological Survey of India (ASI).

That December, the penny dropped. An Empowered Group of Ministers (EgoM) was set up to 'collate the *National Population Register* under the Citizenship Act, 1955, and the *Unique Identification Number project* of the Department of IT'.[116] *Our hairy outsider muscling into the neighborhood turned out to be a separated-at-birth twin.*

So how were we taken in, in 2009? I still believe that there was good reason why, when we conceived our project and then did fieldwork in seven states in 2010–2011, we located our 'ambivalence' in the internecine row between Aadhaar and the NPR. I've talked about it earlier in this essay, so shall only add that this almighty row confused not only us, but also many bureaucrats at state and district levels who often assumed that the NPR was simply one of the numerous registrars empaneled by the UIDAI. Indeed, in the solitary reference the UIDAI's 2009 working paper makes to the NPR, at the bottom of a section titled 'Enrolment Strategy in Rural and Urban India', this is just how it represents their connection. Reiterating Aadhaar's 'pro-rural/pro-poor' approach to enrolment, the paper names rural registrars – like NREGA, RSBY and PDS – as 'government agencies with large rural networks and significant bases among the poor', which in the cities would be 'LIC and Passports'. To this, in an oh-by-the-way line, it adds that 'in addition to these enrollers, the UIDAI will also partner with the Registrar General of India (RGI) – who will prepare the National Population Register through the Census 2011 – to reach as many residents as possible and enroll them into the UID database', pointing out snootily that this may 'require incorporating some additional procedures into the RGI data collection mechanism, in order to make it UID-ready'.[117]

Mission creep is revealed as not creep at all, but as integral to the design. It becomes a fascinating, if at times chilling, exercise of historical revisionism to see Aadhaar and the NPR as, far from being opposed, indeed *planned in unison*, as two halves of the same picture: one to do with residents, as a populational anonymization, and the other to work over the same data to create a visibility apparatus for citizenship that would also weed out the illegal migrants.

The fifth meeting of the EgoM on April 27, 2007 linked the proposed UID with the Household Survey of Rural Development and the individual state PDS databases. On June 15, the Planning Commission was asked to set up the Authority by an executive order. The IT Department was further asked to 'work out modalities for linkage with [the] Election Commission', in addition to firming up the rural development and PDS linkages. That November, the EgoM agreed on the urgent need to create an 'identity related resident database, regardless of whether the database is created on a *de novo* collection of data or

116 *Puttaswamy* v *UOI*, Section 7.
117 UIDAI, *UIDAI Strategy Overview*, Section 3.2.

is based on an already existing data (such as the Election Commission's Voter List)', and on the parallel need to 'create an institutional mechanism that would 'own' the database' and be responsible for its maintenance and updating. The next meeting (for which there is no date mentioned) clearly set up the separated-at-birth twins: to 'consider topics relating to collating the National Population Register (NPR) and UID schemes, *including methodology, effective implementation techniques, identification of the institutional mechanism stated above, and the time schedule* for putting the scheme into operation'.[118]

The die was thus cast. On January 28, 2009, the UIDAI was formed under the Planning Commission by an executive order. The creep that ensued was, one may now speculate in hindsight, the main reason for the crisis of legitimacy that Aadhaar faced: arguably as a direct result of this design ambivalence, in problems in the 'collation' that went beyond issues of methodology or implementation technique, which began to affect legitimacy. A 2010 bill to set up a National Identification Authority of India bit the dust in Parliament, nixed by the Yashwant Sinha-led Standing Committee on Finance. A second bill failed in 2016 when it was sought to be smuggled into Parliament as a money bill, and it squeaked into legality only in 2017 with the epic Supreme Court judgment.

None of this apparently stopped the project from hoovering up, between 2006 and 2012, a growing mountain of big data by an astonishingly diverse set of both government and private agencies, with the UIDAI very much its public face. By mid-2013, around the time our Identity Project came to an end, there was enough evidence of the extent of poison that had entered Drèze's metaphorical well. Notwithstanding the UIDAI's own strenuous assertion that it has always kept its data confidential – a requirement that would be enshrined in 2016 under Article 29(1) of the Aadhaar Act, that 'no core biometric information, collected or created under this Act, shall be shared with anyone for any reason whatsoever; or used for any purpose other than generation of Aadhaar numbers and authentication' – news has consistently circulated about the uses to which its data was being leaked. In February 2013, the Deputy Director General of the UIDAI, Ashok Dalwai, said that data could be shared with security agencies, particularly for cases relating to national security, on the basis of court orders.[119]

IV

We, the Narrative Community: Possibilities of Diffuse Speech

There is, inevitably, another – perhaps somewhat more subversive – way of telling this story, of what *else* happened in this very time. I too begin with Ramnath's point of departure, but I shall focus on a slightly different aspect of the 'We the People' phrase that has received comparatively little legal attention, namely the 'we' in the *plural*. Conventionally, it is of course the 'productive individual' – or its opposite, the incarcerated identity-tagged

---

118 *Puttaswamy* v *UOI*, Section 9 (ii).
119 'UIDAI to Share Data with Police for Investigations', *The Hindu*, 6 February 2013, https://www.thehindu.com/news/national/karnataka/uidai-to-share-data-with-police-for-investigations/article4383068.ece.

individual – who remains the *par excellence* citizen, both as exemplary contributor to nation-building and the abstracted carrier of human rights. Ambedkar, for example, explicitly argued for why the entire object of fundamental rights and the very purpose of prescribing the economic structure of society was, says Jayal, to 'protect the liberty of the individual from invasion by other individuals'.[120]

What I want to focus on are other less-discussed modes in which individuated citizenship also occurred. It was produced, if rather surprisingly, in the *we*-ness of the people – and in the way elements of the multitude, such as *groups, communities* and *collectives, could come together to claim citizenship-like rights through *simulating several of the characteristics of the individual citizen.*

This capacity of collectives to behave like a multi-bodied individual, extensively discussed in theories of group psychology and politically by several strands of the Frankfurt School, has triggered, since colonial times, a major struggle over the meanings that could be attached to political subjecthood. The tension between the 'citizen' and the 'people' came through modernity to be manifested as a tug-of-war between isolatable and identifiable individuation on one side, and diverse amorphous collectives on the other. A longer historical tension over where the nation's imagination lay – whether in discrete individual subjects capable of incarnating and acting on their rights under Articles 19 and 21 (and who thus possessed complete control over their SPD) or in fuzzy social groups and communities – would create in the early 2000s a brand new digital iteration of a hoary problem of colonial vintage.[121] Over the past two decades, this battle over the dis/embodied subject has also substantially defined the *extent* to which social rights such as defined by the Directive Principles – including and especially those of the right to fuzzy or blurred self-description – were seen as having been enabled (or disabled) by the link of biometric to basic demographic data.

The question who is a legal person? has vexed courts in India. We know that, although a 'person' is always an individual, various entities can have 'juridical personality' – including, at different points, animals, rivers, corporations and even, as recently seen, deities. Such legal persons are attributed the characteristics of conscious individuals: if they have a name and a reasonable capacity to say 'I', they can be 'clothed with legal personality'.[122]

---

120 For Ambedkar, she says, the four premises of political democracy were: first, that the individual is an end in himself; second, that the individual has inalienable rights guaranteed by the Constitution; third, that the individual should not have to relinquish any of these rights as a condition of receiving a privilege; and, fourth, that the state should not delegate its powers to private persons to govern others. See Jayal, *Citizenship and its Discontents*, p. 148.

121 Jayal writes: 'This accounts for the preoccupation, in the political discourse of late colonial India, with specifying exactly how, on what terms, and to what extent the relationship of the citizen to the state may be mediated by community. The idea that communities possessed political agency found articulation in their negotiations with the colonial state for a greater institutional presence, with political and legislative representation being viewed as the preeminent form that citizenship could take'. See Jayal, *Citizenship and its Discontents*, pp. 199–200.

122 See the legal services advice being offered here: http://www.legalservicesindia.com/article/2316/Meaning-and-Kind-of-Person.html.

One might presume therefore that collectives with individual-like characteristics seeking legal visibility would have to 'incorporate' themselves and become 'artificial, juristic or fictitious' persons. If one did, one would presume incorrectly. And thus emerges another political story because, for all their newness, the categories Nishant Shah proposes earlier in this essay – between a 'data subject' produced as a blurred entity and a 'quantified self' who can be 'mined for data and information, ranging from genetic blue-prints to socio-cultural profiles' – reveal a considerably longer genesis in the social sciences in India. The pendular movement between *blurred* and *quantified* individuality is critically dependent on the degree to which individuation is able to access, speak for, and mediate communities – as Sudipta Kaviraj shows in his famous outlining of fuzzy and enumerated communities in his celebrated 1992 text, 'The Imaginary Institution of India'.

The arrival of the modern national state, writes Kaviraj, led to the 'relentless project of enumeration – the endless counting of its citizens, territories, resources, majorities, minorities, institutions, activities, import, export, incomes, projects, births, deaths, diseases [...] every conceivable quantifiable thing'.[123] Although Europe may have managed to make a connection between a rationalist view of society and a 'world that is wholly, unsurpassably, classified, enumerated – a world securely distributed into tables', India had a slightly different problem when it encountered rampant enumeration.

On the other hand, although independent India did see the rise of a 'deeply individualistic language which speaks of atomistic individuals who enter into relations with each other on the basis of a purely rational calculation of advantages', it also saw something else – the possibility of an 'easy, intuitive transfer of a language of *possession* from individuals to the more problematic individuality of the nation'. It was the individuality of the nation that in turn disbursed such individuality to diverse entities, and while some of them were actual, enumerated, human beings, at other times they were also primordial (unenumerated, fuzzy) communities.

These communities now produced a form of speech that had marked differences from those of the individual. It was a part of a narrative mode that 'does not [...] aspire to be a universal form of discourse (but) draws lines, distributes people, unlike rational theoretical discourse which attempts to unite them in an abstract universe of ideal consensus'.[124] 'Narratives', he concludes, 'are not for all to hear, for all to participate in to an equal degree'. It is, in short, a very different form of narrative, violating the founding purpose of conventional narratives, which is to open meaning out to the world, comprehensible to all. Narratives aspire, in their very nature, to be universal. Kaviraj's narratives are none of those. Just as his 'fuzzy' community remains elusive to enumeration, creating significant challenges to their legal 'personhood', so it appears that the narratives of such a community – 'not for all to hear' – create significant challenges to the concept of speech as defined by the doctrine of free speech.

---

123   Sudipta Kaviraj, 'The Imaginary Institution of India', in Sudipta Kaviraj, *The Imaginary Institution of India: Politics and Ideas*, New York: Columbia University Press, 2010, p. 199.
124   Kaviraj, 'The Imaginary Institution of India', p. 201.

I want here to introduce a concept I shall name *diffuse speech* – speech that does not have an identifiable speaker and an identifiable listener, but works with a kind of amalgam of the two – that works in conditions rather different from those imagined in Article 19(1)(a). Diffuse speech, I propose, is often unable to (or more commonly refuses to) produce the two conditions that appear essential for 19(1): a person who could say (i) 'Yes, I said this, I take responsibility' and (ii) 'I understand the consequences'. Diffuse speech is neither: it is speech without an identifiable speaking source whose sole purpose is to define a fuzzy community.[125]

If diffuse speech does not have an 'I-said-this' speaker, it also does not have a conventional speech recipient whose main purpose is to merely receive. Recipients of free speech are, within the doctrinal limitations of the right, primarily those who possess the right to information, a necessary condition to make informed choices or to participate intelligently in the democratic process. A well-known legal dissertation on free speech argues that speech-recipients and audiences are the *primary object* of free speech concern. Their right to information is the primary right, from which derives the right of speakers to speak.[126] Neither category plays such a role in Kaviraj's narrative. However, his fuzzy narrative communities bring in numerous actors (interpreters, decoders, or carriers, for example), who are – in a form well known to Indian storytelling traditions – neither purely speakers nor pure listeners but an amalgam of both: where the generation of speech becomes indistinguishable from its endorsement and perpetuation.

Kaviraj's conception of community was of course a 'primordial' one, his context that of national communities. Narrative, for him, had only a provisional and temporary use since narratives of the nation had a strictly curtailed function, for there were things they could do and things they couldn't. He therefore outlined their purpose carefully: narratives were a mode by which to enable communities to reproduce themselves by telling stories about themselves. They were above all 'practical things', 'interpretations of the world and its history which issue in a call to change it'; a *transaction*, a *contract* between a self and an audience.[127] They were able to speak with eloquence about freedom, sacrifice and glory, but were typically 'vague about the more concrete and contestable questions of distribution, equality, power, the actual unequal ordering of the past society or of the future one'. For all its self-avowed boundaries, Kaviraj's narrative contract may well have directly anticipated peer-to-peer networks. As we turn to these, we may also take forward his primary focus, of how specific communities become a variation, a subset, mirroring the national community (literally the 'we' of the 'people') as we now focus on the birth of virtual communities from the late 90s on.

---

125 Although certain kinds of unsourced speech have been legally recognized (e.g., rumor or fake news) – and dealt with by holding the carriers of such speech responsible (e.g., newspapers or after the Information Technology Rules, 2011 that defined digital 'intermediaries', email, hosting, and blogging services) – as well as certain modes of sourced but not conscious or responsible speech (e.g. in 2010 when the Supreme Court banned Deception Detection Tests like polygraph, narcoanalysis, and brain-mapping), these did not exhaust the problems posed by diffuse speech.
126 Eric Barendt, *Freedom of Speech*, Oxford: Clarendon Press, 1985, pp. 26–27.
127 Kaviraj, 'The Imaginary Institution of India', p. 200.

'Liking', Personhood, Terrorism

The person*hood* of the legal person was a key concern when the Information Technology Act was passed in October 2000. New challenges emerged over how the conscious-individual-citizen paradigm could be virtually reproduced, and much debate occurred about the legal acceptability of digital signatures and born-digital documents such as emails. Inevitably, the problem of virtual identities came up in what was still quaintly described as 'cyberspace', especially blurry alter egos commonly described as 'cyborgs' (ambiguously human and ambiguously gendered mutant figures on the edges of legality). Internet porn and cyber deaths dominated debate, Julian Dibbell's 1993 text 'A Rape in Cyberspace, or How an Evil Clown, a Haitian Trickster Spirit, Two Wizards, and a Cast of Dozens Turned a Database into a Society'[128] was still compulsory reading, and the classic cyber controversy of the time was the notorious 2004 Delhi Public School MMS scandal when students circulated a video clip that was put up on auction on the then-popular site Bazee.com.[129] Inevitably, the IT Act also individuated its chosen bad guy against whom it was mobilizing the might of the state. It was the faceless 'cyber-hacker' who was declared the Enemy of the People, and the target of Section 66 of the IT Act was anyone who caused 'wrongful loss or damage to the public' or altered information in a computer that might 'diminish its value or utility'.[130]

A lot of this changed in 2006 when an entirely new, far more complex and elusive, category of public actor emerged with the birth of social media: Orkut's multilingual Indian iteration, on August 31, literally the day after the seventh of many furious meetings taking place among the EgoM. Orkut launched a revolution that, by 2010, had jumped to 83 million internet users overall, 60 percent of whom were on social media.[131] Although Orkut led the way it would have a short shelf life, being replaced within two years on the frontlines by Facebook.

Three major and foundational events in the epochal month of February 2009 would shape the decade to come. There is little that brings the three together other than their simultaneity, and the fact that they were all defined by the emerging threat posed by the shadowy individual-as-amorphous-public. The first we have discussed: it was the ceremonial unveiling of the UIDAI's heavy artillery in the battle over bodily individuation. A very different kind of event, at a very different register, occurred as one of the earliest effective uses of Facebook for subversive community action. In a high-visibility and stunningly successful campaign against a Hindu right-wing organization's targeting of young people celebrating Valentine's Day, a 'Consortium of Pub-Going, Loose and

---

128 https://smg.media.mit.edu/library/dibbell1993.html
129 Also discussed in more detail by Nishant Shah in his essay in this volume.
130 Section 66 of the IT Act ('Hacking with computer system'): 'Whoever with the intent to cause or knowing that he is likely to cause wrongful loss or damage to the public or any person destroys or deletes or alters any information residing in a computer resource or diminishes its value or utility or affects it injuriously by any means, commits hack'. For details, see https://www.meity.gov.in/content/offences.
131 Open Source Center Media Aid, *Overview of Leading Indian Social Media*, 21 December 2010, https://fas.org/irp/dni/osc/india-social.pdf.

Forward Women' put out a call to send gifts of pink knickers to that organization, as a satirical send-up of the khaki shorts that was the uniform of the Rashtriya Swayamsevak Sangh (RSS).[132] The event was in itself relatively small, but it did indicate the growing threat of online community action, and does therefore contextualize the signing off by the President of India, also that February, of a draconian amendment to the IT Act. That amendment, numbered 66A, took direct aim at social media when it threatened imprisonment to anyone sending 'information that is grossly offensive' or 'causing annoyance, inconvenience, danger, obstruction, insult, injury, criminal intimidation, enmity, hatred or ill will' via 'a computer, computer system, computer resource or communication device including attachments in text, images, audio, video and any other electronic record'.[133]

Two years later, in November 2012 following the death of Bal Thackeray, supreme leader of the right-wing Shiv Sena party of Bombay, when the Sena organized its ritual *bandh* (a popular/general strike), a young woman from the town of Palghar named Shaheen Dhadha wrote a Facebook post. In that post, she wondered whether it was right to close down the city like this, and whether Thackeray was a martyr of the stature of Bhagat Singh and Sukhdev. Later that day, another young woman also from Palghar, Rinu Srinivasan, clicked 'like' on Shaheen's Facebook post. Shaheen was of course expressing her personal opinion, and was thus squarely within the ambit of Article 19(1)(a) that is precisely meant to protect such speech. Rinu on the other hand wasn't expressing any opinion other than to endorse Shaheen's view. The following day, however, Mumbai Police made no distinction between the two: they arrested both Shaheen and Rinu under the Section 66A.

Some months earlier, a chemistry professor from Calcutta's well-known Jadavpur University named Ambikesh Mahapatra had been arrested for forwarding to friends, and for uploading to his Facebook account, some cartoons of Bengal's Chief Minister Mamata Banerjee that had apparently referenced Satyajit Ray's film, *Sonar Kella*. [134] In his case the charge wasn't clear, and he was quickly released and awarded compensation by the West Bengal Human Rights Commission. The problem was once again the source of the speech – they weren't his cartoons, he was simply forwarding them, he said.

A somewhat more serious and more significant incident occurred in December 2014, when another man was arrested, also under 66A. This man, only known by his Twitter handle Shami Witness, was arrested because he apparently had pro-ISIS views but – and this was his main crime – also because he had 17,000 followers to whom he was 'aggregating information', in the words of Karnataka's Director General of Police.[135] The

---

132   Wikipedia, https://en.wikipedia.org/wiki/Pink_Chaddi_Campaign.
133   https://cis-india.org/internet-governance/resources/section-66A-information-technology-act.
134   # Mayank Jain, 'Mamata is Suppressing all Dissent, Claims Jadavpur Professor Arrested for Sharing a Cartoon', *Scroll*, 12 March 2015, https://scroll.in/article/712933/mamata-is-suppressing-all-dissent-claims-jadavpur-professor-arrested-for-sharing-a-cartoon.
135   See 'Youth has Confessed to Operating Pro-IS Twitter Account: Karnataka DGP', *Free Press Journal*, 1 June 2019, https://www.freepressjournal.in/india/youth-has-confessed-to-operating-pro-is-twitter-account-karnataka-dgp.

police came to know of this man only when Britain's Channel 4 interviewed him, and although they withheld his identity and blurred his voice and image, they revealed that he lived in Bangalore, had the first name of Mehdi and worked in a leading IT company. He could hardly have done a better job of giving himself away. The next morning, Shami Witness tweeted that he expected to be arrested any moment, and when the police finally arrived, he apparently asked them why they took so long.

I wasn't able to figure out whether he has been released or not, but it was widely accepted that there was no real legal case against him. There were nevertheless two curious facts about his situation. One, his spectacular voluntary 'coming out'. And, two, an argument that applies as much to Rinu's 'Like' as to Mahapatra's forward: whatever his personal views, Shami Witness had not expressed any of them on Twitter, but had only confined himself to aggregating and retweeting information that was already on the internet and thus already in the public domain. In the Channel 4 interview, Shami Witness vehemently asserted his position: 'I haven't harmed anybody. I haven't broken any law...I haven't raised any war or any violence against the public of India. I haven't waged war against any allies of India'.[136]

In 2012, directly inspired by the outrageous arrest of the two women in Palghar, a 24-year-old second-year student at the Delhi University's Faculty of Law named Shreya Singhal challenged the validity of Section 66A in the Supreme Court. Three years later in March 2015 and shortly after the Shami Witness episode, the Supreme Court acceded to Singhal's petition and struck down Section 66A.[137]

As we look at forwards, memes, and other forms of post-authorial diffuse speech, we also go into the somewhat wilder zone of power that was also part of 66A but elusive to the free speech doctrine. Shami Witness' main point – and indeed the key allegation of Karnataka Police – was that he was an aggregator (he had, said the police charge sheet, 35,000 pages and 122,000 tweets on his account). His defense allows us to reopen the online equivalent of the transactional-contractual apparatus that was a key part of Kaviraj's narrative community, namely an amalgamation of speaker and recipient into a narrative whose primary purpose, re-quoting Kaviraj, was to 'draw lines, distribute people'. Justice Rohinton Nariman's judgment on the 2015 Supreme Court case reveals some awareness of this problem, suggesting that Section 66A raises questions that may be additional to those of the black-letter interpretation of Article 19(1)(a). In the narrow sense, Nariman has no hesitation in agreeing with the petitioners, since the 'reasonable restrictions' doctrine of Article 19(2) outlines eight precise categories that might be evoked and no more, and Section 66A falls outside of those.[138]

---

136 # 'ISIS Propagandist Shami Witness: Man Charged in India, Channel 4, 1 June 2015, https://www.
        channel4.com/news/isis-shami-witness-medhi-masroor-biswas-charged.
137 Shreya Singhal v UOI, WP (Criminal) No. 167 of 2012, (24 March 2015), https://indiankanoon.org/
        doc/110813550/.
138 These are: (1) the sovereignty and integrity of India, (2) the security of the State, (3) friendly relations
        with foreign States, (4) public order, (5) decency (6) morality or in relation to contempt of court, (7)
        defamation (8) incitement to an offence. See https://indiankanoon.org/doc/493243/.

But there was more to this. The astonishing idea that information is indifferent to content but only defined by the medium of storage makes sense to many who aren't only students of Marshall McLuhan. Such a concept of information is, for example, the source of a commonly held view of the police that the mere existence of information is sufficient to read meaning into it and to charge someone with a crime. This happened in the legal trials of S.A.R. Geelani some years ago as Shuddhabrata Sengupta has shown us,[139] and clearly happened again in the Safoora Zargar instance.

There are further consequences. Content is bred through circulation: *something becomes so because sufficient numbers of people believe that it is so.* Ganeshas thus drink milk because enough numbers of people believe it, and there is (to quote another Supreme Court judgment in a rather different case) *'no dispute before this Court [...] that the birth of Lord Ram is ascribed to have taken place at Ayodhya*, as described in Valmiki's Ramayan. (The only thing) being disputed is whether the [...] site below the central dome of the Babri Masjid is the place of birth of Lord Ram'.[140]

But there would be another way to tell even this story, as the 2000s went on. The further possibility of nonuniversal narratives generating communities through purely horizontal circulation – that there is no content prior to, or following, the disseminative act – would enable Shami Witness, along with numerous other models of communication, from pornography to fan address, to state his case. It would also enable an entirely new career for 'the people' generating new kinds of nonuniversal narrative communities. Such communities may well need a reinvoking of the Directive Principles as they take the meaning of citizenship to its liminal extremes.

V.

Zones of Occupation

On August 4, 2019 (less than a year before the time of writing and four months before Shaheen Bagh, when Article 370 of the Constitution was abrogated by the Parliament of India, a total internet shutdown was imposed on the state of Kashmir as a 'preventive measure'. Between January 2012 and March 2020, India recorded 385 internet shutdowns, the largest number imposed by any country. Of these, 237 were preventive, imposed in anticipation of law-and-order problems. Kashmir was the longest, lasting over 213 days, and also the most lethal.

By 2019, India also led the world in the number of official takedown requests made to Facebook, Twitter, Google, Microsoft and Wikimedia, nearly all of them directed at

---

139 Shuddhabrata Sengupta, 'Media Trials and Courtroom Tribulations: The Battle of Images, Words and Shadows in the 13 December Case', in *13 December, A Reader: The Strange Case of the Attack on the Indian Parliament*, New Delhi: Penguin Books, 2006.
140 *M Siddiq (D) Thr Lrs* v *Mahant Suresh Das & Ors*, Civil Appeals Nos 10866-10867 of 2010 (2019), https://www.sci.gov.in/pdf/JUD_2.pdf.

Facebook alone (70,815 out of the total of 77,620 requests).[141] There are of course similarities between takedown requests and shutdowns in that both deny access rights, but there are some crucial differences. In the instance of takedown requests, it has been easier to apply the freedom of speech doctrine and to apply Article 19(1)(a), as has been asserted in at least four judgments so far.[142] Shutdowns, on the other hand, *include* but also *exceed* the free speech doctrine with an additional spatialization aspect, when regions, districts or at times entire states, and not just specific individuals, are informationally blanked out. One consequence is a spillover of the right to speech into the right to *access space*, to peacefully assemble in it, or to travel through it, as Article 19(1)(a) now comes alongside Section 144 of the Code of Criminal Procedure (CrPC). Shutdowns thus appear to force diffuse speech into diffuse space. Analogue in the time of curfew forces a return also to the underground and subterranean, to movement through alleys and by-lanes rather than known highways, alongside longer histories of occupation.

In September 2015, wireless internet and voice services shut down for a week without public notification in the district of Churachandpur in Manipur, following protests by Kuki groups opposing the introduction of Inner Line Permits. The protests led to arson and violent clashes, apparently in part as a result of the shutdowns, and nine people died in police firing. In an astonishing display of physical occupation, for an entire year the bodies of the nine dead were kept on public display in mauve coffins under a shamiana, in front of which daily speeches occurred under a sign that said 'Hills & Valley as separate entities: the new normal, learn to live with it'. Apparently, a poster pinned on the wall of Churachandpur police station outside which three of the nine were killed still remains there.[143]

Physical occupation took a new turn in the months that followed August 2019, when the official curfew shaded into a people's *hartal*.[144] It was more than a ban in Kashmir: it was, says journalist Anuradha Bhasin, editor of the newspaper *Kashmir Times*, a 'communication blockade' that even in Kashmir was without precedent. The government did not make the shutdown orders public, leaving people in the dark not only as to what was happening but under which legal statute. 'Kashmiris are not new to curfews', says

141 Paul Bischoff, 'Which Government Censors the Tech Giants the Most?', 19 October 2021, https://www.comparitech.com/blog/vpn-privacy/tech-giant-censorship/.
142 *Faheema Shirin R.K.* v *State of Kerala*, WP (C) 19716/2019-L (19 September 2019), https://indiankanoon.org/doc/188439981/; *Banashree Gogoi* v *Union of India and 7 Ors*, GAHC010310492019, Case No.: PIL 78/2019 (19 December 2019), https://indiankanoon.org/doc/175955438/; *Anuradha Bhasin* v *Union of India*, Writ Petition (Civil) No. 1031 of 2019 (10 January 2020), https://indiankanoon.org/doc/82461587/; *Foundation for Media Professionals* v *Union Territory of Jammu and Kashmir*, Writ Petition (Civil) of 2020 (D. No. 10817 of 2020) (11 May 2020), (https://indiankanoon.org/doc/123992151/.
143 Esha Roy, 'As Nine Bodies Await Burial, Manipur Trenched in Politics of Dead and Living', *Indian Express*, 29 August 2016, https://indianexpress.com/article/india/india-news-india/manipur-violence-protests-in-churachandpur-manipur-deaths-2999507/.
144 In South Asia, the term *hartal* refers to the closure of shops and offices as a protest or mark of sorrow.

Bhasin in an interview with *Frontline*,[145] but the scale of the shutdown was such that 'a kind of civil disobedience' has set in, as 'people have dug their heels in'.

When *Kashmir Times* found itself unable to publish its Srinagar edition after August 6, Bhasin moved court. At that time this was a straightforward freedom of speech issue. All she wanted was to publish her paper. This however couldn't happen unless there was 'free and safe movement of reporters and journalists and other media personnel [...] to report and publish news', which also included the right to unfettered movement. Which meant that when the Supreme Court finally came up with its judgment on *Anuradha Bhasin* v *Union of India* in January 2020, the legal aspects of internet shutdowns proved rather messier.

The judgment moved around between Articles 19(1)(a) and (g), the Temporary Suspension of Telecom Services Rules of 2017 (TSTS) (adapting the Indian Telegraph Act, 1885), and Section 144 of the CrPC prohibiting public assembly. Solicitor General Tushar Mehta 'vehemently opposed selective access to internet services' claiming that the government didn't have the technology, for which he was rapped on the knuckle by the Court, saying that 'if such a contention is accepted, the Government would have a free pass to put a complete internet blockage every time'.[146] Perhaps the most far-out instance of technological unilateralism was the Solicitor General's argument that, since orders for Section 144 had never been published, they 'could not be accorded the force of law'.[147] He was once more chastised and informed that 'the necessity of publication of law is a part of the rule of natural justice'. Then came the question of freedom of speech, and things got even more bizarre. The judgment pointed out that since 'none of the counsels have argued for declaring the right to access the internet as a fundamental right', it was deliberately 'not expressing any view on the same', but confining itself to 'declaring that the right to freedom of speech and expression under Article 19(1)(a), and the right to carry on any trade or business under 19(1)(g) [...] is constitutionally protected'. When it specifically underlined the right to a free press under this doctrine – which was Anuradha Bhasin's primary reason to go to court – Mehta argued this time that 'the jurisprudence on free speech relating to newspapers cannot be applied to the internet' since 'newspapers only allowed one-way communication' whereas 'the internet makes two-way communication'.[148]

Expressing frustration at the moving goalposts, the judgment noted that 'law and technology seldom mix like oil and water [...] there is a consistent criticism that the development of technology is not met by equivalent movement in the law'.[149] In this case the problem was that 'morning to night we are encapsulated within the cyberspace and our most basic activities are enabled by the use of internet'. In trying to bring down the

---

145 Divya Trivedi, 'Anuradha Bhasin: 'Impossible for Journalists to Function', *Frontline*, 27 September 2019, https://frontline.thehindu.com/cover-story/impossible-for-journalists-to-function/article29382196.ece.

146 *Bhasin* v *UOI*, No. 75.

147 *Bhasin* v *UOI*, No. 8B: Contentions.

148 *Bhasin* v *UOI*, No. 8B: Contentions.

149 *Bhasin* v *UOI*, No. 24.

scale and extent of the legal sledgehammer on display into something justiciable, the court ruled: (1) 'freedom of speech and expression and the freedom to practice any profession or carry on any trade, business or occupation over the medium of internet enjoys constitutional protection';[150] (2) on the TSTS Rules, that any order 'suspending internet services indefinitely is impermissible';[151] and (3) on Section 144, that the 'power under Section 144 [...] cannot be used to suppress legitimate expression of opinion or grievance or exercise of any democratic rights'.[152] As a result of the judgment, some kind of spotty internet was made available to the troubled state. Medianama lists out what was achieved: only 2G connectivity and only in selected districts; 400 kiosks; wired broadband only to companies providing software services and only after Mac-binding. All social media websites, peer-to-peer apps and VPNs were explicitly prohibited.[153]

And then, in a brief aside that nobody seems to have quite discussed, the judgment brought up what may well have been the true purpose of the plethora of unpublished Rules and Acts the government was bringing to bear. Its purpose, said the Court, was to produce a 'chilling effect', a category that had not yet been adequately explored in Indian law.[154] The basic principle of a chilling effect was to restrict a person from exercising his protected right 'due to the ambiguous nature of an overbroad statute'. Even though the state may perform a constitutional action, if the 'panopticon concerns' and the 'comparative harm' potentially caused by 'impugned restrictions due to their broad-based nature' was not tempered judicially, its eventual effect would become a 'self-proclaiming instrument' causing a 'great burden on free speech'.

'What will happen when the lid is off?', wonders Anuradha Bhasin. In an astonishing counterresponse to the shutdown, she says, the people had apparently decided to 'refuse to allow the Indian government to show 'normalcy''. Protesting against government claims that there was 'no curfew or restrictions in Kashmir', says a PUCL report, people 'convert(ed) the state-initiated curfew to lock down the valley (into) a people's *hartal* as a spontaneous act to register their protest and resistance'.[155]

Diffuse speech now becomes an amalgam of speech with assembly. This long history of a connection has often been lost to the excessive *individuation* of the free-speaking 'person', but its reintroduction of public space – a direct, if unintended, consequence of shutdowns – also apparently recalled longer histories, as they returned people to the very origins of the theory of the public sphere.

150 *Bhasin* v *UOI*, No. 152: Conclusion.
151 *Bhasin* v *UOI*, No. 152: Conclusion.
152 *Bhasin* v *UOI*, No. 140.
153 Soumyarendra Barik, '2G Internet on Postpaid, Broadband Partially Restored in J&K for Accessing Only 'White-Listed' Websites', Medianama, 15 January 2020,
     https://www.medianama.com/2020/01/223-partial-internet-restoration-jammu-kashmir/.
154 *Bhasin* v *UOI*, Nos 146, 147, 148.
155 People's Union of Civil Liberties, *Imprisoned Resistance - 5th August and its Aftermath*, 2019, https://www.pucl.org/reports/imprisoned-resistance-5th-august-and-its-aftermath.

Manuel Castells points out how an amorphous iteration of the old public sphere worked when he discusses the first-ever internet shutdown the world had seen: the week-long 2011 blackout across Cairo amid the Tahrir Square protests. A new kind of 'networked' public space amalgamated the internet, the mobile phone, 'pre-existing social networks, street demonstrations, occupations of public squares and Friday gatherings around the mosques'.[156] Its primary purpose was to 'create community to overcome fear':[157] fear here generated primarily by network failure. One direct consequence was the resolute return to analogue spaces, to physical contact, and to the many ancestors of networked communication, including 'rumours, sermons, pamphlets, and manifestos, spread from person to person, from the pulpit, from the press, or by whatever means of communication were available'.[158]

Moving from Tahrir Square to the *Indignados* in Spain,[159] Castells points to another feature of the rebirth of networked communities: their assertion of leaderlessness. 'There was no formal decision, but everybody agreed in practice [...] there would be no leaders, either locally or nationally. Not even spokespersons were recognized'.

> The source of this ancient, anarchist principle, usually betrayed in history, was not ideological in the case of this movement, although it became a fundamental principle, enforced by the large majority of the movement's actors. It was present in the experience of Internet networks in which horizontality is the norm, and there is little need for leadership because the coordination functions can be exercised by the network itself through interaction between its nodes.[160]

From roughly 2014, India saw numerous protest movements following the principle known worldwide now as *horizontalism* (or *horizontalidad*, the term coined in Argentina in 2001). The principle's emphasis is on leaderlessness – the primary condition of diffuse speech – and on occupation, both *analogue* and *offline*. All of these movements can directly and straightforwardly be viewed as a protest against digital identity. They are at once protests against the technological unilateralism of the state, a reappropriation of the physical manifestation of the abstracted 'people' as well as a popular re-concretization of the body that – like the corpses on public display for a year in Churachandpur – collectively add up to become also a bid to retake popular sovereignty.

Zones of Mediatized Control

Between 2014 and 2019, these movements took place most prominently on university campuses, where an actual, physical, analogue space existed that literally stood for freedom,

---

156 Manuel Castells, *Networks of Outrage and Hope: Social Movements in the Internet Age*, Cambridge, UK: Polity Press, 2015, p. 57.
157 Castells, *Networks of Outrage and Hope*, p. 10.
158 Castells, *Networks of Outrage and Hope*, p. 15.
159 A 2011 movement in Spain, of major protests, demonstrations, and occupations against austerity policies, which began around local and regional elections. While the issue was local, it pioneered (and lent its name to) a new and increasingly global mode of networked protest.
160 Castells, *Networks of Outrage and Hope*, p. 132.

as JNU's now-famous Freedom Square epitomized. In 2019, they spilled out into the streets and into the several occupy initiatives often led by women. Although these were not, or not only, Kaviraj's primordial communities, they included several features of his fuzzy and nonuniversal narratives, *possessing its one key feature, namely their antagonism to individuated identity.*

Several of their strategies of returning to analogue, both as identity and as space, occur in the context of extreme mediatization, and with it of extreme identification and surveillance practices. G. Arunima, who teaches at JNU, names 'at least three kinds of camera forms that proliferate in universities [...] CCTVs, photos and videos taken by security personnel or the administration, those taken by students, and finally a proposal that classrooms could have cameras to facilitate MOOC (Massive Open Online Course) courses'.[161] In addition to these, campuses are 'awash with cameras and users... Needless to say, the proliferation of cameras and users has democratised photography in the last decade in a manner that may have been unthinkable earlier'.

What it has also led to, says Arunima, is the production of students' visual counter-archive as part of what she calls 'resistance aesthetics'. Such an aesthetics is 'enmeshed within cultural modes and histories of protests and prior histories of opposing institutional authority', and is often resolutely analogue.

> [It] would bring together protests, speeches, marches, fasts, dharnas (sit-ins), and other forms of visual resistance, such as cartoons and posters, all of which are designed to counter administrative authority. Since now many campus protests, following administrative orders, are routinely videographed by security staff, the archive of resistance is also an attempt by student protestors to maintain their own visual record of the events. This counter-archive, I would suggest, should be read more like [...] an ethical mode of witnessing, rather than as connected only to the 'objectivity' of the mechanical eye.[162]

Revisiting Technological Unilateralism in the Era of Aarogya Setu

'Today identity is embedded with vertical solutions and often conflated with entitlement.'

– Pramod K. Verma, technology developer and former Chief Technology Officer, Aadhaar[163]

By the middle of 2020, as the first wave of pandemic lockdowns came to an end, the 'chilling effect' of various techno-legal initiatives had become very much a reality. Even as COVID-19

---

161 G. Arunima, 'Cameras, Campuses and the Future of Politics in an Era of Imaging Technologies', *Contributions to Indian Sociology* 54.1 (2020): 16.
162 Arunima, 'Cameras, Campuses and the Future of Politics', pp. 17–18.
163 # Pramod K. Verma, Architecting Platforms for Innovation https://www.slideshare.net/indiastack/architecting-platforms-for-innovation

positive cases escalated – even as Mumbai alone exceeded all of China in the number of cases – the regulatory impulses of the state grew. In Karnataka, the Seva Sindhu portal sought to integrate all of the state's Common Service Centres, and made registration compulsory to enter the state. It was not alone: by this time, most states had their equivalent border controls. Aarogya Setu itself, originally set up specifically to fight COVID-19, grew in the time it took to write this essay into a platform that would integrate telemedicine video consultations, an essential building block for India's National Health Stack. This Health Stack on its side proposed to build on the legacy of India Stack – a series of API-based collaborations permitting Aadhaar verification platforms, an E-KYC mechanism, Unified Payments Interface, a Digilocker, and much else.

It was astonishing to see the Aadhaar template being reprised. Aadhaar was a Planning Commission project, Aarogya Setu a Niti Aayog initiative. The first was a lean-and-mean identity provider and authenticator, the second merely a COVID-19 contact-tracing app. Both were voluntary except you could do practically nothing without either. Both became effectively gateways into a complex network of services: Aadhaar into the Unified Payments area and Aarogya Setu into the health economy.

What did perhaps change was the absence of any sense of optimism beneath the high-pressure sales talk flooding iSPIRT's many websites. In their presentation on the further integration of the National Health Stack with Aarogya Setu, the two project leaders, Arnab Kumar, Program Director of Frontier Technologies at NITI Aayog, Jay Dutta, Senior Vice President at MakeMyTrip. com, and a private volunteer who developed the app[164] spoke of this as an opportunity that they had 'stumbled upon', a possible initial building block that could – 'if people are interested' – survive beyond COVID-19. As with Aadhaar, here too there appeared to be little regulation available, given that the Personal Data Protection Bill, 2019 was yet to be passed into law.[165]

The chill then really lies in the unknown, as we anticipate the possible future of what this essay has tried to track: namely the sovereign body in its troubled interaction with the changing historical definitions of citizenship. As the 'people' become state property, as ownership becomes a direct manifestation of the data it controls, the right to access their data has become considerably more complicated than simply a right to free speech extending to the internet: it extends into the right to life, and the right to analogue spaces.

Contrary to the assertive, aspirational 'coming out' that is central to Digital India's self-image, much recent politics is defined by its very opposite: of making identifiable speaking voices elusive, making spaces ephemeral, defining a fuzzy leaderlessness to political self-assertion. Such elusiveness in turn contextualizes the overly visible incarceration process with which the state has shown off the example of Safoora Zargar and the several young people arrested

---

164 Aditi Agrawal, 'Aarogya Setu Will Include Telemedicine, Greater Personalisation; May Act as Building Block for India Health Stack', Medianama, 22 April 2020, https://www.medianama.com/2020/04/223-aarogya-setu-upcoming-features/.
165 August 2022 update: the draft Personal Data Protection Bill has been officially withdrawn by the government, and sent back to the drawing board.

under the UAPA. Together with the heavy-handed assertion that identity is only what the state provides, such overt displays of control in pandemic times only open up the long colonial ancestry in the assertion, central to sovereign states, that a body has only one identity with no choice in the matter.

'SLOW VIOLENCE' AND VACANT CITIZENSHIP: THE EXCESSES OF INDIA'S DIGITAL GOVERNANCE

NAFIS AZIZ HASAN

Introductory Note

This essay emerged from a recent encounter with the tumultuous world of technology producers working to transition the Indian state into the realm of the digital. Expecting to be schooled in the technical apparatus of the transition, I interviewed, in 2018 and 2019, multiple engineers and technical experts in various roles, capacities, and inclinations. Yet, instead of a grandiose telling of the potential transformation to governance and life, these conversations revealed an anxiety about data, about the imminent dangers of the transition, and the sheer unpreparedness to tackle the still largely unknown but creeping threats that data posed. Categorized as hacks, leaks, malware, or SQL injections, these experts nervously warned that the gov.in was under siege from within and without. Far from the total and uncritical adoption of digital forms, these experts advised a cautious use of technological products, prescribing ways to wipe out one's digital trail. Indeed, many made elaborate arrangements to leave no trail of their personal information on the computer systems they worked on.

In these conversations, the source of this danger was somewhat unspecified and, when named, not consistent. Sometimes it was Israeli hackers exploiting their weak information technology (IT) laws, sharpening their jacking skills on poorly protected Indian systems; other times it was simply bad design. Yet, the crisis was palpable and the discourse of the imminent danger was reaching scalar proportions. State governments were being forced to discuss it in their Question Hour and senior officials were laying out a counterstrategy in the form of hiring an army of ethical hackers to preempt and foil potential attacks. Media reports and other writing were bolstering these fears by quantifying casualties: 'Over 22k Indian Websites, 114 Govt Portals Hacked between Apr 2017-Jan 2018', read one newspaper report.[1]

Standing for a moment outside this threatening present, one begins to see that the dangers being alluded to are in response to an original expectation from the juggernaut of digitization. This was an expectation of mobility, where information firmly lodged in government documents turns into mobile data, available as a knowledge input in the many decisions that make government. The deviance of data from this linear path toward something else is a phenomenon that comes after decades of the digitization machine at work, possibly a reason for the grave reactions toward it. There is a robust, if brief, history of the datafication of government, which is not often recalled but is a reference point of the current predicament.

---

1   'Over 22k Indian Websites, 114 Govt Portals Hacked between Apr 2017-Jan 2018', 7 March 2018, https://www.business-standard.com/article/current-affairs/over-22k-indian-websites-114-govt-portals-hacked-between-apr-2017-jan-2018-118030700870_1.html.

Historically speaking, what we see now is a situation I term excess. Excess or the excesses of digitization become a vantage point to illuminate the historical conditions and trajectory of digitization as a changing technopolitical assemblage of people, ideas, and technologies and their effects beyond expected outcomes. Other people interested in this history have asked and convincingly pointed out to the many political choices that have led to the present. In other words, we have some scholarly excavations of *why* digitization is in the state it is in. Somewhat uniquely, this essay asks not why but *how* we reached here. Also uniquely, the story of this how is revealed through a technological object: database management systems as a conglomeration of code and algorithms that came to define and direct the mobility of data, the dividing line between analogue and digital.

Relating the story of the present through a technical object doesn't mean getting lost in the intricate technical details of management systems, fascinating as that might be. This essay aims to strike a balance. On the one hand, it is eager to point out remarkable shifts in technical configurations that initiated an altogether new direction and scale of the digital. The one big moment this essay highlights is the revolutionary innovation in coding data through algebraic relations that allowed manipulating it from a distance. To some, this may seem as a primitive technological past of the 80s and 90s. Yet, the reason I focus on revolutionary design of relational databases is because not much has changed in use by governments. There are very few examples of the use of non-relational databases in government (India's biometric project Aadhaar is one example) and it seems like a procurement problem with governments all over the world, not just in India.[2] On the other hand, the essay works hard to illuminate the social and political dimensions of these purportedly technical changes. How does an algebraic relation used to arrange data change our relations with each other and with institutions? Such a hyphenated inquiry encounters political concepts: neoliberal politics, rights, citizenship, access, and takes them head on. Unending servers of data at the 400-odd National Informatics Centres (NICs) strewn across India, leaching in and out of myriad computer systems, unsettle notions of neoliberalism exclusively built on a separation between state and market. Excesses in the form of hacks, leaks, and errors in data produce new obligations on individuals needing this data to exercise their basic rights. Excess offers a vantage point from where to view citizenship practiced and experienced as a tryst with broken data.

This essay is not simply about the social life of databasing techniques, even though a significant amount of space is dedicated to telling that story. It is, at its very core, the thick description of a total social fact that pervades all forms of datafication. Social facts are things external to individuals and specific situations, but have significant effects on material life. Databasing techniques are similarly concealed, but central to the movement of data, so as to not be seen or recognized as critical components to the story of digitization. Yet, as this essay reveals, they constitute the basis for the materiality of information. They give cata a form and interpretive possibilities. They also, as this essay shows, make data potentially dangerous, going beyond the conditions of its arrangement.

2   For instance, see Shira Ovide, 'A Fix-It Job for Government Tech', 24 November 2021, https://www. nytimes.com/2021/11/24/technology/government-tech.html.

I.

Remaking Government in the Realm of the Digital-

The Techno-Politics of Neoliberalism

In 1993, Infosys recorded revenue of $5 million.[3] One year later, that had jumped to $9 million on the back of Finacle – a banking system that centralized customer data to a back-end database system, while allowing a proliferation of service at myriad front ends: at the branch, in the home, or online. In a short period of time, Finacle went from 10 banks to 100, and then rocketed to 1,000 banks across 150 countries.[4] A year later, in 1994, the automobile company Maruti introduced an Oracle database to keep track of a million moving parts in its Gurgaon manufacturing assembly, significantly reducing production time.[5] Likewise, bourses in the mid-90s like the National Stock Exchange, the Delhi Stock Exchange, and the Pune Stock Exchange introduced a dual database and screen-based order-and-quote trading system that made multisited access possible.[6]

What explains this momentous transformation in the sheer extent of data transactions in these diverse domains? Service, during this time, got a new name. From hugely deficit, long-waiting lines of poor service experience, India began to see quicker, multiple points of service access. Underlying this emergence of what has been called 'modern services' was a revolution in data storage design that crucially allowed access to data from locations other than where it was physically located.

In 1973, Edgar Codd, a computer engineer at IBM in San Jose, California, invented a new 'relational' way of storing data that would fundamentally transform how data was being accessed across the world. Called the relational database management system or RDBMS, he developed a system of symbols borrowed from algebra to define multiple relationships between dimensions of data. The format in which the data now came to be stored was the table, as opposed to a tree-like or hierarchical structure. This did two things to revolutionize access. It brought about 'data independence', that is, a separation of the application querying data from the structure of data storage itself, and it allowed access to data without the need for an underlying knowledge of where the data is stored on a disk.

This meant that one did not have to be a trained computer engineer to query a database. People with less technical knowledge (and possibly more business knowledge) could also formulate queries. With rapid increases in information communication through networks,

3   'Infosys Annual Report, 1993–94', April 1994, https://www.infosys.com/investors/reports-filings/
     annual-report/annual/documents/infosys-ar-94.pdf.
4   George Chacko, 'INFOSYS: New Game, New Rules: A Case Study', *Management Research News* 27.8/9
     (2004): 1–25.
5   'New System for Maruti Launched', *The Times of India*, 25 October 1994, sec. In Brief, ProQuest
     Historical Newspapers.
6   'Pune Bourse Goes Online', *The Times of India*, 19 March 1996, ProQuest Historical Newspapers.

widespread querying became possible from locations away from the data source. This gave businesses in the United States a phenomenal opportunity to analyze information from multiple locations and make decisions about stocking, pulling out, and pricing practically in real time. Between 1973, when Codd developed this model, and the early 80s, the market for RDBMS grew to, by one estimate, about $130 million.[7]

RDBMS has sometimes been named, retrospectively, as a 'disruptive' technology. Materially, databases have been over the past 40 years surrounded, supplemented, and displaced by other forms of record keeping. Conceptually, digitization, or the process of turning analogue data into digital forms, is more often than not talked about, thought, and imagined as things that are encoded and represented in databases. The computer scientist, Paul Dourish,[8] echoing an entanglement between prior technologies like writing and the practices they engender, says that 'when the database is a tool for encoding aspects of the world, the world increasingly seems to us as a collection of opportunities for databasing'. RDBMS, and its 'disruption', was not simply a technical infrastructure, but rather an *assemblage of technical choices and political outcomes*. Studying it as a *cultural* phenomenon (as I do in this essay) has thus involved identifying it within a triad of database functions, infrastructural arrangements, and informational practice.

When this disruption reached India in the late 80s and early 90s, it was initially brought to life by IBM on the back of Rajiv Gandhi's New Computer Policy that, after stonewalling foreign investments for a decade, now permitted their entry into technology production. As it did so, India found itself on the brink of another disruption. In 1991, when Prime Minister P.V. Narasimha Rao, after years of debate, finally dropped the axe on the liberalization policy, RDBMS was just about picking up. Indeed, this essay makes the (provocative) argument that the trajectory of post-liberalization would soon be fundamentally entwined with the trajectory of RDBMS as the infrastructure that came to define neoliberalism began to coalesce into its backbone, namely India's growing service sector. Such an argument departs from the conventional history of technology development in India, mostly presented (for example, in a recent book by Mohan Sukumar)[9] as the mute result of dramatic political choices. Likewise, liberalization has itself been conventionally viewed through a political economic lens of a withering state and emerging markets, and less often in its cultural impact on personhood.

While emphasizing what I see as the tectonic effects of a single technology, I do not elide the political; indeed, I hope to provide something of a techno-political account of post-liberalization in India: the ways in which political actions are embedded within technical forms and, conversely, technical objects shape political questions. Techno-politics, in its contemporary usage, often reveals engineering or infrastructure projects as vehicles for political goals and forms of power. It thus foregrounds political abstractions in a very

---

7   Martin Campbell-Kelly, 'The RDBMS Industry: A Northern California Perspective', *IEEE Annals of the History of Computing* 34.4 (2012): 19.
8   Paul Dourish, 'No SQL: The Shifting Materialities of Database Technology', *Computational Culture*, 4 November 2014, p. 2.
9   Arun Mohan Sukumar, *Midnight's Machines: A Political History of Technology in India*, New Delhi: Penguin Viking, 2019.

material way. As a form of postcolonial computing, RDBMS can be seen as an assemblage of technologies, techniques, and desires undergirding shifts in neoliberal governmentality, enabled by significant interventions in multiple definitions of personhood that, in turn, define both privacy and surveillance as well as widen the domains of economic rights as these extend to the identification and targeting of beneficiaries. The *forms* of data that RDBMS helped produce across domains of life, including health, land, labor, and leisure, as well as the *channels* of circulation it opened up – from home to kiosk to data center and back – created a *radically new experience of citizenship*. The changes in the early 90s that many have seen as nothing less than a social revolution with significant legal, economic, and constitutional consequences were, I argue, undergirded by databasing technologies.

Let us consider some of the ways in which the entry of RDBMS helps account for the momentous changes that occurred in the 90s. One view on neoliberalism sees it as taking place autonomously, in what Thomas Friedman names 'golden enclaves' existing outside state institutions.[10] A look at the 'national' career of technologies suggests otherwise – the founding of the call center industry in India that peaked in the late 90s, for example.

At its core, call centers allowed a translocation of services, produced in one (geographic, territorial, sovereign) region and consumed in another. What, we may ask, were the technologies that drove this? A lot of focus has been on the internet and networks in general, but young men and women in Bangalore, Gurgaon, and Mumbai were also accessing data that was stored thousands of miles away. Some were, inevitably, stealing that data and selling it to other companies – such as the famous case of an HSBC employee stealing bank information and money in 2006[11] – but most of them were simply accessing personal, sensitive, financial data of their British or American customers through application interfaces that connected them to databases in those countries. Without several of the features of RDBMS, none of this would be possible.

Crucial here is also the role of service providers contracted to run call centers, build and run technology to access their client data, and offer services. The costing models, the lynchpin of the business of offshoring services, made sense only when Indian companies built their own technology and then charged their customers on a pay-per-use model. Companies like Genpact and Mphasis were now buying proprietary RDBMS from companies like Oracle and Microsoft to run their centers. Without that, it would have been prohibitively expensive to import RDBMS and to make the call center business profitable for firms abroad.

The point of this example is to show that tracing the career of technologies of neoliberalism such as RDBMS can *reconceptualize neoliberalism itself*, taking it away from Friedman's golden enclaves and into entangled governmental policies (allowing the purchase of offshore database management systems in this case). It gives us another, *opposite*, way to think about

10   Thomas Friedman, "Will India Seize the Moment?", *Seattle Post-Intelligencer*, 1924, 23 March 2004.
11   Miles <a href="http://Brignall">Brignall](https://www.theguardian.com/profile/milesbrignall), 'HSBC Indian Call Centre Worker Accused of Hacking into Accounts', *The Guardian*, 29 June 2006, https://www.theguardian.com/money/2006/jun/29/business.india.

the history of the present. Calls among neoliberalism's leading promoters, such as the World Bank, have often been framed around advice like the trite 'less government more governance' line. But growing scholarship on both liberalism and neoliberalism has shown that lesser or leaner government does not necessarily translate into either less regulation or weaker states.[12] Indeed, it proliferates the sites for regulation and domination by creating autonomous entities of government that are not part of the formal state apparatus but are instead guided by an enterprise logic. This is indeed the *techne* of neoliberalism, in which states ends up allying themselves with a range of other groups and forces, and seek to set up 'multiole chains of enrolment'[13] that mask the state's persistent presence through 'government-at-a-distance' approaches to governance.

An oft-cited example of neoliberal governmentality, government-organized non-governmental organizations (more popularly referred to by the sonic acronym GoNGOs) too have been innate to the transformations of government, and mediate governance into the several new distributive possibilities that technological infrastructures increasingly allow.

RDBMS apparently illuminates this better than these new institutions can do on their own. To take one example,[14] in 2012, Mother NGO or MNGO, set up by Chief Minister Sheila Dixit's government in Delhi, conducted a massive GIS survey of Delhi's homeless population to map their geographical coordinates and to create locative identities in the absence of residential ones. Inevitably, the data generated by the handheld GIS tracking devices that its surveyors used night after night (nighttime location being a credible way, the surveyors fathomed, to determine what they called 'most visited location') was stored on an RDBMS. Such collection and storage thus allowed access to multiple interested actors, including contracted surveyors, representatives of MNGO, organizations working for and with the homeless in Delhi, bureaucrats of the Delhi Urban Shelter Improvement Board, and the chief minister's office in the Delhi secretariat. Every one of these actors could, via authenticating logins and interfaces, access locative IDs in real time. This allowed a previously unfathomable level of control and realignment of all of these agencies, and it also enabled a previously unimaginable partnership between state and non-state actors that challenged most received notions of either lesser government or more governance.

'Participation', another keyword freely doled out as a neoliberal expectation, also centrally features in projects that are on their face foundationally located in welfare, such as the Mahatma Gandhi National Rural Employment Guarantee Act, 2005 (MGNREGA), an Indian labor law and social security measure, often presented as an antidote to neoliberalism. MGNREGA's entire logic of social auditing, a much-celebrated aspect of its accountability

---

12   Andrew Barry, Thomas Osborne and Nikolas Rose (eds), *Foucault and Political Reason: Liberalism, Neoliberalism and Rationalities of Government*, Chicago: University of Chicago Press, 1996.
13   Barry et al., *Foucault and Political Reason*, p. 12.
14   This example has been drawn from my research for The Identity Project in 2011 and 2012, in which, among other things, I focused on the Aadhaar enrolments of Delhi's homeless population. See Ashish Rajadhyaksha (ed), *In the Wake of Aadhaar: The Digital Ecosystem of Governance in India*, Bangalore: Centre for the Study of Culture and Society, 2013. Aadhaar is the Government of India's biometric identity project for its billion plus residents.

mechanisms, was enabled mainly by the ability of government officials and other multiple beneficiaries to query an RDBMS database (for example, nodal agencies both at district and central levels supervising the status of work, payment, fund utilization and fund requirement). This data helps government and citizens alike to in turn generate reports through which both participation and accountability are ensured.

Digital Governance as a Stratigraphic System

My aim is not to pick a random set of government endeavors and show the value of RDBMS in them. My own examples, of call centers (a symbol of India decidedly on the route to becoming a service economy) and MGNREGA (as a prime example of welfare, at once a state-directed identification for future dole and a means of enabling participatory governance) are mainly to outline the latter career of two concepts – service and welfare – that have been foundationally connected to the grand narrative of India's tryst, and eventual failure, with an industrial economy. Atul Kohli's argument about liberalizing reforms as neither helping nor hurting India's industrial growth[15] is telling because it opens up a space to think about the *copresence of welfare with a neoliberal service economy*, despite the two being organized around different logics. That RDBMS undergirds elements of *both* welfare and service points to its centrality in shaping our populational experience as a whole.

What I want to take on here, as a specific object of focus, is the career of data and its storage within the story of the digitization of administrative government in India. This is a site where both the potential and the risk of RDBMS is at its most apparent. If RDBMS is the concealed infrastructure of big data, there is another concealment at play here: the vulnerabilities in data produced as a result of changes to its storage design. The career of RDBMS in government shows us that the modularity in the arrangement of data and better reach and access sits side by side with the risks this arrangement of data poses. When data was locked up on a computer – as it was in the earlier DBMS system – it had remained secure. Any threat of manipulation had in part been averted by the need to understand the basic structure of the data, something that was no longer necessary with RDBMS.

Nowhere were the perils more acutely felt than in government itself. Although the Indian state has been on the RDBMS wagon since the 90s, its bureaucrats and their consultants have only recently ratcheted up the conversation on data security. Although I recount older concerns with data security later in this essay, and while I show that security was thought about as early as the 80s, it appears that these did not curtail the movement of data that RDBMS brought forth. The trade-off (between data proliferation and security) is most evident in the digitization of the apparatus of governance itself. It also raises basic questions around how the proliferation of governmental data might be viewed within the present-day excesses of big data. Was there a *weakening* of the formidable forms of knowledge and control governments once possessed, and thus a phenomenological crisis in the state as RDBMS disperses data across locations and people?

---

15   Atul Kohli, 'Politics of Economic Growth in India, 1980–2005 Part II: The 1990s and Beyond', *Economic & Political Weekly*, 41.13 (2006): 1251–1259.

This is a story that unfolds in a more or less stratigraphic manner.[16] The paper files of colonial-style bureaucracy had a system – which database engineers hired by the Planning Commission in the late 70s and 80s abstracted and on top of which they built databases to serve the needs of their massive planning exercises. When other innovations, primarily RDBMS (but also Graphical User Interfaces GUIs and other forms of networked databases), were in turn built on top of *that*, it changed the organization itself and with it the flow of fast-digitizing administrative data. A new set of relations now emerged in the bureaucratic workplace, alongside an accretion of its functions and processes, each changing at different speeds.

What we now saw was significant: a slow descent into chaos, instantiated by spectacular leaks and hacks, mundane system breakdowns, errors and loss of data, all of which reveal diverse layers of techno-politics congealed beneath the benevolent-sounding term 'electronic governance'. Viewing the digitization of government in archaeological fashion, as a series of layers, offers a history of the present. Although the researcher's access to details of any single layer remains always incomplete, a through-line emerges *across* the layers, centered on the *choice* and *availability* of data management infrastructure with their accompanying political possibilities. Let me try to provide an outline of each of these layers, which map onto the sections below.

As far back as in the early 70s, India's Planning Commission – dogged by its recent history of 'failed' plans and frustrated by the poor quality of information available to it from various sectors of the economy – had sought 'data improvement' by constituting various committees. Since much of this information pertained to numbers, and since number-crunching organizations like the Indian Statistical Institute were already using computers and automatic calculators, the Commission decided early on to build computerized information systems. Yet the organizational forms of bureaucracy within which this information lay was notoriously opaque, with complex rules and minute levels of writing and inscriptions. This information was embedded in writing files and records with intimate channels of circulation and comprehension. The Commission soon realized that, before computerizing information, they had to first help bureaucrats in myriad ministries identify and digitize information most relevant to planning.

As I browse through the noting, comments, rebuttals, and replies that constitute the paperwork of these debates, now archived in another bureaucracy (the National Archives of India), a growing turf battle is discernible between scientists and bureaucrats. At the heart of these debates is the question of control over information. Thus, when budding Commission-supported computer scientists began considering, in the 70s, how to develop a digital information system that would aid the Indian bureaucracy in its production of knowledge about the world, as well as how to make that information available to other bureaucracies away from sites of action, they ran into two specific problems. First, *what* information from specific bureaucracies should be digitized and mobilized for action and *who* should decide this? Second, *how* should bureaucracies share this information, through what means, how much, and how often?

---

16   I thank Christopher Kelty at UCLA for suggesting that layers of technological forms could be thought of as strata of a geological formation.

Attempts at digitizing (and subsequently computerizing) information on which public bureaucracies depended for their existence set loose a fundamental transformation in the nature of the information itself. In hindsight, the crisis was initially one of boundaries. If information production had so far worked through opaque rules and rituals of writing, all of which demarcated bureaucracy from the rest of society, how would the relationship of bureaucracy and society change when information once lodged in office registers now became untethered and mobile?

In the initial years of digitization, this relationship did not change very much. Early attempts at dislodging data concealed in dusty registers of district offices were, as I describe below, thwarted by available infrastructure. While these attempts aimed to make information move so that some center (either at state or national level) could see this information as data, movement began to be constrained by an overbearing fidelity to the organizational design of bureaucracy, to its hierarchies and rules, as well as to the computational design of information systems. In contrast, 30 odd years later, the mobility of information as data, in the era of let's say Aadhaar, not only clogs the information highway, it storms into the lanes, cracks, and crevices of daily life.

There is no single metric to determine the extent to which government work has been digitized. But a range of examples exist that point to a huge transition into the digital sphere. A technical director from India's National Informatics Center (NIC), which has spearheaded this transition since the 70s, told me that NIC servers receive over two million emails per day addressed to government employees.[17] He said this makes @NIC.in the largest email service in the world. In 2016, the business magazine *The Ken* carried a long piece on the 'appification of the Indian *sarkar*' (appification of the Indian government), pointing out that the Centre for Development of Advanced Computing or C-DAC was 'churning out five or six apps every month. Read that again: five or six new apps every month'.[18] To point out how much data that must be producing, the writer says: 'It's happening at a scale so massive that there really is no comparison. Just for perspective, the United States of America has a total of 218 apps in its directory'.[19] A land records digitization index, published by the National Council for Applied Economic Research (NCAER) in February 2020, shows that, barring four states, all other states in India have some form of digital land records.[20]

Trying to excavate a chronology of digitization through reading technological infrastructures shows how RDBMS enabled a foundational national policy on the electronification of governance – the National e-Governance Plan (NeGP), a set of projects that includes the

---

17   Personal interview with the Director of NIC Shillong, Timothy Dkhar, in September 2019.
18   Venkat Ananth, 'Government of India: The World's Biggest App Factory', *The Ken*, 17 October 2016,
      https://the-ken.com/story/government-india-worlds-biggest-app-factory/.
19   Ananth, 'Government of India'.
20   National Council of Applied Economic Research, *The NCAER Land Records and Services Index (N-LRSI) 2020*,
      Report 20200201, February 2020, https://www.ncaer.org/publication_details.php?pID=317.

controversial Aadhaar project, to electronically provide governance at different scales.[21] Much has been said about its conception of governance, about the financial investments it has attracted, and the kind of relations between people and states this has engendered. Very little, however, has been said (at least among people studying it as policy) about its technological structure, which at its very core instantiates a first, and eventually lasting, example of RDBMS in action within the domain of digital governance.

The NeGP structure is outlined in more detail later in this essay. In brief, however, it is made up of a core network of State Data Centres (or SDCs) — physical locations that contain the databases along with applications for storage, retrieval and manipulation of data, and maintaining cyber security — connected with intranets. SDCs further connected, through State Wide Area Networks (SWANs), to Common Service Centres (CSCs) that delivered services to multiple publics spread across thousands of geographical locations. The NeGP's infrastructure *is* the form that a neoliberalized state in India has taken, made possible because of the distributed nature of RDBMS.

Digital Excess

But transition into the digital sphere has been only one side of the story. Many of the examples I have pointed to above include within them reports of things gone awry. Of the two million emails received each day, 80 percent are some form of spam. In fact, the same director of the NIC mentioned above, runs a team whose sole job is to monitor the software that filters out spam and prevents it from reaching the email accounts of government employees. He says most of these attacks come in from countries with 'weak or no IT Acts', such as Israel, and many carry malware of various kinds, such as an 'SQL injection' that corrupts databases and 'key loggers' that copy everything typed onto another server.[22] Such information, when identified, is supposed to be sent to the India office of the Computer Emergency Response Team (CERT), but that doesn't happen every time. In early 2018, the Indian Parliament was informed that '114 government websites were hacked during April 2017 to January 2018'.[23] Land record databases are, as we see below, being constantly reported as compromised. While hacking is used as a generic term to suggest multiple forms of divergences, the dissonance caused by the abundant production of data is also felt deeply within the daily working of bureaucracy in other forms, including errors and breakdowns.

In response to this excess, government agencies are hard at work to prevent leakage. Cutting across multiple overlapping attempts is the hiring of armies of 'ethical hackers' by the NIC and the renewed call (for example, in the overarching Personal Data Protection Bill, 2019)

---

21   The National e-Governance Plan is an initiative of the Government of India to make all government services available to the citizens of India via electronic media. For details, see https://www.meity.gov.in/divisions/national-e-governance-plan.
22   Personal interview with the Director of NIC Shillong, Timothy Dkhar, in September 2019.
23   'Over 22k Indian Websites, 114 Govt Portals Hacked'.

for a return to the localization of data.[24] As a policy, the Data Protection Bill appears at times almost like a throwback to an era when organizational and computational limitations had also restricted the movement of data to local districts. The 'local' for the Data Protection Bill is of course not a subnational administrative unit, but rather the boundary of the nation. Nevertheless, in laying out rules to *curb* the movement of data, new policies are retrospectively consciously constraining the technical possibilities of RDBMS, thereby producing new political outcomes.

This is hardly the first time that governments have sought to legally control data movement in the name of security. In addition to recommending laws (not carried out until this present Bill), 'third party audits' and software logs to track changes made to databases had been introduced in the past. A common element connecting these myriad attempts has been the securing of data while *ensuring* its mobility. The proposed Bill, on the other hand, appears to want to secure data by *restricting* mobility.

Empirically tracing the emergence of information-as-data in the career of public bureaucracy reveals the consequences that it has had on the very existence of the bureaucratic institution. How did we reach a situation where data becomes unknowable and, in its mobility, uncontrollable? From static information, stored in registers controlled by a document keeper, to this onslaught of data – has this gone out of hand? To trace an implosive, if not regressive, element in the historical journey of a technology as it got applied to government is also to diverge from the overbearing, hagiographical, mode of writing technology's history in India. As some critiques of science try to do, I hope to show that along the more familiar, national narrative of teleological technological modernity, lies a counter story of a phenomenological crisis in some of society's most formidable organizational forms.

Citizenship as Responsibility: Two Views

My focus so far has been on the effects of RDBMS on the *form* of the state. But if RDBMS is also *rearranging* the administrative state itself, what effect might this have on our understanding of a citizenship premised on state-endowed rights and entitlements? I have been developing an idea of service as a form of value which the technical arrangement of RDBMS sets into motion. I intend now to conceptualize what a service-based approach to *citizenship* might look like. I do this by thinking about how technical configurations like RDBMS aid us in forming neoliberal subjects with particular characteristics, and how this in turn produces an altered terrain of citizenship: for instance, a shift from rights to responsibility by shifting older patterns of power by attributing new technical responsibilities to citizens.

Citizenship has been discussed as rights demanded from the state, whether as consumers

---

24 See 'Chapter 6: Transfer of Personal Data Outside India', in Committee of Experts under the Chairmanship of Justice B.N. Srikrishna, *A Free and Fair Digital Economy: Protecting Privacy, Empowering Indians*, Ministry of Electronics and Information Technology, Government of India, 2018, https://www.meity.gov.in/writereaddata/files/Data_Protection_Committee_Report.pdf.. Also see,Parminder Jeet Singh, 'Bringing Data under the Rule of Law', *The Hindu*, 20 September 2018, https://www.thehindu.com/opinion/op-ed/bringing-data-under-the-rule-of-law/article24988755.ece.

of services or as groups demanding affirmative action, but less often as *responsibilities* that the state attempts to place on citizens or citizens on themselves. Projects of development have often been thought of as collective national projects demanding contributions from all citizens, and yet the question of responsibility has not received adequate interest.

Individual responsibility, self-responsibility, or *responsibilization*, as new forms in which the governed are encouraged, freely and rationally, to conduct themselves,[25] are a neoliberal hallmark in which citizenship recasts itself from a strictly juridical-legal relationship into a biopolitical mode centered on the capacity and resources of individuals to propel their own governance. The government, thus, in anthropologist Aihwa Ong's terms, applies an 'optimizing'[26] technique to produce knowledge of its populations that crucially depends on an ethic of responsibility among its citizens.

Such an ethic of responsibility, one that technical arrangements such as RDBMS actively produce, is one of entrepreneurial governance producing entrepreneurial citizens. The stories of both people and institutions affected by RDBMS that I chart here point to a new breed of citizens working at the service of knowledge production and for a more precise government of the people. The many engineers, management consultants, computer scientists, and technicians appearing on the Planning Commission's horizon right from the 70s, who continued to become permanent members of the government system, were also examples of such entrepreneurial responsibility, as were the business consultants and marketing men who spearheaded RDBMS into India and who took to multiple channels to advertise its positive effects.

I have in mind people like Narasimhiah Seshagiri,[27] who built a network before the internet that could relay information about planning and development from one corner of the country to the other, and J. G. Krishnayya, a management consultant, who went to great lengths in getting the government to adopt a 'systems thinking' approach that could make planning and decision-making quicker. While pointing to specific kinds of individuals, I am interested in uncovering a proliferating ethic that rendered the problem of governmentality into a problem needing technical solutions through entrepreneurial design. This ethic, I intend to show, arose alongside the availability of databasing infrastructures: making a rarely-discussed reconfiguration of citizenship, bureaucracy, and technology in the redefining of the means of delivering welfare.

Entrepreneurial citizens generate projects that posit new relations between themselves and those that govern them in the form of an intervention or enterprise. The entrepreneurial ethic I find in the people that emerged alongside databasing technologies of governance is

25   Barry et al., *Foucault and Political Reason.*
26   Aihwa Ong, *Neoliberalism as Exception: Mutations in Citizenship and Sovereignty,* Durham: Duke University Press, 2006, p. 6.
27   Narasimhiah Seshagiri was a computer scientist under whose supervision the NIC was set up in the late 70s. Impressed by NIC's ability to set up an Information Management System for the ninth Asian Games held in 1982 in Delhi, the then Prime Minister Rajiv Gandhi adopted Seshagiri's policy on computers that set the stage for much of the e-governance to come. See Sukumar, *Midnight's Machines.*

similar to, and yet different from, innovating entrepreneurs such as those that the computer science researcher Lilly Irani describes in her recent book.[28] Like her innovators, these entrepreneurs focused on 'progressive futures *for others* through organizations, know-how, and resourcefulness' and have cultivated 'an ethos of collaboration, experimental life, empathic civic interest, and the monitoring of possibility'.[29] Unlike her innovators, the entrepreneurs I describe were more limited to transforming 'thinking' within administrative structures. Krishnayya, mentioned above, is a great example to think about the ethic of responsibility that entrepreneurs brought to government systems. Even before he was officially contracted by the Planning Commission to help build their systems, Krishnayya had already begun thinking and writing about what a systems approach to government would look like. The titles of his papers, which he sent to the government, sometimes unsolicited, reveal his sense of responsibility toward 'improving' government for a larger good. For instance, his papers titled 'Information Services in Administrative Agencies', 'A User Oriented On-Line Computer System to Assist Decisions and Analysis in Area Development Planning', 'Fail-Soft Information Systems in Government' were all written in direct and interventionist language and were meant to provide practical and yet transformative advice on how to change things for the future. He prescribed both 'a new philosophy of information in government' and ways to operationalize that philosophy through the design of data and systems.[30] In Section II, I describe the development of this entrepreneurial ethos, propelled by new techniques of organizing data, which drove the datafication of a large number of government programs, from land management to identity and health records.

What we shall also see further on in this essay is a flip side to the story: excessive digitization and situations of disarray that point to another kind of responsibilization, marking a different form of citizenship. This is less associated with grand entrepreneurship and more with *repairing data affected by digital excess*. As I show in the case of a land records database, state processes download the labor of corrections onto farmers, who are then mired in a circuitous process of correcting errors ascribed to their data. In this process, their claims on the state vis-à-vis benefits and entitlements is temporarily halted, making for a shift from 'thick' or substantive citizenship to 'thin' and unsubstantiated citizenship.[31]

Such responsibility is not only about keeping one's data updated, which would have been the citizen's responsibility under neoliberalism proper, but a different responsibility – one that nevertheless emerges from the fallout of that same neoliberal vision. For the kinds of *labor of repair* which I describe later in this essay are not bestowed onto citizens (like rights) but are instead tacitly elided by the state and its agents and shifted onto citizens. As men and women across the country are busy repairing their data, damaged as a result

28   Lilly Irani, *Chasing Innovation: Making Entrepreneurial Citizens in Modern India*, Princeton: Princeton University Press, 2019.
29   Irani, *Chasing Innovation*, p. 7.
30   'Computerized Data Bank' - Consultancy Assistance from Institutions (1976), File No. M-12038/3/76 – M&I, National Archives of India.
31   'Thick' and 'Thin' is one of the many binaries in which forms of citizenship have come to be expressed, as recounted by Niraja Gopal Jayal, *Citizenship and its Discontents: An Indian History*, Cambridge, MA: Harvard University Press, 2013, p. 3.

of the excesses of digitization, *citizenship is experienced as a form of violence*. This is not structural, spectacular, or episodic forms of violence that scholars of the state have alerted us to, but what I call a form of 'slow violence' given the slow and concealed way repair creeps into a citizen's life.

II.

THE PLANNING COMMISSION'S QUEST FOR 'DATA IMPROVEMENT'

Many years before data governance came to be synonymous with the digital, the Planning Commission's Monitoring and Information Division (M&I) had begun seriously thinking about an 'Information System' that envisaged nodes and flow of data. The conceptual and logical work generated around building this system – the debates over data and its flow – revealed the people in charge of building the system, their biases and preferences. Most of all, it revealed their undying belief in technology churning government inside out, their urge to make its ugly belly transparent, and to reveal the numerous offices and procedures that the Commission thought did not work, all to find ways to order and standardize them. Inevitably, the information system in the Commission became a record of a failure to stay the course of its mandate.

The failure was evidenced in three different ways in the forecasting and planning of the Commission's third annual plan. First, in the unavailability of recorded information by the 'sectors' critical to planning for the economy referred to as 'gaps in data'. This related primarily to agriculture and industries as the two main assets of economic production in the country. Second, in a 'time-lag': in the unavailability of recorded information in time for the Commission to make their plans. Third, in a disjuncture between the 'formats' in which information was recorded and sent from the sectors and of the Commission's own recording methods – a problem of both 'retrieval' and 'release'.[32] All three added up to an informational crisis, one that the Planning Commission sought to resolve bureaucratically. The Planning Commission set up committees, but soon realized the need for technical consultancy to change the way data was created, digitized, circulated, and made available to the planning and reporting needs of the Commission.

The profile of the prosaically named 'Data Improvement' Committees now began to change from career bureaucrats and statisticians to computer scientists and management consultants. The administration of India's future, the archive suggests, was being wired to a network of computers and their information capacities. Aside from the *zeitgeist* of computerization in the 70s – silicon bling in dreary bureaucracy – and the conceptual as well as logical break from the past that computerization apparently allowed, it was eventually the limitation of the technical intervention, the limitation of databasing, that both defined and curtailed the Planning Commission's work.

---

32   Planning Commission, 'Standing Committee for Directing and Reviewing Improvement of Data Base for Planning and Policy Making', Vol. I, 1978, File No. O-11-17/1/78-M&I, National Archives of India.

The limitation pertained both to *storage* and *access*. Before Codd had developed the RDBMS, units of data stored on a computer system could be traced out only by following a tree-like hierarchy of the system itself — Folder-File-Data — and were thus dependent on the configuration of the system, which in turn was under the purview of database administrators rather than users. This storage method limited its spread and access because dependence on the computer structure meant editing data could happen only on the system on which it was stored. At best, data could be read through remote connections to the storage computer, but this depended on the speed of the network and also the spread of the computer nodes, both of which lacked capacity. These limitations pervaded all decisions. From the prickly question of the centralization of data in the Commission to its existence in individual departments, from the meddling of engineers in bureaucratic decisions to the very transition from paper to the digital, the initial designs of digital stayed close to the paper system.

In April 1976, the Commission did what possibly no government agency in India had done before. It sent out a call for proposals to build its Computerized Data Bank. In a few months, it received detailed responses from five institutions: the Indian Institutes of Management in Ahmedabad and Calcutta, the Indian Institute of Technology Delhi, the Administrative Staff College of India, Hyderabad, and the Systems Research Institute, Pune. The Commission's members weighed these proposals, gave each a sharp but generous review, and eventually decided, by June 1977, to give up the outsourcing plan altogether and to construct the data bank itself. That was a bold move for an organization that had very little experience with computerization, and they did eventually end up hiring 'outside' expertise. For now, at least, the Commission closed its doors to institutions eager to partner with it.

Yet, J. Krishnayya, the charismatic engineer from Massachusetts Institute of Technology (MIT) with some years of global IT consultancy behind him, and at the time the executive director and founder of Systems Research Institute that had sent the Commission new ideas on how to modernize its information system, continued to point the Commission to where it might go wrong with its plan to build a system. Not mincing his words, Krishnayya wrote an emphatic letter in May 1997 to the economist Raj Krishna, who had just joined the Commission as a member, in which he offered critical comments on the data repository that the Commission proposed to build itself, at least in the initial phases. A conversation ensued that would point to a lasting problem in the digitization of information: a problem that was to rankle in organizational design and would hover over the entire career of electronic governance in India. This was the problem of the *location* of data that the Commission was now aiming to centralize into a data bank. Should control of digitized data rest with individual departments or should it be centralized in a data bank? If planning by the Commission was essentially a centralized activity, should data follow suit? There was also the question of the form that the technology should take. Should technology *disrupt* the organizational form of government or should it map onto an existing morphology?

Krishnayya wrote matter of factly that the advice he had earlier given to the Commission, in the proposal in response to their call, was:

NOT TO BYPASS the Sectoral Divisions, but rather to link them into a network [with decentralized computer equipment]. The alternative, which is being followed now, is to construct a large central data bank administratively in one Division in the hope others will use it. Won't happen! People want to control the information they use themselves. It will be a huge boondoggle eventually, and much wasted effort.[33]

In their response in June 1977, the Commission defended its decisions:

The sectoral divisions are not being bypassed, but their information needs have been examined separately and an integrated system is being developed which would meet all these needs. The inputs for Data Bank would be collected and fed into the Data Bank by the individual Divisions. The role of the M&I Division is only that of helping in the identification, analysis and examination of information needs, design and development of the Data Bank, and later, it would be of coordinating the operation of the Data Bank by the Divisions concerned. It will, therefore, be seen that the Data Bank would not be "administered" by one Division but would only be coordinated.[34]

In the inaugural issue of *sacm*, a monthly magazine that Krishnayya and his colleagues had started in 1979, he defined the problem facing the nascent attempt at digitizing government as a concern with the 'application of System Analysis in Government, to problems of government, and government agencies, in the fields of Industry, Forestry, Irrigation, Agriculture, Communications, Transport, Urban development, etc.'[35]

sacm aimed, uniquely, to begin a conversation about what would work for government *per se* without necessarily transitioning 'solutions' from the private sector to government. Nothing like *sacm* exists today, and the fate of that magazine is unclear. It does appear that its editors had aimed to generate ideas for the use of technology from within the contours and organizational depths of government itself. They invited government officers to contribute to the discussion of system analysis – a phrase that came to be used to describe both IT and organizational systems. Its inaugural issue, which incorporated papers from the file on building a centralized data bank for government, provides a clear description of what system design stood for at the time.

One essential principle that the editors of *sacm* proposed, for large computerized information systems in government, was the *decentralization of data*. This was to them an adequate response to the decentralized structure of decision-making among government organizations. This belief came to them from multiple and classic texts on organizations and system design, such as Katz and Kahn's 1966 book *The Social Psychology of*

---

33   Planning Commission, 'Standing Committee for Directing and Reviewing Improvement of Data base for Planning and Policy Making'.
34   Planning Commission, 'Standing Committee for Directing and Reviewing Improvement of Data base for Planning and Policy Making'.
35   J.G. Krishnayya et al. (eds), *sacm: A Monthly Magazine,* Pune: Systems Research Institute, 1979, p. 1.

Organizations and J.G. Miller's 1978 book *Living Systems*. Another principle that SRI recommended in the pages of *sacm* was 'distribution', in response to a question of where information should be processed if it is to be made available 'at the appropriate time and frequency and in the appropriate form to appropriate stakeholders'[36]. The editors defined the different scales at which decisions were taken as 'echelons', saying:

> *Information-processing* capabilities needed to be 'distributed among the various echelons', depending on (a) the analytic capability required at each echelon, (b) the combined economics of processing and transmitting information. This meant that each echelon owns a certain amount of information-processing capability, though not necessarily a mechanized device.[37]

Going further, to show a slew of negative effects of the opposite, that is, a centralized information system, the editors said that if centralized,

> the raw data travels a greater distance [in terms of both time and space]. When the raw data travels more, there could be the following consequences: (i) the delays are greater, (ii) more errors creep in, (iii) communication costs more, (iv) in general the reliability is lower, (v) the context or the relevance [the metalanguage] of the data may get lost, (vi) inappropriate aggregation may result, (vii) reaction time with regard to new data ideas is long.[38]

Importantly, they also pointed to the 'political consequences of centralized processing' in which they said that centralization led to the concentration of power at the center and a reduction in morale and decision-making of people in the echelons.

Essentially, Krishnayya's critique was that the Planning Commission's data bank was counterintuitive to how governance in India worked. If the Commission's focus was to create a centralized data bank even as they strengthened the information systems of individual sectors, then its design needed to understand what kind of storing, retrieval, and processing of data would happen at which scale. Questions abounded on the technical capacities and structure of the devices that the Commission was putting together.[39] While discussing the need for rephasing projects based on changing commitments and demands, the Commission notes: 'How and where the cuts on the past commitments be affected and how to tailor the present budget accordingly [...] is a problem situation to which an information system should respond'.[40] In part this drew from Krishnayya's philosophy that system design be based on fidelity to organizational forms. There was another reason why *sacm* was recommending decentralized storage of data: the databasing capacities available at the time. Technically, *sacm* recommended a database management system (DBMS),

---

36 Krishnayya et al., *sacm*, p. 1.
37 Krishnayya et al., *sacm*, p. 1.
38 Krishnayya et al, *sacm*, p. 2.
39 Unnamed File, File No. O-11717/5/75 M&I, National Archives of India.
40 Krishnayya et al, *sacm*, p. 2.

an IMAGE database system for its QUERY language. They claimed that the IMAGE DBMS was a ready-to-use tool for information management and hence ideal for a decentralized information structure. They, therefore, recommended installing the DBMS on minicomputers, with an RTE-III operating system that had a file manager, and installing these minis at the same levels as where decision-making in government was taking place. This, they believed, was a viable structure, and it would not disrupt the forays that the government had already made in decentralizing decision-making.

Until then, only large-scale, general-purpose computers had been used for all information processing applications. These monoliths had constrained the information system structure to the extent that, even in organizations where decision-making had been significantly decentralized, most information processing functions nevertheless remained centralized. With the rapid advance of minicomputer technology emerged 'minis' packed with powerful features, suitable for a location with small to medium requirements. Corporate users now had the attractive alternative of constructing, at all stages, networks of mini data centers, each equipped with low input/output devices and modular memory devices appropriate to the information processing echelons. Distributed minicomputer-based systems further developed the characteristic of 'adding-on' whenever additional processing capability was called for, thus allowing for possible technical evolution to stay in step with growing organizations.[41]

The Commission's centralized data bank inevitably ran into problems. It could not get individual departments to digitize their data in the formats that it had created, nor to reengineer their processes in ways that could streamline the flow of data from departments in the states and districts to the centralized data bank in New Delhi's Yojana Bhawan.[42]

Notes from a 1975 annual plan meeting between representatives from the 'Industries Sector', Centrally Sponsored Programs of the Department of Mines, and the Planning Commission point to some of the urgency and frustration evident among members of the Commission. That the Commission found that sectors could improve their control on the information they generated can be inferred from the following statement:

> It was significant to note that the distribution of allocations vis-à-vis the strategies for project implementation i.e., holding the project, slowing it down or shelving it, was being handled through negotiations. Given the Data Base the same could have been achieved through recourse to a simple linear programming algorithm.[43]

Later, in early 1978, the Commission ran into more problems with collecting data from the sectoral departments, even in the filling out of minimum standardized data record sheets.

---

41   Unnamed File, File No. O-11717/5/75 M&I, National Archives of India.
42   Yojana Bhavan, which translates to Planning Office, is a physical building which housed India's Planning Commission since its inception in March 1950.
43   Planning Commission, 'Setting up of a National Informatics Centre - Proposal from the Electronics Commission', 1977, File No. 11017/5/77 M&I, National Archives of India.

However, even if this had been sorted out, the flow and access of data would continue to be severely restricted in the absence of technical infrastructure to connect to the main computer in which all the data was purportedly stored. In this regard, some, if not all, of Krishnayya's ominous statements about the centralized data bank would ring true.

But just when the Commission's plans were failing, a new project emerged in sight. This was the creation of the National Informatics Centre, or the now-common sight NIC, housed under the Electronics Commission and partly funded by a grant from the United Nations Development Programme (UNDP).[44] Since the NIC was a cocreation of the UNDP and the Electronics Commission, with the blessings of the Planning Commission, technical consultancy from across the world was being made available to put it together. An entire file dedicated to the debates, meetings, and decisions around the planning for NIC reveals the gigantic infrastructural changes it was bringing to life. UNDP described it as a project of 'very great national importance – the scale and complexity of this project makes it a pioneering experiment', and went on to justify NIC as follows:

> A crucial requirement for national socio-economic planning and planned management is the availability of an extensive information system based on reliable data. Only then does it become possible to develop and to analyze policy options by employing, modeling and forecasting techniques.[45]

NIC's ambition was to conceptualize an information design and the flow of that information through the networks that it built, the most popular being the NICNET – a network before the internet that aimed to connect district offices across the country to a center. At first, NIC was less an organization and more like a network of computers. With the emergence of the NIC, it appears that Krishnayya's idea of a decentralized information architecture that connected departments through a network was finally being taken seriously. It is, however, most closely associated with the computer scientist N. Seshagiri, one of its prominent executive directors. For NIC, in addition to establishing a supercomputer host in Yojana Bhawan in New Delhi which linked to several minicomputers in various sectors, there was also the work of building sectoral or department-wise data systems. This involved digitizing information in these sectors, and then creating a database management system for individual sets of data. NIC's job was to create a standardized sectoral DBMS allowing sector-wise comparison, even when the data itself was stored in the Planning Commission's supercomputer.

NIC launched this project with three priority data banks, or information systems, for three sectors that the Commission identified as having a 'pronounced influence on the national economy,[46] namely agriculture, manpower, and industry and technology. In each, the idea

---

44   The Electronics Commission has an interesting genesis as it was directly set up by M.G.K. Menon with the prime minister's blessings.
45   Unnamed File. File No. O-11717/5/75 M&I, National Archives of India.
46   'Setting up of a National Informatics Centre - Proposal from the Electronics Commission', File No. 11017/5/77 M&I, National Archives of India.

was to create a consolidated sector-wise data bank. So, for agriculture, information that would be related to agricultural products, geological data, meteorological data, oceanographical data, and hydrological data was collected as independent sets, with the NIC aiming to create a common system for all this data.

NIC's goal was to achieve standardization by improving the way data could be classified *across* sectors. Classification of data in a hierarchical, tree-wise structure, a condition of DBMS, was necessary for easy retrievability. Ravi K. Zutshi, a consultant at the Planning Commission, noted that a coding structure was to be devised for classification that would distinguish between sectors, projects, and various categorizations that have to be incorporated in the database.[47] A hierarchical coding structure was developed: (1) Industries Code; (2) Category Subcode; (3) Project Code; and (4) File Code. Different projects would then fall under one of these categories and would be given an individual number. A project code dictionary would have to be developed to provide easy access to the specific project in the centralized database. Since a number of files of information would be associated with every DBMS, a structure to name the files would also be needed. Zutshi proposec a hierarchy of 'Sector File-Project File-Company File-Scheme File'. Other categories, beyond the main ones, pertained to reasons for escalation and delay, and included a 'scarce resource subcode'. Based on this categorization, project reports were printed out and mace available to the Commission. In this way, data was made mobile in a standardized and tabularized format. These sectoral DBMS databases were to be hosted on a main computer in New Delhi, purchased by the UNDP, and linked to minicomputers in states and districts.

The Commission's centralized data bank did eventually take off, but the infrastructural work of creating a network that would link the supercomputer with the minis, of designing the format for data storage in the DBMS, and, most importantly, of getting departments to input data in these formats appeared monumental in comparison to the amount of data actually transacted. The data bank, even when up and running, allowed for the transference of only a small proportion of data (compared to the Commission's planning needs) and that too with glitches and delays. So, even when the digital had replaced the slow and unpredictable flow of paper that had frustrated the Commission in the first place, and created the need for a computerized data bank, its success was constrained by the vagaries of available infrastructure, the creative but tenuous arrangement of a network that produced only a trickle of data.

There were also political consequences, which resulted in something of a technical artifice. Organizationally, the NIC was imagined as a relationship between the Planning Commission and Electronics Commission. But that relationship was choppy from the very start. There are notes from Planning Commission members suggesting that the Electronic Commission, via the people developing the NIC, was trying to go beyond its mandate and decide what 'information' should be generated by the sectors. They were merely 'physical technicians', and it would be 'odd' if they gave suggestions like that. Apparently, the noting suggests, the Electronics Commission was obstructing the development of decentralized databases by individual departments and agencies.

---

47   'Setting up of a National Informatics Centre'.

Essentially, the Planning Commission aimed to create a separation between the people and the departments that would plan the data to be collected, stored, and retrieved, and those, such as the NIC, who implemented these plans by looking after the technical aspect of the information system. Such a conceptual-technical split has characterized the politics of NIC's work with government departments and has over the years led to a gap between intent and outcome, evident from the checkered nature of digitization projects in government.

III.

DATA EXCESS: RELATIONAL DATABASE MANAGEMENT AND DATA PROLIFERATION

Technical Specifics of RDBMS

The storage of data from a tree-based or network structure to one of rows and columns opened up possibilities for the arrangement and access to data that had not been fathomable before that. In database terminology, RDBMS changed the way 'entities', or pieces of information about the real world, could be represented and expressed. Such 'entities' included 'real' or non-digital representations of the world such as ledgers of land records, and 'relations' referred to the connection between them. RDBMS is, says one writer, a set of 'relational database systems—which organize information conceptually in a similar manner to the tabular layout of a spreadsheet, but with concurrent access, transactional reliability, and a flexible querying interface' that 'ultimately became the dominant technology for storage and retrieval of structured data in commercial businesses and the de facto standard on the web', providing the 'technical core of a vast, global transformation of enterprise data processing and management'.[48] Rather than using pointers between entities in a network relation, and thereby enforcing some sort of referential link between entities (such as the hierarchical relation in the DBMS that the Planning Commission had built in the 70s), storage of data in tabular formats was not based on prior referential connection, but rather on the possibility of expressing those connections whenever desired. This difference can also be understood as the attempt of the networked model to mimic a real-world physical relationship into symbolic, tabular forms.

These differences between DBMS and RDBMS started becoming apparent to me as I began meeting database administrators.[49] Most, if not all, were part of the NIC which has since grown from being a small part of the Planning Commission into a full-fledged organization. Most were young engineers who had worked for a few years on contract for the NIC or elsewhere, and had slowly been elevated into permanent employees. Many spoke about data security, some

---

48   Michael Castelle, 'Relational and Non-Relational Models in the Entextualization of Bureaucracy', *Computational Culture* 3 (November 2013). http://computationalculture.net/relational-and-non-relational-models-in-the-entextualization-of-bureaucracy/.
49   This was between August and September 2019 at the NIC in Shillong.

about design. In between rough sketches of tables, my notebook began to carry statements such as 'design is both art and science', 'a good designer sees the database in his mind before he sets about building the database'. Called an 'entity-relation' (or E-R) diagram, these young database administrators (DBAs) claimed that they would use paper and pen to labor over the multiple relations that now appeared possible between 'entities'.

Since the NIC builds databases for government departments that already have some form of storage mechanism in a physical format, drawing the E-R meant having to understand, from the ledgers and registers waiting to be digitized and databased, what relations existed between the entities. Engineers call this 'domain knowledge', accrued over many years of hanging out with staff whose work they aimed to digitize. I saw this repeatedly across departments. One or two DBAs would have developed close ties with some staff in the government office and that connection would seem to power the progress of the database projects.

Once the E-R was established through flowchart-like diagrams, the actual project began. Unlike a tree or network-based database structure, the E-R did not determine structure by itself, but instead showed all the relations possible between entities. Based on these relational possibilities, the entities were ordered into tables, with other constraints in mind, such as not increasing the columns of a table beyond 15. This was the background of tables. The front itself was an interactive screen that allowed for various combinations of the entities to be seen. Codd, when pioneering the database model, had stressed on this feature of RDBMS,[50] and indeed the fact that people using it did not have to worry about the ordering of the tables or the E-R relations would be a critical component of its commercial success.

A critical aspect of this symbolic view of data was the technique of indexing or pulling up different sets of records and presenting them in a picture that allowed them to be viewed together in different combinations. Without indexing, databases had to be queried one record at a time, defeating the very purpose it was set up for, namely quick access to different slices of data. Indexes are built using unique identifiers (or the 'primary key' in database language) for every record. A 'pointer' with the location of the record in the disk on which the database is stored is created, so that querying a record means going directly to where that record is located. While the index itself is large, querying times reduce, taking us to the next inevitable level of multiple higher-level indices, created with pointers to an underlying index, and then to the data tables. This combined index structure, allowing a faster search, the addition, modification or deletion of records, or the 'B-Tree index', was invented in the 70s. In Castelle's words, 'without this technique, relational models would likely have remained as inefficient as their detractors often predicted'.[51]

Such a relational model brought with it new ways of organizing data on a disk, and newer and faster ways of accessing individual records of that data. It also importantly brought about an accessible interface to the 'casual user' now no longer limited to the programmer and independent from the structure of the data on the disk. This software interface, along

50   Castelle, 'Relational and Non-Relational Models'.
51   Castelle, 'Relational and Non-Relational Models'.

with larger random access devices (that allowed for many more locations for storing data tables), allowed for simultaneous work on the data from different locations, not possible in the prior models. This in turn enabled 'on-line transaction processing' or OLAP, made possible by the RDBMS defining criteria for online transactions.

The value of RDBMS began to be seen against the acronym ACID. It is worth understanding what ACID actually means, since this defines the expectations that corporate organizations have for RDBMS. *Atomicity* is meant to indicate that 'individual transactions either occur or – if aborted – have no effect; *Consistency* – the data appears in correct, valid state all the time; *Isolation* – transactions are isolated from one another; this is equivalent to the appearance of serialized execution; *Durability* – successful transactions persist and do not disappear or become corrupted in the case of failures'.[52]

At the heart of ACID was the desire for a robust system that would ensure 'information retrieval' of rapidly changing entities which organizational theorists had identified since the 50s as central to bureaucratic organizations. Yet, it wasn't information in its entirety that was needed to be available all the time. Instead, like the management consultant Peter Drucker said of the business executive, 'problems have to be presented to him in a form which allows him to act, that is stripped of everything not pertaining to the business of the moment'.[53] By making databases ACID-compliant, information retrieval could happen selectively.

RDBMS and the Entrepreneurial Spirit

Inevitably, the arrival of RDBMS in India became complicated. Given that it was specifically designed for commercial use in the US, its adoption by industry in India matched expectations. But, what of the government? Did government in India need or use OLAP and, by extension, did it need the support that RDBMS was intended to provide? Older engineers are surprised when I ask the question. To them, RDBMS has become so ubiquitous that it does not warrant discussion. They remember the NIC switching from DBMS to RDBMS as a natural progression of things, from the older to the newer. It was hard to get people to think about what value RDBMS was actually adding to their work. It began to appear that the significant leap in the digitization of India's government, paralleling the growth of RDBMS in the country, was simply viewed in evolutionary terms.

While this is chronologically true, I shall challenge the assumption that RDBMS meets the same requirements in government as in the corporations it was meant for. More importantly, when one pays attention to *what* is digitized within government and *how* that stands in relation to its physical form, one finds that RDBMS may not have after all been employed in government for the reasons for it had been originally invented. Let us question its efficacy, in relation to the risk that is posed by digital data, by returning to the instances of leakage I had introduced at the beginning of this essay.

52   Castelle, 'Relational and Non-Relational Models'.
53   David Alan Grier, 'The Relational Database and the Concept of the Information System', *IEEE Annals of the History of Computing* 34.4 (2012): 13.

First, however, a short description of the promises and perils of RDBMS and the entrepreneurial spirit it gave rise to as it entered India in the 90s. In several of the statements of its early promoters can also be read a call for responsibility as a potential for better governance of the nation. Such a spirit would be further tied to the arrival of 'experts', different from incumbent bureaucrats and managers, leading eventually, I suggest below in my example of the digitization of land ownership data, to a further weakening of control over data. Most significantly, it would lead to an ensuing shift in responsibility – from entrepreneurs to citizen-beneficiaries governed, in large measure, by new citizenship responsibilities arising from the excesses of entrepreneurial overattention to digitization.

The ten-year period between the late 80s and late 90s marked heightened activity in the marketing of RDBMS in India. According to a NASSCOM study, domestic RDBMS sales went up by 90 percent in 1994–95 compared to the previous year.[54] The 200 firms established by the mid-80s in the US database industry selling 'DBMS software, tools, and related products', emerging out of the heady California 'start-up' days, were making forays into other markets, particularly in South and Southeast Asia.[55] Firms like IBM, Oracle, Ingres, Informix, and Sybase had had an established presence in India by the mid-90s. Informix, started by a computer engineer at UC Berkeley named Roger Sippal, tied up with the Indian software firm IDM in 1989, the same year that it started offering OLAP transactions with Informix Online.[56] Informix was the first to create an SQL-based RDBMS for DOS in 1986. The *Times of India* reported this alliance as revolutionary, for it 'gives users decision-making powers by offering them access to information regardless of database location or desktop platform [...] helping define standards that will make technology more accessible and affordable to users'.[57]

Meanwhile, Sybase, best known for aiding the computerization of Wall Street in the mid-80s with its RDBMS software product made exclusively for Sun Microsystems' client-server configuration, tied up with Hindustan Computers Ltd., better known as HCL, to expand their database sales in Southeast Asia. The alliance specifically offered 'a Sybase solution along with database consulting, training and programming services'.[58] Even though it was IBM where knowledge of relational technology was first generated (Codd was at IBM when he wrote his pioneering paper),[59] it was Oracle that would be credited with the commercial success of RDBMS.[60] In May 1991, Oracle opened a liaison office to 'coordinate localization for India [...] as a market with a lot of exciting potential'.[61] Its major customer in India was the government – the Centre for Railway Information Systems (CRIS), All India Institute

54 Dewang Mehta, 'India on the Global Pathway', *Times of India*, 7 February 1996, ProQuest Historical Newspapers.
55 Campbell-Kelly, 'The RDBMS Industry', p. 18.
56 'IDM-Informix Tie-up', *Times of India*, 24 December 1989, ProQuest Historical Newspapers.
57 'IDM-Informix Tie-up'.
58 Aprajita Sikri, 'A US-Indian Database Venture', *India Abroad*, 1 June 1990, ProQuest Historical Newspapers.
59 Campbell-Kelly, 'The RDBMS Industry', p. 21.
60 Campbell-Kelly, 'The RDBMS Industry', p. 22.
61 'Oracle Opens India Liaison Office', *Dataquest*, 1991, https://itihaasa.com/describe/artefact/001_001_0568?referenceYear=1991.

of Medical Sciences (AIIMS), Steel Authority of India (SAIL), and Centre for Development of Telematics (C-DoT).[62] By 1993, Oracle had set up a fully functional Indian subsidiary, and Indian companies like Infosys, TCS, and others had begun manufacturing and selling RDBMS software.

RDBMS was also recognized and circulated as a specific computer skill, along with programming languages of the day, and advertisements for both students and faculty were put out regularly.[63] Job calls for 'programmers and system managers who had experience with RDBMS' and even more specifically with Oracle or Ingres, were widely placed for both local and multinational companies.[64] *Times of India*'s 'On the Move' section that tracked hiring and movement of corporate honchos, lists in 1993 the hiring by Datamatics of a general manager for RDBMS.[65] In editorials, writers waxed eloquent about its transformational possibilities. Madhu Valluri, a regular contributor to the *Times of India*, wrote, for example, about how a computer system developed in the US to track and communicate environmental disasters could provide an 'insight into what's actually going on around us [...] at a touch of a key'.[66] Valluri complained that 'today, not a single state government has access to instant information about the chemical composition of its rivers. Neither there is any biological information of its marine life'[67], and setting up RDBMS systems would enable all of that.

Outside government, RDBMS was deployed in multiple industries – automobiles (for instance, Maruti introduced Oracle RDBMS in 1994 to keep track of millions of moving parts in its Gurgaon manufacturing assembly) and, most visibly, the financial sector comprising banks, stock exchanges, and other financial institutions. Further examples include deployment for a 'screen-based order-and-quote trading system'[68] for the National Stock Exchange, Delhi Stock Exchange, and Pune Stock Exchange. In the late 90s, after its success with Finacle, Infosys created BANCS 2000, an RDBMS for the banking sector offering an information system and decision support system under one roof[69] that was later described as 'a core on-line transaction product operating in 300 sites for 22 banks in seven countries'.[70]

A specific challenge to the banking sector was posed by nationalized banks. Tata Consultancy Services was already in the fray for the automation of nationalized banks, which constituted

---

62   'Oracle Opens India Liaison Office'.
63   'Nalanda Computer Education for RDBMS', *The Times of India*, 29 May 1991, ProQuest Historical Newspapers.
64   'Overseas Appointments', *The Times of India*, 20 September 1992, ProQuest Historical Newspapers; 'Appointments,' *The Times of India*, 6 April 1993, ProQuest Historical Newspapers; 'Tata Unisys Ltd', *The Times of India*, 28 December 1993, ProQuest Historical Newspapers.
65   'On the Move', *The Times of India*, 22 March 1993, ProQuest Historical Newspapers.
66   Madhu Valluri, 'How Info-tech can Help Environment', *The Times of India*, 14 April 1993, ProQuest Historical Newspapers.
67   Valluri, 'How Info-tech can Help Environment'.
68   'Pune Bourse Goes Online'.
69   '4-Day Conference Opens', *The Times of India*, 8 February 1996, ProQuest Historical Newspapers.
70   Rajesh Y.P., 'Software Firms Eye a Pie in Banking', *News - India Times*, 10 July 1998, ProQuest Historical Newspapers

by one estimate a market share of INR 250 crore.[71] What these companies offered was a powerful RDBMS that would conduct the operations of 'calculation of demand and time liability, fund and non-fund based advances such as loans, overdrafts and letters of credit. The software also took care of remittances, safe keeping operations and foreign exchange accounts'.[72] Another writer speculated that a computerized system in nationalized banks 'should be able to handle five to 10 million customer accounts and eight to 10 lakh transactions per day and at the same time provide acceptable response time per transaction'. He recommended a key technical requirement, a 'relational database management system [...] providing parallel server rollback and recovery along with features like two phase commit'.[73] All that was missing was a 'concerted marketing thrust' to get banks to show 'enthusiasm for computerization'.

This luminous career of RDBMS in private corporations, particularly financial ones, gave it a veneer of efficacy that was now being sought to be transferred into the realm of government. As with the nationalized banks mentioned above, commentators of the time found it surprising that governments were not adopting RDBMS as rapidly as they ought to have. To interrogate this roadblock – and thus to also interrogate the assumption that since RDBMS was 'good' for multisited organizations with a requirement for high transaction capability, like banks, it would also necessarily be beneficial for government – we need to make a distinction between *transaction-based* government services operating in multiple locations in huge volumes (such as the Indian railways online ticketing, an oft-repeated example) and the daily work of writing, recording, and filing inside government bureaucracies, the focus of technology-mediated 'transparency' reforms (such as the management of land records through databases, discussed below). While the former lends itself to RDBMS use, it is the latter that requires us to question RDBMS' efficacy. Land records, when digitized, are not transacted online in the same way that bank functions are, nor is there any 'intelligence' generated from their arrangement in an RDBMS upon which the government acts. A land records database is as much controlled by a paper economy as the physical records had once been. These sites, I argue, have also engendered greater risk of leakage, leading to data excesses.

An example of successful use of RDBMS in transacting services offered by the government is that of the digitization of the railways booking system. By the 90s, the Indian Railways Passenger Reservation System (PRS), one of the largest and most important information systems of the Indian Railways (itself the world's largest railway network) had begun to totter. Even while it was a functioning system, although it had expanded to computerized ticket reservation, it nevertheless required visits to the train station or to a PRS reservation office, and often the assistance of tourist operators. With low-cost airlines offering competitive prices and easier ways of booking tickets over the internet, the challenge before CRIS was

71   Moneesh Narula, 'Bank Automation Gets Competitive', *The Times of India*, 4 September 1993, ProQuest Historical Documents.
72   Narula, 'Bank Automation Gets Competitive'.
73   T. Narayanaswami, 'The Central Solution', *The Times of India*, 7 May 1996, ProQuest Historical Documents.

to make a system on which PRS could be accessible from many more locations, including the home, and flexible enough to accommodate real-time updates. In other words, to meet the 'service' aspiration of upwardly mobile middle-class passengers. Unsurprisingly, these demands were believed to have been met by an RDBMS system.[74]

Yet not everyone was convinced. A top official at CRIS said, 'the benefits of emerging from changing over to a RDBMS from the current flat file system might not be commensurate with the resources expended'.[75] Other sceptics within the ministry questioned its efficacy, or whether the need for passengers for 'more avenues for reservation services' could have been 'met without disturbing the core of the system: in fact, world-wide, major high-volume ticketing systems were still being run on file-based platforms, rather than DBMSs'.[76] Even as RDBMS in the railway reservation system has been seen as an important technology, a minority belief in the department has remained that the volume of transactions produced with ticket reservation going online with the Indian Railways Catering and Tourism Corporation (IRCTC) was possible even without RDBMS. Even so, RDBMS made possible a scale and distribution of service delivery that had been hitherto unfathomable before the use of relational systems.

What should be more visible to any researcher of electronic governance in India, but is rarely the focus of analysis, is where the technical possibilities offered by RDBMS have produced spillover effects that have hurt rather than helped the entrepreneurial imagination of governance. In these situations, RDBMS lends itself to performative impulses that substitute for the more straightforward practical opportunities that have defined what we have named the entrepreneurial spirit. From a purely empirical stance, such situations also depict the incommensurability of RDBMS for the linear hierarchies of administrative governance. But its continued and even celebrated uses for these exact purposes calls for an accounting of its *effects* which, I argue, are to be found in the shifting terrain of citizen responsibility in and of the data produced for their governance.

My main example to describe these shifts is the system of land records management that began to be used from the late 90s to centralize ownership data with RDBMS. Historically, the recording of landownership was a colonial enterprise, as has been widely documented. It was usually the responsibility of village accountants who had custodial control over their production and maintenance, and who became powerful figures in village economies as

---

74   In the words of the international authors presenting a case study of PRS transformation in Milwaukee, 'RDBMS-based data management, in place of the older file-based data management sub-system was being used. A decade ago, RDBMSs had been expensive and resource-intensive, and the desired user response times had been difficult to obtain in large RDBMS-based applications. Nowadays, hardware resources were no longer a constraint, and the flexible data structures possible with an RDBMS core would greatly enhance overall application flexibility'. See Shirish C. Srivastava, Sharat Mathur and Thompson Teo, 'Modernization of Passenger Reservation System: Indian Railway's Dilemma, *ICIS 2006 Proceedings* 98 (2006). http://aisel.aisnet.org/icis2006/98.

75   Srivastava et al., 'Modernization of Passenger Reservation System', p. 434.

76   Srivastava et al., 'Modernization of Passenger Reservation System', p. 437.

a result.[77] In the late 80s, and following the World Bank's belief inspired by claims made by the Peruvian economist Hernando de Soto that securing property titles could eradicate poverty, many countries vigorously took up the challenge to 'clean up' their records. Such a cleanup, often powered by the belief that the physical form of the record was in a mess, sought to digitize the record, usually in a first phase dedicated to 'conclusive titling' of land, followed by a documentary system that gave owners full and legal title over land (unlike the present, colonial-origin presumptive titling of land in India which does not guarantee individual title). Modernization of land records was closely linked to the belief that databases could provide the clarity needed to what were considered opaque practices of record keeping by village accountants. The concept was first formalized by the Planning Commission when India's Prime Minister Manmohan Singh was still its deputy chairman.[78]

In came a number of technology companies aiming to digitize land records. In Karnataka, Comat technologies first built a Fox Base DBMS system in the late 90s but then quickly transitioned into an RDBMS when it became more affordable.[79] The same RDBMS database has existed since then, and other than offering itself as a digital registry for printing copies of land records, it has not been used for much else.

None of the original aims — creating a market in land, analyzing the extent of land types under the supervision of the government, all of which an RDBMS could enable one to do — have even been attempted. The printing of digitized records, its primary purpose, had been possible even with a file-based structure of storing data. In Haryana's Kurukshetra, where a database was created around the same time as Bangalore, the architect, now the director of the NIC in Kurukshetra, complained that as a young employee building the database in the RDBMS 'environment' there were multiple opportunities for 'analytics', but he had not been given the opportunity to explore any of this.[80] On the one hand, senior bureaucrats have claimed that land records have been modernized through technology, and have received national and international appreciation for this. On the other hand, the undergirding of this apparent modernization with RDBMS has not been exploited to perform any kind of analytical work on the records. The irony of this is not lost on observers, who point out that India's prowess in IT does not seem to be applied to its modern land records.[81] In essence, even when land records *were* digitized, their production was never separated from the dense practices of paper-based verification and authentication. The figures and numbers seen in the database are only the symbolic representation of an intricate process of record creation located between the field and the office.

---

77   R.S. Smith, 'Rule-by-Records and Rule-by-Reports: Complementary Aspects of British Imperial Rule of Law', *Contributions to Indian sociology* 19.1 (1985): 153–176.
78   D.C. Wadhwa, 'Guaranteeing Title to Land', *Economic and Political Weekly* 37.47 (2002): 4704.
79   Personal conversation with the cofounder of Comat Technologies, Ravi Ranjan, in August 2019 in Bangalore.
80   Personal conversation with the director of NIC Kurukshetra in July 2018.
81   At the India Land and Development Conference 2020, Tim Hanstead, the CEO of Landesa, pointed out that it was ironical that India leads the world in IT, but in the 20 years that the program on land modernization has seen, very little progress has been achieved.

Locating Excesses of Digitization in the Structure of RDBMS

Even while RDBMS databases have not made land governance more 'intelligent' – arguably the key purpose for which these databases were set up and aggressively marketed – has it made the *management* of that data more risky? In this transition from records in physical registers to records on a database, multiple aspects of control have been compromised. First, the already existing gap between what is actually happening on a piece of land and what records signify has only further widened. The reason usually lies in the very processes that had brought database to life for, even as databases marked a disjuncture from the practices of village accountants, its original architects depended on those very accountants to verify the first version of digital records. They were often nothing but physical records typed by young men and women working on poorly paid contracts for the government. Verification took so long that the status of the land had often changed by the time digital records were finally approved.[82] Far from becoming intelligent, the quality of information in fact suffered, not to mention the copious amount of time invested in sorting out these errors.

A second, more technical, question lay around storage and access, and the potential for manipulation. The RDBMS for land records in Karnataka includes an entity called 'surnoc' or survey number character denoted by a '*'. This asterisk had been included in the database as an identifier for the first parcel of land split from a bigger plot. For instance, for survey number 32, if a *hissa* or split is recorded by one of the joint owners, the first split gets survey number 32* to differentiate it from the original number 32. This convention was originally created when the database was built, and it was discovered that previously split land was not being given a separate record. What the database architect didn't consider was that putting in a * for any survey number in the database – that is entering a * in the surnoc column – generated a *new* legitimate record that could be legitimately used for legitimate transactions.

A senior bureaucrat explained how in an office in his charge, a series of such offenses came to light when a new database operator accidentally gave a farmer the 'wrong' version of the record, that is, a version created by a 'surnoc' or duplicate to an original survey number. On the basis of this new record, the unscrupulous operator, according to the bureaucrat, took loans that the farmer was shocked to now discover. On hearing this, the bureaucrat telephoned the main operator manning the centralized database and asked him to dig out all cases in which new false records were created using the surnoc. A litany of cases emerged, operators were fired, and conniving village accountants slapped with criminal cases. The bureaucrat ended this story by saying that this problem has now been fixed by another new and more tech-savvy commissioner of land records in the state.

These were only some of the instances of the many problems that RDBMS databases had created. Even with the new commissioner, multiple cases arose of 'breaking into' the

---

82   This was made apparent to me in conversations with the architect of the Bhoomi database in Bangalore, in August 2019.

database to make changes. A case was reported in 2018 in which 19 acres of government wasteland were transferred to a private individual.[83] The report also claimed that it was the third reported time such a 'breach' had occurred in which government land was transferred to private people. It is interesting that the commissioner chose to respond by differentiating a 'breach' from a 'hack', saying that the 'Bhoomi software cannot be *hacked* at all'[84] and that 'in both cases, some person has *breached* the security and logged into the system to change the database'.[85] It could not be hacked from outside the institution because it wasn't online (there has only recently been some move to create an online database for Bhoomi), and not because there was anything inherently insecure about it. In the literature, a 'security breach' includes '*unauthorized data observation, incorrect data modification, and data unavailability*'.[86] The records in Bhoomi have been found to be replete with missing information – discovered, on several occasions, in different versions of records printed at different points in time.

More importantly, the commissioner's remarks obscure the fact that it was the very village-level records in their physical registers, and their process of being databased and stored in the subdistrict, that created the conditions for this violation. Databasing by its very nature, and particularly RDBMS with its tables and easy format, provides the opportunity to access and change data. In database terminology, such kinds of invasion are called 'direct attacks' as 'the attacker can easily attack the database as it does not have any protection mechanism'.[87] The not-so-user-friendly file-based structure of the database is often more secure against intervention, an unintended consequence of design since a user needed to know the structure of the database in order to access it. In RDBMS, on the other hand, any access to the SQL program that interfaces the data behind it also allows access to database tables.

One way of securing such access was by introducing an encryption key that made the data unreadable, as the commissioner eventually said about the land record data under Bhoomi: 'As a first step, we are encrypting the whole of Bhoomi data. This will prevent even officials from seeing the database'.[88] Encryption has been a long-standing method for securing data in RDBMS, the literature pointing to many kinds of tools and techniques for such

---

83   Akshatha M, 'Land Sharks Hack Bhoomi Data, Shift Government Land Title', *The Economic Times*, 10 September 2018, https://economictimes.indiatimes.com/news/politics-and-nation/land-sharks-hack-bhoomi-data-shift-government-land-title/articleshow/65749538.cms.
84   Bhoomi software, introduced to digitize land records, came into being in 2002.
85   Akshatha, 'Land Sharks Hack Bhoomi Data'.
86   Elisa Bertino and Ravi Sandhu, 'Database Security—Concepts, Approaches, and Challenges', *IEEE Transactions on Dependable and Secure Computing* 2.1 (2005): 2.
87   Michael Geertz and Madhavi Gandhi, 'Security Re-engineering for Databases: Concepts and Techniques', in Michael Geertz and Sushil Jajodia (eds) *Handbook of Database Security: Applications and Trends*, New York: Springer, 2008, pp. 267–298.
88   Geertz and Gandhi, 'Security Re-engineering for Databases'.

encryption to prevent 'intrusion'.[89] There have also been critiques of encryption itself, such as the argument that it can 'significantly degrade the system performance and application response time'.[90] Encryption remains at best an incomplete solution to the basic problem of 'security threats' that Geertz and Jajodia suggest arise from the following basic fact:

> Today's often mission-critical databases no longer contain only data used for day-to-day processing by organization; as new applications are being added, it is possible for organizations to collect and store vast amounts of data quickly and efficiently and to make the data readily accessible to the public, typically through Web-based applications.[91]

Scholarship on data security often starts with such observations: 'As organizations increase their reliance on, possibly distributed, information systems for daily business, they become more vulnerable to security breaches even as they gain productivity and efficiency advantaged'.[92] Even though Bhoomi does not (so far) operate on the web, its data is spread across databases connected via leased lines located in multiple subdistricts, and there are plans to connect them into a centralized web-based architecture. In this situation, encryption is admittedly a way forward, but it has its limits.

Data finds new locations with RDBMS, even as concerns for data security recommend limiting 'access' points or making the data unreadable through encryption. This ability of data to be located in multiple locations in the same tabular formats allows for *an imagination of modularity*, alongside a *replicability of homogenous form across varied contexts*.

Such an imagination would, in 2006, undergird the ambitious NeGP: a densely packed policy for digitizing all government administration and services across many domains of life. The NeGP is often seen as having brought together a trinity of material forms in its effusive modernization project. Called 'core IT infrastructure', this included leased internet lines integrated into a State Wide Area Network or SWAN that offered high speed connectivity between web applications offered at CSCs but which were actually stored in SDCs. This was an institutional arrangement for the maintenance of databases and networks at a single fixed location in the state capital. Front-ends of the application, producing say birth and death certificates available at CSCs, would be produced through SWAN's link to a back-end linked to a data center in the state capital. All this operated entirely on a client-server model enabled by RDBMS.

---

89   Harshavardhan Kayarkar, 'Classification of Various Security Techniques in Databases and their Comparative Analysis', *arXiv preprint arXiv* 1206.4124 (2012): 1 and Seul-Gi Choi and Sung-Bae Cho, 'Evolutionary Reinforcement Learning for Adaptively Detecting Database Intrusions', *Logic Journal of the IGPL* 28.4 (2020): 449–460.
90   Y. Khmelevsky, 'Information and Data Protection Within a RDBMS', *Condensed Matter Physics* 11.4 (2008): 761–765.
91   Michael Geertz and Sushil Jajodia (eds) *Handbook of Database Security: Applications and Trends*, New York: Springer, 2008, p. v.
92   Bertino and Sandhu, 'Database Security, p. 2.

A guidelines document lists several features expected of RDBMS for developing applications stored in SDC. The RDBMS should, it says, 'support data base partitioning and parallel processing', 'have support for generation, consumption of XML data and XML based query capabilities', 'allow multi-dimensional OLAP capabilities for Data Warehousing'.[93] It further suggests that the RDBMS should adopt industry standards to ensure interoperability between databases.[94]

A couple of years after RDBMS began to be employed for applications, a study conducted by two computer scientists for 14 e-government services in the state of Himachal Pradesh in north India in 2010 concluded that 'the development of e-government applications invariably lacks conforming to standard database design parameters'.[95] They found several problems of multiple parameters of database design, important among them being the absence of primary or foreign keys which greatly reduced the 'referential integrity' or the validity of the relation between two tables, absence of a 'constraint mechanism' to verify data that can enter a database and 'poor E-R design' that pointed to the fact that databases had not 'developed any conceptual schema and databases are designed on ad hoc manner'.[96] The last two aspects pointed to reduced security measures in the databases, as unverified data entries and poor E-R design could make databases open to breaches or attacks. Many of the databases were made by the NIC in Himachal Pradesh, and it is possible to find similar problems with databases in other states as the NIC is known to share its design principles.

Repair of Data and the 'Slow' Violence of Excess

That databases being built for government are falling short on design and security is one aspect of the problem. A more trenchant issue is the 'breakdown' of data produced by the *excess* of the technical structure of RDBMS, as we have seen with Bhoomi. A significant and under-discussed aspect of this breakdown is the labor involved in the repair and correction of data, and the way such labor has been shifted onto the citizens. Claims to citizenship through access to rights and entitlements depend increasingly critically on this responsibility of repair, so that for many people citizenship is experienced only through the practice of data repair.

This is not the same as the neoliberal impulse of responsibilization, where citizens keep their data updated in their own best interest. What I am trying to point to is an unintended fallout of this impulse – a fallout of precisely the opportunity promoted by RDBMS, through technologies of government to sort out citizen-subject relations in a discrete and transactable fashion. Just as claims to rights and entitlements are made unequally, repair too is practiced unevenly. This is not a problem of capacity, rather it is the concealment of data error within ongoing material disruptions between citizens and states. When citizens are required to

---

93   'eDistrict Mission Mode Project Under the National eGovernance Plan. Pilot Implementation Guidelines',
        Department of Information Technology, Government of India, January 2009, https://www.meity.gov.in/
        writereaddata/files/eDistGuidelines_Feb09(rev1).pdf.
94   'eDistrict Mission Mode Project Under the National eGovernance Plan'.
95   Amar Jeet Singh and Rajesh Chauhan, 'E-Government Databases: A Retrospective Study', Indian
        Journal of Computer Science and Engineering 1.2 (2010): 72.
96   Singh and Chauhan, 'E-Government Databases', p. 71.

bear the responsibility of repair, it is not a visible transfer of responsibility, rather it is a tacit, neglected, fringe encounter, embroiled within ongoing material disruptions between the citizen and the state.

Before I turn to the empirical example to support all that I am saying here, let me propose one final outcome of this form of unintended responsibility emerging from relations produced *through* the very technical opportunities that RDBMS offers. Violence, disaster, and breakdown are familiar experiences when negotiating with states. Experiencing citizenship-through-repair is often not a spectacular crisis or disaster, nor is it a stark infrastructural breakdown or the choking of infrastructural time. Repairing data is instead best viewed as temporal vacuity, a state of limbo, a temporary break from ongoing relationships. It is not structural violence in the usual way of describing state procedures (though there is some overlap). Nor is it spectacular violence. I propose to think of it as a temporary, circuitous low-grade suffering, and so a form of 'slow' violence that scholars have begun to attribute to the slow-moving temporalities of suffering.[97] *Such violence of data repair, as a mechanism of citizenship, is slow because it proceeds at a speed that distances suffering from its original causes.* Repair is embedded in familiar structures so that citizens are unable to any more distinguish the repair of data from the other bureaucratic processes within which they are often mired.

I continue, as I now explicate this pattern of digitization and data repair, with my example of land records digitization and its database-driven excesses. We turn now to the repair work that goes into data rehabilitation. The split experienced between the digital record itself and the paperwork that continues to surround it is experienced by farmers as a form of harassment – often physical, involving multiple trips to offices, courts, hiring and paying advocates, waiting for months sometimes years to have their errors resolved. It produces a growing disjunction between the overt promise of transparent, speedy, and clear databases, and the substantive experience of vacuity produced by the errors – a form of ironic, symbolic violence.

A few pointed out that people have been urged, since the turn of the millennium, to become 'e-citizens', to conduct their business with the state online. Encrypted, barcoded, digitally signed land records can be printed out from internet cafes boasted a young engineer, a Bhoomi consultant. But, as often is the case, when it was revealed that the record has something amiss – a name wrong, the extent of land incorrect, missing information about the crops on land, in essence a record paralyzed in an identification-based ecosystem of entitlements – people were asked to go back into the dreary world of paper records and fish out from the dense physicality of the paper record room the claims about who you are and what you own.

The rehabilitation of these digital errors opens up another side of the process, namely the administrative-legal procedures of record keeping and record rehabilitation. In order for an error to be corrected, it must first be made legible to the bureaucracy. This is done by reinscribing it as a 'dispute' between the owner of land and the head of the office to which

---

97   Rob Nixon, *Slow Violence and the Environmentalism of the Poor*, Cambridge, MA: Harvard University Press, 2011.

the record belongs. A dispute calls for a specific arrangement of documentary material with specific inscriptional work, described below.

Once presented as a dispute, it is put through a revenue court process in the office of a senior bureaucrat, higher than the head of the office in which the error, now renamed dispute, is lodged. The court process takes its own discursive path, ending up in an order that either accepts the applicant's request for correction or rejects it by asking for more supporting documents. If accepted, it comes back to the office where a 'mutation' process begins to make changes in the digital record. This entire process points to why a digital error cannot be corrected digitally, since an error is not identified simply as a typographical error and thus becomes a much more complex legal problem.

A specific feature of the correction process is that the law, on which the bureaucratic process is based, makes it incumbent on the *owner* to prove to the bureaucrats that there is indeed a correct version of the data that is identified as erroneous. This is irrespective of the source of the error. The effects of such a transfer of responsibility were made starkly apparent to me in a conversation between an owner and a Bhoomi operator who had just made an error on his application for change in the record. The operator had incorrectly entered the wrong name for a particular record, and the application had now left her 'login' which meant that she could no longer edit it. As part of the state government's ever-evolving strategy of gaining further control on the production of the record, deleting an application at the office level was not an option any more. When the next bureaucrat in Bhoomi's workflow sequence received it and verified the owner's name on the screen with what was in the copy of an older paper document, the *Aakar Band* provided as part of the application, she marked the application as an error. At this point the application left the 'mutation' flow and went into a 'dispute' list of cases that now needed a scanned court order to be put back into the mutation process. The owner in question was, in the operator's words, 'scolding' her for making this mistake as he would now have to run around to have it corrected. The owner bears the brunt of the state's centralizing logic that, as becomes further evident, draws heavily on a colonial logic in which an owner's rights are presumptive on her ability to prove at every point in time that her records are indeed correct, in order to continue to validate the authenticity of the record and thus to produce the ethos of fairness and transparency attached to data transaction.

The correction of records often involves chasing files in a circular fashion as they move within multiple government offices and as clients move from office to office. Not every record holder makes all these trips in person. Sometimes these are mediated by brokers or advocates who represent record holders in revenue courts, or by office clerks themselves for a fee. Essentially, record holders have to strike a balance between bearing the burden of running around by themselves at the cost of losing out on working on their farms or paying bribes to have it done for them. This depends on the socioeconomic status of the owners, with rich landowners (identified locally as people owning 15-20 acres of land) being able to afford bribes to hire mediators to do the job. How soon a dispute will come up for hearing depends on how networked the advocate hired is with the office clerks and how much money the record holder is willing to pay to get the job done. Even when admitted, cases take multiple hearings to finally produce an order. The magistrate sometimes asks the record holder or his representative to return with more documents to bolster the file. Building a file becomes an accretive process, and the only way documents are accepted is through physical submission to the magistrate.

The Bhoomi operator, whose case I described above, said that 'caseworkers' – clerks of the processual side of bureaucracy – do not work on these files quickly enough. For them it is often merely a 'drop in an ocean of files', and they need to be adequately compensated for the job. Once an application is marked as 'dispute', it falls out of the First-in-First-Out (FIFO) system (a much-advertised feature of Bhoomi), after which it depends completely on the whim of the caseworker. There is no accountability mechanism to track when an error file will come up for hearing and resolution, thus making people visit offices multiple times to check on the status. Court sessions are often cancelled because the office head is busy with other pressing work, but there is no way for record holders to know that unless they read the notice board. As a result, offices teem with large numbers of record holders hovering around the desks of office clerks in charge of handling the correction file, or in front of the court room where, in performative fashion, the head of the office will receive documents from them to add to their file as proof of their ownership.

For citizens, repairing Bhoomi data and thereby recovering their status as claimants of substantive citizenship (as opposed to legally ascribed thin citizenship) requires stepping back into the quagmire of paper bureaucracy. Here is where the first kind of entrepreneurial responsibility, of the kind that technical configurations such as RDBMS have spurred, trails off and the burdensome responsibility of the citizen emerges. The digital service of maintaining land records is put on hold until resolutions are received. This is a critical moment of reconnection with a past that had been ostensibly discontinued when the storage and dissemination of records had been made digital. The back-and-forth between owning data and being a legitimate subject of citizen services, and being saddled with the burden of repairing data and losing that status, depicts the experience of slow violence emerging in these interactions.

IV.

CONTAINING EXCESS OR RETURN TO THE LOCAL

One startling aspect of the proposed Personal Data Protection Bill in India in 2018 was its suggestion that the movement of data be curtailed by compelling organizations to store data *locally*.[98] The Justice B.N. Srikrishna Committee report on data privacy says: 'A policy of storage and processing of personal data within the territorial jurisdiction of a country is advocated to ensure effective enforcement and to secure the critical interests of the nation state.'[99]

---

98   See Committee of Experts under the Chairmanship of Justice B.N. Srikrishna, *A Free and Fair Digital Economy*. Hereafter referred to as the Srikrishna report.
99   Srikrishna report, p. 82.

'Local' here meant *national*: that is, data produced in the country should remain in the country. If this becomes law, it will singlehandedly upend the relationship between technological infrastructures and globalization. There are many technologies of globalization, and databases are one of them. As Benjamin Baez argues, databases are 'informational technologies leading to a new communication system, one increasingly speaking a universal, digital language and integrating globally the production and distribution of the words, sounds, and images of our culture'.[100] In other words, databases are what make movement from local to global possible. Recall that RDBMS was a commercial success because it was marketed as a solution to the problem of organizational spread *across* geographies. In Grier's words, 'Cocd developed a structure that allowed business people to focus on certain kinds of relationships. These relationships determined how businesses thought about their customers, their bills, and their employees' *across regions*.[101] In fact, Grier compares the organization of the World Wide Web to Codd's relationship structure: 'It [the Web] was clearly built upon the ideas that Codd developed. Those ideas could be seen in the databases that supported the Web, spreadsheets, and even in the organization of data scratched hastily on a pad of paper'.[102] If RDBMS (or other such technological infrastructures) are now restricted to national borders, the change they will inevitably undergo is right now unfathomable.

Going 'local' is the Indian government's most aggressive strategy yet to prevent what I am calling 'excess', but it is definitely not the instance where the state has tried to comprehend data security. At the heart of data localization is the question of whether security is inherently related to the physical proximity of data. What distinguishes the Indian government's past attempts at data security has been that control over data has actually *centered on its mobility, not its containment*, arising from the foundational concern for keeping *movement* of data alive. Whether it was in the calls for legislation to counter the risks of data theft as early as the 70s, as I discuss below, or the development of a multination standardized framework for conducting information technology audits in government, security has been thought of in terms of speed and mobility of data. Calls for localization as a form of containment in a bid to counter excess can transform the entire attempt at digitization that this essay has tracked since the mid-70s. In this section, we trace past attempts at securing data against excesses to point to different strategies employed, by both state and non-state, and contrast these with the present attempt at data localization. This is not an argument either for or against data localization, rather it shows how, in returning to an imagination of immobility of data when it exists in physical registers, we are seeing a return to an earlier imagination. This return is even more startling when viewed against India's ongoing history of securing data through emphasizing mobility while searching for ways to limit excess.

A starting point for tracing the genealogy of the government's concerns with data security could be the early years of information digitization, in the late 70s, when multiple

100 Benjamin Baez, *Technologies of Government: Politics and Power in the "Information Age"*, Charlotte, North Carolina: Information Age Publishing, 2014.
101 Grier, 'The Relational Database', p. 16.
102 Grier, 'The Relational Database', p. 16.

government agencies first began experimenting with centralized data centers. A seminar conducted at the Indian Institute of Public Administration in 1979, perhaps the first time that security threats to India's steady march toward digitization were discussed, opened with an evocative lecture on the perils to privacy. Justice Krishna Iyer, who would retire the following year as judge of the Kerala High Court, made an emphatic appeal to his audience (whom he addressed as 'Scientists, Sociologists, Administrators and Friends') to think seriously about the security of data: 'The problem before us is temporal – how to tame and train electronic power for the Human Cause but this is also a problem of value judgement and moral consciousness – a profound commitment to the dignity of man and progress of the world community.'[103]

The need for data's *transcendence from the territorial* – which the authors of the Personal Data Protection Bill today suggest needs to be curbed through a legal prevention of the flow of data – is already identified in this early talk by Krishna Iyer. The threat of security emerged from the fear that data may go out of hand, leading to a situation of data excess:

> The consequence of the combined achievements of the computing and communications technologies is that data collection and transmission is becoming massive in its quantity and apparently limitless in its capability. Its speed increases as its cost diminishes. Unrestrained by law, it will know no national borders [...] the notion that the State can control flows of information, difficult enough with paper and manual files becomes more difficult with instantaneous transmission of information through computer terminals in other countries.[104]

Even so, Krishna Iyer did not recommend localizing data in the way the Personal Data Protection Bill recommends. His expectation from the law was to provide what he called 'pre-emptive action' against attacks on security, sometimes belied by his distrust of the 'average lawyer and judge' whom he considered 'illiterate about designing privacy legislation suitable for the computer age'. Nevertheless, he believed that strong legal safeguards for security was the only way forward.

It is an irony that having given this lecture at the very beginning of the massive digitization attempts of the Indian state, Krishna Iyer would, toward the end of his life, fight a bitter war against Aadhaar for breaching personal security.[105] What followed, in the years after his lecture, were state-led interventions for instilling security that ranged from creating committees and reports to hiring 'ethical hackers'. Soon after Krishna Iyer's lecture, in 1980, a Committee/Panel of Specialists in the Department of Electronics, set up in the Electronic Commission to advise it on 'problems of ensuring security of information while using electronic data processing (EDP) equipment', submitted its final report.[106] The report consisted of the work of

103 'Setting up of a National Informatics Centre'.
104 'Setting up of a National Informatics Centre'. Emphasis is mine.
105 'Why Late Justice Krishna Iyer Opposed Biometric Aadhaar', *ToxicsWatch*, 10 December 2014, http://www.toxicswatch.org/2014/12/why-late-justice-krishna-iyer-opposed.html.
106 'Setting up of a National Informatics Centre'.

six working group committees to draft guidelines on various aspects of security. These groups included members from the NIC, the Intelligence Bureau, the army, scientists from Tata Institute of Fundamental Research (TIFR), and civil servants. The report that they produced was detailed, covering multiple aspects of data production and communication. But as a Special Invitee to the final meeting of the committee from the Ministry of Law and Justice pointed out, data processing activity in India in general was at an early stage and depended heavily on the experience of the West, discernible from the list of references. The language used to justify the report seemed, he appeared to suggest, out of place with the nascent nature of database development in the country. In hindsight, we may now infer that this was possibly only appropriate to the later moment of RDBMS development. It said, 'shared resources and jointly used data have become the normal mode of computer operations', which made the issue of data security or 'the protection of data against unauthorized disclosure, modification, restriction, or destruction' especially critical.[107]

The synchronous use of data was hardly a feature of the databases operating in India at the time. Neither was a 'direct interaction with computer' – once the prerogative of the programmer or operator, now a 'common place activity for the most casual of computer users' – much in evidence.[108] It appeared that data security in the 80s was seeking solutions to problems that had not yet arrived. Even so, there was detailed focus on the problems arising from making data mobile, as members of this committee braced themselves for the excesses of data that they realized would soon arise from the multiple paths that data would traverse across the country. Under the subsection 'Data Base Security and Communications', the report explained:

> When multiple users are accessing centralized data through terminal devices from remote locations linked to a central computer system via telephone lines or other communication links, a number of security problems arise. When we have to deal with a large population of users, massive amount of data, many communications links and a vast array of functions [...] safeguards are necessary.[109]

This was before the internet, and so the committee focused on dial-up, leased, satellite, or radio microwave links. Their focus on how to safeguard these communication links remains valid, for data for many e-governance projects continues to be sent on leased lines, both to data centers and to front-end locations. They envisaged the role of both Posts and Telegraphs and of Telecommunications to be one of 'ensur(ing) security of data which will traverse the communication links between the men and the computers'.[110] Much of the imagined movement was through 'switched communication links' which 'pass through the public telephone exchange network' or a 'dedicated communication link' which offered a 'dedicated line between two or more computers or between a computer and a remote terminal, using

107 'Setting up of a National Informatics Centre'.
108 'Setting up of a National Informatics Centre'.
109 'Setting up of a National Informatics Centre', p. 19.
110 'Setting up of a National Informatics Centre', p. 21.

data modems'.[111] Securing the former was considered difficult, since movement depended on large number of people (telephone operators) and did not involve more than physically locking the 'cabinets' (nodes through which data passed).

In sum, the report envisaged a situation of data mobility through the infrastructure of the time and recommended ways by which such existing infrastructure, like the telephone switch system, could be made more secure. It also made a few generic recommendations about securing the operational apparatus, such as physically securing the site of operations, creating access protocols for personnel, backing up computer hardware and data tapes and discs, and classifying data depending on the security risks they pose and the mechanisms to control access. The report dedicated a few pages to laying out risk, recommending 'Communications Line Safeguards' as against 'penetration techniques' such as 'masquerading', 'eavesdropping', 'piggybacking' and 'Line Grabbing'. The focus was on securing data as it travelled across sites, and it forewarned the breaches and attacks that government data could suffer (and indeed did suffer in the decades that followed).

A third, and more direct, involvement with managing the risks associated with data has been the government's investment in auditing the infrastructure of digitization, including software code and data banks. Here, too, the focus was not on curtailing the movement of data, but on checking for risks in a limited way.

For digital infrastructures, an 'audit' includes common physical and selective checking, but also includes specific digital interventions such as maintaining automated audit logs to connect movement of data with users. The physical auditing of data is part of every digitization project that the government undertakes every time manual data transforms into a digital platform. In the digitization of land records in Karnataka, for example, digitized data was, we saw, made online only after its verification by village accountants, and in some cases by district commissioners, sometimes causing problems such as how to keep the database 'live' and in sync with reality. Even so, physical audit at the moment of transitioning from manual to digital continues.

A second kind of audit practice is the recording audit logs that track the history of change made to the data in the database tables. This, as a NIC DBA explained to me, is a critical component of the database, to track what changes have been made to core data and by whom. DBAs usually store the audit log in a separate table that contains columns for user id, IP address (to track from where the change was made), what changes were made (addition, deletion, modification), and the exact time at which this was done. This table is usually accessible to the 'super admin' of the database. Sometimes, to get around server space constraints, audit logs are stored in a separate database and a 'dirty flag' is used to highlight changes. A claim that I heard repeated several times by people critical of government databases is that they didn't maintain robust audit logs, making the breach of government databases not so difficult. In any case, audit logs seem to be a critical component, applied across the board, of maintaining security within databases.

111 'Setting up of a National Informatics Centre', p. 21.

A fourth type of audit practice that has emerged after the digital infrastructure of the NeGP is of third party auditing or TPA, particularly of the SWAN. This emphasis continues the focus on securing communication links from the pre-internet days, and is on how to ensure both mobility and security. Even some of the language is the same, of 'penetration testing' and 'vulnerability testing'. The difference with older attempts is that large private corporations are involved in both creating of the network and its security management.

According to a Request for Proposals for the selection of a TPA:

> SWAN (State Wide Area Network) is envisaged as the converged backbone network for data, voice and video communications throughout the State/UT and is expected to cater to the information communication requirements of all the departments. Key focus of the SWAN project is on high service delivery. As per SWAN policy, all States/UTs are implementing SWAN under two Options. Under the first Option, the State is to select a suitable Public Private Partnership (PPP) model and get the SWAN commissioned and operated for 5 years by a private Network Operator. In the second Option, the SWAN for the States/UTs would be set up and operated for 5 years by the National Informatics Centre (NIC). In either of the Options a Third Party Auditor (TPA) is required.[112]

The document then outlines the work that a TPA will be expected to undertake:

> Third Party Audit shall include monitoring the performance of the SWAN with a view to ensure desired Quality of Service (QoS) by the Network Operator and bandwidth service provider, as defined in the respective SLA's, signed between the State/UT Government, and Bandwidth Service Provider, Network Operator. These Guidelines define the broad areas of work, which TPA shall perform for a period of five years from the date of final acceptance test of the network.[113]

PriceWaterhouseCoopers or PwC is, for example, a popular TPA in many government departments, though other firms also compete for that position. Bureaucrats generally take pride in naming these companies. Beyond physical verification, database audit logs, and employing third party vendors, some national organizations are also involved in the creation of audit protocols which were applied across multiple departments. The Comptroller & Auditor General (CAG) of India is a 'supreme audit institution' or SAI, one of a set of government audit institutions around the world. As a SAI, it has led a cross-country working group on IT audits since the 80s, through which, a senior director of a NIC told me enthusiastically, it has been auditing data quality, the process of data entry and data validation of major government schemes such as the National Rural Employment Guarantee Scheme (NREGS). He added that government departments are happy with CAG's involvement because they have an oversight on the NIC.

---

112 'Request for Proposal (RFP) For Selection of SWAN TPA', https://www.meity.gov.in/writereaddata/files/An8_Indicative_SWAN.pdf.
113 'Request for Proposal (RFP) For Selection of SWAN TPA', p. 8.

A handbook published on IT audit by the working group states the need for such audits as a:

> natural response to the increasingly computerized operations of governments and public sector organizations. While the increasing use of IT has led to improving business efficiency and effectiveness of service delivery, it has also brought with it risks and vulnerabilities associated with computerized databases and business applications, which typically define an automated working environment. The role of IT audit in providing assurance that appropriate processes are in place to manage the relevant IT risks and vulnerabilities is crucial if the SAI is to meaningfully report on the efficiency and effectiveness of government and public sector operations. In the IT audit environment, processes, tools, oversight, and other ways to manage a function are also referred to as controls.[114]

The objectives of the CAG audit are related to data integrity, by which they mean the data that is used in decision-making and operating organizations' core function. An 'audit can definitively identify risks to data integrity, abuse and privacy, and also provide assurance that mitigating controls are in place'.[115] The focus on integrity is in the service of ensuring mobility. The handbook points out that computers today communicate with each other and exchange data over networks, both public and private. It also acknowledges that:

> employing overseas service providers is a common form of outsourcing, especially in a cloud computing environment, even though this poses risks involving foreign regulations on information storage and transfer may limit what can be stored and how it can be processed, data may be used by law enforcement of a foreign country without the knowledge of the organization, privacy and security standards may not always be commensurate, and disputes because of the different legal jurisdictions cannot be totally avoided.[116]

But instead of clamping down on overseas data operations, it recommends a 'strategy on contracting services to overseas vendors'[117] which asks the organization to make itself aware of overseas laws and regulations, reports on a vendor's past performance, and on 'deviations from the Service Level Agreement and outsourcing contract'[118] among other things.

In all these instances, we see actions dedicated to data mobility rather than its containment. They give us a new vantage point from where the current calls for the localization of data in order to secure it might be viewed.

To summarize the main arguments of this essay. The phenomenon of data excess, and its effects on the ability of governments to control information, is linked to the emergence

---

114 'WGITA – IDI Handbook on IT Audit for Supreme Audit Institutions', February 2014, https://icisa.cag.gov.in/resource_files/c60986ef8dd5d4f658df077c1b5dceb7.PDF.
115 'WGITA – IDI Handbook on IT Audit', p. 1.
116 'WGITA – IDI Handbook on IT Audit', p. 39.
117 'WGITA – IDI Handbook on IT Audit', p. 90.
118 'WGITA – IDI Handbook on IT Audit', p. 90.

of relational databases (among other technologies like networks), which have created infrastructure for data proliferation without necessarily ramping up expected efficiencies such as those produced in the corporate sector. Instead, the phenomenon of data excess forces citizen-beneficiaries to engage in repairing their data, producing moments of vacant citizenship, a situation I term 'slow violence'.

The examples I have provided in this chapter are of classic bureaucracies (the bureaucracy concerned with land has been my chief example) that have undergone a significant change in their information-producing capacities with the introduction of RDBMS. Classic forms of bureaucracy have been described as 'a remarkable form of human organization that has enabled modern governments and corporations to provide previously unimaginable benefits to humans around the world'.[119] The question that the disruption in the flow of data that RDBMS poses is whether the organizational form of the bureaucracy will survive in the way it was imagined. In other words, in a networked digital age, does bureaucracy remain an efficient and effective apparatus for managing human affairs if its control on the information it produces is weakening?

Multiple bureaucrats in the land bureaucracy in Karnataka told me that after the land records went digital, the bureaucrats know *less* about the lands under their jurisdiction. Digital records have proliferated, but not necessarily aided bureaucracies in control. Is declining governmental effectiveness punctuated by disastrous events like a data breach, an outcome of the digital transformation that has been sweeping government since the Commission built its first centralized database?

---

119 Nils Gilman, Jesse Goldhammer and Steven Weber, 'Can You Secure an Iron Cage?', *Limn*, Issue 8, February 2017, https://limn.it/articles/can-you-secure-an-iron-cage/.

ABOUT THE BOOK: *AN INTERNET FROM INDIA*

One of the thorniest questions you can ask authors is: 'What is the book about?' The instinctive tendency is to give detailed, nuanced, specific answers that explain vantage points, offer disciplinary specificity, political commitment, alongside the anecdotal excitement that makes books possible. But here we choose not to do that, knowing well that each of us might then give a different version of the book, and also because we could lose a potential reader who has probably had enough of the book before even opening it. So we look at each other and we vaguely say, 'It is about the internet'. It is almost an inside joke at this point because all of us have invested much time in debunking the idea that there is a singular internet, emphasizing in our different ways that the internet has to be layered across multiple stacks of hardware, software, wetware, infrastructure, and governance.

It also hits home hard because we have all, at different points, argued for more nuance when talking about digital technologies. We have emphasized that the digital is much more than just the internet, just as the internet is in turn more than social media. The book is much more than the internet as it looks at processes of digitization, mediated interaction, digital governance and regulation, and the messy and hybrid bureaucracies of digital infrastructure. And yet, 'It is about the internet' feels like a phrase to stand by, precisely because it is such a non-descriptor that it demands both explanations and imaginations to make it come to life.

What does it mean to write a book about the internet in a world where it is theoretically possible to say everything about the internet? The title of the book already gives some clues about what to expect: *Overload, Creep, Excess.* These three terms are not necessarily connected to the internet, though (as we will argue through the three long sections) they remain defining characteristics of the internet as we know it. They might not be the buzzwords through which the internet is being described and coded right now, but we nevertheless hope that they may yet become the analytic frameworks – or at least curious pathways – to make sense of the state of the internet(s) today. The sections further anchor the argument by locating various debates, histories, and materialities in the geopolitical region of India. In so doing, they recognize the deep-seated irony of trying to localize and nationalize a technological medium and a rhetorical imaginary that was resolutely developed to transcend physical and territorial boundaries as arbitrary and redundant as nation-state.

And yet, while working on different drafts of the sections and discussing them with different groups, when we said, 'It is about the internet', people would always suggest that it is about 'the internet in India'. It seemed necessary to say that, either because of the ways in which internet imaginaries always produce noncanonical geographies as exceptional states, or because the idea of a free-floating internet that escapes all bounded signifiers is too terrifying. Whatever the reason, the idea of India was continually brought back into the conversation.

It is admittedly true that the cases, histories, timelines, and events in this book draw from the unfolding of internet technologies in India. However, these developments are neither disconnected nor distanced from the global shape of the internet. Almost all the incidents and phenomena are shaped through, influenced by, and have in some cases even pioneered global internet debates and governance propositions. Sometimes this was because the sheer size, scale, and scope of digital networks in India saw questions arise here before their global time, making India the proverbial canary in the coal mine of the toxic gas buildups that we have now learned to identify especially on social media spaces.

Even as we have resisted 'India'-specificity we have also baulked at the prospect that this may be a working theory of the internet in the world. We are neither media theorists nor media philosophers, and none of us has any ambitions of creating a universal framework such as this. We are shaped in our scholarships, practice, and interventions by engaging with the internet in India. And even though we spend time in three different continents, between India, the Netherlands, and the United States, and despite the fact that the book was conceived at different times in Hong Kong, Bangalore, and Amsterdam, it still anchors itself in the temporal development of India, even as India's geospatial imagination of itself changed, in its internal geography as well as in its relationship with the 'rest of the world'.

The book is therefore about how we saw *An Internet from* India, but not necessarily *in* India, and it has global resonances and extensions that are both beyond its scope as well as our ambitions for it. Our historical timeline will find an implicit parallel with developments elsewhere, and both the validity and urgency of what we discuss will hopefully be carried forward, perhaps by others watching another internet from another location who may make connections.

The Glossary

Even this remains an inadequate answer to the question of what this book is about. This glossary furthers that question, in part by largely ignoring it and also perhaps by reframing it: not reframing what the book is about, but how you might talk about 'An Internet from India' so it doesn't just perform yet another analysis of the technology through its global language and vocabulary.

If anything, this is a book that tries to read the unfolding of the internet over a 24-year period and produces an account that is not about well-documented trajectories of data, code, algorithms, networks, databases, infrastructure, or investments. Many experts better equipped than us, perhaps also more engaged with these debates, have already done this and we learn from them. However, we still feel that there are a set of framings that do not feature easily or even remain absent from books about the internet. So fast-moving, deeply complex, and profoundly impactful has the internet been that much intellectual energy and effort goes into understanding – explaining and predicting – the technology in terms set by the technology. The *critique*, then, as well as its unravelling, are often done in the same language and framework as the narratives being questioned and resisted. To narrate the internet is, typically, to inadvertently fall back on the very terms and conditions it sets for itself. Trying to make sense of these terms and conditions requires adapting to the language within which they are set out, because, you know, YOLO and FOMO.

Positioned as we are (reluctantly but strategically) in the catchall disciplines of 'digital cultures', our attempt instead is to try and make sense of some of the urgent, emergent, critical, and knotty problems of the internet as we see them unfold from India. Each section tries to establish why the section exists, and what might be the confounding questions of the day that we keep trying to understand through a *faux* historicization and a cultural analysis of this thing that we call the internet. Before you reach those sections, it might perhaps make life easier to have a glossary of unexpected things you might find. It serves the function of reminding you (and us, really), again and again, that this is not a book about the internet, but about reading and understanding the problems around the internet(s) in India, and hence you might encounter terms that might not necessarily be expected in this reading like Overload, Creep, and Excess.

While the titular terms will have their day, and we will expand on them, this glossary bears the unbearable weight of signaling what we think are unexpected concepts that you might encounter in this book, while also refusing to take any definitional responsibility, given that we each approach them differently in ways both *ad hoc* and strategically mutable. This then is not a glossary as much as it is a cautionary manual, an invitation to look out for these concepts and unpack them with us as you read. If that is too difficult to parse, consider this the equivalent of the microaggressive 'Terms and Conditions' that precede all digital usage. Instead of taking your data, we hope that we will at least be able to gather your attention.

Body

At the heart of the debates on the internet has been the body. Even without the theoretical apparatus of the cyborg and the post-human or the disciplinary framings of computer-human interaction and digital cultures, the body is central to the internet both as a source of inspiration and a verification of its outcomes. While these essays don't necessarily theorize the body in our digitally enmeshed networks, it appears in multiple ways across the book. There is the flesh-and-bone body, the 'natural person' (using the language of the Personal Data Protection Bill, 2019), that is capable of being incarcerated, or subjected to 'civil death' when its link to its digital avatar is switched off, or made '*conditional, on a compulsory barter* [...] [which] compels citizens to give up their biometrics 'voluntarily', allow [their] biometrics and demographic information to be stored by the State and private operators and then used for a process termed 'authentication'' (as described by the Supreme Court judgment on Aadhaar in 2018 in *Justice K.S. Puttaswamy (retd) and Another* v *Union of India and Others*). There is the 'inviolate personality' possessing a 'natural right' to privacy that can never be taken away by any law, according to another Supreme Court judgment on privacy in 2017 (in *Justice K.S. Puttaswamy (retd) and Another* v *Union of India and Others*). And there are the numerous preventive detention regulations that allow such a body to be denied of its basic right to self-determination if it is seen as threatening public order, or the security and integrity of India. Such a body is directly implicated when discussing post-pandemic contact tracing e-health technologies, the most prominent among them being Aarogya Setu, which exemplified the creep of the internet in unprecedented private and personal forms.

The disconnected body presents itself as the endpoint justification of a variety of policies and regulations, from the Information Technology Act, 2000 that sought to connect the body into the digital networks by granting it access to the internet blackouts which saw hyperconnected bodies as threats to governance and sovereignty, and thus threats to regulating access. The traces of the body become apparent in the empty signifiers of database regulation and management, so that the streams of the body, passing through bureaucratic assemblages, dismiss and empty the body of its liveness, signaling an evacuation of meaning that comes with a technocratic organizing of the world.

The essays are confronted with (and in turn confront readers with) different renderings of the body, both in its hyper-presence as well as in its glaring absence when thinking through the internet as it develops to become a site of severe digital contestation and reconciliation in contemporary times.

Bureaucracy

Given the rhetoric of the internet as an efficient organizing machine, creating order and control through a careful parsing and archiving of the world's information, it comes as a surprise that so many of the pauses in the essays are about its bureaucratization.

A central feature of the digital turn of governance has however been the overcoming of the proverbial 'last mile', a communications term typically used as a means of leapfrogging bureaucratic and procedural holdups, leakages, and corrupt intermediaries, to directly reach intended recipients either through their bank accounts, through point-of-service devices, or other biometric mechanisms. The painstaking introduction of the clumsy systems of a Relational Database Management System (RDBMS) profoundly changed the very experience of citizenship as they favor specific forms of data that reshape the relationship of the state and the subject. Such a reshaping redefines bureaucratic (mis) management, as it creates new conditions of 'slow violence' that often linger long beyond the original structures that created them.

Bureaucracy similarly shows up, in unexpected ways, in conversations around freedom of speech and censorship, where the entire domain of what can and cannot be said eventually boils down to a bureaucratic arrangement of Section 79 of the Information Technology Act, 2000, and to responsibilities of 'data fiduciaries', despite the chilling effects it can produce on free speech. And equally unexpectedly, the movement of bodies over space becomes a question of bureaucratic calibration of the distinction between bodies and data, in, for example, the crisis of sovereignty in Kashmir when physical curfew was superimposed by a wholesale internet blackout. The neoliberal model of slick, postmodern flows of information confronting slow-moving, often counterproductive, and clumsy bureaucracies of governance is one that the different essays here often encounter and structure themselves around, the better to understand the paradoxical slowness of regulation, the enduring need for welfare, and the futility of control exercised by increasingly totalitarian information regimes.

Citizenship

In most prominent narratives of the internet, the unit of human operator is the user. The user has been so scrubbed of specificity and history that it allows us to imagine the global community of operators who, contrary to all evidence, are posited as undifferentiable. In contrast, our account of the book is heavily reliant and hugely embedded in conditions of citizenship.

Citizenship was difficult to define in post-Partition India given the massive numbers of people who could potentially have turned stateless, and so – nearly a decade after Independence – India put together its first Citizenship Act in 1955 declaring in effect that all those who resided in India could qualify for citizenship. This was modified in 2003, introducing the concept of the 'illegal migrant' and also making it necessary for the parents of putative citizens to prove that they were born in India. In 2019, further modification of the Act to specifically target Muslims led to major protests that contextualize several of the concerns of this book.

Creep theorizes citizenship by looking at the complex constitutional and jurisprudence challenges that emerging internet practices and subjectivities have thrown in quick succession. Particularly in the last decade, the continued replaying of 'the citizen + internet = terrorist' formula sees the profound ways in which the development of the internet, primarily as a nation-building exercise and then as a policing vehicle, is changing the very definitions of who gets to be counted as a citizen.

The Aadhaar project – India's largest biometric identification project – to which all the essays refer, is a prime example of database citizenship engineered to meet new imaginations of the future nation. *Excess* marks for us how excessive digitization and its demands of care and repair, the continued updating and maintaining of personal records by the personal user, creates new conditions of 'thing' and how they 'unsubstantiate' citizenship. *Overload* theorizes a citizenship that is almost relegated to the realm of affect, producing the 'Youser' which is an amalgamation of the user and their data, governed and shaped by algorithmic curation seemingly without human autonomy and agency. The essays are thus bookended by citizenship as each struggles to understand how rights and responsibilities get realized in this new space, while also addressing the changing nature of violence and erasure that are presented by a growing number of digital crises.

Crises

Bruno Latour, in his exposition of the 'Actor-Network Theory', had famously postulated that technologies make themselves visible in the moments of their breaking or their failure. The three essays here might argue that the internet doesn't quite break but is nevertheless kept on the verge of breaking so that the gap between 'almost working' and 'not quite working' remains a narrow one. The internet, it would seem, is largely a *response to crises*, is thus itself in a state of crisis, and creates crises. Such a circularity, making the internet not just an attribute of crisis but as synonymous with crises, is evident across this book. If we were in the habit of memeing (which we are, you will see), we would already have created an internet/crisis meme with a cat dressed as Michel Foucault on it. Data might be the new currency, but crises, in our accounts, are definitely the lifeblood of the internet.

While we do not attempt a definition of the term crises, we do examine the ways in which the internet is not only made visible in times of crises, but that new crises are also made visible only because of the internet. This leads to the ironic set of regulations that seek to control the internet when physical conditions of law and order break down, and try and organize the geographical state of things in order to control and contain the excesses and overloads of the creepy internet.

Disconnection

So much of the discourse on the internet has been about getting everybody on to the information superhighway that it comes as a shock when a major focus here is on *dis*connection. All of us engage with multiple conditions and materialities of connectivity. In *Overload*, we look at the Free Basics campaign that sought to preserve net neutrality as a precondition for universal access. In *Creep*, we discuss the hyperconnectivity of COVID-19 pandemic access. In *Excess*, we show how new citizenship can become bereft of meaning: an explanation without a signification, in the newly arranged databases of governance.

And yet, in these explorations of access and connectivity looms the figure of disconnection. Sometimes it is willful, as in the case of internet blackouts, at other times it is accidental, a by-product of procedural bureaucracy, and on yet other occasions it is weaponized, as in the deployment of 'fake news' and 'terrorism' by controlled media during the student protests in New Delhi in 2016. Disconnection simultaneously invokes the traditional 'last mile' subject — one in part not-yet-connected, in part the new subject of control — to be disconnected, and in that duality offers witness to the idiosyncrasies and imaginaries of the internet from India.

Governance

Maybe 'governance' should not be in the list of unsuspecting words to talk about the internet. Or so we thought, given that so much of the internet seems to be nothing more than an exercise in governance that accidentally happens to be about technology. Especially against the backdrop of the biometric citizenship project Aadhaar, against which all three sections stage themselves, it becomes inevitable to not just look at the governance of the internet but also the ways in which governance itself is being shaped by the emergence and unfolding of the internet (as in the 'Minimum Government, Maximum Governance' tagline of the Bharatiya Janata Party government). While *Excess* provides almost a full-frontal view of the ways in which technological arrangements led to the emergence of entire units of governance and administration, *Overload* looks at the landmark DPS MMS (Delhi Public School Multimedia Messaging Service) viral porn clip as a trigger point for understanding the remit of governance in online spaces, and *Creep* exposes the ways in which data protection laws reshape the entire domain of what is private and free speech, further defining the tenuous terrain of 'larger public interest'. Governance became an unusual term in this discourse because unlike the larger discourse of 'What shall we do with the internet?', this book significantly focuses on what we shall do with ourselves now that the internet is doing things to us.

ICT4D

Information and Communication Technologies for Development (ICT4D) might perhaps be the one phrase that comes from particular geopolitical relationships that internets from India have that may not always be intelligible to a global reader. It is an infrastructural term. It immediately orients the internets in a particular direction — of progress, of economic uplift, of societal reform, and of a close alignment with the national agenda for development. ICT4D becomes important because it rescues internets from partisanship and shows how, despite the different track records in protecting fundamental civil liberties and human rights, governments position internets in startlingly similar ways.

The invasive Aadhaar project, widely accused of stripping marginalized groups of their citizenship, was initiated by a different regime and its intentions were continued by its successors. The suspension of free speech is not something that is peculiar to the current administration, but it was continually deployed to control efforts to organize without state permission. The tracking of suspicious persons began even before the current markets of surveillance governance, but it has become naturalized in the post-pandemic era.

All the essays continue to focus on, and are informed by, the developmental schemes of the Indian government — from the National Rural Employment Guarantee Scheme (NREGS) to the Information Technology Acts, from the National Identity Cards Rules to Aadhaar, from the Personal Data Protection Bill to COVID-19 patient tracking tools. The specter of developmentalism looms large, mostly because contrary to popular belief so much of the internet is still at the behest and under the supervision of the state and its 'Make in India' or 'India Shining' imaginations, which might easily resonate with other geographies that too want to make themselves great again.

Nation-state

A common claim is that the earliest modern imaginations of the Indian nation came from cinema. The industry of cinema predates the industry of nation-building, and although the idea of statehood and its relationship of nation to citizens might have been codified in the Constitution, its popular understanding was formulated through film. It can be argued, then, that the imaginary of a future India finds its input from the internets of the present. So clear has been the hope of present-day internets as leap-frogging the developmental era that digitalization has been not only a process of translation but of world building itself. The digital future is the cog around which the rest of the nation has to be reconfigured. This is most apparent in the discussions around land record digitization in RDBMS, which show how the very act of creating digital records is an act of creating digital dependence, which set up a clear trajectory of digital literacy which cannot be reversed or questioned.

The idea of the nation-state and its enduring control of internet technologies to establish its dominion and power are also present in the continued conversations around protests, politics, and the policies that have been enacted, trying to make sense of the bodies, collectives, and communities that will have to be shaped (sometimes with force, often insidiously) to fit into the digital nation-state that is currently being built. National borders as also borders of data move alongside concepts such as data sovereignty and localization used in the Data Protection Bill, 2021.

The focus on nation-state is additionally helpful because while the mainstream focus in digital cultures has been in the critique of Big Tech, the state is not necessarily recognized as one of the Big Techs. As a service provider and as one of its largest regulators, it is important to recognize the history of the nation-state with technologies of incarceration and penalization, and how that relationship is only amplified and strengthened in its partnerships with Big Tech, producing a sinister nexus of opaque control.

Promises

The promises of the internet are boundless. We have all bought into them, despite evidence to the contrary. Ever since the declaration of the World Wide Web, the promises have been offered and renewed, even as each one of them has not quite lived up to the expectations. What were these promises, and how did they evolve and change, even as the intention of technology met the design of implementation? We do not pretend to track these different and differed promises, but it is important to understand that the myriad 'presents' of the internet were all mobilized around the promises of a 'future'. We write from that future to the past, trying to make sense of what happened and how it may have been that we got here. The intriguing part of these failed promises is that, despite their continued failure, they still continue to linger. The imaginaries change, but the promissory note of the internets never seems to get outdated. The sections in this book tell what the current promises are, and try and reverse engineer them to see where they began and how they perhaps unfolded.

Protests

It would seem, in the current state of public participation and political discord, that protests are what the internet was made for. And cats. And, of course, porn. However, the essays in this book are particularly interested and invested in a different idea of a protest — not protests as mobilized and organized by the different Web 2.0 technologies, but protests as possible only because of the internet. There has been a spectacular coming together of multiple voices and communities that would have found no voice or expression beyond the internet. The public squares of internets made protests possible. And, ironically, many of the problematic stakeholders of the internets became unusual allies in these protests. The unfolding of the #MeToo movement and the subsequent #LoSHA conversations in India are a prime example of a conversation that always simmered offline, stayed in whisper circles, and suddenly created a public discourse through distributed participation. In a very different vein, it was the digital doctoring of a video of protest in a student movement in 2019, and the viral spread of this manipulation, that prompted tens of thousands of students across the country to participate in what became one of the most landmark student movements in recent years. The essays center the idea that protests — either through bureaucratic excess or because of political deficits — continue to both mark and be shaped by the techno-politics of internets, and that even as protests go through their life cycles, they keep on prolonging the life cycle of internets, by both expanding the scope of the network and by inviting new modes of policy and practice to find their feet. The ephemera of protests translates into the infrastructure of the internets.

Subjectivity

The subject of digital studies is the subject of digital usage. Much attention has been given to the idea of the user, the peer, the digital native, the networked individual, that makes the nodes of the computational networks come to life. Especially with social media penetrations, and the forced move to digitize everything pandemic, leading to zoom fatigue and platform exhaustion, it is increasingly clear that even if the internet might have been made for cats, it predominantly shapes individual subjectivity. In this book, we try a different provocation. Through the three essays, we suggest that the user, rather than this individuated, self-affirming, information-mongering self, has in fact been evacuated of meaning, agency, and autonomy because of the ways in which the person is *installed* in digital networks. This is most evident in *Excess*, where the subject is literally hollowed out and recreated as a flattened conduit of information transfer by emphasizing database relationality over individual relationships.

Creep looks at the same subject being leaked into multiple streams, each being regulated as a discrete data entity that then maps back on to the subject, making it subject to technological governance without direct interface with the regulation. *Overload* gives us the idea of a Youser — a subject position that becomes a necessary point in cybernetic feedback loop of algorithmic agencies and networked actions. The subjectivity that gets mapped in these essays is not one that gives particular hope, given the extraordinary powers of exception that are ascribed to digital transformation technologies. At the same time, subjectivity is, in its evacuation, presented as something needing careful reconstruction. Through the different sections of this book, we also try and show the potentials for protest, reframing, and rekindling the digital subject in new negotiations with the state of the internet.

Vacancies

At the heart of our explorations of the different entities involved in the shape of tech right now — the state, the subject, the collective, the law — we keep stumbling over the idea that these are *older forms evacuated of meaning*. In many ways, writing this book has been an exercise of epistemological anxiety, for it does feel like several well-known terms of the past do not any longer sit right, and that the digital transformation in which they are all engaged has also transformed them structurally. In *Overload*, this is presented as a 'silent but dramatic transformation', where the relationship with informational scale has already changed the idea of the person who is supposed to have this relationship. *Creep* proposes that the new matrices of verification-oriented digital citizenship present themselves as empty containers, waiting to be filled with new subjects who can be verified by opaque technological protocols. *Excess* sees how a mandatory interpellation of digital users in the repair and maintenance of their own data sets, performing the labor of keeping themselves alive, creates a 'vacant citizenship' that makes them participate in practices of slow violence. The digital was supposed to fill the gaps in governance and social construction, but it seems to instead produce vacancies, which can be filled only by those who can bear the affordances of digital verification and the burden of digitization, and it has clear consequences on the futures that are being predicated on the promise of digitization.

****

This glossary is our way of leading you into some of the questions that tie these three essays together. It is also a way of finding our limits, of trying to figure out why equally urgent and related questions – postcolonial legacies of carceral states, structures of surveillance, logic of economic expansion, new technologies like blockchain, emergence of locally controlled and nationally walled internets, processes of gentrification, emergence of pirate technologies, debates around data ownership, responsibilities of tech platforms, and eroding space for civic action to name a few – are not a part of this book, even though they become the larger landscape within which this book makes sense. We hope that this glossary produces an intentionality to the reading of the different essays, and to making connections not only between the texts but also with readers who are now invited to add to the glossary by unpacking, identifying, and highlighting terms that might irrigate an account of the internet(s) from their own locations.

ANNOTATED TIMELINE

Timelines are chronological devices, giving the impression of progress. Yet, the timeline of events that we curate here is less to depict a story of progress or disrepair, and more to portray a snapshot of defining moments in the public life of the digital encounters that we trace in this book. These moments appear in the form of letters, court judgements, plans and policies, working together with the archive, provide something of a window into the key problems that motivate this book. They coalesce around the total and unprecedented re-organization of social and political life that has been mediated by digital technologies. Every event in this timeline thus points to an upheaval in the order of things, producing new problems in the world, and, for us, new opportunity to excavate the life-worlds of techno-political interventions.

Consider this timeline a roving flashlight then, selectively illuminating the torrid twenty years of digital governance and its prequel. It is not intended to be comprehensive. It is a curatorial accompaniment to the text, showcasing our authorial choices, our reading of the past. It is at the same time an invitation to readers to unpick up these moments, chart their own genealogies and, of course, to add to them. Some interventions are more well-known than others. The lesser-known ones are equally critical to our story of why the past twenty years need the attention and space this book offers.

1975: The National Informatics Center (NIC) is set up. An institution that brought irreversible change to the information generating and organizing capacities of the government, the NIC was set up under the Department of Electronics to digitize government offices. NIC's founder Narasimhiah Seshagiri developed an internet before the Internet to create a distributed network of information sharing offices. In many important ways, this book (and the third essay in particular) tracks the excesses of this pioneering ambition.

1976: Jaswanth Krishnayya's May 15 1976 *aide memoire* to the Planning Commission on setting up 'information systems and a computerized data bank'. A systems thinker, Krishnayya may be considered as a prototype of today's ubiquitous management consultant of the sort dotting government offices. But, as is revealed in this defining letter, Krishnayya wasn't just purveying technology to the civil servants of India's Planning Commission. He was offering a paradigm shift, an ontological change in the information gathering and organizing model of government, a vision that game to define the material transformation in the sinews of government. This is a rare opportunity to glimpse the thought-work that accompanied digital change, something that is lost as technology interventions become more 'plug and play' in the decades to come.

1984: New Computer Policy of the Department of Electronics. One of Rajiv Gandhi first decisions on taking over Prime Ministership was to afford special status to the information technology industry, laying the foundations for the famous IT revolution a decade later. The New Computer Policy included reduced import duties for peripherals, foreign equity participation, liberalized import of computers and recognition of software as a separate industry, setting up the informational infrastructure that forms the background in this book.

1998: Launch of the Simputer by four scientists from the Indian Institute of Science. This was low-cost, smart-card-compliant, handheld end-user device using the IMLI (or 'information mark-up language interface') on a touchscreen intended to revolutionise a digital grassroots in India. According to Vijay Chandru, one of the four founders, it was imagined alongside two other equally revolutionary inventions, one, the Wireless-in-Local-Loop (WLL) technology set up in 2001 as part of the SARI (Sustainable Access in Rural India) project of Ashok Jhunjhunwala at the Indian institute of Technology, Chennai, often seen as the moment when mobile telephony took root in India, with kiosks providing telephone, Internet and other stand-alone computer services to villagers, and in 2002 of computational linguistics with the Language Technologies Research Centre at the Indian Institute of Informational Technology. Together, these were going to be the technologies for democratizing information in India.

In many ways, the problems of the Simputer were not hardware or design problems. They were, rather, that the digital ecosystem – like Aadhaar, for instance – had not yet been built. They were a cog without a wheel, without a system to support it. The Simputer nevertheless proved to be a key antecedent to complex e-governance systems, anticipating a complex legal ecosystem including, for example, the draft Personal Data Protection Bill, 2019.

1999: DISNIC-PLAN, A NICNET Based Distributed Database for Micro-level Planning. The first attempt to connect offices and introduce real time relay of data from the 200+ districts of India to the headquarters of the Planning Commission in Delhi. This was a distributed database, pre-empting relational database management systems. This book has explored the geography of this network, as it aimed to make data mobile and yet curtail its movement by mirroring the hierarchical structure of government. Debates around the localization of data, which is referenced across the chapters of this book, are reminiscent of this pioneering model of containing data within the geography of the district.

1999: New Telecom Policy. NICNet, established by the National Informatics Centre in 1995, as an inter-operability platform between government institutions, was also accompanied by the availability of the first public Internet service on 15th August 1995, by the Videsh Sanchar Nigam Limited (VSNL). In 1999, the New Telecom Policy spelled out Universal Services as among its main objectives, leading to India becoming a signatory to the USOF (Universal Services Obligation Fund), receiving funds to encourage universal access. In 2003, the USO was given statutory status, and in 2004 the Broadband policy act further consolidated the idea that digital connectivity is a fundamental right. It is important to emphasise that the history of universal access is and should remain central state responsibility, and that the current idea of universal access as administered by private telecoms, as in the partnership with Reliance Jio or the backdoor negotiation with Free Basics are an abdication of state responsibility to offer universal access and obligatory services.

2000: Information Technology Act passed. Although a technological regulation document, this Act is clearly an origin point of cultural and political expressions of technology. Throughout the book, across the essays, the different conditions of access, expression, speech, security, and integrity keep on drawing from this earliest historical document about regulation of the Internet. See especially its Section 3 on Electronic Governance, its licensing structure for electronic certification, its Section 43 announcing draconian penalties for 'computer contaminants', its cyber-regulation structure, its section 66 that brought the concept of 'hacking' for the first time into legal terminology, its emphasis on 'sovereignty and integrity of India', and finally its outlining of 'service providers' and their accountability. Subsequent annotations and amendments merely reinforce the centrality that ICTs have gained in imagining the apparatus of a digital India. It is important to trace many of the cultural, organisational, and bureaucratic events back to this Act that sought to contain and control the then emerging Internet networks.

2003: The revised Citizenship Amendment Act. This is the Act that first conceives the Rules on Registration of Citizens and Issue of National Identity Cards that would become the National Population Register. The 2003 Rules were the first time when a 'Local Register of Indian Citizens' was defined, when 'individuals whose Citizenship is doubtful' would be weeded out. It was also the first time that illegal migrants or foreigners become central to defining citizenship.

2005: The Right to Information Act. This Act, though not quite about the digital technologies or infrastructure is critical in understanding the expectations and the ambitions of building a nation-wide internet infrastructure. RTI forced the government to recognise digital platforms as the only way of giving access to public information, thus precipitating massive digital reforms and e-governance initiatives in the very working of governments. It also suddenly changed government bureaucracy, replacing older structures with several new agents, using database logics to produce new interfaces and transactions for spreading of information. The institution of RTI also led to concerns around privacy, because a non-discrete scrutiny of public information could, it became apparent, lead to adverse consequences for those who had not consented for their data to be used beyond a particular context.

2006: The Personal Data Protection Bill. The PDP, introduced to the Rajya Sabha in 2006, was the first recognition of the unregulated nature of personal data online. The Bill significantly anticipates and identifies the ways in which personal data can be harvested, consolidated, and often weaponised against users, in ways both unpredictable and uncontrollable. Ironically the PDP Bill was targeted at private use of citizen data but did not pose any questions to the state's own ambitions of data surveillance and extraction. Thus, the most vulnerable data subjects – the YOUsers caught in the matrices of digitalisation – remained without agency and understanding of what happens to their data and how it can be used against them.

2006: National E-Governance Plan. An ambitious and multi-pronged plan to digitize various facets of governance, radically re-imagining the location and scale at which government would operate. Aadhaar (see below) might be its most experiential and controversial project, but the plan, as a whole, marshalled a new technological architecture that included service centre nodes, fibre-optic networks and stable data centres. The NeGP, as it came to be known, offers some of the best instances of RDBMS-led datafication of government, and is frequently upgraded with new ways of reconfiguring service. It is thus a historical index to track the development of techno-legal mechanisms for the practice of government and the re-figuration of the individual as a citizen-recipient.

2006. Orkut's multi-lingual Indian iteration. The moment of the introduction of social media in India. Within the next four years India had 83 million internet users, sixty percent of whom had some kind of social media existence. Although Orkut led the way it would have a short shelf life, being replaced within two years on the frontlines by Facebook.

2007: RSBY (Rashtriya Swasthya Bima Yojana, or National Health Insurance Scheme) announced as a cashless Mediclaim for the poor. One of the first experiments to convert the slew of Centrally Sponsored Schemes to move to the cashless system, this health insurance system for the poor was imagining over multiple financial gateways of e-commerce and payments. It also introducing the idea of digital money to a largely disconnected population. A history of the Internet in India is also perhaps the history of shaping the image of the benefactor, and experimenting in their onboarding onto the Internet by shifting their basic services online, as we have seen both in the case of demonetization as well as Aadhaar.

2008: Amendments to the IT ACT – the presentation of cyber security. These amendments primarily addressed cyber-security. The first conversations around data transfer and safety, for which the 2004 Delhi Public School User Generated Pornography case was a central marker, resurfaced and found a resolution in these amendments. Of particular interest for this book are the sections that look at cyber-security, not in terms of keeping users safe but to keep data safe *from* users, and from their ability to corrupt, steal or manipulate digital data. The legacy of controlling users in order to keep the technologies safe, unfolds in many of the cases in this book, including 'Whatsapp Lynch Mobs' – where social media platform, ascribed both responsibility and accountability, in turn starts a 'user literacy' campaign to control user behaviour. Cyber security is critical also because it began allowing dissident voices to be examined from a national data security lens, bringing in new layers of control and silencing.

2008: Second Administrative Reform Commission, Eleventh Report, Promoting e-Governance. Another landmark in the turn towards datafication of government. Dedicating an entire report to electronic governance at the same time as the appearance of the NeGP (see above), suggests not just a firm resolve to a digital transition, but also the digital reform of Indian administration as a whole. E-governance became a relay point through which corporate and managerial idioms of transparency and efficiency, would shift from government to governance. It followed a series of financial crises during the late 1980s, and now planned for a new organizational structure that would shrink bureaucracy to the backend, foregrounding instead new bridges between service centres and clients. A managerial ideal of heightened efficiency suggested not so much a transformation as a transcendence of politics.

2009: Launch of Aadhar. In February of this month, the Unique Identification Authority of India (UIDAI) was started, initially within the Planning Commission, with former Infosys co-founded and CEO Nandan Nilekani in charge. A year earlier Nilekani had published his book *Imagining India: Ideas for the New Century*, which had laid out several of the revolutionary concepts around portable and bodily identity for every Indian resident, that he would now be tasked with implementing. The first UIDAI Working Paper, *Creating a Unique Identity for Every Resident in India*, effectively outlines a new biopolitical definition of residency, by ensuring repeatedly that the Aadhar number would be itself a dumb number containing no intelligence; it was not an identity card; and it was portable.

2009: DoT issued blockage of porn websites. Pornography has been one of the poster children for Internet regulation. The Department of Telecommunication's continued attempts at blocking porn and censoring 'obscene content' has continually been rebuffed, and has never quite worked. The 2009 blocking of porn websites was the first national attempt that showed the inefficacy of content filtering online, and also the power of distributed content networks which could easily surpass the different content filters, as is discussed in the case of the Savita Bhabhi controversies. In many ways, the failure at content filtering and censorship can be seen as the trigger point for the government mediators to start looking at other forms of information shaping which lead to the reliance on Internet shutdowns and information blackouts as blanket strategies for blocking and censoring information.

2011: Intermediary Liability Act. A major moment in the arrival of new telecom companies as performers of state-like activities, this Act. saw a new tacit arrangement of the public and the private in which social media platforms, made liable for the actions of their users, got enfranchised as independent and autonomous bodies of governance with Terms of Service taking precedence over independent judgements on censorship and agency. Not only did this produce a chilling effect, as self-censorship and arbitrary blocking became common, but it also registered new ways in which these companies began to lobby for and shape the future of the Internet, as in the Free Basics campaign and the fight to retain Net Neutrality. The Intermediary Liability Act also needs to be recognised as the precursor to the regimes of Internet blackouts and shutdowns, and disconnection which superseded the safeguards against censorship in older media technology regulations.

2015: Digital India campaign launched. Major initiative rhetorically linking digital technologies with national identity. Like many countries that have become production and service hubs for global IT industries, this campaign was focussed on the economic wealth that global outsourcing can bring the country. Digital India started ostentatiously, as an economic alliance and collaboration building project, but it also suggested a new kind of intentionality on the part of the state. Activities that were seen to be using digital technologies to disrupt, question, or challenge the overt intentionalities of development and economic wealth-creation, were seen as problematic and even traitorous (threatening to the 'security and integrity of India'). This extended to arrests of activists, institutional prohibitions including harassment of digital groups demanding social justice, and governmental crackdowns on dissenting voices and communities.

2015: The landmark 'Shreya Singhal' judgment. A second-year law student, outraged by the arrest of two young women for putting up (or simply 'liking') Facebook posts, challenged the draconian section 66A of the Information Technology Act, and won. That amendment, which had taken direct aim at social media in threatening imprisonment to anyone sending 'information that is grossly offensive' or 'causing annoyance, inconvenience, danger, obstruction, insult, injury, criminal intimidation, enmity, hatred or ill will' via 'a computer, computer system, computer resource or communication device including attachments in text, image, audio, video and any other electronic record', was struck down by the Court. However, the Court retained the equally draconian 69A that authorized the government to block any information 'in the interest of sovereignty and integrity of India, defence of India, security of the State, friendly relations with foreign States or public order or for preventing incitement to the commission of any cognizable offence'. A growing split in the two halves of the 'reasonable restrictions' on the right to free speech became increasingly clear, defining the uses of the Unlawful Activities (Prevention) Act and the conditions under which preventive detention began to be used.

2016: Prohibition of Discriminatory Tariffs for Data Services Regulation. India does not have any specific legislations regarding Net Neutrality. However, in 2016, the Telecom Regulatory Authority of India (TRAI) passed this new regulation after public consultations about the regulatory framework for Over-the-top (OTT) services. This effectively makes net neutrality a fundamental right and aligns India with many other countries that seek to keep the Internet services neutral and agnostic to the kinds of use and user. This regulation came into effect because of the ways in which private corporations (Airtel in 2014, Free Basics in 2015) were trying to fork the Indian Internet into basic and luxury services, intending to create a multi-tier userbase with differing advantages and services.

2016: The India Stack takes shape. taking Aadhar into a new era of 'presenceless, paperless, cashless and consent', with the launch of United Payments Interface (UPI), catapulting India into the age of digital payments. UPI works on increasingly integrating the banking system with a real-time mobile payments system, to to enable interoperability between money custodians, payment rails and front-end payment applications. Aadhar's API is increasingly made available to build larger numbers of apps.

2017: K.S. Puttuswamy Judgment on the right to privacy. In asserting such a right, the Supreme Court came up with several new conceptions of the biopolitical subject, now defined as a 'natural person' who possesses a bodily right to privacy, which is 'a natural right' and 'inalienable'. It was also at the same time transactable, thus laying the foundations for data exchange and commodification. It is an underlying current through this book that the regulation around data privacy and data security also contribute to the regimes of data surveillance and data capitalisation by enforcing data as discrete computational set that create the user in what we are calling a YouSer.

2017: Temporary Suspension of Telecom Services (Public Emergency or Public Safety) Rules, 2017, amendment to the 1855 Telegraph Act. Section 144 of the Code of Criminal Procedure (CrPC) allows local magistrates to direct properties like cellphones and mobile towers to be used in specific ways. The PAAS agitations in Gujarat was the first time that the Internet telecommunication was included under this, and infrastructure regulation was used as a way of information spreading. This was challenged in court and eventually, in 2017, the Telecom Internet Suspension Rules were formulated and codified as a part of the Telegraph Act, which made it possible for Internet shutdowns to be normalized, making India top the lists of the longest and largest number of Internet shutdowns in the world. Under the Telegraph Act amendment, shutdowns are often seen as modes of limiting speech, but its origin in the CrPC is a stark reminder that this is an infrastructure shaping that curtails free speech and a new form of censorship and control through infrastructural development.

2018: K.S. Puttaswamy Judgment on Aadhar: the landmark judgment on the validity of the Aadhar Act is best remembered for Justice D.Y. Chandrachud's dissenting judgment. While the Act was passed, Chandrachud outlined a grim picture in which, for all the emphasis on privacy and data protection, when rights that are 'freely exercised, liberties freely enjoyed, entitlements granted by the Constitution and laws' become 'conditional, on a compulsory barter', then the 'barter compels the citizens to give up their biometrics 'voluntarily', allow their biometrics and demographic information to be stored by the State and private operators and then used for a process termed 'authentication''. It also allows for an extraordinary ability of the state to perform 'civil death' through turning off a digital resource at will.

2018: M/S United India Insurance… vs Jai Prakash Tayal (26th Feb 2018). A case on genetic data privacy and the weaponization of individual genetic data became an unlikely focal point to connect technological data and biological data to ensure protection for the individual. Digital data is often seen as discrete and separate from the embodied user that it refers to and, in this judgement, data (digital or otherwise) was established as intrinsic to the privacy and integrity of a person. The establishment of data as thus fundamental to personhood, leads to interesting questions around bodily security, safety, and individual safety in the face of continued data leaks and instances of trolling and doxing online. It perhaps can be seen as the first recognition of a Youser – a combination of multiple data streams – and its negotiations with agency and autonomy in the complex field of data regulation and security.

2019: Personal Data Protection Bill based on the committee recommendations led by Justice B.N. Srikrishna. It contains the government of India's most recent response to the kinds of data overload, creep and excesses that this book aims to document. It sought to create a legal framework for the protection of personal data, through the creation of data fiduciaries and, more starkly, by proposing localization strategies to contain data within the geographic boundaries of the nation. In the ensuing public debate, some saw data localisation as an attempt to bring back the rule of law to our digital and datafied existence, whereas for others, this was an extension of the long arm of the state as a mode of surveillance or economic protectionism. Against the long-standing attempts by the government to secure data, starting in the 1970s, where the mobility of data was never compromised, this latest intervention suggests limiting the spread of data. As such, it is reminiscent of old information architectures that mapped data onto specific categories, such as the 'district'. As far as government's access to data is concerned, the situation has not changed much from the prior version of the Bill (see above), where the government continues to have unchecked access to public and personal data. As of the moment of completing this book, the Bill has been withdrawn and will be fundamentally redrafted.

2019: Sabka Sath, Sabka Vikas, Sabka Vishwas ('The support of all, the advancement of all, the faith of all'). The slogan adopted by the Bharatiya Janata Party in 2019 has led to interesting socio-political and cultural arguments about who the intended 'everybody' is. The proposition of a 'greater good for everybody' has often been used to reinforce draconian authoritarian and surveillance practices, perhaps the most visible during the e-management of the covid19 pandemic in India. The idea that the greater good requires intrusive governance standards and that development becomes the ambition for all digitalisation also is used as justification for state generated crises like demonetization that led to a massive shift towards virtualisation of the financial ecosystem or extended lockdowns that isolated entire communities in the case of the abrogation of the constitution and reformulation of Kashmir, clearly show how the Internet is often used as a means of defining the greater good that fits specific political expressions of control and power.

2019: The revised Unlawful Activities (Prevention Act). specifically targets individuals as terrorists. A new kind of individual is born, alongside the 'natural person' and the 'data principal'. Together with the further amendment to the Citizenship Act, now targeting Muslims with its own ruling that only migrants who entered India from 'Afghanistan, Bangladesh or Pakistan... before the 31st day of December, 2014' would be allowed if they 'belonging to Hindu, Sikh, Buddhist, Jain, Parsi or Christian community', and the National Register of Citizenship, this led to major protests across India, and especially in Delhi.

2020 Anuradha Bhasin vs. Union of India and Ors. The landmark judgement from the Supreme court upheld that blanket Internet shutdowns were constitutional breaches because they hampered the fundamental rights of self-determination, commerce, and freedom of speech and expression. It recognised the Internet has a central and non-optional infrastructure in contemporary acts of being and realising one's citizenship and hence deemed Internet shutdowns illegal. It thus introduced the language of necessity and proportionality on to the regulation of the Internet infrastructure, and particularly Internet access. It also established that the Internet has a peculiar relationship with crises: It generates them and is also the tool for making interventions in times of crises, and that the very act of being online might be seen as entering a state of crisis. This is particularly critical to understanding that access to technology, which is often heralded as a universal right, is inherently suspicious and hence needs to be controlled with greater discretion, through public and private means, enabling both governments and private corporations to capitalise on different forms of Internet infrastructure regulation.

2021: New Intermediary Guidelines and Digital Media Ethics Code "2021 Rules" establish two provisions for content moderation and regulation on the Internet in India: Rule 4(4) on Content Filtering Mandate and Rule 4(2) on Traceability Mandate. The question of misinformation and conspiracy theories, accelerated by the supposition that all information is now subject to relative truth value, leads to these draconian principles. The Content Filtering Mandate overrides all end-to-end encryption and allows all digital content to be offered for review to authority. The traceability mandate emphasises the 'real name' principles that social media giants have already enforced on users, and 'enables the identification of the first originator of the information on its computer resource', thus implementing the

2009 Decryption Rules that allow authorities to request interception or monitoring of any decrypted digital information. These technological solutions claim to not compromise the K.S. Puttaswamy judgement that establishes the right of privacy as a fundamental right and allows new forms of information overload management tools and systems for the government. The monitoring of contemptuous comments, as in the case of the Agrima-Mishra controversy, or the prosecution of individuals who have made critical comments as in the case of Kanhaiya Kumar, were precursors to the establishment of these rules and show how these draconian measures are slowly leading to erasure of free-speech rights.

THE ARCHIVE

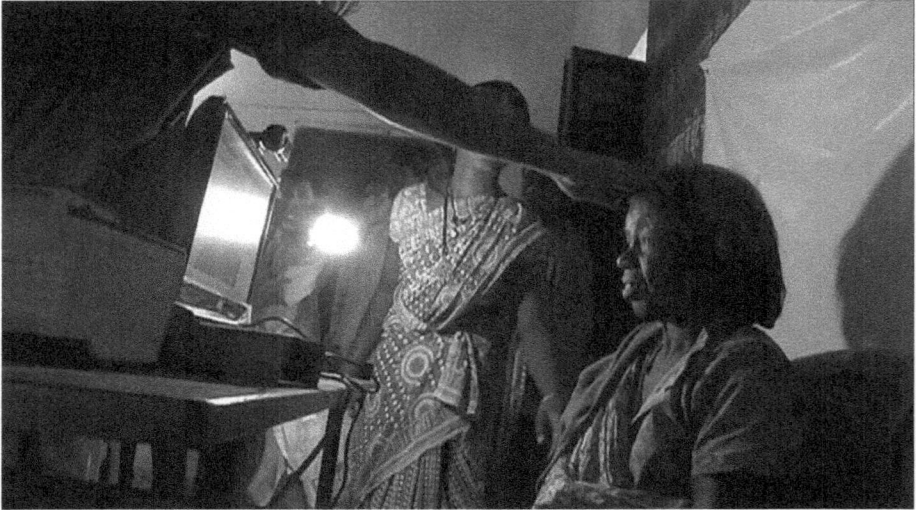

Fig 0: March 2011, Ratu Block, Ranchi. A tribal woman gets enrolled in Aadhaar, in the first year of its full operation across Bihar. Inage taken in the first stage of the CSCS Identity project field work.

SECTION 1

Box 7.4.1

Major Government Initiatives in the IT Sector

- Setting up of a new Ministry of Information Technology in October 1999, which was re-christened as Ministry of Communication and Information Technology in September 2001 given the increasing convergence between communication and IT.
- Setting up of National Task Force on Human Resources Development in IT in July 2000. The report of the Task Force is before the Government.
- Creation of an IT Venture Capital Fund of Rs. 100 crore in 1999.
- Upgradation of the Education and Research Network (ERNET) connecting various universities and regional engineering colleges (RECs) through a high speed network.
- Upgrading all RECs to the level of National Institutes of Technology.
- Enactment of a comprehensive law called the Information Technology (IT) Act, 2000, which provides legal recognition for transactions through electronic data interchange.
- Lowering custom duties on IT products, allowing 100 per cent foreign direct investment (FDI) in the sector, raising the limit on the issue of American Depository Receipts/Global Depository Receipts (ADR/GDR) by stock swap from $50 million to $100 million or up to ten times the company's export earnings in the previous year.
- Computerisation of government departments by spending up to 3 per cent of the budget on IT. Many e-governance applications were initiated. A number of government portals were hosted. Technology development and content creation in Indian languages were promoted.
- The Government initiated moves to set up 487 Community Information Centres at the block headquarters in the northeastern states and Sikkim for bridging the digital divide.
- The Media Lab Asia project was initiated in 2001 for taking IT to masses.
- Human resource development (HRD) for the IT sector was promoted through a multi-pronged approach revolving around increasing the availability and improving the quality of education. Many states set up Indian Institutes of Information Technology (IIITs) as centres of excellence.
- Research and development (R&D) in the emerging areas of technology and supercomputing are being pursued.

---

of 25 per cent in production and 46.5 per cent in exports. While software sector registered an impressive CAGR of 50 per cent, the growth in the hardware sector lagged at 10 per cent. The performance of the industry during Ninth Plan period is given in Table 7.4.1.

STRATEGY FOR THE TENTH PLAN

Hardware Development

7.4.5   The major reasons for the stagnant growth in IT hardware production are distorted tariff structure, poor infrastructure, high cost of finance and stiff competition from multinational corporations (MNCs). This sector is likely to face even harder competition after 2005 when the zero duty regime comes into place in line with the Information Technology Agreement of the World Trade Organisation (ITA-WTO). Although under this regime, import duty on finished products would come down to zero, it is unlikely that duties on various inputs such as chemicals and metals used in hardware production would also be brought down to zero. In such a scenario, the viability of domestic manufacturing will be adversely affected. A comprehensive package

---

Fig 1. The Tenth Five-year Plan, 2002-07, and usually seen as the point when e-governance was launched in India. It saw the implementation of the Information Technology Act of 2000 and the founding of the Ministry of Information Technology, the mass computerisation of government departments and the launch of the ERNET linking academic and research institutions in India.

ORDER UNDER SECTION 144 OF THE CODE OF CRIMINAL PROCEDURE 19

Whereas it has been made to appear before me that the Jat reservation agitation has sprea throughout the District Hisar. There are ongoing instances and further likelihood of block Railway track, highway and other roads by the agitators. Similarly, there is likelihood of (to public property and commission of cognizable offences related to safety and security o: individuals and property. This has caused a great inconvenience to the general public and adversely affected the essential services and supply of commodities. Many gatherings of t agitators are being facilitated by way of spreading disinformation and rumours through va social media such as Whatsapp, Facebook, Twitter, Instagram, Flickr, Tumblr, Google+, (mobile phones. Similarly, SMS services on mobile phones are being used to spread disinformation and for facilitating gatherings of agitators. As per reports received, there is imminent danger of disturbance of public tranquility due to inflammatory material being transmitted/ circulated to the public through social media/ messaging services on internet 2G/3G/Edge/ GPRS.

This order is issued to prevent any disturbance of peace and public order in the jurisdiction of Haryana and shall remain in effect till further orders.

This Order is being passed ex-parte in view of the emergent situation.

In case of violation of the aforesaid order, person found guilty shall be liable to be punished as per Section 188 of the Indian Penal Code.

Given under my hand and the seal of the court this day, 18th February 2016.

District Magistrate
Hisar.

No. 1194-1256 /PA IMA , dated 18|02|2016
A copy of the above is forwarded to the following for information and necessary action please:-
1. The Deputy Director General, TERM Cell (H), Ambala.
2. All Telecom Service Providers operating in Haryana Telecom Circle.
3. The Chief Secretary to Govt. Haryana. (For information)
4. The Addl. Chief Secretary to Govt. Haryana, Home Department, Chandigarh. (For information)
5. The Director General of Police, Haryana, Panchkula. (For information)
6. The Addl. Director General of Police, CID (H) Panchkula. (For information)
7. Divisional Commissioner, Hisar
8. District & Session Judge, Hisar
9. All District Magistrates in the state.
10. The Superintendent of Police Hisar with 5 spare copies
11. SDM Hisar/Hansi/Barwala.
12. CTM Hisar.
13. Civil Surgeon Hisar.
14. All Tehsildars/Naib Tehsildars in District Hisar.
15. All BDPOs in District Hisar.
16. DIPRO Hisar.
17. PA to DM Hisar

Fig 2. February 2016, Hisar, Haryana. Internet shutdown under Section 144 directly targeting 'WhatsApp, Facebook, Twitter, Instagram, Flickr, Tumblr and Google +'. This occurred in the wake of protests by the Jat community for inclusion of their caste under the Other Backward castes (OBC) community.

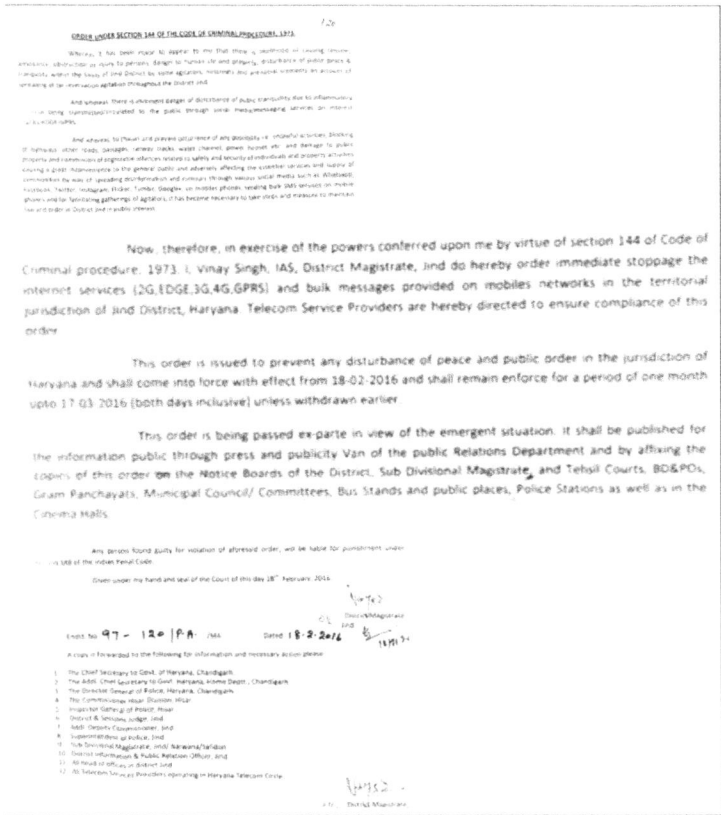

Fig 3. February 2016, Jind district, Haryana. District Magistrate Order for internet shutdown under Section 144 of the Indian Criminal Procedure Code, in the wake of major agitations by farmers in Punjab and neighbouring states.

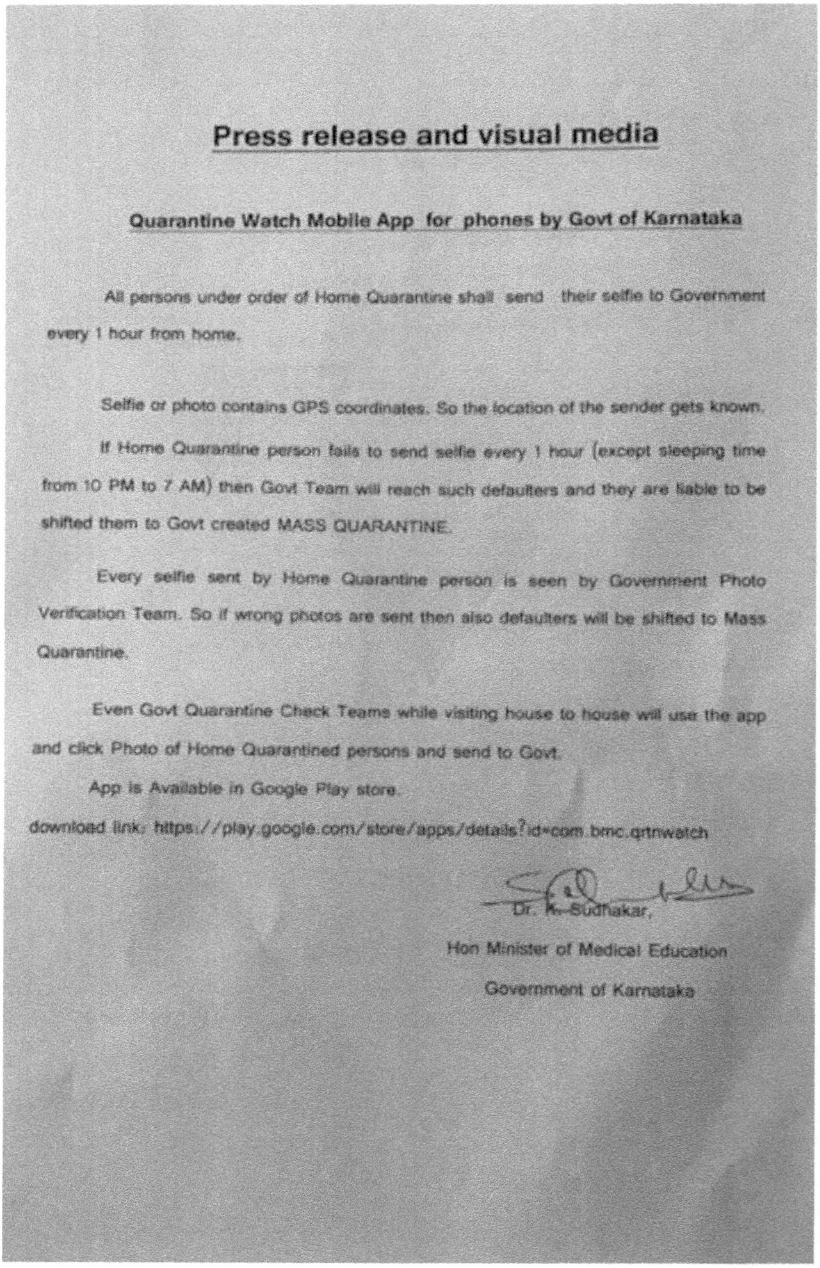

Press release and visual media

Quarantine Watch Mobile App for phones by Govt of Karnataka

All persons under order of Home Quarantine shall send their selfie to Government every 1 hour from home.

Selfie or photo contains GPS coordinates. So the location of the sender gets known.

If Home Quarantine person fails to send selfie every 1 hour (except sleeping time from 10 PM to 7 AM) then Govt Team will reach such defaulters and they are liable to be shifted them to Govt created MASS QUARANTINE.

Every selfie sent by Home Quarantine person is seen by Government Photo Verification Team. So if wrong photos are sent then also defaulters will be shifted to Mass Quarantine.

Even Govt Quarantine Check Teams while visiting house to house will use the app and click Photo of Home Quarantined persons and send to Govt.

App is Available in Google Play store.

download link: https://play.google.com/store/apps/details?id=com.bmc.qrtnwatch

Dr. K. Sudhakar,

Hon Minister of Medical Education

Government of Karnataka

Fig 4. March 2020, Bangalore. Karnataka government guidelines for self-quarantining using the Quarantine Watch mobile app during the first COVID lockdown.

'While investigating Jamia and NE riot cases, Delhi Police has done its job sincerely and impartially. All the arrests made have been based on analysis of scientific and forensic evidence, including video footages, technical & other footprints.

Delhi Police is committed to upholding the Rule of Law and bringing the conspirators, abettors and culprits of NE riots to books and secure justice to the innocent victims. It will not be deterred by the false propaganda and rumors floated by some vested elements who try to twist facts to their convenience. We continue to work tirelessly and relentlessly towards our motto ..Shanti, Seva and Nyaya.

Jai Hind'

Fig 5. March 2020, Delhi. Delhi police put out a Twitter post, following the arrest of the student activist Safoora Zargar, for her role in the protests against the Citizenship Amendment Act, 2019.

MOST IMMEDIATE

F. No. 101/2/1/2020-CA.IV
भारत सरकार /Government of India
मंत्रिमण्डल सचिवालय /Cabinet Secretariat
राष्ट्रपति भवन /Rashtrapati Bhawan
***

New Delhi, the 3rd April, 2020

Subject: Constitution of Committee for developing and implementing a Citizen App technology platform for combating COVID-19.

In response to the COVID-19 pandemic, a wide range of technology products and applications have come up to bring citizens onto a common platform. Technology experts, academicians and private companies have also reached out to the Government offering solutions and services. Developing a single nation-wide technology platform on-boarding all citizens can be a powerful tool in combating the pandemic.

2.   In view of the above, it has been decided to create an enabling mechanism through a public private partnership model to develop and implement a Citizen App technology platform, on-boarding all citizens in combating COVID-19, evaluating and converging related technology solutions and suggestions. A Committee is constituted comprising of the following:

   i.   Shri R.S. Sharma, Chairman, TRAI
   ii.   Professor K. Vijay Raghvan, Principal Scientific Advisor to Govt. of India
   iii. Shri Ajay Prakash Sawhney, Secretary, M/o Electronics & Information Technology
   iv.   Shri Anshu Prakash, Secretary, D/o Telecommunications
   v.   Shri Anand Mahindra, Chairman, Mahindra & Mahindra
   vi.   Shri N. Chandrasekaran, Chairman, Tata Sons
   vii. Professor V. Kamakoti, Member, NSAB, IIT Chennai

3.   M/o Electronics & Information Technology will provide secretarial support to the Committee. The Committee will be further assisted by Shri Manharsinh Yadav, Deputy Secretary, Prime Minister's Office.

4.   The Committee may co-opt any member as per requirement. The Committee shall complete its work within 3 months.

(Amrapali Kata)
Deputy Secretary to the Govt. of India
Tel: 2301 3507

To,

   1.   Shri R.S. Sharma, Chairman, TRAI
   2.   Professor K. Vijay Raghvan, Principal Scientific Advisor to Govt. of India
   3.   Shri Ajay Prakash Sawhney, Secretary, M/o Electronics & Information Technology
   4.   Shri Anshu Prakash, Secretary, D/o Telecommunications
   5.   Shri Anand Mahindra, Chairman, Mahindra & Mahindra
   6.   Shri N. Chandrasekaran, Chairman, Tata Sons
   7.   Professor V. Kamakoti, Member, NSAB, IIT Chennai
   8.   Shri Manharsinh, Deputy Secretary, Prime Minister's Office

Copy, for information, to:

   1. Dr. Hardik Shah, Deputy Secretary, Prime Minister's Office w.r.t. O.M. No. 5239411/2020 dated 02.04.2020.
   2. SO to Cabinet Secretary

Fig 6

Fig 6. April 2020, Delhi. The Cabinet Secretariat of the President of India announces a Committee for implementing what is explicitly described as a 'citizen app', ostensibly for combating COVID.

Broadcast Engineering Consultants India
Limited (Under Ministry Of Information
and Broadcasting) (544/17, Sector #2,
Noida- 201307

Tender No. 46CIL/PROJ/ITH&AV/Healthcare/2020 Dated: 10-04-2020

Corrigendum / Addendum No. 3

Subject: Corrigendum to Expression of Interest for EMPANELMENT OF AGENCY FOR SUPPLY OF
HEALTHCARE EQUIPMENTS

Tender No. BECIL/PROJ/ITH&AV/Healthcare/2020 Dated: 10-04-2020

1.   The following items are included in the EOI and their Technical specifications are attached as
Appendix to this corrigendum.
     a) HAND HELD THERMAL IMAGING SYSTEM
     b) OPTICAL THERMAL FEVER SENSING SYSTEM
     c) COVID - 19 PATIENT TRACKING TOOL
2.   The Pre – Bid question of all the prospective bidders are attached as Appendix to this
corrigendum.
3.   The Important Dates of EOI has been changed as below:

COVID -19 PATIENT TRACKING TOOL

S.No	Specifications
1.	Intelligence investigation platform & tactical tool to detect, prevent and investigate threats to national security using CDR, IPDR, Tower, Mobile Phone Forensics Data.
2.	Should be an advanced analytics and intelligence software that uses Telecom & Internet Data to identify suspect Locations, Associations & Behaviour.
3.	Should Trace contacts & connections of infected persons
4.	Should Identify unknowing contacts with infected persons.
5.	Should be able to Geo locate possible COVID-19 infected persons
6.	Location based Analysis - Easily Geo- Fence an area of interest (eg Meeting place, airport, mosque, railway station, bus stand etc) and identify all the people present at the location at the time of event
7.	Should allow Investigator to identify the how many cell towers from different service providers are covering an incident place or a location on a map.
8.	Should Identify the movement of COVID infected suspects, their cross-border movements, the people they come in contact with etc.
9.	Trace where this person has been and if he or she has been to areas known for being high risk locations.
10.	Should be able to Easily Identify close contacts, frequent contacts as well as occasional contacts such as Uber drivers etc.
11.	Should be able to collect information like where the suspect has spent most of his/her time and who all he or she has met. Zero in on connections with Watch List suspects
12.	Should be able to Identify a suspects behaviour, see what he or she does on specific days of the week, where does he or she order food from, where does the suspect go for regular walks, where does he/she work during the day, where does he/she sleep at night etc.

Fig 7. April 2020, Delhi. Broadcast Engineering Consultants India, Ministry of Information & Broadcasting, puts out a call for a Covid Tracking tool that is directly a surveillance app, which should be able to 'identify close contacts, frequent contacts as well as occasional Contacts', 'collect information like where the suspect has spent most of his/her time and who all he or she has met', 'zero in on connections with Watch List suspects', 'Identify a suspects behaviour, see what he or she does on specific days of the week, where does he or she order food from, where does the suspect go for regular walks, where does he/she work during the day, where does he/she sleep at night etc'.

SECTION 2

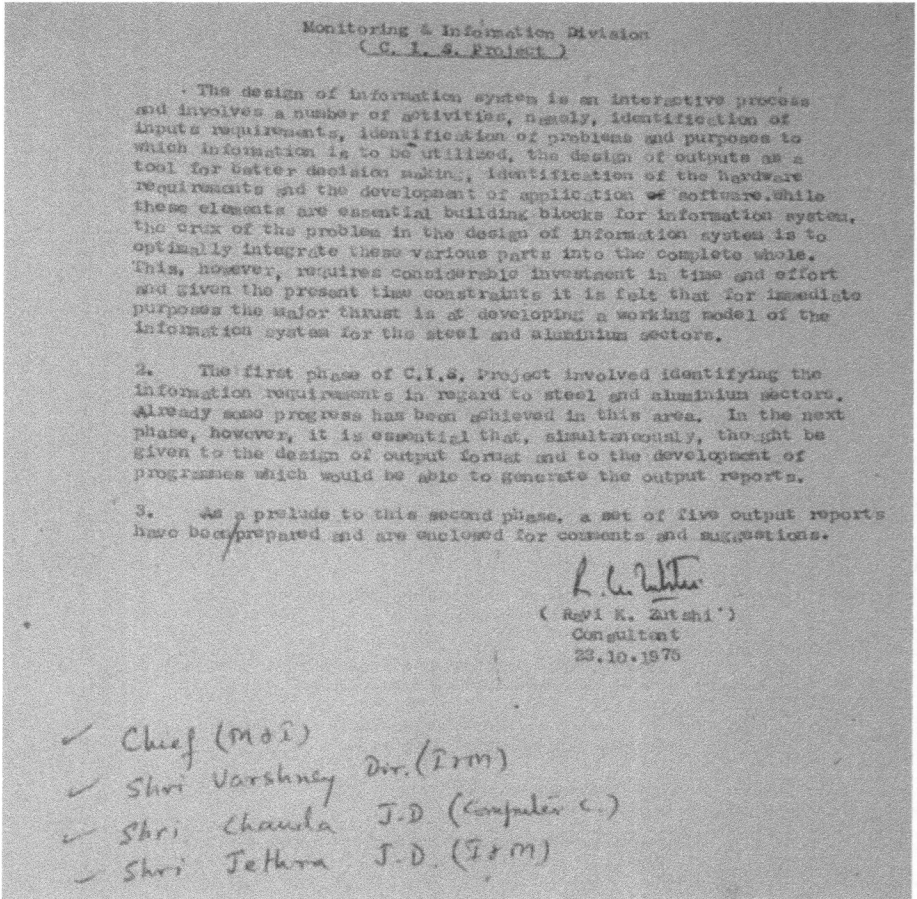

Fig 8. October 1975. One of the earliest project outlines for the management of a centralised data system by the Planning Commission.

PUBLIC ACCOUNTS COMMITTEE
(1975-76)

(FIFTH LOK SABHA)

TWO HUNDRED AND TWENTY-FIRST REPORT

COMPUTERISATION IN GOVERNMENT
DEPARTMENTS

DEPARTMENT OF ELECTRONICS

LOK SABHA SECRETARIAT
NEW DELHI

CHAPTER V

DATA SECURITY

5.1. For an expert bent on crime, it is said cracking a computer system's defence is only 'as difficult as doing a hard Sunday crossword puzzle'. According to a story entitled 'Waiting for the Great Computer Rip-off' published in FORTUNE, July, '74, ZARF, a joint project of the U.S. Air Force and MITRE Corporation—a defence research out-fit, is said to have 'subverted everyone of the system's (Multies)** safeguards' which has been designed' with security as an upper most consideration. This is an instance of the vulnerability of the modern electronic data processing systems. Until not long ago computer manufacturers and users saw little reason to fear that an unscrupulous person at one terminal could be able to read, alter or delete another user's data or tamper with the intricate programmes that manipulate this data. But in the recent years even the manufacturers have come to acknowledge that it is not very difficult for some one with a lot of skill to do things like that even with the most secured systems now in existence. Robert Courtney the man responsible for safeguards that go into IBM equipment is stated to have classified computer related risks into 6 categories. Among these he has mentioned the "category that includes remote manipulation of the system by outsiders".

5.2. There are various subtle methods by which unauthorised persons can have access to the information sorted in the computers.

"The programmers who write the software can subvert supposed protective features or instal "trapdoors" for subsequent entry. Operators may have daily opportunity to tamper with data or files. Maintenance men may incorporate subversive instructions into the test programmes they employ to test for mal-functions. Wiretaps and various bugging devices can intercept data transmissions or even pick up electromagnetic emanations from wires and terminals. The tappers may use intercepted passwords to "masquerade" as legitimate users, or may even insert "piggyback" data into legitimate transmissions. Sometimes legitimate users borrow passwords to masquerade or

**A new computer system designed by Honeywell Inc.

155

493 LS—11.

Fig 9. April 1976, Delhi. Parliament of India Public Accounts Committee 1975-97: the first explicit governmental concern about hacking and data security.

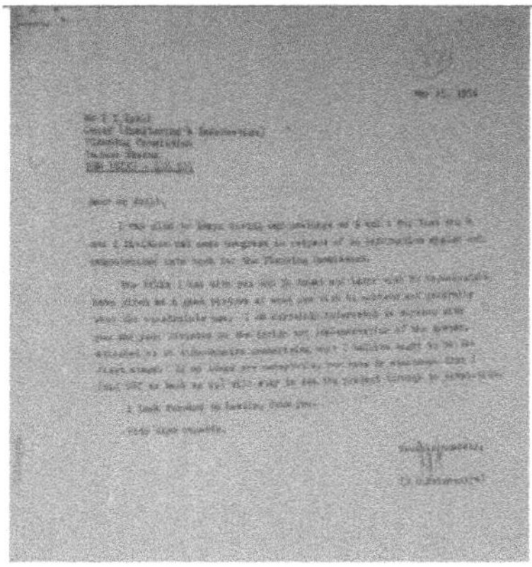

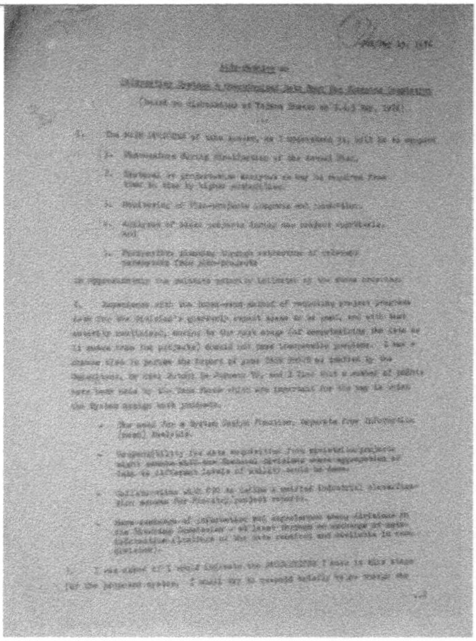

Fig 10. May 1976. J.G. Krishnayya's aide memoire on the design of an information system for a computerised data bank by the Planning Commission.

NICNET

NICNET — A Hierarchic Distributed Computer Communication Network for Decision Support in the Indian Government

N. Seshagiri, K.K.K. Kutty, N. Vijayaditya,
Y.K. Sharma, D.P. Bobde, M. Moni

National Informatics Centre
Department of Electronics, Government of India
New Delhi 110 003

A decision support information system for the Indian Government is being evolved, based on the design of a predominantly query-based computer network with hierarchic distributed databases and random access communication. The four level hierarchy spans 439 districts at the lowest level, the Central Government headquarters in New Delhi, the set of 32 State Capitals and Union Territories, and the set of four Regional Centres.

With interference tolerance and random access as two guiding principles behind the choice, Spread Spectrum transmission and Code Division Multiple Access system of satellite communication was adopted. Each node of the network is a 32-bit computer which is capable of local bulk storage of up to three units of 300 megabytes each for purposes of query-accessible distributed databases. The design and implementation of such a distributed database has endowed the network with the capability to distribute the data related to such databases over various nodes in the network so as to be able to accept a query from any of the nodes.

1. INTRODUCTION

From the genesis of the concept of the National Informatics Centre (NIC) in 1973 to its nucleation in 1975 followed by the commissioning of NICNET in 1977, it was a phase of innovation penetrating through barriers of conservatism in Governmental organisations.

The NIC, now an organisation structured around nearly 2000 personnel, including nearly 1500 computer specialists, is giving full-fledged Management Information System (MIS) and computerisation services to several Ministries/Departments and associated organisations in the Central and State Governments by catalysing the growth of computerisation where none existed earlier. The most important function of NIC is to put to use the new technology of computer networking to enable efficient exchange of information between the Centre and the States, between the States and their Districts and among the

Fig 11. 1987. N. Seshagiri et al: in many ways a founding document for the NICNET, outlining a hierarchical networked system for all arms of the Government by the National Informatics Centre, together with a distributed DBMS system.

1990 – NICNET forecasts

Indian Journal of Radio & Space Physics
Vol. 19, October & December 1990, pp. 281-296

621·39

281- 96.

Global compunication — A 15-year technology forecast

N. Seshagiri

National Informatics Centre, Planning Commission, A-Block, CGO Complex, Lodi Road, New Delhi 110 003

A technology forecast for 1990-2005 A.D. is made for the global compunication technology, which is a synergetic merger of computer technology and communication technology. The trends in global compunication as it metamorphoses the office, the factory and the home services, are forecast, utilising the Harvard Map of Information products and services as well as Kobayashi's concept of integration of computer and communication. From the experience of setting up a nation-wide computer-communication network, NICNET, based on very small aperture terminals (VSATs) and spread spectrum code division multiple access technology, certain VSAT technology trends are analysed. In this product environment, the emerging profile of integrated services digital network (ISDN) is outlined based on a seven-layer protocol and broad-band application spectrum. Supplementary forecasts are made on trends in value added network, switched optical communication, cellular mobile communication, and personal communication network.

1 Introduction

In his treatise 'Understanding Media', Marshall McLuhan predicted, 25 years ago, a world-wide coalescence of human activities into a single community tending to a "Global Village". Such a coalescence is already perceptible as global communication is increasing in complexity, variety and volume of interaction between the various countries of the world. Global networks of computers are already bringing about an information exchange between countries. This infrastructure is fostering increased international trade. The convergence of computer technology and communication technology is already becoming visible in the form of facsimile service, automatic bank teller machines, international television, answering machines, compact disks, among others.

Kobayashi[1] evolved a concept of integration of computer and communication (C&C) in which he forecast the features of communication technology which would be derived from computer technology and vice versa. Building up on this concept, the system of global compunication access that is likely to evolve in the next fifteen years has been derived as shown in Fig.1. Basically this forecast is a combination of three functional elements: (a) terminals interfacing with people, (b) conventional transparent communication network, and (c) computer oriented information and communication service centres.

The transmission systems assumed are: (a) Terrestrial communication (Tercom): microwave/millimetre wave system, optical fibre cable system, coaxial cable system, paired cable system and submarine cable system, and (b) Satellite communication (Satcom): point-to-point communication with Ka-band (20-30 GHz) hubless very small aperture terminals (VSATs) and ADSATs with onboard switching facility (OBS), remote sensing satellites with OBS and high precision digital photography equipment, and mass media satellites for broadcasting.

Local area networks (LANs) in offices, factories and homes are connected to meteropolitan area switching systems. These switching systems also connect communication and information processing centres (CIPCs) (Videotex, data processing, databases, etc.), value added network (VAN) communication and information processing centres as well as radio and television broadcasting stations. The LAN and CIPC are connected to subscriber access systems which, in turn, along with VAN, are connected to the switch. The output of the switch multiplexes the radio base stations. Throughout, integrated services digital network (ISDN) will be the main infrastructure.

Broadcasting stations are connected directly to the transmission system. The radio base stations and the broadcasting station along with remote sensing satellites, point-to-point compunication satellites and mass media satellites provide the mobile compunication links for air transport, marine transport, surface transport and individual communication.

281

Fig 12. December 1990. N. Seshagiri's forecast for what the future holds for NIC, especially in regard to ISDNs creating a diversity of networks with different priorities, as against a single, hierarchical and centralised network.

DISNIC-PLAN : A NICNET Based Distributed Database for Micro-level Planning in India

M.Moni
National Informatics Centre, New Delhi
E-Mail: moni@hub.nic.in

Micro-level Planning is gaining momentum in developing countries. The Planning steps, the data needs, the institutional requirements, the macro-micro linkages and the information flows are necessary to make the planning process effective. Indian planning and development process is aheading for a change from the centralised to more of decentralised approach in order to give due recognition to the micro-level needs and potentials in decision making. The committee on Study Group on Information Gap, constituted by the Planning Commission, Government of India, in 1989 has recommended for the creation of data bases on (i) Plan Information, (ii) Plan Monitoring, and (iii) Plan Evaluation, in districts. This committee has also recommended to develop databases with respect to (i) Socio-economic, (ii) Agro-economic, (iii) Infrastructure, (iv) Demographic, and (v) Natural resources.

A "village" or a "cluster of villages" is considered as a "suitable and manageable" geographic unit for planned development within the framework of district planning. Since India has its varied spatial peculiarities over different types of terrain, natural resources, climate, socio-economic conditions, political ideologies, etc., the micro-level planning and modeling requires a comprehensive village level spatial and non-spatial information system.

With the establishment of NICNET nodes in all 500 districts of India, which are the basic administrative spatial units at the sub-state level and also consistent with the decentralised planning concepts of the Government of India, National Informatics Centre(NIC) has launched "DISNIC - a NICNET based district government informatics programme" for strengthening planning and development, covering 28 sectors such as agriculture, animal husbandry, irrigation, industry, education, environment, energy, rural development, etc., at the local levels. An integrated approach for database development across different sectors has been adopted, as it is essential for planning and development.

The National Informatics Centre, through its DISNIC-PLAN Programme, has created a distributed database on village level information for about 6 lakhs villages, in the country, using its NICNET facilities at 500 district nodes. Project activities have been taken-up to link these databases with the spatial database in the form of maps to provide an effective spatial analysis under Geographical Information System(GIS) environment. Further, development of INTRANET site over NICNET National Info-Highway, on DISNIC-PLAN Programme has also been undertaken.

Proceedings of the 22nd VLDB Conference
Mumbai(Bombay), India, 1996

586   Fig 13

Fig 13. 1996. Two decades after J.G. Krishnayya's initial outlines, the National informatics Centre outlines DISNIC, a decentralized information architecture that connected departments through a network enabling micro-level, village-centered, planning.

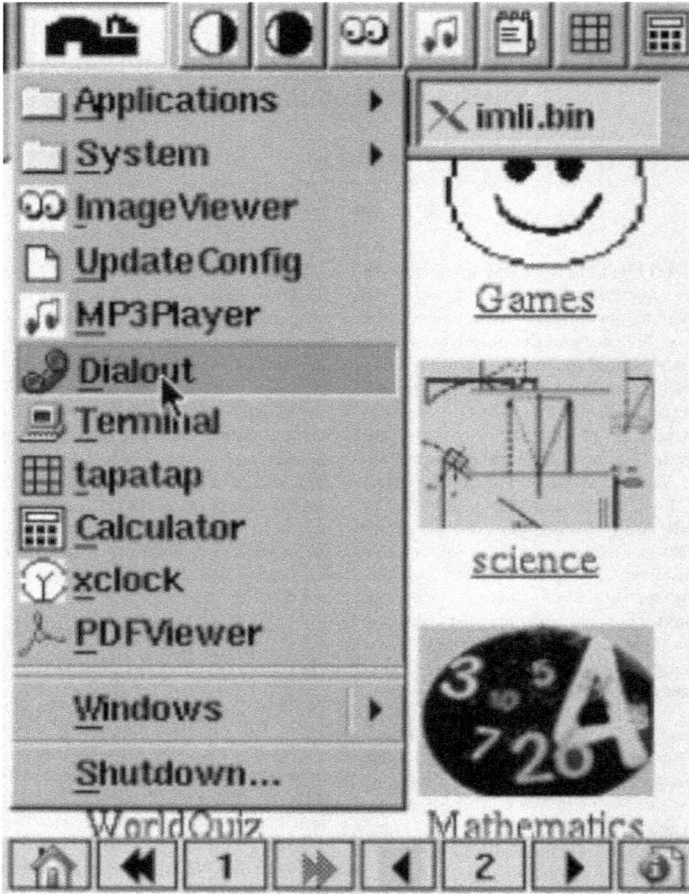

Fig 14. 1999, Bangalore. Visual interface for the Simputer, a handheld smartcard-compliant device invented by scientists from the Indian Institute of Science.

66. (*1*) Whoever with the intent to cause or knowing that he is likely to cause wrongful loss or damage to the public or any person destroys or deletes or alters any information residing in a computer resource or diminishes its value or utility or affects it injuriously by any means, commits hacking.

(*2*) Whoever commits hacking shall be punished with imprisonment up to three years, or with fine which may extend upto two lakh rupees, or with both.

Directions of Controller to a subscriber to extend facilities to decrypt information.

69. (*1*) If the Controller is satisfied that it is necessary or expedient so to do in the interest of the sovereignty or integrity of India, the security of the State, friendly relations with foreign States or public order or for preventing incitement to the commission of any cognizable offence, for reasons to be recorded in writing, by order, direct any agency of the Government to intercept any information transmitted through any computer resource.

Fig 15. June 2000, Delhi. The Information Technology Act, including its Sections 66A and 69A, digitally upgrading, and also significantly transforming, the right to free speech.

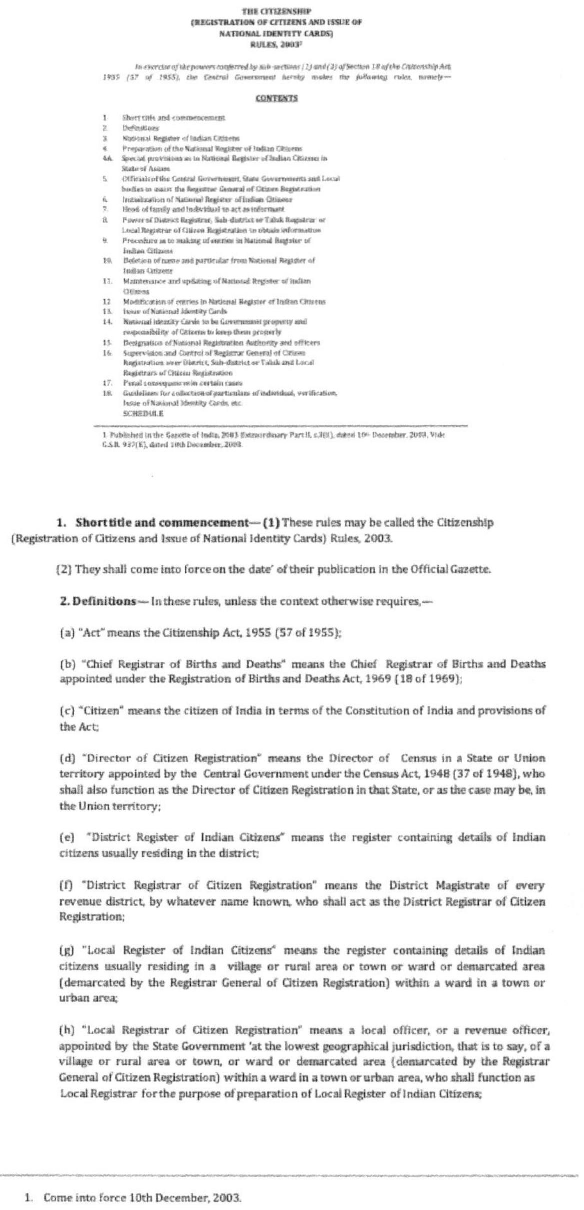

THE CITIZENSHIP
(REGISTRATION OF CITIZENS AND ISSUE OF
NATIONAL IDENTITY CARDS)
RULES, 2003[1]

In exercise of the powers conferred by sub-sections (1) and (3) of Section 18 of the Citizenship Act, 1955 (57 of 1955), the Central Government hereby makes the following rules, namely—

CONTENTS

---

1. Published in the Gazette of India, 2003 Extraordinary Part II, s.3(i), dated 10th December, 2003, Vide G.S.R. 937(E), dated 10th December, 2003.

1. Short title and commencement— (1) These rules may be called the Citizenship (Registration of Citizens and Issue of National Identity Cards) Rules, 2003.

(2) They shall come into force on the date[*] of their publication in the Official Gazette.

2. Definitions— In these rules, unless the context otherwise requires,—

(a) "Act" means the Citizenship Act, 1955 (57 of 1955);

(b) "Chief Registrar of Births and Deaths" means the Chief Registrar of Births and Deaths appointed under the Registration of Births and Deaths Act, 1969 (18 of 1969);

(c) "Citizen" means the citizen of India in terms of the Constitution of India and provisions of the Act;

(d) "Director of Citizen Registration" means the Director of Census in a State or Union territory appointed by the Central Government under the Census Act, 1948 (37 of 1948), who shall also function as the Director of Citizen Registration in that State, or as the case may be, in the Union territory;

(e) "District Register of Indian Citizens" means the register containing details of Indian citizens usually residing in the district;

(f) "District Registrar of Citizen Registration" means the District Magistrate of every revenue district, by whatever name known, who shall act as the District Registrar of Citizen Registration;

(g) "Local Register of Indian Citizens" means the register containing details of Indian citizens usually residing in a village or rural area or town or ward or demarcated area (demarcated by the Registrar General of Citizen Registration) within a ward in a town or urban area;

(h) "Local Registrar of Citizen Registration" means a local officer, or a revenue officer, appointed by the State Government 'at the lowest geographical jurisdiction, that is to say, of a village or rural area or town, or ward or demarcated area (demarcated by the Registrar General of Citizen Registration) within a ward in a town or urban area, who shall function as Local Registrar for the purpose of preparation of Local Register of Indian Citizens;

---

1.   Come into force 10th December, 2003.

Fig 16. December 2003, Delhi. The first major amendment to the 1955 Citizenship Act, with the Citizenship Registration and National Identity Cards Rules.

Table 8.1: Whose "Transparency and Efficiency"?

Taluks / Villages / Respondents	Pre- Bhoomi		Post Bhoomi		Other details
	RTC (copy/correction)	Mutation	RTC (copy/correction)	Mutation or *khata* change	
Locations: 3 Villages in a relatively less intensively urbanizing taluk. **Respondents:** Local politicians: 3 (current and former Village Presidents) Taluk and village level officials: 4 (RI: 1, VAs: 3) Small farmers: 10 Brokers: 2	Rs.5 to Rs.100 Immediate	Rs. 1000 2-4 days	Rs.15 + Rs.35 plus expenses of Rs. 100 for agent to visit the taluk office Time taken is 2-3 months	Rs.3000 in addition to transport expenses for several visits. While there is an official one-month rule, in reality this normally extends to 3-4 months.	Bribes are on a transaction basis
Locations: 2 villages in an urbanized taluk in the city's peri-urban area. **Respondents** Taluk and village officials: 5 Politicians: 5 Small and medium farmers: 10 Brokers	Rs.3 to Rs.50 Immediate	Rs. 500 to Rs. 5000 2-4 days	Rs 15 (individual) and Rs. 100 processed via an agent. Correction for individual is not possible due to the need to visit the office for 10 days. Application via an agent is Rs.300.	Rs.3000 to Rs.5000 If there is a problem, the amount can go upto Rs. 15,000 to Rs.20,000	**Bribes on an acre basis** Investors from Andhra Pradesh, and large developers and layouts catering to NRIs and IT firms, dominate the land market.
Location: 2 villages in an urbanized and in some parts, very rapidly urbanizing taluk in the city's peri-urban area. **Respondents**	Time limit = 1 or 2 days Cost Rs.5 to Rs.50 Fewer corrections were required in the manual system. In those cases, a correction could be made immediately if needed. Previously, the medium	Rs.500 to Rs. 5000 depending on the size of land and the complexity of *khata* involved. Following are categories of land sanctions:	The fees depend on the type of work and the reality of visiting the taluk office. Copy of RTC: Rs.15 (fee) and a bus ticket of Rs.40. There is the additional problem of equipment downtime at the kiosk.	The bribe ranges between Rs. 1000 and Rs.3000. Here, the lower amount is for those seen as 'small farmers' with no significant problems. But having land with no 'problem' is rare, as most small farmers are situated on	**Bribes on an acre basis**

Bhoomi   *-VIII. 16-*

Fig 17. 2004, Bangalore. Major report on the consequences of Bhoomi, or the digitization of land records, and the nature of change pre-and post-Bhoomi. Information and Communications Technologies for Development: A Comparative Analysis of Impacts and Costs from India: report funded by The Department of Information Technology (DIT) and Infosys Technologies, Bangalore.

Web Services & Localisation: A Way forward to Realise Digital Inclusion and Development in Rural India[*]

Madaswamy Moni
Deputy Director General
National Informatics Centre
Government of India
moni@nic.in

1   Digital Economy – An Economic Transformation, Now Intensifying

Most of rural India is yet to accept the idea of an inclusive India, and presents a baffling dichotomy of images: poverty and growing potential of rural markets, where over 70 % of the Indian population lives. Rural India desires to take advantage of "knowledge-intensive" techniques for sustainability of its stakeholders: farm and non-farm linkages, through grassroots level information access (contents) and grassroots level access to information (networking). India is also a highly multilingual country with more than 20 officially recognized languages and hundreds of dialects in use, and only 5% of the Indian populace speaking the English language. Breaking the language barrier is like providing an essential infrastructure for good governance, peace & prosperity at grassroots level. Rural connectivity is strength, wealth, and progress and hence to face the SWOT in respect of:

- Reaching the unreached : Public Services

- From digital divide to digital opportunities for sustainable development and economic growth

- Fostering agricultural growth, poverty reduction and sustainable resources use

- Sustainable development & earth care policies - water, energy, education, health, agriculture & rural development, biodiversity

- A Cluster of villages - sustainable societies in viable rural space

This has led to a growth of supply capacity through capital-augmenting technological change, which in turn, changed the capital and labour markets, and has generated greatest demand in: Web Services Development, User Interface Design, Business Domain Expertise, Security Expertise, Mobile Application Development, and Ubiquitous Computing. Indian IT & ITES industries have tremendous potential to become an engine of growth and productivity improvement, through localisation, for all sectors of the economy. Data may need to be abstracted from more than 200 different document formats (HTML, PDF, Word, PPT, etc) encountered on the Web. An economic transformation - digital economy - is now intensifying and leading to a rapid economic growth in India [1].

2   ICT Diffusion for Development with a Rural Focus

The Indian government has initiated several Digital Initiatives: Digital Networks for Farmers (DNF), as a follow up of ISDA95 [2] recommendations, to ensure digital inclusion for fostering rural prosperity and reducing spatial disparities in India. Rural India should be given a chance through Digital Networks for Farmers (DNF), DISNIC Programme, e-Cooperatives, and digital SMEs. [2], [3], [4] and [5] dealt with the Digital Initiatives, so as to help 'bridge theory and reality at grassroots':

- e-Cooperatives & CoopNet : an Internet enterprise development programme for fostering agricultural and rural industries;

- AGMARKNET : A network connecting about 2500 Agricultural Produces Wholesale Markets to transmit daily market prices of more than 300 commodities and 2000 varieties – facilitating a DATAWAREHOUSE for rural empowerment to achieve 24-7-365-Supply–Chain; with a road map to cover 7000 and 32000 rural markets (http://agmarknet.nic.in)

---

[*]Published in CSI Communications (India), March 2006

Fig 18. March 2006. The National Informatics Centre's Digital inclusion project targeting rural India as well as arguing for localisation of data, coinciding with the first meetings of the National E-Governance Plan the same year.

GUIDELINES FOR NATIONAL ROLLOUT eDistrict

1. BACKGROUND

a. NeGP was approved by the Government in May 2006, with the following vision:

> "Make all Government Services accessible to the common man in his locality, through common service delivery outlets and ensure efficiency, transparency and reliability of such services at affordable costs to realize the basic needs of the common man".

b. To realize this vision, 27 Central, State and Integrated Mission Mode projects (MMPs) along with 8 support components were identified and approved under NeGP **(Annexure II).** States have been given flexibility to identify upto 5 additional state-specific projects, which are particularly relevant for the economic development of the State. NeGP also envisages creation of the core IT infrastructure in the form of SWANs, SDCs and one lakh front ends namely CSCs in rural areas across the country to deliver public services electronically.

c. **e-District** is one of the 27 MMPs under NeGP, with the Department of Information Technology (DIT), Government of India (GoI) as the nodal Department, to be implemented by State Government or their designated agencies. **This MMP aims at electronic delivery of identified high volume citizen centric services, at district and sub-district level, those are not part of any other MMP.** To achieve these objectives service levels and outcomes for each of these services will be clearly laid down by the concerned State, with a view to improving the efficiency and effectiveness of the service delivery. The MMP envisages leveraging and utilizing the four pillars of e-infrastructure namely, SDCs, SWANs, SSDGs and CSCs, optimally to deliver public services electronically to citizens at their door steps. Initially only those high volume citizen-centric services will be taken up for implementation which have high priority for the State. New services will be added to the portfolio subsequently, once the demand for the initial set of e-enabled services increases.

2. OBJECTIVES

The objectives of the e District Mission Mode Project are to ensure the following:

a. Undertake backend computerization of District and Tehsil level offices to ensure electronic delivery of high volume citizen centric services at the district level.

Fig 19. May 2006. The National E-Governance Plan (NeGP) outlines for creating e-districts, namely the electronic delivery 'high volume citizen-centric services' at the district level that are not included in any of its other 39 mission-mode projects.

Draft Document   Person Identification Codification

Report of Expert Committee on Metadata and Data Standards
For
Person Identification

1.0 Scope

1.1 Objective of Person Identification Codification

To identify each and every person uniquely at the national level to ensure interoperability of information related to individuals collected by various Govt./non Gov. organization. Also to ensure data integrity and smooth horizontal and vertical data exchange related to the individuals across the domain applications.

1.2 Description

a. Identification of generic data elements for person identification and their business formats

b. Mechanism for the codification / nomenclature of the generic data elements to reflect parent-child relationship among them

c. Identification of code directories and their ownerships for updation.

d. Identification of attributes of the code directories on the basis of identified generic data elements

e. Standardization of values in the code directories

f. Identification of Person Identification attributes

g. Identification of metadata Qualifiers

h. Preparation of metadata of the data elements

i. Metadata and Data Standards implementation steps / procedure in domain applications

1.3 Approach to be adopted:

Phase 1

a. Mechanism of codification of data elements

b. Identify generic data elements for person identity

c. Identify code directories & their ownership

d. Identify basic qualifiers for metadata

e. Describe metadata of identified data elements

Version 0.8	Date : 29/08/2008	Page 4 of 64

Fig 20. 2008. Expert Committee on Metadata and Data Standards to 'identify each and every person uniquely at the national level' to ensure 'interoperability of information related to individuals collected by various Govt./non Gov. organizations'.

GOVERNMENT OF INDIA

SECOND ADMINISTRATIVE REFORMS COMMISSION

ELEVENTH REPORT

PROMOTING e-GOVERNANCE
The SMART Way Forward

DECEMBER 2008

PREFACE

In his *Grundlegung Zur Metaphysik de Sitton*, Immanual Kant says, *"So act a treat humanity, whether in their own person or in that of any other, in every case an end withal, never as means only"*. Kant's observation is even more valid today. ' citizens are ends in themselves, rather than as means to other ends. The colonial v of the Government used to be as a 'controller' and 'ruler'. It is now that of a coordin and provider. Government is responsible for providing certain services to the citizens, like an organisation is responsible for managing a value chain that leads to output. Busir corporations have discovered over the last few decades that information technology make the value chain more efficient and lead to quality improvements and cost savir Similarly, Governments have discovered that information technology can make the provis of services to the citizen more efficient and transparent, can save costs and lead to a hig level of efficiency.

e-Governance is in essence, the application of Information and Communicati Technology to government functioning in order to create 'Simple, Moral, Accounta Responsive and Transparent'[1] (SMART) governance. In this report on e-Governance, Second Administrative Reforms Commission (ARC) has tried to analyse the successes failures of e-Governance initiatives in India and at the global level, in order to extrapo the best practices, key reform principles and recommendations that can help the governm to implement a new paradigm of governance in the country. This new paradigm wo focus on the use of information technology to bring public services to the doorsteps of citizens and businesses on the basis of revolutionary changes in our institutional structu procedures and practices that would transform the relationships between our three le of government, our businesses and our citizens.

The revolution in Information and Communications Technology (ICT) has brou a whole new agenda for governance into the realm of possibility. e-Governance compr decisional processes and the use of ICT for wider participation of citizens in public affa Citizens are participants in e-Governanc. The purpose of implementing e-Governanc to improve governance processes and outcomes with a view to improving the delivery public services to citizens. Some authors have defined e-Governance as the e-business of

Paragraph 43, Report of the Working Group on Convergence and E-Governance for The Tenth Five Year Plan (2002-20971, Planning Commission, November 2001

Fig 21. December 2008, Delhi. Second Administrative Reforms Commission, report on 'Promoting E-Governance, the SMART Way Forward' introducing the concept of 'SMART' (Simple, Moral, Accountable, Responsive and Transparent'), also transforming governance into a form of service providing, with significant consequences to social and economic rights.

2

Annexure 1

(TO BE PUBLISHED IN PART-I, SECTION-2 OF THE GAZETTE OF INDIA)

GOVERNMENT OF INDIA
PLANNING COMMISSION

Yojana Bhawan, Sansad Marg,
New Delhi, 28th January,2009

NOTIFICATION

No. A-43011/02/2009-Admn.I: In pursuance of Empowered Group of Ministers' fourth meeting, dated 4th November 2008, the **Unique Identification Authority of India (UIDAI)** is hereby constituted and notified as an attached office under aegis of Planning Commission with following terms of reference and initial core staff composition:-

COMPOSITION:

2. UIDAI shall be set up with an initial core team of 115 officials and staff as per details given below:

Post	Level	No. of Posts
UID Authority of India		
Director General & Mission Director	Additional Secretary Govt. of India	1
Deputy Director General (DDG)	Joint Secretary, Govt. of India	1
Assistant Director General (ADG)	Director, Govt. of India	1
Support Staff		
PS	PS	3
Peon	Peon	2
Driver	Driver	2
	Total Manpower	10
State /UT Units of UIDAI		
State / UT UID Commissioner	Joint Secretary, Govt. of India	35
Support Staff		
PS	PS	35
Peon	Peon	35
	Total Manpower	105
Grand Total		**115**

Fig 22   Page 1 of 52

Fig 22. 2009, Delhi. The Planning Commission produces the original founding document of the Unique identification Authority of India (UIDAI).

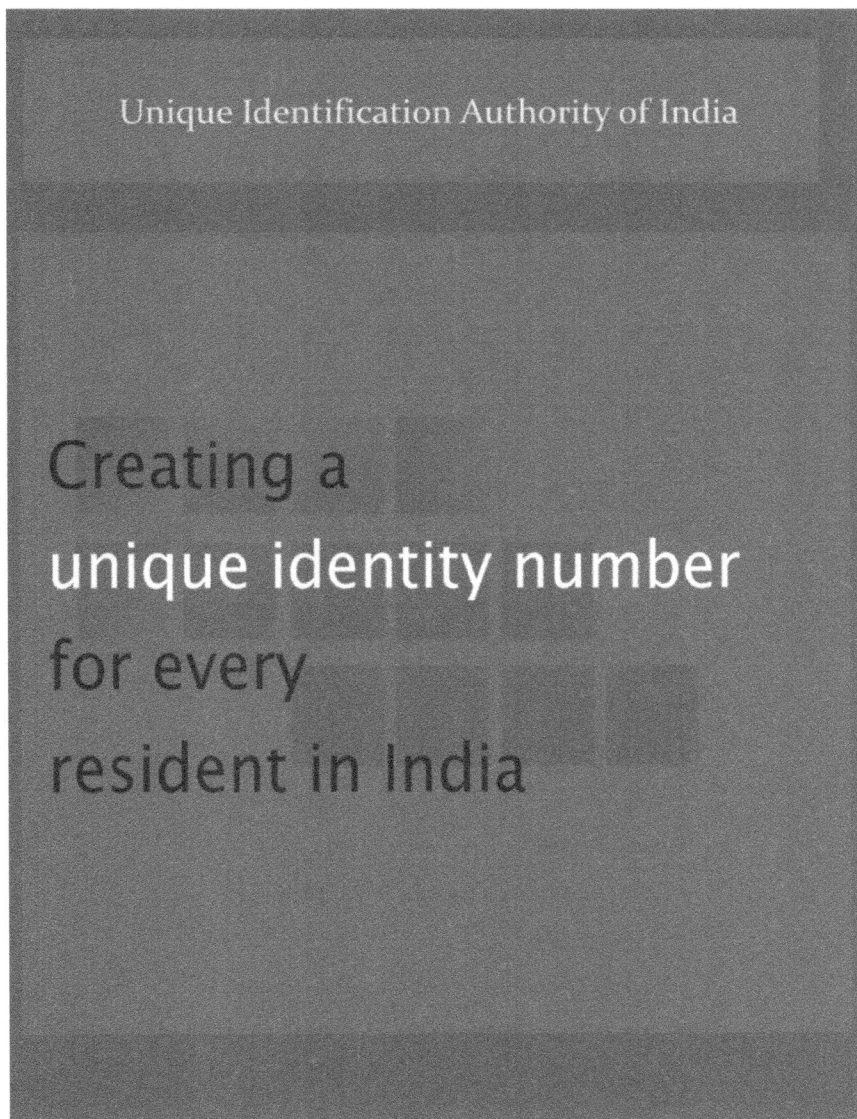

Unique Identification Authority of India

Creating a
unique identity number
for every
resident in India

Fig 23. April 2010. Inaugural document of the UIDAI, 'Creating a Unique identity Number for Every resident in India' (UIDAI Working paper 1.1), outlining a 'new approach to identity'. This document does not exist on UIDAI's database any longer. Also: the Aadhaar enrolment ecosystem as envisaged in the initial document, as a public-private partnership, leading to several questions about the security of the data.

duplicate and fake identities, and (b) can be verified and authenticated in an easy, cost-effective way. The UIDAI's approach will keep in mind the learnings from the government's previous efforts at issuing identity.

The UIDAI will be created as a statutory body under a separate legislation to fulfil its objectives. The law will also stipulate rules, regulations, processes and protocols to be followed by different agencies partnering with the Authority in issuing and verifying unique identity numbers.

Executive Summary

Overview

In India, an inability to prove identity is one of the biggest barriers preventing the poor from accessing benefits and subsidies. Public as well as private sector agencies across the country typically require proof of identity before providing individuals with services. But till date, there remains no nationally accepted, verified identity number that both residents and agencies can use with ease and confidence.

As a result, every time an individual tries to access a benefit or service, they must undergo a full cycle of identity verification. Different service providers also often have different requirements in the documents they demand, the forms that require filling out, and the information they collect on the individual.

Such duplication of effort and 'identity silos' increase overall costs of identification, and cause extreme inconvenience to the individual. This approach is especially unfair to India's poor and underprivileged residents, who usually lack documentation, and find it difficult to meet the costs of multiple verification processes.

There are clearly, immense benefits from a mechanism that uniquely identifies a person, and ensures instant identity verification. The need to prove identity only once will bring down transaction costs for the poor. A clear identity number would also transform the delivery of social welfare programs by making them more inclusive of communities now cut off from such benefits due to their lack of identification. It would enable the government to shift from indirect to direct benefits, and help verify whether the intended beneficiaries actually receive funds/subsidies.

A single, universal identity number will also be transformational in eliminating fraud and duplicate identities, since individuals will no longer be able to represent themselves differently to different agencies. This will result in significant savings to the state exchequer. As an example, the Ministry of Petroleum and Natural Gas can save over Rs.1200 crores a year in subsidies now reportedly lost on LPG cylinders registered under duplicate or ghost identities.

Features of the UIDAI model

The UID number will only provide identity: The UIDAI's purview will be limited to the issue of unique identification numbers linked to a person's demographic and biometric information. The UID number will only guarantee identity, not rights, benefits or entitlements.

The UID will prove identity, not citizenship: All residents in the country can be issued a unique ID. The UID is proof of identity and does not confer citizenship.

A pro-poor approach: The UIDAI envisions full enrolment of residents, with a focus on enrolling India's poor and underprivileged communities. The Registrars that the Authority plans to partner with in its first phase – the NREGA, RSBY, and PDS – will help bring large numbers of the poor and underprivileged into the UID system. The UID method of authentication will also improve service delivery for the poor.

Enrolment of residents with proper verification: Existing identity databases in India are fraught with problems of fraud and duplicate/ghost beneficiaries. To prevent this from seeping into the UIDAI database, the Authority plans to enrol residents into its database with proper verification of their demographic and biometric information. This will ensure that the data collected is clean from the start of the program.

However, much of the poor and underserved population lack identity documents, and the UID may be the first form of identification they have access to. The Authority will ensure that the Know Your Resident (KYR) standards don't become a barrier for enrolling the poor, and will devise suitable procedures to ensure their inclusion without compromising the integrity of the data.

A partnership model: The UIDAI approach leverages the existing infrastructure of government and private agencies across India. The UIDAI will be the regulatory authority managing a Central ID Data Repository (CIDR), which will issue UID numbers, update resident information, and authenticate the identity of residents as required.

In addition, the Authority will partner with agencies such as central and state departments and private sector agencies who will be 'Registrars' for the UIDAI. Registrars will process UID applications, and connect to the CIDR to de-duplicate resident information and receive UID numbers. These Registrars can either be enrollers, or will appoint agencies as enrollers, who

- Name

- Date of birth

- Place of birth

- Gender

- Father's name[1]

- Father's UID number (optional for adult residents)

- Mother's name

- Mother's UID number (optional for adult residents)

- Address (Permanent and Present)

- Expiry date

- Photograph

- Finger prints

Fig 24.1 June 2010. Aadhar Working paper on its envisaged role in the Public Distribution System (PDS) for food security. Coming on the heels of the Right to Food campaign and the National food security Bill that was even then being drafted, it made an already controversial Targeted Public Distribution System defined by poverty levels even more problematic.

Envisioning a role for Aadhaar in the Public Distribution System

Unique Identification Authority of India
Planning Commission,
Government of India

Unique Identification Authority of India

2 Areas for PDS reform

The Indian government and the Department of Food and Public Distribution have pinpointed critical aspects of the PDS that need reform, for the program to function more effectively. These include:

i) Beneficiary identification, and addressing inclusion/exclusion errors
ii) Addressing diversions and leakages
iii) Managing foodgrain storage and ensuring timely distribution
iv) Effective accountability and monitoring, and enabling community monitoring
v) Mechanisms for grievance redressal
vi) Ensuring food security

2.1 A role for Aadhaar within the PDS

Aadhaar can be a potent tool for the government, in making the PDS more effective across these identified areas. The following features of the number would be instrumental for delivering food entitlements to the beneficiary:

i) **One Aadhaar = one beneficiary:** Aadhaar is a unique number, and no resident can have a duplicate number since it is linked to their individual biometrics. Using Aadhaar to identify beneficiaries in PDS databases will eliminate duplicate and fake beneficiaries from the rolls, and make identification for entitlements far more effective.

ii) **Portability in identification:** Aadhaar is a universal number, and agencies and services can contact the central Unique Identification database from anywhere in the country to confirm a beneficiary's identity. The number thus gives individuals a universal, portable form of identification.

iii) **Aadhaar-based authentication to confirm entitlement delivered to the beneficiary:** Aadhaar enables remote, online biometric and demographic authentication of identity. Such Aadhaar-based authentication can take place in real-time, and can even be performed through a mobile phone. Using Aadhaar for real-time identity verification at the FPS, when beneficiaries collect their entitlements, will help governments verify that the benefits reached the person they were meant for.

One challenge here is ensuring that such authentication is carried out at the FPS. Governments can ensure that Aadhaar-based authentication is implemented by the FPS owner by **linking future FPS allocations to authenticated offtake by beneficiaries**. The fewer Aadhaar-based authentications happen at the outlet, the less grain the FPS receives from the government. This will give the FPS owner a strong incentive to ensure

_____
This meets the recommendations of the Planning Commission and Wadhwa Committee, which have suggested biometric authentication of beneficiaries while delivering food entitlements.

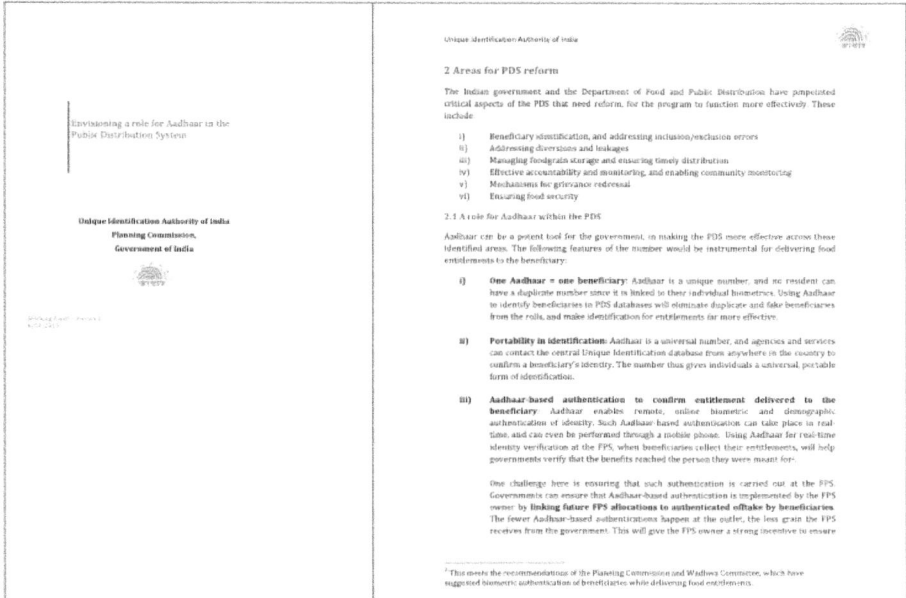

Fig 24.2. 2011. Aadhar and National Population demographic data forms. Aadhar's data limited to name, age, address and 9for minors) relationship to enroller. Notably, the linking of Aadhar to bank account was kept optional. NPR by contrast had 12 datasets.

भारतीय विशिष्ट पहचान प्राधिकरण
योजना आयोग, भारत सरकार

आधार

ENROLMENT FORM (आवेदन पत्र)

Please use CAPITAL letters (कृपया स्पष्ट अक्षरों में भरें)
Date (दिनांक): _ _ / _ _ / _ _ _ _

Part A – Primary Details / (क) प्राथमिक जानकारी
Name: (नाम)

Date of Birth: If not known, Age ___
जन्म तिथि _ _/ _ _ /_ _ _ _   दिये नहीं पता, आयु ___

Gender   ☐ Male   ☐ Female   ☐ Transgender
लिंग   पुरुष   स्त्री   ट्रांसजेंडर

Residential address: आवासीय पता
C/O

House No. and name: घर संख्या और नाम

Street No. and name: गली/सड़क संख्या और नाम

Landmark: मुख्य पहचान

Village / Town / City: ग्राम / शहर

District: जिला

State: Pin code: ☐☐☐☐☐☐
राज्य   पिन कोड

Part B - Relation Details (compulsory for children less than 5 years of age)
(ख) रिश्तेदार की जानकारी (5 साल आयु से कम बच्चों के लिए अनिवार्य)
Name: नाम
Relationship (Mother, Father, Wife, Husband or Guardians), AADHAAR/enrolment number:
रिश्ता (माता, पिता, पत्नी, पति या संरक्षक)   आधार / आवेदन क्रमांक

Part C - Additional Information / (ग) (अन्य जानकारी)
Phone No. / Mobile No. (optional): फोन क्रमांक / मोबाइल क्रमांक (ऐच्छिक)
Email (optional): ईमेल (ऐच्छिक)

Part D - Financial Information / (घ) (वित्तीय जानकारी)
☐ I want to link my existing bank A/c to Aadhaar.
मैं चाहता / चाहती हूँ कि मेरे वर्तमान बैंक खाते को आधार के साथ जोड़ दिया जाए।
Branch (शाखा)   A/c No. (खाता संख्या)
Name (नाम)   IFSC Code (आईएफएससी कोड)

Census of India 2011 | Household Schedule | Confidential when filled | Use only arabic numbers as indicated here | 0 1 2 3 4 5

	Age at marriage	Religion	Scheduled Caste (SC)/ Scheduled Tribe (ST)	Disability	Mother tongue	Other languages known	Literacy status
urrent arital atus	In completed years	(Write name of the religion in full)	8(a) Is this person SC/ST? If 'YES' give code in box SC....1	9(a) Is this person mentally / physically disabled? Yes-1/No-2	write name of the mother tongue in full	write upto two languages in order of proficiency excluding mother tongue	literate ...1 illiterate ...2

Fig 25. 2011. Aadhar and National Population demographic data forms. Aadhar's data limited to name, age, address and 9for minors) relationship to enroller. Notably, the linking of Aadhar to bank account was kept optional. NPR by contrast had 12 datasets.

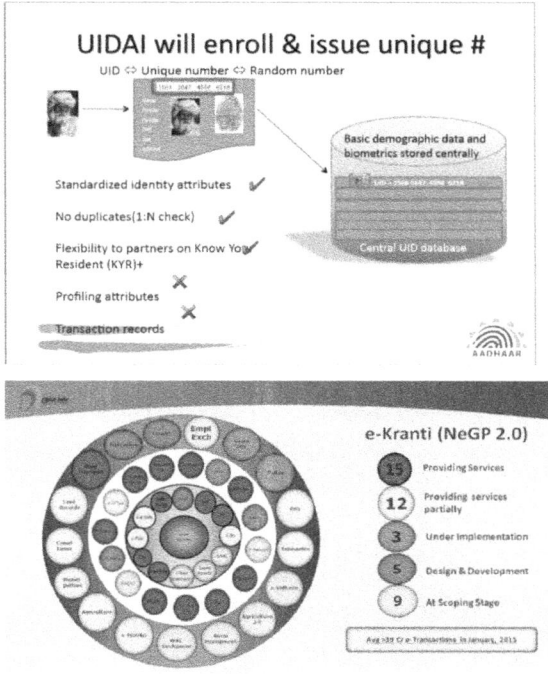

Fig 26. 2015. UIDAI workflow pattern, juxtaposed with the big picture image of E-Kranti (the E-Revolution), the second stage of the National E-Governance Plan. Defined by the famous slogan that it is about 'transformation, not translation', and that it is an 'integrated' set of services based on 'infrastructure on demand', run largely on cloud and mobile applications.

Fig 27. 2016. Free Basics, a collaborative project between Facebook and the Government of India widely viewed as threatening the neutrality of the internet, mounts a direct signature drive to ask people to write to the Telecom Regulatory Authority of India.

the person (Sections 23(2)(g) of the Aadhaar Act and Regulation 27 and 28 of the Aadhaar (Enrolment and Updates) Act, 2016).

(d) By making Aadhaar compulsory for other activities such as air travel, rail travel, directorship in companies, services and benefits extended by State governments and municipal corporations etc. there will be virtually no zone of activity left where the citizen is not under the gaze of the State. This will have a chilling effect on the citizen.

(e) In such a society, there is little or no personal autonomy. The State is pervasive, and dignity of the individual stands extinguished.

(f) This is an inversion of the accountability in the Right to Information age: instead of the State being transparent to the citizen, it is the citizen who is rendered transparent to the State.

383) Mr. Sibal also added that accountability of governments and the state is a phenomenon which is accepted across the world. In furtherance of the Right to information Act, 2005 was passed intended to ensure transparency and state accountability. Through Aadhaar, on the other hand, the state seeks transparency and accountability of an individual's multifarious

Writ Petition (Civil) No. 494 of 2012 & connected matters ***Page 450 of 567***

Fig 28. September 2018, Delhi. Supreme Court of India, Justice K.S. Puttaswamy (Retd) versus Union of India, on the legal validity of the Aadhar Bill. Dissenting judgment by Y.V. Chandrachud, on the ubiquity of Aadhaar control of everyday life, and the 'chilling effect' of the 'gaze of the state'.

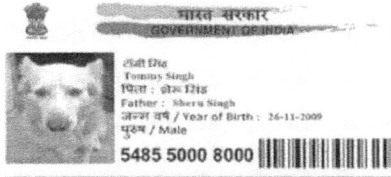

House of Parliament	Lok Sabha
Question No.	666
Ministry	MEITY
Date	June 26, 2019
Question asked by	Sunil Kumar Mondal
Political Party	Trinamool Congress
Question answered by	Ravishankar Prasad
Type of question	Unstarred Question
Subhead	Issuance of Aadhaar Card
Question	(a) Whether the Government has separate details of Aadhaar cards issued to all women, children, senior citizens, persons with a disability, unskilled and unorganised workers, nomadic tribes and such other persons who do not have any permanent dwelling house; and (b) If so, the details thereof and if not, the reasons therefor?
Answer	(a) and (b): Unique Identification Authority of India (UIDAI) only collects name, gender, date of birth, address and other relevant information at the time of enrolment for Aadhaar of an individual in accordance with Section 2 (k) of Aadhaar (Targeted Delivery of Financial and other Subsidies, Benefits and Services) Act, 2016 and the Aadhaar (Enrolment & Update) Regulations 3-6 thereunder. UIDAI do not collect information regarding race, religion, caste, tribe etc.

Fig 29. June 2019, Delhi. Lok Sabha Parliamentary question on the nature of data Aadhar collects, and the answer 'UIDAI do not collect information regarding race, religion, caste, tribe etc'. This was part of the original Aadhar Act, 2016. This clashes with several of the KYC-Plus data generated, which specifically ask for Caste data as well as economic category information. Alongside all of these is the famous dog, 'Tommy Singh', for whom an Aadhar card was created.

Section 3

UID Registrar	Primary Access[1]	Additional Acces[2]	Potential Overlap	Effective Enrolment
	Crore Residents			
LPG (Oil PSU)	8.4[3]	16.8[4]	20%	20.2
LIC (Life Insurance)	13.5	13.5	50%	13.5
PAN Cards	4.0	-	75%	1.0
Passports	6.0	-	80%	1.2
Urban Enrolment				35.9
Lic (Life Insurance)	3.5	3.5	90%	0.7
NREGA	10.0	20.0	10%	27.0
BPL Ration Cards	7.0	21.0	60%	11.2
State BPL/APL	15.0	45.0	50%	30.0
Old Age Pensioners	1.5	1.0	70%	0.8
Women/Child Welfare	1.0	2.0	70%	0.9
Social Welfare	1.0	2.0	70%	0.9
RSBY	0.5	1.0	70%	0.5
Rural Enrolment				72.0
Total Enrolment				107.9

In addition to these enrollers, the UIDAI will also partner with the Registrar General of India (RGI) – who will prepare the National Population Register through the Census 2011 – to reach as many residents as possible and enrol them into the UID database. This may require incorporating some additional procedures into the RGI data collection mechanism, in order to make it UID-ready.

Fig 30. 2009-2012. Tensions rise around state control and social media. (Above) The UIDAI's outlining of their partner registrars, and sidelining the NPR as 'also' one of the UIDAI's partners, on condition that the NPR 'incorporat(es) some additional procedures into the RGI data collection mechanism, in order to make it UID-ready'. Below left: the original 2012 Facebook post that led to the Supreme Court case known as the 'Shreya Singhal case', challenging the validity of Section 66A of the Information Technology Act, 2000.

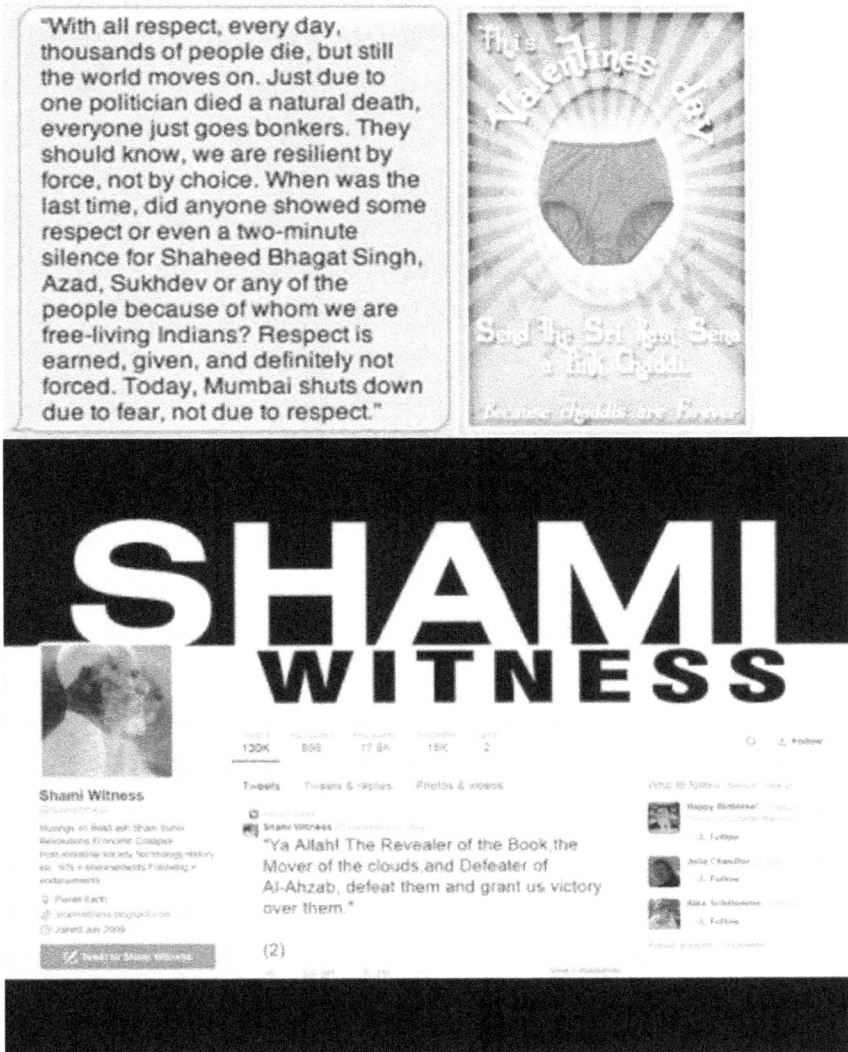

"With all respect, every day, thousands of people die, but still the world moves on. Just due to one politician died a natural death, everyone just goes bonkers. They should know, we are resilient by force, not by choice. When was the last time, did anyone showed some respect or even a two-minute silence for Shaheed Bhagat Singh, Azad, Sukhdev or any of the people because of whom we are free-living Indians? Respect is earned, given, and definitely not forced. Today, Mumbai shuts down due to fear, not due to respect."

This Valentines day...

Send the Sri Ram Sene a Pink Chaddi

Because chaddis are Forever

SHAMI WITNESS

Shami Witness

"Ya Allah! The Revealer of the Book, the Mover of the clouds, and Defeater of Al-Ahzab, defeat them and grant us victory over them."

(2)

Fig 31. (Top left) the original Facebook post that led to the Shreya Singhal judgment. (Top right) The 'Pink Chaddi' campaign by a 'Consortium of Pub-Going, Loose and Forward Women', as a rejoinder to a Hindu right-wing organization's targeting of young people celebrating Valentine's Day, asking for gifts of pink knickers be sent to that organization. (Below): Twitter reposts by 'Shami Witness' in 2014, arrested for pro-ISIS views for whom he was 'aggregating information', in the words of Karnataka's Director General of Police.

MEMORANDUM OF UNDERSTANDING
BETWEEN THE UNIQUE IDENTIFICATION AUTHORITY OF INDIA
AND
THE NATIONAL COALITION OF ORGANISATIONS FOR SECURITY OF
MIGRANT WORKERS

TO ENABLE THE ENROLLMENT OF MIGRANT WORKERS

This Memorandum of Understanding (MoU) has been executed on the 29th day of July, 2010 between the **Unique Identification Authority of India** (hereinafter referred to as "UIDAI") and the **National Coalition of Organisations for Security of Migrant Workers** (hereinafter referred to together as the "Coalition"). The Coalition has authorized "**Aajeevika Bureau**" (hereinafter referred to as "Aajeevika") as the signatory for the Coalition and a representative "Working Group" selected from members of the coalition as the endorsing signatories to this MoU.

Preamble

Whereas, the Government of India has set up the UIDAI with the mandate to issue unique identification numbers (hereinafter "AADHAAR") to all residents of India (hereinafter "UID project").

Whereas, it is the mandate of the UIDAI to take special measures to ensure that AADHAAR is made available to poor and marginalised persons, including street/orphaned children, widows and other disadvantaged women, migrant workers, the homeless, senior citizens, nomadic communities, including tribals, and the differently abled. AADHAAR may enable such marginalized communities access to various government schemes designed for them as well as to banking and other financial services.

Whereas, the UIDAI seeks to collaborate with Civil Society Organizations (CSOs) serving the marginalized communities in developing outreach strategies and action plans to help their inclusion.

Whereas, the UIDAI and the Coalition have agreed to formalize their outreach partnership for expanding inclusion of migrant workers through this MoU.

The Parties

The UIDAI is implementing the UID project through a network of 'Registrars' across the country. Registrars are departments or agencies of the Central or State Government/Union territory, public sector undertakings, and other agencies and organisations, which, in the normal course of implementation of some of their programs, activities or operations interact with residents. Examples of such Registrars are Rural Development Department (for MGREGS) or Civil Supplies and Consumer Affairs Department (for PDS), insurance companies such as Life Insurance Corporation, and Banks such as the State Bank of India.

Fig 32. July 2010. The UIDAI signs a memorandum of Understanding with the National Coalition of Organisations for Security of Migrant Workers, specifically providing for enabling migrants to register with Aadhar. This was a critical demonstration of how 'portable identities' worked. A decade later this would be a major issue in March 2020, when the first Covid lockdown was declared and millions of such migrants found themselves without support in their workplaces but were unable to travel home because they could not prove their home address.

(v) "Information" includes data, message, text, images, sound, voice, codes, computer programmes, software and databases or micro film or computer generated micro fiche."

Two things will be noticed. The first is that the definition is an inclusive one. Second, the definition does not refer to what the content of information can be. In fact, it refers only to the medium through which such information is disseminated. It is clear, therefore, that the petitioners are correct in saying that the public's right to know is directly affected by Section 66A. Information of all kinds is roped in - such information may have scientific, literary or artistic value, it may refer to current events, it may be obscene or seditious. That such information may cause annoyance or inconvenience to some is how the offence is made out. It is clear that the right of the people to know - the market place of ideas - which the internet provides to persons of all kinds is what attracts Section 66A. That the information sent has to be annoying, inconvenient, grossly offensive etc., also shows that no distinction is made between mere discussion or advocacy of a particular point of view which may be annoying or inconvenient or grossly offensive to some and incitement by which such words lead to an imminent causal connection with public disorder, security of State etc. The petitioners are right in saying that Section 66A in creating an offence against persons who use the internet and annoy or cause inconvenience to others very clearly affects the freedom of speech and expression of the citizenry of India at large in that such speech or expression is directly curbed by the creation of the offence contained in Section 66A.

Fig 33. 2015, Delhi. Supreme Court of India Shreya Singhal vs U.O.I on 24 March, 2015, defineds what 'information' is defined by the Information Technology Act.

Fig 34. September 2015, Manipur. The Churachandpur protests, following protests by Kuki groups opposing the introduction of Inner Line Permits, led to a week-long internet shutdown. Nine people died in police firing widely seen as directly instigated by that shutdown. In an astonishing display of physical occupation, for an entire year the bodies of the nine dead were kept on public display in mauve coffins under a shamiana, in front of which daily speeches occurred under a sign that said 'Hills & Valley as separate entities: the new normal, learn to live with it'.

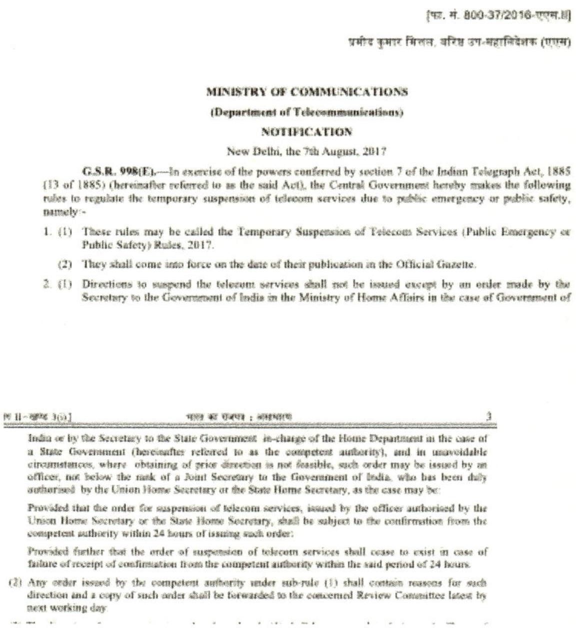

[फा. नं. 800-37/2016-एएस.II]

प्रमोद कुमार मित्तल, वरिष्ठ उप-महानिदेशक (एएस)

MINISTRY OF COMMUNICATIONS
(Department of Telecommunications)
NOTIFICATION

New Delhi, the 7th August, 2017

G.S.R. 998(E).—In exercise of the powers conferred by section 7 of the Indian Telegraph Act, 1885 (13 of 1885) (hereinafter referred to as the said Act), the Central Government hereby makes the following rules to regulate the temporary suspension of telecom services due to public emergency or public safety, namely:-

1. (1) These rules may be called the Temporary Suspension of Telecom Services (Public Emergency or Public Safety) Rules, 2017.

   (2) They shall come into force on the date of their publication in the Official Gazette.

2. (1) Directions to suspend the telecom services shall not be issued except by an order made by the Secretary to the Government of India in the Ministry of Home Affairs in the case of Government of

---

[भाग II—खंड 3(i)]   भारत का राजपत्र : असाधारण   3

India or by the Secretary to the State Government in-charge of the Home Department in the case of a State Government (hereinafter referred to as the competent authority), and in unavoidable circumstances, where obtaining of prior direction is not feasible, such order may be issued by an officer, not below the rank of a Joint Secretary to the Government of India, who has been duly authorised by the Union Home Secretary or the State Home Secretary, as the case may be:

Provided that the order for suspension of telecom services, issued by the officer authorised by the Union Home Secretary or the State Home Secretary, shall be subject to the confirmation from the competent authority within 24 hours of issuing such order:

Provided further that the order of suspension of telecom services shall cease to exist in case of failure of receipt of confirmation from the competent authority within the said period of 24 hours.

(2) Any order issued by the competent authority under sub-rule (1) shall contain reasons for such direction and a copy of such order shall be forwarded to the concerned Review Committee latest by next working day.

Fig 35. August 2017, Delhi. the Temporary Shutdown of Telecom Services (TSTS) Rules are passed.

from de-identification which involves the masking or removal of identifiers from data sets to make identification more difficult.[100] Given the pace of technological advancement, it is desirable not to precisely define or prescribe standards which anonymisation must meet in the law. It is appropriate to leave it to the DPA to specify standards for anonymisation and data sets that meet these standards need not be governed by the law because they cease to be personal data.

A general standard in the definition of anonymisation regarding the possibility of identification, should be sufficient to guide the DPA in prescribing these standards. While the possibility of identification must be eliminated for a data set to be exempted from the rigours of the law, any absolute standard requiring the elimination of every risk including extremely remote risks of re-identification may be too high a barrier and may have the effect of minimal privacy gains at the cost of greater benefits from the use of such data sets.[101]

For other techniques of removing or masking identifiers from data including pseudonymisation, we adopt the term de-identification. The use of such techniques is encouraged and forms an important component of privacy by design. Despite the removal of identifiers from data, de-identified data carries with it a higher risk of re-identification.[102] Hence it is appropriate to continue to treat de-identified data as personal data. Here again, the precise standards that these processes must meet will be specified by the DPA from time to time. In addition to technical standards, this could also include specification of measures for safekeeping of the key or additional information that could lead to re-identification from pseudonymised data.

(b) Sensitive Personal Data

Most data protection legislations set out the rules or grounds in accordance with which personal data may be processed to prevent any harm to data principals. However, it has been observed that despite the existence of such rules or grounds, the processing of certain types of data (usually relating to an integral part of an individual's identity) [103] could result in greater harm to the individual. Consequently, processing of these types of data will require stricter rules or grounds in law to minimise such harm.

While there has been no clear-cut approach towards categorising sensitive personal data, some authors have suggested a contextual approach, i.e., where any personal data can become sensitive depending on the circumstances and the manner in which it is being processed.[104]

---

[100] Mark Elliot, Elaine Mackey, Kieron O'Hara and Caroline Tudor, The Anonymisation Decision-Making Framework (UKAN, 2016) at p.16.
[101] Polonetsky, Tene and Finch, Shades of Gray: Seeing the Full Spectrum of Practical Data De-identification, 56 Santa Clara Law Review (2016) at p. 619.
[102] Mark Elliot, Elaine Mackey, Kieron O'Hara and Caroline Tudor, The Anonymisation Decision-Making Framework (UKAN, 2016) at p.16.
[103] Edward J. Bloustein, Privacy as an Aspect of Human Dignity- An Answer to Dean Prosser (New York University, School of Law, 1964).
[104] Helen Nissenbaum, Privacy as Contextual Integrity, 79(11) Washington Law Review (2004).

Fig 36.1. 2018. The Justice B.N. Srikrishna Committee (aka A Free and Fair Digital Economy: Protecting Privacy, Empowering Indians, Ministry of Electronics and Information Technology) outlined what it considers 'Sensitive Personal Data', namely the data that should be the primary concerns of the draft Data Protection Bill that followed in 2019

However, this approach may place significant burden on data fiduciaries and regulatory resources as they would have to determine whether the personal data in question is sensitive or not, and whether it is capable of causing great harm to the individual, on a case by case basis. Therefore, by identifying certain types of data as sensitive in the law itself, and setting out specific obligations that must be met by the data fiduciary while processing such data, potentially significant harms may be pre-empted.

Data sensitivity, in one view, can depend on the legal and sociological context of a country.[105] However, certain categories of personal data are capable of giving rise to privacy harms regardless of context and an objective method of identifying such kinds of data becomes necessary. Hence, we have considered the following criteria to categorise what is 'sensitive':

(i)   the likelihood that processing of a category of personal data would cause significant harm to the data principal;
(ii)   any expectation of confidentiality that might be applicable to that category of personal data;
(iii)   whether a significantly discernible class of data principals could suffer harm of a similar or relatable nature;[106]
(iv)   the adequacy of general rules to personal data.

Based on the above criteria, the Committee has thought fit to categorise the following as sensitive personal data under a data protection law:

a.   Passwords;
b.   Financial data;
c.   Health data;
d.   Official identifiers which would include government issued identity cards;
e.   Sex life and sexual orientation;
f.   Biometric and genetic data;
g.   Transgender status or intersex status;[107]
h.   Caste or tribe; and
i.   Religious or political beliefs or affiliations.

---

[105] See Karen McCullagh, Data Sensitivity: Proposals for Resolving the Conundrum, 2(4) Journal of International Commercial Law and Technology (2007) at p. 191.
[106] Please note that these factors are adapted from those identified by Paul Ohm in Sensitive Information, 88 Southern California Law Review (2015) at p. 35.
[107] Personal data revealing the condition of a person as being transgender or intersex should be protected as sensitive personal data. The additional protection afforded by this categorisation is required due to the discrimination that they may be subjected to in society. Such persons are free to reveal their status voluntarily. We understand a transgender person to be one whose gender does not match the gender assigned to them at birth. On the other hand, an intersex person is one who is neither wholly female nor wholly male, or a combination of female or male, or neither female nor male (this may be due to physical, hormonal or genetic features).

Fig 36.2 (continued)

Bill No. 373 of 2019

THE PERSONAL DATA PROTECTION BILL, 2019

ARRANGEMENT OF CLAUSES

6

CHAPTER II

OBLIGATIONS OF DATA FIDUCIARY

Prohibition of processing of personal data. 4. No personal data shall be processed by any person, except for any specific, clear and lawful purpose.

Limitation on purpose of processing of personal data. 5. Every person processing personal data of a data principal shall process such personal data—

(a) in a fair and reasonable manner and ensure the privacy of the data principal; and

(b) for the purpose consented to by the data principal or which is incidental to or connected with such purpose, and which the data principal would reasonably expect that such personal data shall be used for, having regard to the purpose, and in the context and circumstances in which the personal data was collected.

Limitation on collection of personal data. 6. The personal data shall be collected only to the extent that is necessary for the purposes of processing of such personal data.

Requirement of notice for collection or processing of personal data. 7. (1) Every data fiduciary shall give to the data principal a notice, at the time of collection of the personal data, or if the data is not collected from the data principal, as soon as reasonably practicable, containing the following information, namely:—

(a) the purposes for which the personal data is to be processed;

(b) the nature and categories of personal data being collected;

(c) the identity and contact details of the data fiduciary and the contact details of the data protection officer, if applicable;

(d) the right of the data principal to withdraw his consent, and the procedure for such withdrawal, if the personal data is intended to be processed on the basis of consent;

(e) the basis for such processing, and the consequences of the failure to provide such personal data, if the processing of the personal data is based on the grounds specified in sections 12 to 14;

(f) the source of such collection, if the personal data is not collected from the data principal;

CHAPTER VIII

EXEMPTIONS

20   **35.** Where the Central Government is satisfied that it is necessary or expedient,—

Power of Central Government to exempt any agency of Government from application of Act.

(i) in the interest of sovereignty and integrity of India, the security of the State, friendly relations with foreign States, public order; or

(ii) for preventing incitement to the commission of any cognizable offence relating to sovereignty and integrity of India, the security of the State, friendly relations with foreign States, public order,

25

it may, by order, for reasons to be recorded in writing, direct that all or any of the provisions of this Act shall not apply to any agency of the Government in respect of processing of such personal data, as may be specified in the order subject to such procedure, safeguards and oversight mechanism to be followed by the agency, as may be prescribed.

30   *Explanation.*—For the purposes of this section,—

(i) the term "cognizable offence" means the offence as defined in clause (c) of section 2 of the Code of Criminal Procedure, 1973;

(ii) the expression "processing of such personal data" includes sharing by or sharing with such agency of the Government by any data fiduciary, data
35   processor or data principal.

Fig 37. 2019, Delhi. The final draft of the Privacy Bill, formally withdrawn in August 2022. This had followed the Supreme Court judgment of 2017 establishing privacy to be part of Article 21 of the Indian Constitution. Key sections, involving Data Fiduciaries, the localisation of data, and the exemptions that allow Central Government violation of privacy, were among its contentious issues.

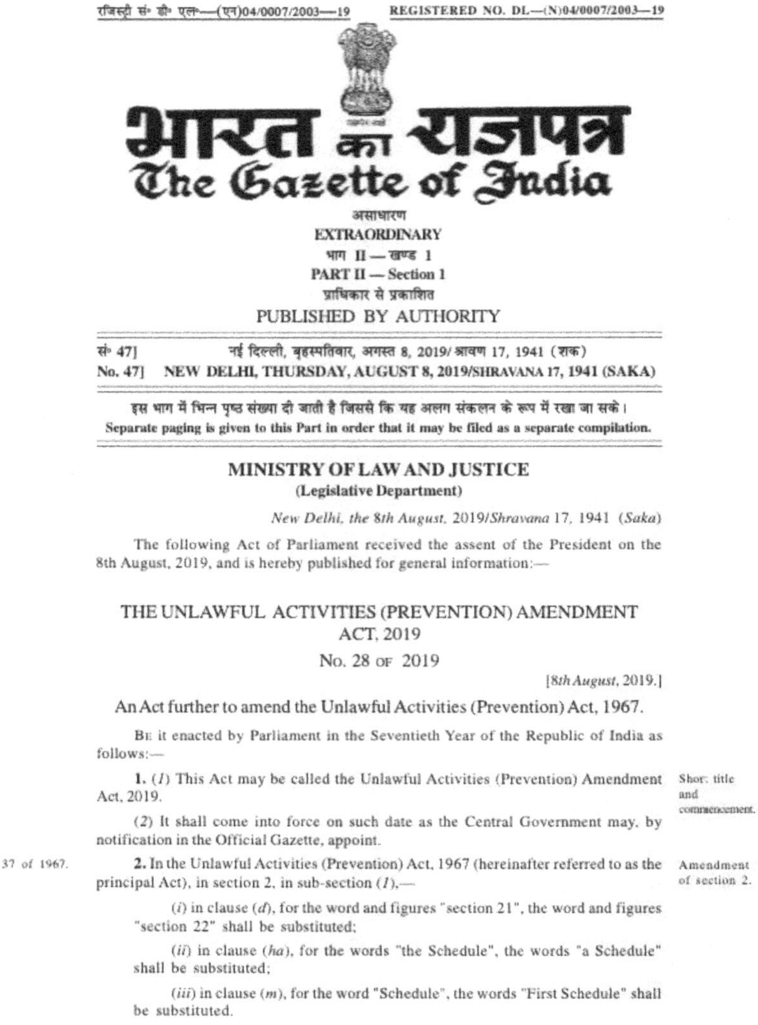

रजिस्ट्री सं॰ डी॰ एल॰—(एन)04/0007/2003—19   REGISTERED NO. DL—(N)04/0007/2003—19

भारत का राजपत्र
The Gazette of India

असाधारण
EXTRAORDINARY
भाग II — खण्ड 1
PART II — Section 1
प्राधिकार से प्रकाशित
PUBLISHED BY AUTHORITY

सं॰ 47]   नई दिल्ली, बृहस्पतिवार, अगस्त 8, 2019/श्रावण 17, 1941 (शक)
No. 47]   NEW DELHI, THURSDAY, AUGUST 8, 2019/SHRAVANA 17, 1941 (SAKA)

इस भाग में भिन्न पृष्ठ संख्या दी जाती है जिससे कि यह अलग संकलन के रूप में रखा जा सके।
Separate paging is given to this Part in order that it may be filed as a separate compilation.

MINISTRY OF LAW AND JUSTICE
(Legislative Department)

New Delhi, the 8th August, 2019/Shravana 17, 1941 (Saka)

The following Act of Parliament received the assent of the President on the 8th August, 2019, and is hereby published for general information:—

THE UNLAWFUL ACTIVITIES (PREVENTION) AMENDMENT ACT, 2019
No. 28 of 2019

[*8th August*, 2019.]

An Act further to amend the Unlawful Activities (Prevention) Act, 1967.

BE it enacted by Parliament in the Seventieth Year of the Republic of India as follows:—

1. (*1*) This Act may be called the Unlawful Activities (Prevention) Amendment Act, 2019.   Short title and commencement.

(*2*) It shall come into force on such date as the Central Government may, by notification in the Official Gazette, appoint.

37 of 1967.   **2.** In the Unlawful Activities (Prevention) Act, 1967 (hereinafter referred to as the principal Act), in section 2, in sub-section (*1*),—   Amendment of section 2.

(*i*) in clause (*d*), for the word and figures "section 21", the word and figures "section 22" shall be substituted;

(*ii*) in clause (*ha*), for the words "the Schedule", the words "a Schedule" shall be substituted;

(*iii*) in clause (*m*), for the word "Schedule", the words "First Schedule" shall be substituted.

Fig 38.1. August 2019. The amendment of the Unlawful Activities Prevention Act, targeting individuals in addition to organizations as 'terrorist'. Fig 38. August 2019. The amendment of the Unlawful Activities Prevention Act, targeting individuals in addition to organizations as 'terrorist'.

Amendment of section 25.

3. In section 25 of the principal Act, in sub-section (*1*), for the words "in which such property is situated, make an order", the words "in which such property is situated, or where the investigation is conducted by an officer of the National Investigation Agency, with the prior approval of the Director General of National Investigation Agency, make an order" shall be substituted.

Amendment of heading of Chapter VI.

4. In Chapter VI of the principal Act, for the Chapter heading, the following Chapter heading shall be substituted, namely:—

"TERRORIST ORGANISATIONS AND INDIVIDUALS".

Amendment of section 35.

5. In section 35 of the principal Act,—

(*i*) in sub-section (*1*),—

(*A*) in clause (*a*), after the words "First Schedule", the words "or the name of an individual in the Fourth Schedule" shall be inserted;

(*B*) in clause (*b*), after the words "United Nations", the words "or the name of an individual in the Fourth Schedule" shall be inserted;

(*C*) in clause (*c*), after the words "First Schedule", the words "or the name of an individual from the Fourth Schedule" shall be inserted;

(*D*) in clause (*d*), after the words "First Schedule", the words "or the Fourth Schedule" shall be inserted;

(*ii*) in sub-section (*2*), for the words "an organisation only if it believes that it is", the words "an organisation or an individual only if it believes that such organisation or individual is" shall be substituted;

(*iii*) in sub-section (*3*), for the words "an organisation shall be deemed to be involved in terrorism if it", the words "an organisation or an individual shall be deemed to be involved in terrorism if such organisation or individual" shall be substituted.

Amendment of section 36.

6. In section 36 of the principal Act,—

(*i*) in the marginal heading, for the words "a terrorist organisation", the words "terrorist organisation or individual" shall be substituted;

(*ii*) in sub-section (*1*), for the words "an organisation from the Schedule", the words "an organisation from the First Schedule, or as the case may be, the name of an individual from the Fourth Schedule" shall be substituted;

(*iii*) in sub-section (*2*),—

(*A*) in clause (*b*), for the words "Schedule as a terrorist organisation", the words "First Schedule as a terrorist organisation, or" shall be substituted;

(*B*) after clause (*b*), the following clause shall be inserted, namely:—

"(*c*) any person affected by inclusion of his name in the Fourth Schedule as a terrorist.";

(*iv*) in sub-section (*5*), for the words "an organisation from the Schedule", the words "an organisation from the First Schedule or the name of an individual from the Fourth Schedule" shall be substituted;

(*v*) in sub-section (*6*), after the words "an organisation", the words "or an individual" shall be inserted;

(*vi*) in sub-section (*7*), for the word "Schedule", the words "First Schedule or the name of an individual from the Fourth Schedule" shall be substituted.

Amendment of section 38.

7. In section 38 of the principal Act, in sub-section (*1*), in the proviso, in clause (*b*), for the word "Schedule", the words "First Schedule" shall be substituted.

Fig 38.2. (Continued)

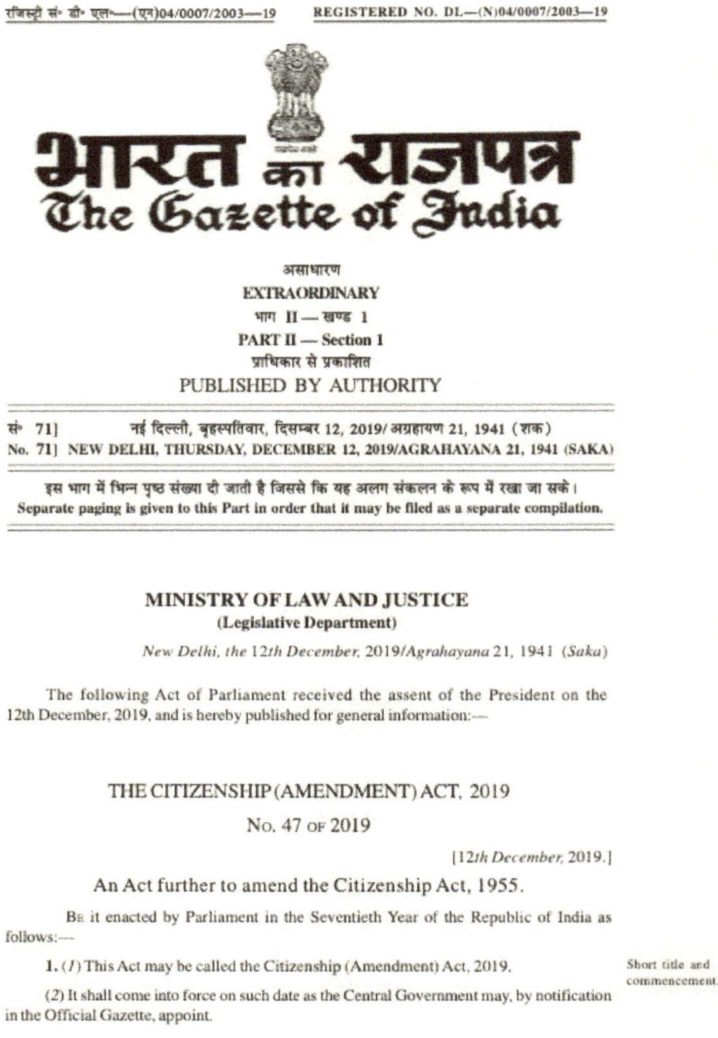

रजिस्ट्री सं॰ डी॰ एल॰—(एन)04/0007/2003—19   REGISTERED NO. DL—(N)04/0007/2003—19

भारत का राजपत्र
The Gazette of India

असाधारण
EXTRAORDINARY
भाग II — खण्ड 1
PART II — Section 1
प्राधिकार से प्रकाशित
PUBLISHED BY AUTHORITY

सं॰ 71]   नई दिल्ली, बृहस्पतिवार, दिसम्बर 12, 2019/ अग्रहायण 21, 1941 (शक)
No. 71] NEW DELHI, THURSDAY, DECEMBER 12, 2019/AGRAHAYANA 21, 1941 (SAKA)

इस भाग में भिन्न पृष्ठ संख्या दी जाती है जिससे कि यह अलग संकलन के रूप में रखा जा सके।
Separate paging is given to this Part in order that it may be filed as a separate compilation.

MINISTRY OF LAW AND JUSTICE
(Legislative Department)

New Delhi, the 12th December, 2019/Agrahayana 21, 1941 (Saka)

The following Act of Parliament received the assent of the President on the 12th December, 2019, and is hereby published for general information:—

THE CITIZENSHIP (AMENDMENT) ACT, 2019

No. 47 OF 2019

[*12th December, 2019.*]

An Act further to amend the Citizenship Act, 1955.

BE it enacted by Parliament in the Seventieth Year of the Republic of India as follows:—

1. (*1*) This Act may be called the Citizenship (Amendment) Act, 2019.   Short title and commencement.

(*2*) It shall come into force on such date as the Central Government may, by notification in the Official Gazette, appoint.

Fig 39.1. December 2019: Citizenship Amendment Act 2019, specifically identifying religions that qualified for Indian citizenship.

Amendment of section 2.

2. In the Citizenship Act, 1955 (hereinafter referred to as the principal Act), in section 2, in sub-section (*1*), in clause (*b*), the following proviso shall be inserted, namely:— *57 of 1955.*

"Provided that any person belonging to Hindu, Sikh, Buddhist, Jain, Parsi or Christian community from Afghanistan, Bangladesh or Pakistan, who entered into India on or before the 31st day of December, 2014 and who has been exempted by the Central Government by or under clause (*c*) of sub-section (2) of section 3 of the Passport (Entry into India) Act, 1920 or from the application of the provisions of the Foreigners Act, 1946 or any rule or order made thereunder, shall not be treated as illegal migrant for the purposes of this Act;". *34 of 1920. 31 of 1946.*

Insertion of new section 6B.

3. After section 6A of the principal Act, the following section shall be inserted, namely:—

Special provisions as to citizenship of person covered by proviso to clause (*b*) of sub-section (*1*) of section 2.

'6B. (*1*) The Central Government or an authority specified by it in this behalf may, subject to such conditions, restrictions and manner as may be prescribed, on an application made in this behalf, grant a certificate of registration or certificate of naturalisation to a person referred to in the proviso to clause (*b*) of sub-section (*1*) of section 2.

(2) Subject to fulfilment of the conditions specified in section 5 or the qualifications for naturalisation under the provisions of the Third Schedule, a person granted the certificate of registration or certificate of naturalisation under sub-section (*1*) shall be deemed to be a citizen of India from the date of his entry into India.

(*3*) On and from the date of commencement of the Citizenship (Amendment) Act, 2019, any proceeding pending against a person under this section in respect of illegal migration or citizenship shall stand abated on conferment of citizenship to him:

Provided that such person shall not be disqualified for making application for citizenship under this section on the ground that the proceeding is pending against him and the Central Government or authority specified by it in this behalf shall not reject his application on that ground if he is otherwise found qualified for grant of citizenship under this section:

Provided further that the person who makes the application for citizenship under this section shall not be deprived of his rights and privileges to which he was entitled on the date of receipt of his application on the ground of making such application.

(*4*) Nothing in this section shall apply to tribal area of Assam, Meghalaya, Mizoram or Tripura as included in the Sixth Schedule to the Constitution and the area covered under "The Inner Line" notified under the Bengal Eastern Frontier Regulation, 1873.'. *Reg. 5 of 1873.*

Amendment of section 7D.

4. In section 7D of the principal Act,—

(*i*) after clause (*d*), the following clause shall be inserted, namely:—

"(*da*) the Overseas Citizen of India Cardholder has violated any of the provisions of this Act or provisions of any other law for time being in force as may be specified by the Central Government in the notification published in the Official Gazette; or";

(*ii*) after clause (*f*), the following proviso shall be inserted, namely:—

"Provided that no order under this section shall be passed unless the Overseas Citizen of India Cardholder has been given a reasonable opportunity of being heard.".

Amendment of section 18.

5. In section 18 of the principal Act, in sub-section (2), after clause (*ee*), the following clause shall be inserted, namely:—

"(*eei*) the conditions, restrictions and manner for granting certificate of registration or certificate of naturalisation under sub-section (*1*) of section 6B;".

Fig 39.2.

भारत सरकार
Government of India
इलेक्ट्रॉनिकी और सूचना प्रौद्योगिकी मंत्रालय
Ministry of Electronics & Information Technology
इलेक्ट्रॉनिक्स निकेतन, 6, सी जी ओ कॉम्पलेक्स, नई दिल्ली-110003
Electronics Niketan, 6, C G O Complex, New Delhi-110003
Website: www.meity.gov.in

संख्या 16(1) /2020-CLES   दिनांक 20.03.2020
No...............................   Date..........................

To

All Social media platforms:

Subject: ADVISORY TO CURB FALSE NEWS / MISINFORMATION ON CORONA VIRUS"

The Corona virus (Covid-19) outbreak has become a global concern with World Health Organisation declaring it a global health emergency. Countries across the world are trying their best to mitigate the spread of corona virus. However, it has been reported in media that there is a trend of circulation of misinformation/false news and sharing anonymous data related to Corona virus in various social media platforms creating panic among public.

2.   Social media platforms are intermediaries as defined under section 2(1)(w) of the Information Technology Act, 2000 and are required to follow due diligence as prescribed in the *Information Technology (Intermediary Guidelines) Rules 2011 notified under section 79 of the IT Act.* They must inform their users not to host, display, upload, modify, publish, transmit, update or share any information that may affect public order and unlawful in any way.

3.   Therefore, Intermediaries are urged to:

(i)   initiate awareness campaign on their platforms for the users not to upload/circulate any false news/misinformation concerning corona virus which are likely to create panic among public and disturb the public order and social tranquillity;

(ii) take immediate action to disable /remove such content hosted on their platforms on priority basis;

(iii) promote dissemination of authentic information related to corona virus as far as possible.

Rakeshi

(Rakesh Maheshwari)
Group Coordinator (Cyber Laws and E-Security)
Email : gccyberlaw@meity.gov.in / cyberlaw@meity.gov.in

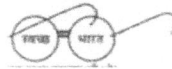

Digital India
Power To Empower

भारत

ELECTRONICS INDIA

Fig 40. August 2019. March 2020, New Delhi. Use of the Information Technology (Intermediary Guidelines) Rules of 2011 to prevent 'false news' on Covid. These rules held 'intermediaries', more precisely 'significant social media intermediaries' (SSMIs), with registered users in India above a notified threshold. In 2021, a year later, these rules were further amended to require SSMIs to 'observe certain additional due diligence such as appointing certain personnel for compliance, enabling identification of the first originator of the information on its platform under certain conditions, and deploying technology-based measures on a best-effort basis to identify certain types of content'

ARSENAL CONSULTING

— ARM YOURSELF —

the email from the person using Varavara Rao's email account, he was actually opening a link to a malicious command and control ("C2") server - see Image 3.

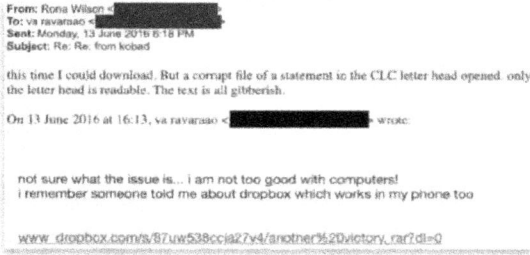

From: Rona Wilson <
To: va ravanrao <
Sent: Monday, 13 June 2016 6:18 PM
Subject: Re: Re: from kobad

this time I could download. But a corrupt file of a statement in the CLC letter head opened. only the letter head is readable. The text is all gibberish.

On 13 June 2016 at 16:13, va ravanao <   > wrote:

not sure what the issue is... i am not too good with computers!
i remember someone told me about dropbox which works in my phone too

www. dropbox.com/s/87uw538ccja27v4/another%20victory. rar?dl=0

Image 1

Image 2

```
<a rel="nofollow" shape="rect" href="http://185.106.122.233/another%20victory.rar" target="
_blank">www.dropbox.com/s/87uw538ccja27v4/another%20victory.rar?dl=0</a>
```

Image 3

Arsenal used a variety of techniques to determine that Mr. Wilson's computer was compromised by the same attacker between June 13, 2016 and April 17, 2018 - just over 22 months. Rebuilding the partial chain of events involved in the compromise of Mr. Wilson's computer (as well as subsequent attacker activity) was quite challenging, in part due to a mixture of both legitimate and illegitimate use of secure deletion tools such as CCleaner, Quick Heal PC Tuner, and SDelete. Rebuilding these events required the use of Arsenal's own digital forensics tools.[9]

Fig 41. March 2020. June 2021. Arsenal Consulting, a Boston-based company specializing in computer forensics, analyses hard disks by several academics, activists and lawyers imprisoned under the UAPA for what has come to be known as the 'Bhima-Koregaon' case, and proves that much of the evidence produced by the police alleging conspiracies to wage war against the Indian state were as a result of malware planted.

Government of Jammu and Kashmir
Home Department
Civil Secretariat, Jammu

Subject: Temporary suspension of Telecom Services-directions reg;

Reference: Letter Nos. JZ/Internet/2020/21 dated 13.01.2020 and KZ/CS/Misc/2020/606 dated 13.01.2020 from IGP, Jammu & IGP, Kashmir, respectively.

Government Order No: Home -03 (TSTS) of 2020
Dated: 14.01.2020

Whereas, the police authorities have brought to notice material relating to the terror modules operating in the UT of J&K, including handlers from across the border, and activities of separatists/ anti-national elements within who are attempting to aid and incite people by transmission of fake news and targeted messages through use of internet to propagate terrorism, indulge in rumour-mongering, support fallacious proxy wars, spread propaganda/ideologies, and cause disaffection and discontent; and

2.   Whereas, based on the intelligence inputs and assessment of the law and order situation obtaining on ground, the law enforcement agencies, while detailing the present situation, have inter-alia reported about the sustained efforts being made by the terrorists to infiltrate from across the border, re-activate their cadres and scale up anti-national activities in Kashmir Division as well as terrorism affected areas of the Jammu Division, by communicating effectively with their operatives within the UT of J&K through Voice on Internet Protocol (VOIP) and encrypted mobile communication through various social media applications to co-ordinate & plan terror acts; and

3.   Whereas, the misuse of data services by anti-national elements has the potential to cause large scale violence and disturb public order which has till now been maintained due to various pre-emptive measures, including restrictions on access to internet with relaxations in a calibrated and gradual manner, after due consideration of the ground situation; and

4.   Whereas, as on date, mobile internet activity of all kinds has been suspended in the UT of J&K. However, internet through fixed line broadband facility exists in Jammu Division while in the Kashmir Division, to facilitate the general public, students, etc., 844 e-terminals have been established besides 69 special counters for tourists, apart from separate terminals for filing of GST returns and application forms for various examinations. Also, among others, a number of Government departments including those

Page 1 of 3

Fig 42. January 2020, Srinagar. State-wide order by the Inspector General of Police for blanket internet shutdown under the Temporary Suspension of Telecom Services (TSTS) Rules, 2017.

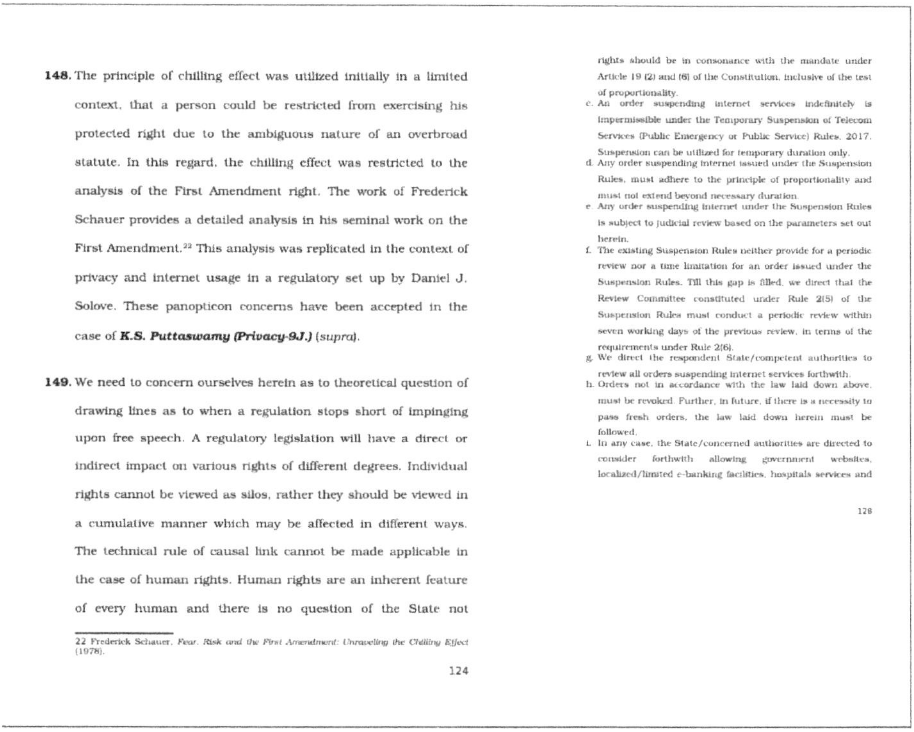

148. The principle of chilling effect was utilized initially in a limited context, that a person could be restricted from exercising his protected right due to the ambiguous nature of an overbroad statute. In this regard, the chilling effect was restricted to the analysis of the First Amendment right. The work of Frederick Schauer provides a detailed analysis in his seminal work on the First Amendment.[22] This analysis was replicated in the context of privacy and internet usage in a regulatory set up by Daniel J. Solove. These panopticon concerns have been accepted in the case of **K.S. Puttaswamy (Privacy-9J.)** (supra).

149. We need to concern ourselves herein as to theoretical question of drawing lines as to when a regulation stops short of impinging upon free speech. A regulatory legislation will have a direct or indirect impact on various rights of different degrees. Individual rights cannot be viewed as silos, rather they should be viewed in a cumulative manner which may be affected in different ways. The technical rule of causal link cannot be made applicable in the case of human rights. Human rights are an inherent feature of every human and there is no question of the State not

22 Frederick Schauer, Fear, Risk and the First Amendment: Unraveling the Chilling Effect (1978).

124

rights should be in consonance with the mandate under Article 19 (2) and (6) of the Constitution, inclusive of the test of proportionality.
c. An order suspending internet services indefinitely is impermissible under the Temporary Suspension of Telecom Services (Public Emergency or Public Service) Rules, 2017. Suspension can be utilized for temporary duration only.
d. Any order suspending internet issued under the Suspension Rules, must adhere to the principle of proportionality and must not extend beyond necessary duration.
e. Any order suspending internet under the Suspension Rules is subject to judicial review based on the parameters set out herein.
f. The existing Suspension Rules neither provide for a periodic review nor a time limitation for an order issued under the Suspension Rules. Till this gap is filled, we direct that the Review Committee constituted under Rule 2(5) of the Suspension Rules must conduct a periodic review within seven working days of the previous review, in terms of the requirements under Rule 2(6).
g. We direct the respondent State/competent authorities to review all orders suspending internet services forthwith.
h. Orders not in accordance with the law laid down above, must be revoked. Further, in future, if there is a necessity to pass fresh orders, the law laid down herein must be followed.
i. In any case, the State/concerned authorities are directed to consider forthwith allowing government websites, localized/limited e-banking facilities, hospitals services and

128

Fig 43. January 2020, Delhi. Supreme Court of India - Anuradha Bhasin vs Union Of India on 10 January, 2020 – the major case involving the legality of internet shutdowns with reference to the 2019 shutdown in Kashmir. Sections 148 and 149 deal with the concept of the 'chilling effect', and its role in suspending free speech.

Government of India
NATIONAL DISASTER MANAGEMENT AUTHORITY
Policy & Plan Division
NDMA Bhawan, A-1, Safdarjung Enclave
New Delhi -110 029

No. 1-29/2020-PP (Pt.II)   Dated : 24th March, 2020

ORDER

Whereas, the National Disaster Management Authority is satisfied that the country is threatened by the spread of COVID-19, which has been declared as a pandemic by the World Health Organisation, and that it is necessary to take effective measures to prevent its spread across the country and for mitigation of the threatening disaster situation;

And whereas, experts, keeping in view the global experiences of countries which have been successful in containing the spread of COVID-19 unlike some others where thousands of people died, have recommended that effective measures for social distancing should be taken to contain the spread of this pandemic;

And whereas, there is a need for consistency in the application and implementation of various measures across the country while ensuring maintenance of essential services and supplies, including health infrastructure;

Now, therefore in exercise of the powers under section 6(2)(i) of the Disaster Management Act, 2005, the National Disaster Management Authority has decided to direct Ministries/ Departments of Government of India, State Governments and State Authorities to take measures for ensuring social distancing so as to prevent the spread of COVID-19 in the country. Necessary guidelines in this regard shall be issued immediately under section 10(2)(l) of the Disaster Management Act, 2005 by the National Executive Committee. These measures shall be in force for a period of twenty one days w. e. f. 25th March, 2020.

Member Secretary, NDMA

To

Union Home Secretary,
North Block, New Delhi-110001

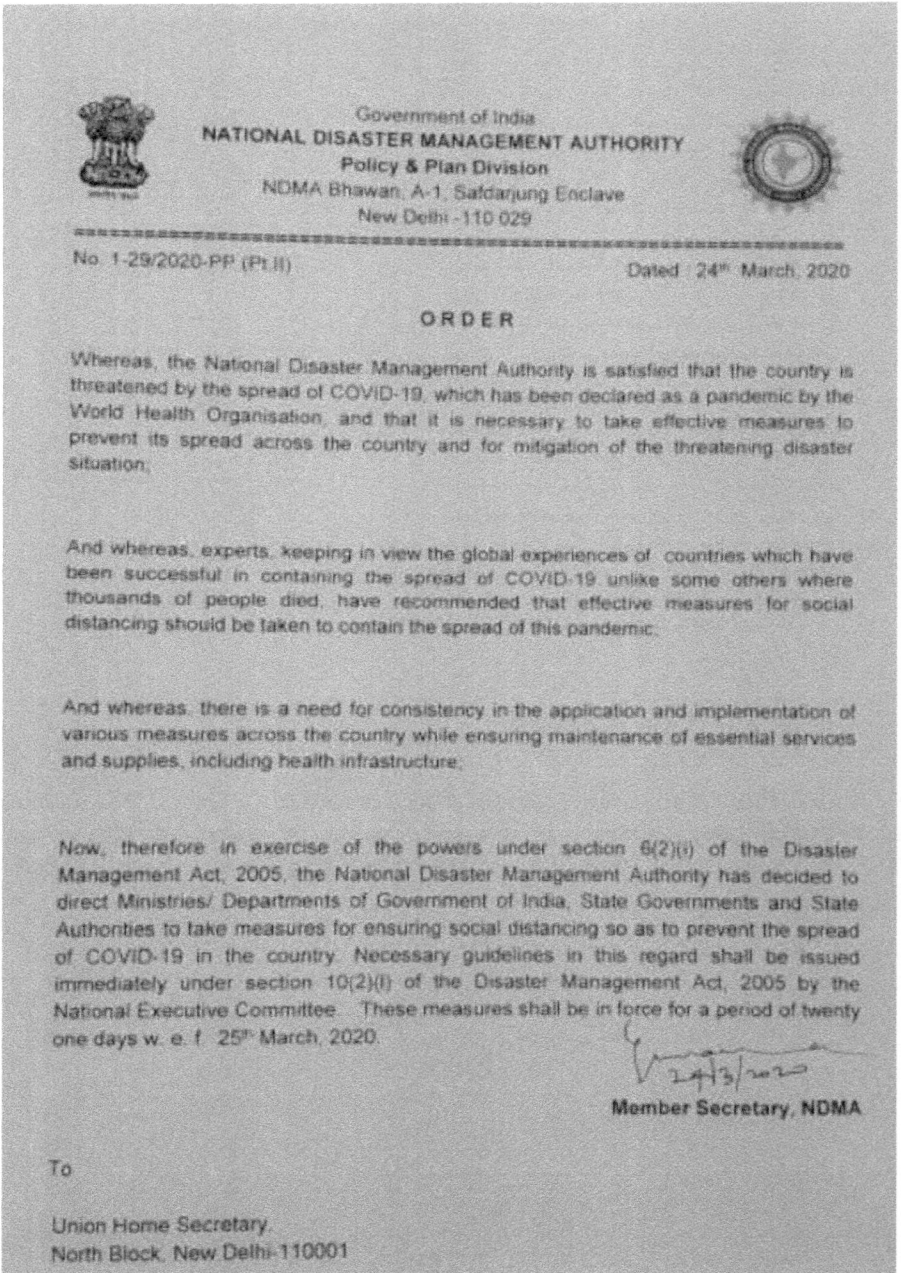

Fig 44. March 2020. The National Disaster Management Act, 2005, is invoked, producing Emergency-like conditions in the name of the pandemic.

CP/X16 1/144/ (Prohibitory Order)/2020

THE COMMISSIONER OF POLICE, GREATER MUMBAI

ORDER
(UNDER SECTION 144 OF CRIMINAL PROCEDURE CODE-1973)

WHEREAS based on the declaration issued by World Health Organization on 11/03/2020 characterizing the outbreak of COVID-19 a global pandemic and the subsequent notifications issued by Government of India and Government of Maharashtra, under the Epidemic Diseases Act, 1897, it has been observed that there is widespread dissemination of fake news, incorrect information, misinformation and other such objectionable content in the form of messages, videos (both edited and self-created), image or memes (both edited and self-created), audio clips and other such forms of communication over internet messaging and social media platforms like WhatsApp, Twitter, Facebook, Tiktok, Instagram etc. Such type of content has been found to have caused panic, confusion among the general public, inciting mistrust towards government functionaries and their actions taken to control the COVID-19 pandemic and also to have created animosity towards various communities.

2. Therefore, it is apprehended that dissemination of such information in any form can lead to a law and order situation and that there is danger to human health or safety or a disturbance of the public tranquility. The undersigned in the capacity of Executive Magistrate is fully satisfied that there are sufficient reasons/grounds for passing prohibitory orders under section 144 of Criminal Procedure Code (CrPC)-1973 to ensure that there is no danger to human health or safety or a disturbance of the public tranquility.

3. WHEREAS it is considered expedient to issue prohibitory order for restricting any dissemination of information through various messaging and social media platforms which is found to be incorrect, derogatory and discriminatory towards a particular community, distortion of facts, causing panic and confusion among the general public, inciting mistrust towards government functionaries and their actions taken in order to prevent spread of the COVID-19 virus and thereby causing danger to human health or safety or disturbance of the public tranquility in the areas under the control of Commissioner of Police, Greater Mumbai.

4. THEREFORE I, Pranaya Ashok, Dy. Commissioner of Police (Operations), Greater Mumbai and Executive Magistrate, vide powers conferred upon me u/sec 144 of the Criminal Procedure Code 1973 (Act II of 1974) r/w the Commissioner of Police Greater Mumbai's Order dated 23/12/1959 u/s 10 sub section (2) of the Maharashtra Police Act 1951 (Mah. Act XXII of 1951), with a view to prevent danger to human life, health or safety or disturbance of the public tranquility, do hereby promulgate an order under section 144 CrPC, in the areas under the control of Commissioner of Police, Greater Mumbai, prohibiting any persons from :

i. dissemination of information through various messaging and social media platforms like WhatsApp, Twitter, Facebook, Tiktok, Instagram etc. And found to be incorrect and distorting faces; or

ii. derogatory and discriminatory towards a particular community; or

iii. causing panic and confusion among the general public; or

iv. inciting mistrust towards government functionaries and their actions taken in order to prevent spread of the COVID-19 virus and thereby causing danger to human health or safety or a disturbance of the public tranquility.

5. All persons designated as "Admin" on messaging and social media platforms, either to self or by allowing any member of the group, shall be personally responsible for any such information being disseminated from a group administered by them.

P.T.O

6. It shall be the personal responsibility of all persons designated as "Admin" on messaging and social media platforms to report any such malicious, incorrect or derogatory content posted by a member of the group to the Police immediately.

7. This order shall come into force, in the areas under the control of Commissioner of Police, Greater Mumbai, with effect from 00.15 hours on 25/05/2020 and ending at 24.00 hours on 08/06/2020 unless withdrawn earlier.

8. Any person contravening this order shall be punishable under section 188 of the Indian Penal Code.

9. As the notice cannot be served individually on all concerned, the order is hereby passed ex-parte. It shall be published for the information of public, through press, or by affixing copies on the Notice Boards of the police stations, Divisional ACsP, Zonal DCsP,

Given under my hand and seal this on 22nd day of the May, 2020 at Mumbai

Office of the
Commissioner of Police,
Greater Mumbai

(Pranaya Ashok)
Dy. Commissioner of Police (Operations)
and Executive Magistrate
Greater Mumbai.

Fig 45. March 2020, Mumbai. After the Covid outbreak, amid widespread rumours about the nature of the disease, but also community information around the availability of hospital beds (often contrasting with official pronouncements), the Commissioner of Police uses Section 144 of the Code of Criminal procedure (right to public assembly) to stop information dissemination under 'Whatsapp, Twitter, Facebook, TikTok, Instagram etc'

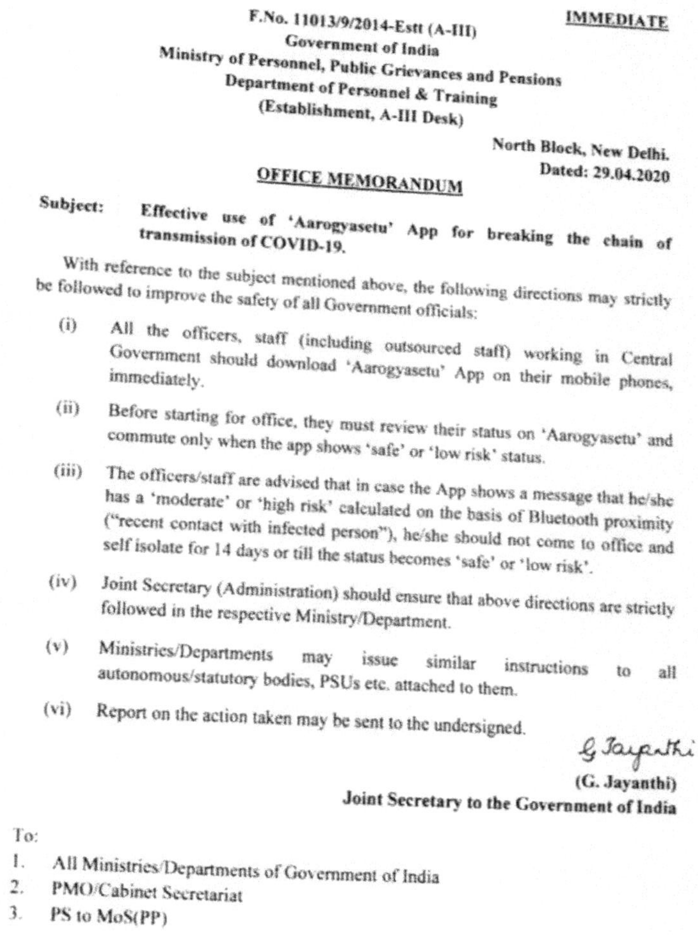

F.No. 11013/9/2014-Estt (A-III)   **IMMEDIATE**
Government of India
Ministry of Personnel, Public Grievances and Pensions
Department of Personnel & Training
(Establishment, A-III Desk)

North Block, New Delhi.

OFFICE MEMORANDUM   Dated: 29.04.2020

Subject: Effective use of 'Aarogyasetu' App for breaking the chain of
transmission of COVID-19.

With reference to the subject mentioned above, the following directions may strictly
be followed to improve the safety of all Government officials:

(i)   All the officers, staff (including outsourced staff) working in Central
Government should download 'Aarogyasetu' App on their mobile phones,
immediately.

(ii)   Before starting for office, they must review their status on 'Aarogyasetu' and
commute only when the app shows 'safe' or 'low risk' status.

(iii)   The officers/staff are advised that in case the App shows a message that he/she
has a 'moderate' or 'high risk' calculated on the basis of Bluetooth proximity
("recent contact with infected person"), he/she should not come to office and
self isolate for 14 days or till the status becomes 'safe' or 'low risk'.

(iv)   Joint Secretary (Administration) should ensure that above directions are strictly
followed in the respective Ministry/Department.

(v)   Ministries/Departments   may   issue   similar   instructions   to   all
autonomous/statutory bodies, PSUs etc. attached to them.

(vi)   Report on the action taken may be sent to the undersigned.

G. Jayanthi.

(G. Jayanthi)
Joint Secretary to the Government of India

To:
1.   All Ministries/Departments of Government of India
2.   PMO/Cabinet Secretariat
3.   PS to MoS(PP)

Fig. 46. April 2020, Delhi. The Covid-tracking app Arogya Setu is rendered mandatory in all government office and for all employees, in contrast to the explicit declarations that the app was not legally mandatory.

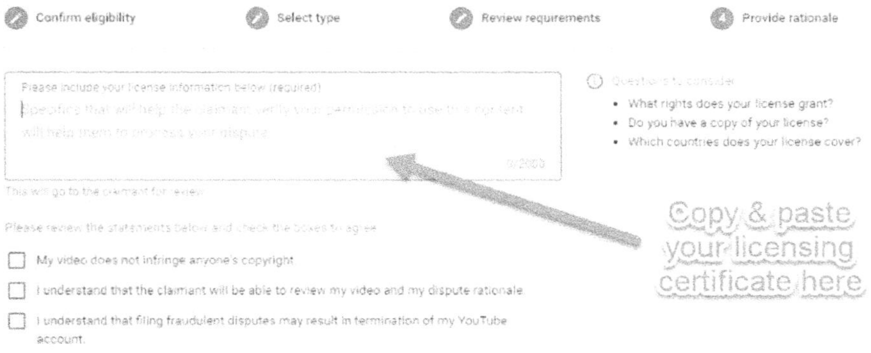

Fig 47. January 2022. Youtube Licensing policy as part of its new Terms of Service

ACKNOWLEDGMENTS

This book has been long in the making. A lot of it happened even before the idea of such a book came together. The authors, old collaborators and friends, thank each other, and will raise a toast whenever it is that we reconvene, someday, in a single space. Nishant expresses his gratitude to the people that made the Centre for Internet & Society possible – Sunil Abraham, Pranesh Prakash, and Nirmita Narsimhan, with whom it all started and grew. There were some incredible scholars whose work framed the Internet and Society history in India through its Researchers At Work series – Asha Achuthan and Namita Malhotra, in particular. Nishant's writing owes its intellectual and emotional debt to different collaborators and interlocutors – Chinmayi Arun, Alexandra Juhasz, Wendy Chun, David Theo Goldberg, Elizabeth Losh, Martin Warnke, Malavika Jairam, Clemens Apprich, Rolien Hyong, and Renee Ridgway, who have all workshopped these different ideas over time. He acknowledges the generous support of the Digital Earth Project at Hivos and the Feminist Internet Research Network at the Association of Progressive Communication, where parts of this work were presented and grew. Ashish Rajadhyaksha recalls the many colleagues who worked, along with his co-authors, on the Identity Project at the Centre for the Study of Culture and Society, and thanks Sruti Chaganti and Kakarala Sitharamam. A special thanks to http://pad.ma, to Lawrence Liang, Shaina Anand and Ashok Sukumaran. The Identity Project was funded by the Ford Foundation, Delhi. For advice on 'following the technology', Nafis Hasan is very grateful to Chris Kelty at UCLA and the wonderful magazine he co-edits, *LIMN,* particularly Issue 8, which set him on the path of excavating the stratigraphy of technical structures that lead to the devastating excesses this book addresses. He is also very thankful for the grants and research positions that have made the writing and editing possible.

The authors all remember the Centre for the Study of Culture and Society, and Tejaswini Niranjana, S.V. Srinivas, and many other faculty and students there. We are grateful to Geert Lovink, Tommaso Campagna, Jasmin Leech and the team of the Institute of Network Cultures for enabling this book. We express our deepest thanks to Ravi Sundaram, Chris Kelty, and Michelle Kasprzak for their detailed, careful, and generous comments on this book, and Chinmayi Arun for the foreword. Finally, we thank Sunaina Dalaya for her copyediting, her attention to detail, and for bringing the book together in such a wonderful way.

BIBLIOGRAPHY

Reports

Dara, Rishabh. 'Intermediary Liability in India: Chilling Effects on Free Expression on the Internet 2011', *The Centre for Internet* & Society, 10 April 2012, https://cis-india.org/internet-governance/intermediary-liability-in-india.

Engelbart, Douglas C. 'Augmenting Human Intellect: A Conceptual Framework', Summary Report, SRI Project No. 3578, Stanford Research Institute, October 1962, https://www.dougengelbart.org/content/view/138.

'Infosys Annual Report, 1993–94', April 1994, https://www.infosys.com/investors/reports-filings/annual-report/annual/documents/infosys-ar-94.pdf.

NAMEDIA, *A Vision for Indian Television*, New Delhi: Media Foundation of the Non-aligned, 1986.

National Council of Applied Economic Research, *The NCAER Land Records and Services Index (N-LRSI) 2020*, Report 20200201, February 2020, https://www.ncaer.org/publication_details.php?pID=317.

People's Union of Civil Liberties, *Imprisoned Resistance - 5th August and its Aftermath*, 2019, https://www.pucl.org/reports/imprisoned-resistance-5th-august-and-its-aftermath.

Reporters Without Borders. '2020 World Press Freedom Index: "Entering a Decisive Decade for Journalism, Exacerbated by Coronavirus"', https://rsf.org/en/2020-world-press-freedom-index-entering-decisive-decade-journalism-exacerbated-coronavirus

Srivastava, Shirish C., Mathur Sharat, and Teo, Thompson. 'Modernization of Passenger Reservation System: Indian Railway's Dilemma, *ICIS 2006 Proceedings* 98 (2006), http://aisel.aisnet.org/icis2006/98.

Swaminathan, R. 'UIDAI-NPR Row: Identity Politics of a Different Kind', Observer Research Foundation, 7 April 2012, https://www.orfonline.org/research/uidai-npr-row-identity-politics-of-a-different-kind/.

Government Documents and Judgments

1976: Planning Commission, 'Computerized Data Bank' - Consultancy Assistance from Institutions, File No. M-12038/3/76 – M&I, National Archives of India.

1977: Planning Commission, 'Setting up of a National Informatics Centre - Proposal from the Electronics Commission', File No. 11017/5/77 M&I, National Archives of India.

1978: Planning Commission, 'Standing Committee for Directing and Reviewing Improvement of Data Base for Planning and Policy Making', Vol. I, File No. O-11-17/1/78-M&I, National Archives of India.

1989: Supreme Court of India, S. Rangarajan Etc v P. Jagjivan Ram, 1989 SCR (2) 204, 1989 SCC (2) 574, 30 March, https://indiankanoon.org/doc/341773/.

2000: 'The Information Technology Act, 2000', The Gazette of India, June, https://www.indiacode.nic.in/bitstream/123456789/13116/1/it_act_2000_updated.pdf.

2003: Citizenship (Registration of Citizens and Issue of National Identity Cards) Rules, 2003, https://censusindia.gov.in/2011-Act&Rules/notifications/citizenship_rules2003.pdf.

2009: 'eDistrict Mission Mode Project Under the National eGovernance Plan. Pilot Implementation Guidelines', Department of Information Technology, Government of India, January, https://www.meity.gov.in/writereaddata/files/eDistGuidelines_Feb09(rev1).pdf.

2009: 'The Information Technology (Amendment) Act, 2008', The Gazette of India, February, https://eprocure.gov.in/cppp/rulesandprocs/kbadqkdlcswfjdelrquehwuxcfmijmuixngudufgbuubgubfug-bububjxcgfvsbdihbgfGhdfgFHytyhRtMTk4NzY=.

2010: UIDAI. Strategy Overview: Creating a Unique Identity Number for Every Resident in India, Planning Commission/UIDAI, Government of India, April.

2010: Supreme Court of India. M Siddiq (D) Thr Lrs v Mahant Suresh Das & Ors, Civil Appeals Nos 10866-10867 of 2010 (2019), https://www.sci.gov.in/pdf/JUD_2.pdf.

2014: 'WGITA – IDI Handbook on IT Audit for Supreme Audit Institutions', February, https://icisa.cag.gov.in/resource_files/c60986ef8dd5d4f658df077c1b5dceb7.PDF.

2015: Supreme Court of India, Shreya Singhal v Union of India, WP (Criminal) No. 167 of 2012 (24 March), https://indiankanoon.org/doc/110813550/.

2016: Aadhaar (Targeted Delivery of Financial and Other Subsidies, Benefits and Services) Act, Ministry of Law and Justice (Legislative Department) New Delhi, 26th March, The Gazette of India, https://uidai.gov.in/images/targeted_delivery_of_financial_and_other_subsidies_benefits_and_services_13072016.pdf.

2016: Telecom Regulatory Authority of India. 'Prohibition of Discriminatory Tariffs for Data Services Regulations, 2016', The Gazette of India, 8 February, https://trai.gov.in/sites/default/files/Regulation_Data_Service.pdf.

2017: Supreme Court of India, K.S. Puttaswamy (Privacy-9J.) v. Union of India, (2017) 10 SCC 1, 24 August, Writ Petition(s)(Civil) No(s). 494/2012, https://indiankanoon.org/doc/60686607/.

2018: Committee of Experts under the Chairmanship of Justice B.N. Srikrishna, A Free and Fair Digital Economy: Protecting Privacy, Empowering Indians, Ministry of Electronics and Information Technology, Government of India.

2018: Supreme Court of India, Justice K.S. Puttaswamy (retd) v Union of India, Writ Petition (C) 494/2012 (2018), https://main.sci.gov.in/supremecourt/2012/35071/35071_2012_Judgement_26-Sep-2018.pdf.

2018: Supreme Court of India, Romila Thapar v Union of India, Writ Petition (Criminal) No. 268 of 2018, 28 September, 2018, https://indiankanoon.org/doc/52834611/.

2019: The Citizenship (Amendment) Act, 2019 No. 47 Of 2019, Ministry of Law and Justice (Legislative Department) New Delhi, The Gazette of India, 12th December. https://egazette.nic.in/WriteReadData/2019/214646.pdf.

2019: Banashree Gogoi v Union of India and 7 Ors, GAHC010310492019, Case No.: PIL 78/2019 (19 December 2019), https://indiankanoon.org/doc/175955438/

2019: Faheema Shirin R.K. v State of Kerala, WP (C) 19716/2019-L (19 September 2019), https://indiankanoon.org/doc/188439981/

2019: The Unlawful Activities (Prevention) (Amendment) Act, Ministry Of Law And Justice (Legislative Department) New Delhi, The Gazette of India, 8 August, 2019, 2588GI.p65 (egazette.nic.in)

2020: Anuradha Bhasin v Union of India, Writ Petition (Civil) No. 1031 of 2019 (10 January 2020), https://indiankanoon.org/doc/82461587/

2020: March 24. The National Disaster Management Act, 2005, order by the National Disaster Management Authority Policy and Plan Division, invoking the National disaster Management Act (2005) for Covid.

2020: 'Notification of the Aarogya Setu Data Access and Knowledge Sharing Protocol, in Light of the COVID-19 Pandemic', Ministry of Electronics and Information Technology, Government of India, 11 May, https://www.meity.gov.in/writereaddata/files/Aarogya_Setu_data_access_knowledge_Protocol. pdf.

2020: Foundation for Media Professionals v Union Territory of Jammu and Kashmir, Writ Petition (Civil) of 2020 (D. No. 10817 of 2020) (11 May 2020), (https://indiankanoon.org/doc/123992151/)

2020: 'Constitution of Committee for Developing and Implementing a Citizen App Technology Platform for Combating Covid-19', Memo issued by Rashtrapati Bhavan, 3 April,

s.d. 'Request for Proposal (RFP) For Selection of SWAN TPA', https://www.meity.gov.in/writereaddata/ files/An8_Indicative_SWAN.pdf.

Books and Journal Essays

Achuthan, Asha. *Re:Wiring Bodies*, Bangalore: Researchers@Work and The Centre for Internet & Society, 2012.

Agamben, Giorgio. *Homo Sacer*, Stanford: Stanford University Press, 1998.

Appadurai, Arjun. *Modernity at Large: Cultural Dimensions of Globalization*, Minneapolis: University of Minnesota Press, 1996.

Apprich, Clemens, Chun, Wendy Hui Kyong, Cramer, Florian, and Steyerl, Hito. *Pattern Discrimination*, Minneapolis: University of Minnesota Press, 2019.

Arunima, G. 'Cameras, Campuses and the Future of Politics in an Era of Imaging Technologies', *Contributions to Indian Sociology* 54.1 (2020): 1–26.

Atanasoski, Neda and Vora, Kalindi. *Surrogate Humanity: Race, Robots, and the Politics of Technological Futures*, Durham: Duke University Press, 2019.

Baez, Benjamin. *Technologies of Government: Politics and Power in the "Information Age"*, Charlotte, North Carolina: Information Age Publishing, 2014.

Barabási, Albert-László. 'Scale-Free Networks: A Decade and Beyond', *Science* 325.5939 (2009): 412–413.

Barendt, Eric. *Freedom of Speech*, Oxford: Clarendon Press, 1985.

Barry, Andrew, Osborne, Thomas, and Rose, Nikolas (eds), *Foucault and Political Reason: Liberalism, Neo-liberalism and Rationalities of Government*, Chicago: University of Chicago Press, 1996.

Baudrillard, Jean. *Simulacra and Simulation*, trans. Sheila Glaser, Ann Arbor: University of Michigan Press, 1983.

Berlant, Lauren. *Cruel Optimism*, Durham: Duke University Press, 2011.

Bertino, Elisa and Sandhu, Ravi. 'Database Security—Concepts, Approaches, and Challenges', *IEEE Transactions on Dependable and Secure Computing* 2.1 (2005): 2–19.

Bhatia, Gautam. 'The Aadhaar Judgment: A Dissent for the Ages', *Indian Constitutional Law and Philosophy*, 27 September 2018, https://indconlawphil.wordpress.com/2018/09/27/the-aadhaar-judgment-a-dissent-for-the-ages/.

———. *The Transformative Constitution: A Radical Biography in Nine Acts*, New Delhi: Harper Collins, 2019.

Blair, Ann M. *Too Much to Know: Managing Scholarly Information before the Modern Age*, New Haven and London: Yale University Press, 2010.

Braidotti, Rosi. *The Posthuman*, New York: Wiley, 2013.

Campbell-Kelly, Martin. 'The RDBMS Industry: A Northern California Perspective', *IEEE Annals of the History of Computing* 34.4 (2012): 19

Castelle, Michael. 'Relational and Non-Relational Models in the Entextualization of Bureaucracy', *Computational Culture* 3 (November 2013). http://computationalculture.net/relational-and-non-relational-models-in-the-entextualization-of-bureaucracy/.

Castells, Manuel. *Networks of Outrage and Hope: Social Movements in the Internet Age*, Cambridge, UK: Polity Press, 2015.

Chatterjee, Partha. 'Beyond the Nation? Or Within?', *Social Text* 56 (1998): 57–69.

———. *A Princely Impostor?: The Kumar of Bhawal and the Secret History of Indian Nationalism*, Princeton, N.J.: Princeton University Press, 2002.

———. 'Democracy and Economic Transformation in India', *Economic & Political Weekly* 43.16 (2008): 53–62.

———. *I am the People: Reflections on Popular Sovereignty Today*, Ranikhet: Permanent Black, 2019.

Choi, Seul-Gi and Cho, Sung-Bae. 'Evolutionary Reinforcement Learning for Adaptively Detecting Database Intrusions', *Logic Journal of the IGPL* 28.4 (2020): 449–460.

Chun, Wendy Hui Kyong. 'The Enduring Ephemeral, or the Future Is a Memory', *Critical Inquiry* 35.1 (2008): 148–171.

———. *Updating to Remain the Same: Habitual New Media*, Cambridge, Massachusetts, and London: The MIT Press, 2016.

Crawford, Kate and Joler, Vladan. 'Anatomy of an AI System: The Amazon Echo as an Anatomical Map of Human Labor, Data and Planetary Resources', *AI Now Institute and Share Lab,* 7 September 2018, https://anatomyof.ai.

Deleuze, Gilles. *Difference and Repetition*, trans. Paul Patton, Columbia: Columbia University Press, 1994.

Dijck, José van and Poell, Thomas. 'Understanding Social Media Logic', *Media and Communication* 1.1 (2013): 2–14.

Dourish, Paul. 'No SQL: The Shifting Materialities of Database Technology', *Computational Culture*, 4 (November 2014): 2.

Ernst, Wolfgang. *Digital Memory and the Archive*, Minneapolis: University of Minnesota Press, 2013.

———. *Sonic Time Machines: Explicit Sound, Sirenic Voices, and Implicit Sonicity,* Amsterdam: University of Amsterdam Press, 2016.

Hoffmann, Anna Lauren, Proferes, Nicholas, and Zimmer, Michael. '"Making the World More Open and Connected": Mark Zuckerberg and the Discursive Construction of Facebook and its Users', *New Media and Society* 20.1 (2016): 199–218.

Fisher, Adam. *Valley of Genius: The Uncensored History of Silicon Valley (As Told by the Hackers, Founders, and Freaks Who Made It Boom)*, New York and Boston: Twelve (The Hatchett Group), 2018.

Fitzpatrick, Kathleen. *Planned Obsolescence: Publishing, Technology, and the Future of the Academy*, New York and London: New York University Press, 2011.

Geertz, Michael and Jajodia, Sushil (eds) *Handbook of Database Security: Applications and Trends*, New York: Springer, 2008.

Geertz, Michael and Gandhi, Madhavi. 'Security Re-engineering for Databases: Concepts and Techniques', in Michael Geertz and Sushil Jajodia (eds) *Handbook of Database Security: Applications and Trends*, New York: Springer, pp. 267–298, 2008.

Ghosh, Atig (ed.), *Branding the Migrant: Arguments of Rights, Welfare and Security*, Kolkata: Frontpage Publications Ltd., 2013.

Gilman, Nils, Goldhammer, Jesse, and Weber, Steven. 'Can You Secure an Iron Cage?', *Limn*, Issue 8, February 2017, https://limn.it/articles/can-you-secure-an-iron-cage/.

Gitelman, Lisa (ed.) *'Raw Data' is an Oxymoron*, Cambridge: MIT Press, 2013.

Gitelman, Lisa. *Paper Knowledge: Towards a Media History of Documents*, Durham: Duke University Press, 2014.

Grier, David Alan. 'The Relational Database and the Concept of the Information System', *IEEE Annals of the History of Computing* 34.4 (2012): 9-17.

Haraway, Donna J. *Simians, Cyborgs and Women: The Reinvention of Nature*, New York and London: Routledge, 1991.

Hertz, Garnet and Parikka, Jussi. 'Zombie Media: Circuit Bending Media Archaeology into an Art Method', *Leonardo* 45.5 (2012): 424–430.

Hörl, Eric, in exchange with Fiegelfeld, Paul, and Kastelan, Cornelia. 'The Anthropocenic Illusion: Sustainability and the Fascination of Control', in Christoph Behnke, Cornelia Kastelan, Valerie Knoll, and Ulf Wuggenig (eds) *Art in the Periphery of the Center*, Berlin: Sternberg Press, 2015, pp. 352–368.

Irani, Lilly. *Chasing Innovation: Making Entrepreneurial Citizens in Modern India*, Princeton: Princeton University Press, 2019.

Jayal, Niraja Gopal. *Citizenship and Its Discontents: An Indian History,* Cambridge, MA: Harvard University Press, 2013, pp. 84–85.

Jayaram, Malavika. 'India's Big Brother Project: The World's Largest Biometrics Identity Program', *Boston Review*, 19 May 2014, https://bostonreview.net/world/malavika-jayaram-india-unique-identification-biometrics.

Kaviraj, Sudipta. 'The Imaginary Institution of India', in Sudipta Kaviraj, *The Imaginary Institution of India: Politics and Ideas*, New York: Columbia University Press, 2010, pp. 167–209.

Kayarkar, Harshavardhan. 'Classification of Various Security Techniques in Databases and their Comparative Analysis', *arXiv preprint arXiv* 1206.4124 (2012).

Khmelevsky, Y. 'Information and Data Protection Within a RDBMS', *Condensed Matter Physics* 11.4 (2008): 761–765.

Kohli, Atul. 'Politics of Economic Growth in India, 1980–2005 Part II: The 1990s and Beyond', *Economic & Political Weekly*, 41.13 (2006): 1251–1259.

Krishnayya, J.G. et al. (eds), sacm: A Monthly Magazine, Pune: Systems Research Institute, 1979.

Lanier, Jaron. *You Are Not a Gadget: A Manifesto*, New York: Alfred A. Knopf, 2010.

Latour, Bruno. 'A Collective of Humans and Nonhumans: Following Daedalus's Labyrinth', in Bruno

———, *Pandora's Hope: Essays on the Reality of Science Studies*, Cambridge, Massachusetts: Harvard University Press, 1999, pp. 183–184.

———. *An Inquiry into Modes of Existence: An Anthropology into the Moderns*, Cambridge, Massachusetts: Harvard University Press, 2013.

Manohar, Swami, 'The Simputer: Access Device for the Masses', http://www.simputer.org/simputer/history/paper.pdf.

Manzano, Maria. *Extensions of First-Order Logic.* Cambridge Tracts in Theoretical Computer Science, Series #19. Cambridge: Cambridge University Press, 1996.

Malhotra, Namita A. *Porn: Law, Video & Technology*, Bangalore: The Centre for Internet & Society, 2011.

Marvin, Carolyn. *When Old Technologies Were New: Thinking About Electric Communication in the Late Nineteenth Century*, Oxford: Oxford University Press, 1988.

Millett, Kate. *Sexual Politics*, Garden City, New York: Doubleday & Co., 1970.

Nandy, Ashis. 'Coming Home: Religion, Mass Violence and the Exiled and Secret Selves of a Citizen-Killer', in Ashis Nandy, *Regimes of Narcissism, Regimes of Despair*, New Delhi: Oxford University Press, 2013.

Nilekani, Nandan. *Imagining India: Ideas for the New Century*, New Delhi: Penguin, 2008.

Nixon, Rob. *Slow Violence and the Environmentalism of the Poor*, Cambridge, MA: Harvard University Press, 2011.

Ong, Aihwa. *Neoliberalism as Exception: Mutations in Citizenship and Sovereignty*, Durham: Duke University Press, 2006.

Rajadhyaksha, Ashish. *The Last Cultural Mile: An Inquiry into Technology and Governance in India*, Bangalore: The Centre for Internet & Society/Researchers@Work, 2011.

———— (ed), *In the Wake of Aadhaar: The Digital Ecosystem of Governance in India*, Bangalore: Centre for the Study of Culture and Society, 2013.

Ramanathan, Usha. 'A State of Surveillance', International Environmental Law Research Centre, 2010, http://www.ielrc.org/content/w1002.pdf.

Ramnath, Kalyani, ''We the People': Seamless Webs and Social Revolution in India's Constituent Assembly Debates', *South Asia Research* 32.1 (2012): 57–70.

Rose, Mark. *Authors and Owners: The Invention of Copyright*, Cambridge, Massachusetts: Harvard University Press, 1993.

Sen, Amartya. 'Markets, State and Social Opportunity', in Amartya Sen, *Development as Freedom*, New York: Alfred A. Knopf, 2000, pp. 126–128.

Sengupta, Shuddhabrata. 'Media Trials and Courtroom Tribulations: The Battle of Images, Words and Shadows in the 13 December Case', in *13 December, A Reader: The Strange Case of the Attack on the Indian Parliament*, New Delhi: Penguin Books, 2006.

Shah, Nishant. 'Subject to Technology: Internet Pornography, Cyber-terrorism and the Indian State', *Inter-Cultural Studies* 8.3 (2007): 349–366.

————. 'In Access: Digital Video and the User', in Joshua Neves and Bhaskar Sarkar (eds) *Asian Video Cultures: In the Penumbra of the Global*, Durham: Duke University Press, 2017, pp. 114–130.

————. 'Identity and Identification: The Individual in the Time of Networked Governance', *Socio-Legal Review* 11.12 (2015): 22–40.

————. '(Dis)information Blackouts: Politics and Practices of Internet Shutdowns', *International Journal of Communication* 15 (2021): 2693–2709.

Singh, Amar Jeet and Chauhan, Rajesh. 'E-Government Databases: A Retrospective Study', Indian Journal of Computer Science and Engineering 1.2 (2010): 66-73.

Smith, R.S. 'Rule-by-Records and Rule-by-Reports: Complementary Aspects of British Imperial Rule of Law', *Contributions to Indian sociology* 19.1 (1985): 153–176.

Star, Susan Leigh. 'The Ethnography of Infrastructure', *American Behavioral Scientist* 43.5 (1999): 377–391.

Sukumar, Arun Mohan. *Midnight's Machines: A Political History of Technology in India*, New Delhi: Penguin Viking, 2019.

Teltumbde, Anant. *The Persistence of Caste: The Khairlanji Murders and India's Hidden Apartheid*, London: Zed Books, 2010.

Thomas, Pooja. 'Museum as Metaphor: The Politics of an Imagined Ahmedabad', in Arvind Rajagopal and Anupama Rao (eds) *Media and Utopia: History, Imagination, and Technology*, New York: Routledge, 2017, pp. 133–148.

Tofler, Alvin, *Future Shock*, New York: Random House, 1970.

Watts, Duncan J. *Small Worlds: The Dynamics of Networks between Order and Randomness*. Princeton Studies in Complexity #36. Princeton: Princeton University Press, 1999.

———. 'Networks, Dynamics, and the Small-World Phenomenon', *American Journal of Sociology* 105.2 (1999): 493–527.

Warnke, Martin and Wedemeyer, Carmen. 'Documenting Artistic Networks: Anna Oppermann's Ensembles are Complex Networks!', *Leonardo* 44.3 (2011): 258–259.

Woodhouse, Edward and Patton, Jason W. 'Design by Society: Science and Technology Studies and the Social Shaping of Design', *Design Issues* 20.3 (2004): 1–12.

Woolf, Virginia. *A Room of One's Own*, London: Hogarth Press, 1929.

News sources

'4-Day Conference Opens', *The Times of India*, 8 February 1996, ProQuest Historical Newspapers.

'After Delhi Metro Opens, You May be Denied Ride Without Mask', Arogya Setu Pass', *The Mint*, 23 April 2020, https://www.livemint.com/news/india/after-delhi-metro-opens-you-may-be-denied-ride-without-mask-aarogya-setu-pass-11587649373682.html.

'Agrima Joshua Case: Maha HM Anil Deshmukh Asks Mumbai Police to Take Legal Action against Comedian over Chhatrapati Shivaji Maharaj Remark', *The Free Press Journal*, 11 July 2020, https://www.freepressjournal.in/mumbai/agrima-joshua-case-maha-hm-anil-deshmukh-asks-mumbai-police-to-take-legal-action-against-comedian-over-chhatrapati-shivaji-maharaj-remark.

'Agrima Joshua Row: Comedian Posts Video Apologizing to Members of Political Parties', *The Free Press Journal*, 11 July 2020, https://www.freepressjournal.in/india/agrima-joshua-row-comedian-posts-video-apologizing-to-members-of-political-parties.

Agrawal, Aditi. 'Aarogya Setu Will Include Telemedicine, Greater Personalisation; May Act as Building Block for India Health Stack', Medianama, 22 April 2020, https://www.medianama.com/2020/04/223-aarogya-setu-upcoming-features/.

Akhauri, Tanvi. 'Shubham Mishra Has Been Arrested, but the Problem of Offence-Taking Still Persists', *shethepeople*, 13 July 2020.

Akshatha M, 'Land Sharks Hack Bhoomi Data, Shift Government Land Title', *The Economic Times*, 10 September 2018, https://economictimes.indiatimes.com/news/politics-and-nation/land-sharks-hack-bhoomi-data-shift-government-land-title/articleshow/65749538.cms.

Ananth, Venkat. 'Government of India: The World's Biggest App Factory', *The Ken*, 17 October 2016, https://the-ken.com/story/government-india-worlds-biggest-app-factory/.

'Appointments,' *The Times of India*, 6 April 1993, ProQuest Historical Newspapers.

Ashar, Hemal. 'Woman With No Travel History, No Symptoms, Whisked Away by BMC', *Mid-day*, 18 April 2020, https://www.mid-day.com/articles/coronavirus-outbreak-woman-with-no-travel-history-no-symptoms-whisked-away-by-bmc/22737204.

Banerjee, Prasid and Nandy, Shreya. 'Govt's Arogya Setu App to be Installed on Smartphones by Default Soon', *The Mint*, 29 April 2020, https://www.livemint.com/technology/apps/govt-s-aarogya-setu-app-to-be-installed-on-smartphones-by-default-soon-11588170539557.html.

Barik, Soumyarendra. '2G Internet on Postpaid, Broadband Partially Restored in J&K for Access-ing Only 'White-Listed' Websites', Medianama, 15 January 2020, https://www.medianama.com/2020/01/223-partial-internet-restoration-jammu-kashmir/.

BBC. 'New Zealand Man Jailed for 21 Months for Sharing Christchurch Shooting Video', *BBC News*, 18 June 2019, https://www.bbc.com/news/world-asia-48671837.

Bhalla, A.S. 'Can High Technology Help Third World 'Take-Off'?', *Economic & Political Weekly* 22.27 (1987): 1082–1086.

Bhatia, Rahul. 'The Inside Story of Facebook's Biggest Setback', *The Guardian*, 12 May 2016, https://www.theguardian.com/technology/2016/may/12/facebook-free-basics-india-zuckerberg.

Bhatti, Bharat, Drèze, Jean, and Khera, Reetika. 'Experiments with Aadhar', *The Hindu*, 27 June 2012, https://www.thehindu.com/opinion/lead/Experiments-with-Aadhaar/article12916184.ece.

Bischoff, Paul. 'Which Government Censors the Tech Giants the Most?', 19 October 2021, https://www.comparitech.com/blog/vpn-privacy/tech-giant-censorship/.

Blake, Aaron. 'Kellyanne Conway Says Donald Trump's Team Has 'Alternative Facts.' Which Pretty Much Says It All', *The Washington Post*, 22 January 2017, https://www.washingtonpost.com/news/the-fix/wp/2017/01/22/kellyanne-conway-says-donald-trumps-team-has-alternate-facts-which-pretty-much-says-it-all/.

Brignall, Miles. 'HSBC Indian Call Centre Worker Accused of Hacking into Accounts', *The Guardian*, 29 June 2006, https://www.theguardian.com/money/2006/jun/29/business.india.

Chacko, George. 'INFOSYS: New Game, New Rules: A Case Study', *Management Research News* 27.8/9 (2004): 1–25.

Chaturvedi, Vinita. 'I Keep a Low Profile to Promote Savita Bhabhi Better: Puneet Agarwal', *The Times of India*, 11 April 2013, https://timesofindia.indiatimes.com/entertainment/hindi/bollywood/news/i-keep-a-low-profile-to-promote-savita-bhabhi-better-puneet-agrawal/articleshow/19493624.cms.

Chauhan, Ashish. 'Jat Fire Tempts Patidars to Action', *The Times of India*, 22 February 2016, https://timesofindia.indiatimes.com/city/ahmedabad/jat-fire-tempts-patidars-to-action/article-show/51086440.cms.

'Comic Joshua Gets Rape Threat for Joke on Chhatrapati Shivaji', *The* Quint, 13 July 2020, https://www.thequint.com/news/india/comic-agrima-joshua-gets-rape-threat-for-joke-on-chhatrapati-shivaji.

David, Nash. 'Digital 'Equality' Not So Equal: Is an Aggressive Facebook Turning Free Basics into a Movement?', *Firstpost*, 24 December 2015, https://www.firstpost.com/india/is-an-aggressive-face-book-turning-free-basics-into-a-movement-2557360.html.

Deshmane, Akshay. 'The Dalit Identity Dilemma', *Frontline*, 28 April 2017, https://frontline.thehindu.com/cover-story/the-dalit-identity-dilemma/article9629313.ece.

DNA, 'Patidar Reservation: Social Media Spreading Sardar Patel Movement Like Wild Fire', 22 August 2015, http://www.dnaindia.com/india/report-patidar-reservation-social-media-spreading-sardar-patel-movement-like-wild-fire-2117056.

Drèze, Jean. 'Unique Facility, or Recipe for Trouble?', *The Hindu*, 25 November 2010, https://www.thehindu.com/opinion/op-ed/Unique-facility-or-recipe-for-trouble/article15714630.ece.

Friedman, Thomas. "Will India Seize the Moment?',' *Seattle Post-Intelligencer*, 1924, 23 March 2004.

Gelineau, Kristen and Gambrell, Jon. 'New Zealand Mosque Shooter is a White Nationalist Who Hates Immigrants, Documents and Video Reveal', *Chicago Tribune*, 15 March 2019, https://www.chicagotribune.com/nation-world/ct-mosque-killer-white-supremacy-20190315-story.html.

Ghosh, Mohul. 'Is #SabKaInternet a Deliberate Attempt by COAI to Confuse People?', *Trak. in*, 2 December 2016, https://trak.in/tags/business/2015/04/22/sabkainternet-deliberate-attempt-coai-to-confuse/.

Goldsmith, Belinda and Beresford, Meka. 'India Most Dangerous Country for Women with Sexual Violence Rife – Global Poll', *Reuters*, 26 June 2018, https://www.reuters.com/article/women-dangerous-poll-idINKBN1JM076.

Graham-McLay, Charlotte. 'Spreading the Mosque Shooting Video is a Crime in New Zealand', *The New York Times*, 21 March 2019. https://www.nytimes.com/2019/03/21/world/asia/new-zealand-attacks-social-media.html.

'Gujarat Shuts Down Internet during Exams', *The Hindu*, 29 February 2016, http://www.thehindu.com/todays-paper/tp-miscellaneous/tp-others/gujarat-shuts-down-internet-during-exam/article8294672.ece.

Hafeez, Sarah. 'Zee News Producer Quits: Video We Shot Had No Pakistan Zindabad Slogan', *The Indian Express*, 22 February 2016, https://indianexpress.com/article/india/india-news-india/zee-news-producer-quits-video-we-shot-had-no-pakistan-zindabad-slogan/.

IANS. 'Google Techie's Lynching in Karnataka: How an Act of Kindness Turned Deadly', *Business Standard*. 16 July 2018, https://www.business-standard.com/article/current-affairs/google-techie-s-lynching-in-karnataka-how-an-act-of-kindness-turned-deadly-118071500351_1.html.

'IDM-Informix Tie-up', *Times of India*, 24 December 1989, ProQuest Historical Newspapers.

'ISIS Propagandist Shami Witness: Man Charged in India, Channel 4, 1 June 2015, https://www.channel4.com/news/isis-shami-witness-medhi-masroor-biswas-charged.

Jain, Mayank. 'Mamata is Suppressing all Dissent, Claims Jadavpur Professor Arrested for Sharing a Cartoon', *Scroll*, 12 March 2015, https://scroll.in/article/712933/mamata-is-suppressing-all-dissent-claims-jadavpur-professor-arrested-for-sharing-a-cartoon.

Jain, Subash. 'Man Arrested for Getting Aadhaar Card for Dog', *Hindustan Times*, 3 July 2015, https://www.hindustantimes.com/india/man-arrested-for-getting-aadhaar-card-for-dog/story-MVtobqWtsrLXm01OkCBSvK.html.

Jaiswal, Nimisha. 'Why Indians Are Turning Down Facebook's Free Internet', *GlobalPost*, 13 January 2016, https://theworld.org/stories/2016-01-13/why-indians-are-turning-down-facebooks-free-internet.

'JNU Sedition Case: Umar Khalid, Kanhaiya Kumar, Other Accused Appear in Court', *The Wire*, 16 March 2021, https://thewire.in/law/jnu-sedition-case-umar-khalid-kanhaiya-kumar-delhi-court.

Johari, Aarefa. 'Gujarat Internet Ban: On Day Six, Citizens Have Had Enough of Being Patronized by the State', *Scroll.in*, 1 September 2015, https://scroll.in/article/752538/gujarat-internet-ban-on-day-six-citizens-have-had-enough-of-being-patronised-by-the-state.

'Journalists Exposing Aadhaar Deserve Award, Not Investigation: Edward Snowden', The News Minute, 9 January 2018,

https://www.thenewsminute.com/article/journalists-exposing-aadhaar-deserve-award-not-investigation-edward-snowden-74409.

Kanwal, Rahul. 'JNU Row: Did a Fake Video Fuel the Anti-national Fire?', *India Today*, 18 February 2016, https://www.indiatoday.in/india/story/panelists-debate-whether-kanhaiya-sedition-video-doctored-or-not-309451-2016-02-18.

Kapur, Devesh, Mukhopadhyay, Partha, and Subramanian, Arvind. 'The Case for Direct Cash Transfers to the Poor', *Economic & Political Weekly* 43.15 (2008): 37–43.

Kateshiya, Gopal. 'Gujarat Protests: Who Are the Patidars, and Why Are They Angry', *The Indian Express*, 27 August 2015, https://indianexpress.com/article/explained/simply-put-who-are-gujarats-patidars-and-why-are-they-angry/.

KK, Sruthijith. 'Govt Bans Popular Toon Porn Site', *Hindustan Times*, 20 June 2009, https://www.hindustantimes.com/entertainment/govt-bans-popular-toon-porn-site/story-M7UO7XgStS9Cfrvfziok6J.html.

Krishna, Gopal. 'Where is WIPRO's 'Strategic Vision on the UIDAI Project' Document?', *Countercurrents*, 7 August 2011, https://www.countercurrents.org/krishna070811.htm.

Matthan, Rahul. 'The Privacy Features That Are Built into Arogya Setu', *The Mint*, 8 April 2020, https://epaper.livemint.com/Home/ShareArticle?OrgId=b5a81ef7.

Mehta, Dewang. 'India on the Global Pathway', *Times of India*, 7 February 1996, ProQuest Historical Newspapers.

Mehta, Ivan. 'India Wants to Build an Ultra-intrusive 'Wristband' to Track Coronavirus Patients' Every Move', *TNW News*, 22 April 2020, https://thenextweb.com/in/2020/04/22/india-wants-to-build-an-ultra-intrusive-wristband-to-track-coronavirus-patients-every-move/.

'Nandan Nilekani, Home Ministry End UIDAI Tiff, to Divide Data Collection', *The Economic Times*, 28 January 2012, https://economictimes.indiatimes.com/news/politics-and-nation/nandan-nilekani-home-ministry-end-uidai-tiff-to-divide-data-collection/articleshow/11655516.cms?utm_source=contentofinterest&utm_medium=text&utm_campaign=cppst.

'Nalanda Computer Education for RDBMS', *The Times of India*, 29 May 1991, ProQuest Historical Newspapers.

Narayanaswami, T., 'The Central Solution', *The Times of India*, 7 May 1996, ProQuest Historical Documents.

Narula, Moneesh. 'Bank Automation Gets Competitive', *The Times of India*, 4 September 1993, ProQuest Historical Documents.

Navlakha, Gautam. ''My Hope Rests on a Speedy and Fair Trial': Gautam Navlakha Before His Surrender', *The Wire*, 14 April 2020, https://thewire.in/rights/gautam-navlakha-bhima-koregaon-nia-surrender.

'New System for Maruti Launched', *The Times of India*, 25 October 1994, sec. In Brief, ProQuest Historical Newspapers.

'On the Move', *The Times of India*, 22 March 1993, ProQuest Historical Newspapers.

'Over 22k Indian Websites, 114 Govt Portals Hacked between Apr 2017-Jan 2018', *Business Standard*, 7 March 2018, https://www.business-standard.com/article/current-affairs/over-22k-indian-websites-114-govt-portals-hacked-between-apr-2017-jan-2018-118030700870_1.html.

'Overseas Appointments', *The Times of India*, 20 September 1992, ProQuest Historical Newspapers.

'Oracle Opens India Liaison Office', *Dataquest*, 1991, https://itihaasa.com/describe/artefact/001_001_0568?referenceYear=1991.

Pandey, Brijesh. 'Natgrid Will Kick in from May 2011. Is the Big Brother Threat for Real?', *Tehelka*, 13 November 2010.

Parthasarthy, Suhrith, Bhatia, Gautam, and Gupta, Apar. 'Privacy Concerns During a Pandemic', *The Hindu*, 29 April 2020, https://www.thehindu.com/opinion/op-ed/privacy-concerns-during-a-pandemic/article31456602.ece.

'PM's Remarks at the Launch of Digital India Week', 1 July 2015, https://www.narendramodi.in/pm-s-remarks-at-the-launch-of-digital-india-week-175128.

Pranesh Prakash, 'Social Media Regulation vs. Suppression of Freedom of Speech', *Kafila Online*, 19 November 2012, https://kafila.online/2012/11/19/social-media-regulation-vs-suppression-of-freedom-of-speech-pranesh-prakash/.

———. 'Adding Insult to Injury', *Outlook India*, 19 November 2012, https://www.outlookindia.com/website/story/adding-insult-to-injury/283033.

'Pune Bourse Goes Online', *The Times of India*, 19 March 1996, ProQuest Historical Newspapers.

Rajagopal, Krishnadas. 'Plea in Supreme Court to Save Academic Freedom', *The Hindu*, 30 March 2021, https://www.thehindu.com/news/national/plea-in-supreme-court-to-save-academic-freedom/article34200750.ece.

Ranjit, Tanisha. 'When and Where is Aarogya Setu Mandatory? We're Keeping Track', Internet Democracy Project, 8 May 2020, https://internetdemocracy.in/2020/05/aarogya-setu-tracker/.

Rajesh Y.P., 'Software Firms Eye a Pie in Banking', *News - India Times*, 10 July 1998, ProQuest.

'Remember Agrima Joshua's Vile Abuser Shubham Mishra? He's Out on Bail Now', *The Free Press Journal*, 18 August 2020, https://www.freepressjournal.in/entertainment/remember-agrima-joshuas-vile-abuser-shubham-mishra-hes-out-on-bail-now.

Reuters. 'Bidar Lynching: He Looked Like Terrorist, Says Villager, Days After WhatsApp Rumour Leads to Death of 1 in rural Karnataka', *Firstpost*, 30 July 2018, https://www.firstpost.com/india/bidar-lynching-he-looked-like-terrorist-says-villager-days-after-whatsapp-rumour-leads-to-death-of-1-in-rural-karnataka-4848181.html.

Rodriguez, Ariana. 'India Bans Adult Cartoon Site SavitaBhabhi.com', *XBIZ Newswire*, 28 June 2009, http://newswire.xbiz.com/view.php?id=109797.

Roy, Esha. 'As Nine Bodies Await Burial, Manipur Trenched in Politics of Dead and Living', *Indian Express*, 29 August 2016, https://indianexpress.com/article/india/india-news-india/manipur-violence-protests-in-churachandpur-manipur-deaths-2999507/.

Sam, Cyril and Thakurta, Paranjoy Guha, 'Part 1: Is Facebook in India Truly Independent of Political Influence? Not Really – It has Backed Modi and BJP', NewsClick, 22 November 2018, https://www.newsclick.in/part-1-facebook-india-truly-independent-political-influence.

Shantha, Sukanya. 'Elgar Parishad: NIA Arrests Hany Babu, 'Pressured Him to Implicate Colleagues, Others,' Says Wife', *The Wire*, 28 July 2020, https://thewire.in/government/nia-bhima-koregaon-hany-babu-arrest-gn-saibaba.

Sharma, Pankul. 'Only Male or Female Can Get PAN Card, Transgenders Told', Times of India, 15 March 2018, http://timesofindia.indiatimes.com/articleshow/63321785.cms?utm_source=contentofinterest&utm_medium=text&utm_campaign=cppst.

Shira Ovide, 'A Fix-It Job for Government Tech', 24 November 2021, https://www.nytimes.com/2021/11/24/technology/government-tech.html.

Sikri, Aprajita. 'A US-Indian Database Venture', *India Abroad*, 1 June 1990, ProQuest.

Singh, Parminder Jeet. 'Bringing Data under the Rule of Law', *The Hindu*, 20 September 2018, https://www.thehindu.com/opinion/op-ed/bringing-data-under-the-rule-of-law/article24988755.ece.

Sircar, Jawhar. 'A Long Look at Exactly Why and How India Failed its Migrant Workers', *The Wire*, 29 May 2020, https://thewire.in/labour/lockdown-migrant-workers-policy-analysis.

Smiley, Lauren. 'How India Pierced Facebook's Free Internet', *Wired*, 1 February 2016, https://www.wired.com/2016/02/how-india-pierced-facebooks-free-internet-program/.

'Stir Over OBC Status: Govt Proposes Talks; Hardik Plays Hardball', *The Indian Express*, 23 August 2015, http://indianexpress.com/article/india/india-others/stir-over-obc-status-govt-proposes-talks-hardik-patel-plays-hard-ball/.

Strang, Ben. 'Thousands Don't Believe Official Christchurch Terror Attacks Story', *RNZ*, 4 April 2019, https://www.rnz.co.nz/news/national/386367/thousands-don-t-believe-official-christchurch-terror-at-tacks-story.

'Tata Unisys Ltd', *The Times of India*, 28 December 1993, ProQuest Historical Newspapers.

'TRAI Tells Reliance to Put Facebook's Free Basics Platform on Hold', *The Free Library*, 23 December 2015, https://www.thefreelibrary.com/TRAI+tells+Reliance+to+put+Facebook%27s+Free+Ba-sics+platform+on+hold-a0438721289.

Trivedi, Divya. 'Anuradha Bhasin: 'Impossible for Journalists to Function', *Frontline*, 27 September 2019, https://frontline.thehindu.com/cover-story/impossible-for-journalists-to-function/article29382196.ece.

'UIDAI to Share Data with Police for Investigations', *The Hindu*, 6 February 2013, https://www.thehindu.com/news/national/karnataka/uidai-to-share-data-with-police-for-investigations/article4383068.ece.

Valluri, Madhu. 'How Info-tech can Help Environment', *The Times of India*, 14 April 1993, ProQuest Historical Newspapers.

Wadhwa, D.C. 'Guaranteeing Title to Land', *Economic and Political Weekly* 37.47 (2002): 4699-4722.

Web We Want. 'Indian Comedians Explain Net Neutrality in Free Basics Battle', 13 January 2016, https://webwewant.org/news/indian-comedians-explain-net-neutrality/.

'Why Late Justice Krishna Iyer Opposed Biometric Aadhaar', *ToxicsWatch*, 10 December 2014, http://www.toxicswatch.org/2014/12/why-late-justice-krishna-iyer-opposed.html.

Yamunan, Sruthisagar and Daniyal, Shoaib. 'As Delhi Police Crack Down on Student Leaders, Courts Cite Lockdown to Justify Lack of Scrutiny', *Scroll*, 29 April 2020, https://scroll.in/article/960591/as-del-hi-police-crack-down-on-student-leaders-court-cites-lockdown-to-justify-lack-of-scrutiny.

About the Authors

Nishant Shah is a feminist, humanist, technologist. He was the cofounder of The Centre for Internet & Society, India. He is currently an endowed professor of aesthetics and cultures of technology at ArtEZ University of the Arts and Radboud University in the Netherlands, a Faculty Associate at the Berkman Klein Centre for Internet & Society, Harvard University, USA, and a Knowledge Partner with the Digital Asia Hub, Hong Kong. His current preoccupations are around questions of digital technologies, narrative practices for collective action, and cultural politics of Artificial Intelligence.

Ashish Rajadhyaksha worked as Senior Fellow at the Centre for the Study of Culture and Society. Although known primarily as a film scholar, he has published widely on digital governance, including the book *The Last Cultural Mile: An Inquiry into Technology and Governance in India* (2011), 'State Power and Technological Citizenship in India: From the Postcolonial to the Digital Age' (with Itty Abraham) in *East Asian Science, Technology and Society: An International Journal* (2015), and *In the Wake of Aadhaar: The Digital Ecoystem of Governance in India* (2013).

Nafis Aziz Hasan has been researching the techno-politics of digital media, material politics of public institutions, and technological policies for governance, with a regional focus on India. One part of his project seeks to offer a historical understanding of digital technology in relation to prior technologies of rule. Another aspect of his work draws on rich ethnographic material on the assemblage of people, processes, and technologies, generated over a decade from across India. His work has appeared in academic journals such as *South Asia*, *Political and Legal Anthropology Review*, and *Economic and Political Weekly*, and popular outlets such as thewire.in, *New Indian Express* and raiot.in. This is his first book.

www.ingramcontent.com/pod-product-compliance
Lightning Source LLC
Chambersburg PA
CBHW021617270326
41931CB00008B/734